Publishing Culture and the "Reading Nation"

Publishing Culture and the "Reading Nation"

German Book History in the Long Nineteenth Century

Edited by Lynne Tatlock

CAMDEN HOUSE

Rochester, New York

First published 2010
by Camden House

Camden House is an imprint of Boydell & Brewer Inc.
668 Mt. Hope Avenue, Rochester, NY 14620, USA
www.camden-house.com
and of Boydell & Brewer Limited
PO Box 9, Woodbridge, Suffolk IP12 3DF, UK
www.boydellandbrewer.com

ISBN-13: 978-1-57113-402-8
ISBN-10: 1-57113-402-6

Library of Congress Cataloging-in-Publication Data

Publishing culture and the "reading nation": German book history in the long
nineteenth century / edited by Lynne Tatlock.
    p. cm. — (Studies in German literature, linguistics, and culture)
Includes bibliographical references and index.
ISBN-13: 978-1-57113-402-8 (acid-free paper)
ISBN-10: 1-57113-402-6 (acid-free paper)
    1. Book industries and trade — Germany — History — 19th century.
2. Books and reading — Germany — History — 19th century. 3. Authors
and publishers — Germany — History — 19th century. 4. Literature
publishing — Germany — History — 19th century. I. Tatlock, Lynne, 1950–.
II. Title. III. Series.
    Z315 .P83 2010
    381'.450020943—dc22
                                                            2010004391

A catalogue record for this title is available from the British Library.

This publication is printed on acid-free paper.
Printed in the United States of America.

Contents

I: Distinction, Affiliation, and Education in Consuming Formats

II: Niche Markets, Reading Socialization, and Gender: Girls as Consumers of Literature, Nation, and Canon

III: Writers and Their Publishers

IV: Elite Culture, Mass Culture, and the Medium of the Book

Illustrations

Acknowledgments

THE IMPETUS TO UNDERTAKE A VOLUME on book history arose from conversations with Jennifer Askey, Kirsten Belgum, and Jana Mikota, three of the participants in the three sessions on publishing that I organized on behalf of the Division on Nineteenth and Early Twentieth Century for the national meeting of the Modern Language Association in December 2007. However, I would also like to acknowledge the members of the MLA division who gave me a free hand in organizing these sessions in the first place: Kirsten Belgum, William C. Donahue, Eric S. Downing, and Irene Kacandes. I also thank Jim Walker, Editorial Director at Camden House, whose early interest in the anthology encouraged me to go forward with the project and whose continued enthusiasm, responsiveness, and support have made every step of the process manageable and thus ensured expeditious completion of the project. I am grateful also to James Hardin at Camden House for his interest in and frank advice on the volume, and also to the anonymous readers at Camden House for generous and useful feedback.

I received excellent assistance in the preparation of the first draft of the manuscript from Faruk Pašić, who attended in particular to proofreading and formatting the notes and bibliography. His work was funded by a summer research grant from the Graduate School of Arts and Sciences at Washington University. I am also beholden to Shelby Carpenter and to the Interdisciplinary Project in the Humanities, which supported her summer work for me. Thanks go as well to Photographic Services at Washington University and especially to David Kilper, who one November afternoon made over sixty photographs of the stack of books featured on the cover.

I am grateful to the authors in the volume for their collegiality and collaboration.

Finally, Joseph F. Loewenstein deserves special thanks for patiently listening to my starts and stops and offering me encouragement along the way.

L. T.
February 2010

Introduction: The Book Trade and "Reading Nation" in the Long Nineteenth Century

Lynne Tatlock

IN BOOK 5 OF *The Hunchback of Notre Dame* (1831), Victor Hugo writes exuberantly of the book as having supplanted architecture and usurped its place as the register of humanity. Conceiving the book in architectural terms, he expansively imagines a "prodigious edifice" that includes all of the products of printing. "The entire human race is on the scaffold; every mind is a mason," his narrator exclaims; "the humblest bores his hole or lays his stone."[1] Himself a prolific writer, Hugo saw his democratizing century as a highpoint in the age of printing and in particular in the history of the book. And he was not wrong to think so.

Literary and cultural critics speak of the "writtenness" or "textualization" of the world in nineteenth-century Europe, an age dominated by literary styles, modes, and movements (historicism, realism, naturalism, literary impressionism) and print media — newspapers, journals, and encyclopedias — that aspired to represent and chronicle in minute and rich detail the totality of the world. Hugo's German contemporary, the novelist and popular historian Gustav Freytag, saw precisely this ability to write things down as a sign of progress. He spoke for middle-class Germans and to their values when he framed German history in his *Bilder aus der deutschen Vergangenheit* (1859–66; Pictures from the German Past) as a process of intellectual emancipation in which the ability to write prose and thus adequately and fully to represent one's own circumstances and to make judgments about them played a critical role, indeed, was the yardstick of national majority.[2] This will to write the world in the "century of words" accompanied and was mutually informed by significant social, cultural, and economic developments, not the least of which were the rapid increase in literacy, industrialization, urbanization, German unification, and the emergence and development of mass markets.[3]

If, however, the romantic, republican Hugo imagined in 1831 an edifice consisting of books and reaching to the sky, approximately one hundred years later, in 1929, at the end of the period addressed by the current volume, the voracious book reviewer Kurt Tucholsky oversaw a much smaller edifice as he humorously despaired of taking account of the precariously leaning tower of books "on his nightstand."[4] In Tucholsky's day, reading was still "viewed as a barometer of society," but, as Gideon Reuveni has demonstrated, in postwar Germany pervasive feelings of decline were expressed in lamentation over a "crisis of the book."[5] Moreover, cultural pundits feared that with the competition posed by other media, the book would no longer function as the central repository of human experience and knowledge; it would cease to be the principal means of "mediation between humans and their surroundings."[6] Nevertheless, as Reuveni outlines, the book market continued to flourish, and if anything, the perception of a crisis of the book in and of itself "reflected the success of the bourgeoisie in achieving a popularization" of a reading culture throughout all social levels, one that imparted and imposed middle-class values on all strata of society, touting the idea of "reading up."[7]

The eleven essays in this anthology examine aspects of German book history, understood broadly, from the late eighteenth century to the Weimar Republic, that is, during the approximately 150 years of the "the long nineteenth century," the period that Hugo might have deemed the age of the book. Through case studies, they explore multiple aspects of what Robert Darnton, in his seminal definition of the interdisciplinary field of book history, terms the "communications circuit."[8]

Darnton's schema conceives of the life cycle of the printed book in terms of the convergence of complex cultural, social, and economic pressures and networks, that is, as a fraught passage from the author to the publisher, the printer, the shippers, the booksellers, and the readers, each step of which influences the others, including the author's future production. Book history allows us to problematize the phases of this life cycle, including the author. Indeed, two articles here concern publications that were generated by multiple authors — the Brockhaus encyclopedia and the *Journal des Luxus und der Moden* (1786–1827; Journal of Luxuries and Fashion); these publications were originally conceived by the *publishers* and therefore are not "authored" in the common understanding of the word.

In the aggregate, this volume aspires to help illuminate the complex field opened up by the "socialization of texts" identified by Finkelstein and McCleery;[9] in keeping with John O. Jorden and Robert L. Patten, moreover, it aims to make the elements in the life cycle of the book "interactive and inter-dependent."[10] In this endeavor it also relies on impetus from the contributing authors' own field of German Studies. Reinhard Wittmann, a German historian of the book, formulates what he terms "literarisches Leben" (literary life) in the final pages of his *Buchmarkt und Lektüre im 18. und 19. Jahrhundert: Beiträge zum literarischen Leben 1750–1880* (1982) in terms like those used by Anglo-American book historians. Similar to the way in which Darnton conceives the communications circuit, Wittmann understands "literary life" as a complex and interrelated network of forces with multiple focal points. "Literary life" is thus a "multicentric phenomenon," a "System mehrerer, einander teilweise schneidender und überlagernder Kreise heterogenen Materials" (system of many circles of heterogeneous materials that in part intersect and overlap).[11] It thus encompasses, in Wittmann's formulation, the historical environment in which literature is produced, distributed, and read, including all of the instances of communication in this process as well as political, social, economic, and cultural influences. Paraphrasing Rudolf Schenda, whose seminal work *Volk ohne Buch* (1970) continues to serve as a rich source for book history in the German context, Wittmann emphasizes, further, that literary life must be seen as a "ständiges prozessuales Miteinander der literarischen Fakten und der gesellschaftlichen Determinanten, ein Geflecht gegenseitiger Bedingungen und Abhängigkeiten, in welchem jedes Element jedes andere konditionieren oder von jedem anderen konditioniert werden kann" (continual processual conglomerate of literary facts and social determinants, a mesh of mutual stipulations and dependencies, in which each element can condition every other one and [in turn] can be conditioned by each of the others).[12] Wittmann notably writes of "literature" — not of books — and the question thus arises here as to what kinds of publications we contributors, trained literary historians, examine in this volume. Here again book history encourages a wide-angle focus.

In his study of English-language books and reading in the Romantic period, English book historian William St Clair asserts, "any study of the consequences of the reading of the past ought to consider the print which was actually read, not some modern selection, whether that selection is derived from judgments of canon or from other modern criteria."[13] In examining some of the phases in the fraught passage of books from authors to publishers to readers and back again, each phase influencing the other, this anthology pays special attention to books that were actually read by the German "reading nation" in the belief that investigation of their history provides a more complete and nuanced picture of book history, literary production, and reading cultures in the shadow of nation-building and class formation in the long nineteenth century.

The term "reading nation" in our title borrows directly from St Clair to signal interest in the actually read, but it is doubly significant in our context. It refers, in St Clair's meaning, to those who regularly read German-language printed books, but also to those who by reading participated in the German national culture that was being made and supported by book production over the course of approximately 150 years. In this second sense, this volume continues and builds, for example, on the work of Kirsten Belgum, Todd Kontje, and Brent O. Peterson by considering that books both addressed and helped to form a national community of readers.[14]

Impulses from literary sociology, studies of the public sphere such as Peter Uwe Hohendahl's *Literarische Kultur im Zeitalter des Liberalismus* (1985), the politics of literature, cultural studies, New Historicism, Franco Moretti's attempts to quantify genres and literary production with "graphs, maps, and trees," and the renewed flourishing of book history invite us to — indeed, make possible — multiple border crossings between the interpretation of texts and the study of their socialization.[15] Georg Jäger's voluminous and comprehensive multi-authored *Geschichte des deutschen Buchhandels im 19. und 20. Jahrhundert*, furthermore, has greatly aided the conception and execution of the present project. When Jäger's history of the book trade is used as a touchstone, it also becomes clear that the products of the periodical press belong to book history. We have considered some of these, too, in this volume in the clear understanding that there is considerable crossover between magazines and books.

The eleven essays that follow have been assembled with an eye to what we as literary critics and historians can learn by examining the broader context of writing, reading, and publishing, and by thinking about the book not only as carrying and shaping texts but also as subject to economies of materials, production, and consumption.[16] The essays are written and should be understood in the light of a complex history of an age in which publishing, writing, and reading expanded exponentially, transforming in step with modernization and playing a critical role in the major social and political developments of that era.

* * *

From the late eighteenth century through the Weimar Republic, the period embraced in this volume by the term the long-nineteenth century, publishing, measured by any standard, boomed in the German territories. Book production doubled in the last half of the eighteenth century and continued to expand.[17] Between 1821 and 1845 the number of book titles tripled, growing from an annual production of 4,505 titles to 14,059.[18] Despite setbacks in times of war and economic downturn and despite struggles with censorship throughout this period, by 1910, thirty-nine years after unification, Germany could boast 31,281 book titles published in a single year, far more than other leading industrial nations, for example France at 12,615, England at 10,804, and the United States of America at 13,470.[19] In 1913, a year before the outbreak of the First World War, Germany still led the world with 34,871 books published in a single year.[20] Even after the turmoil of the war years and their immediate aftermath, Germany experienced sturdy book publication; the year 1927 witnessed a record high of 37,866 titles.[21] To achieve this record within the approximately 130 years since the first reading revolution in the wake of the Enlightenment in the eighteenth century, the book trade had reorganized and industrialized, changing methods of output and marketing and recalibrating its relationship to authors.

The technology of printing improved dramatically in this period. Beginning around 1800 with the advent of the all-metal press, which doubled the printing capacity of the old wooden press, production techniques began to modernize. Friedrich Koenig's high-speed press followed in the 1820s and, a decade later, would be driven by the steam engine and still later by electricity. The rotary press first came into use in the German territories in the 1860s and became more widely used in the 1870s.[22] By 1880 a single press had sixty times the printing capacity of the hand-operated press of 1800.[23] Over the course of the century publishers employed new techniques for reproducing images as well, from wood engravings (as opposed to the woodcut) earlier in the century to various kinds of photomechanical reproduction later on. The invention of the halftone process late in the century, for example, made it possible to reproduce images cheaply in newspapers and magazines. Bookbinding likewise developed from the occupation of a "kramender Handwerksmann" (small-time skilled manual laborer) in the 1780s to an industry that employed significant numbers of workers, both men and women, in the 1890s.[24]

The size of print runs also grew over the course of the century, as can be seen even in the example of the relatively expensive Brockhaus *Conversations-Lexikon*. In 1809 the six volumes of the first edition enjoyed a print run of 2,000; the print run of the fifth edition (1818–20), now ten volumes strong, reached 32,000. By 1870, a total of 300,000 copies of the encyclopedia (including all eleven editions) had been printed.[25] Still more impressively, the sixteen volumes of the third edition of Brockhaus's rival, *Meyers Konversations-Lexikon,* were published in print runs of 130,000 copies in the years 1874–78, and its fourth edition (1885–90) expanded to 200,000 copies.[26]

In step with expanded book production, bookstores, too, increased in number between 1850 and 1865 by 57% and between 1865 and 1879 by 70%.[27] From 1869 to 1890 the number of undertakings in the book trade — understood in the broadest sense — grew from 3,506 to 7,474 — that is, more than doubled in Germany.[28]

New production techniques that increased output made it possible to lower the price of books, even of illustrated books. As books became more affordable, ever more readers had access to them. Reclam, for example, could offer the classics to a broad audience for as little as twenty pfennigs a copy at the end of the nineteenth century. Langewiesche could sell more elaborate books in the first decade of the new century at the still affordable price of 1.80 marks while encouraging consumers to educate themselves by reading.[29] By the end of the century it also became possible to produce affordable books with decorative covers, and publishers could give their customers a choice of book bindings — even for popular literature — ranging from the plain and simple to multi-colored, elaborately designed covers such as those offered by Keils Nachfolger/Union Deutsche Verlagsgesellschaft beginning in the late 1880s, when it re-published *Gartenlaube* (Garden Bower) novels in collected, illustrated editions.[30]

The industrialization of the book trade especially in the last decades of the nineteenth century enabled a second reading revolution, that is, the emergence of a mass readership and thus a mass market for newspapers, magazines, and books. The number of readers had grown astronomically since the mid-eighteenth century. Indeed, as literacy increased over the course of the nineteenth century, the reading revolution of the late eighteenth century, centered in the educated middle class, was superseded by a greater democratization of reading. According to Rudolf Schenda, in 1830 about 30% of the entire population of the German territories over six years of age was literate. Thereafter literacy increased by approximately 10% per decade until virtually everyone could read.[31] With the advent of more readers came new habits of reading as well as new interests and new tastes. As has often been pointed out, reading became "extensive," that is, readers read much more broadly, tending less toward the "intensive" reading (repeated reading of the same small set of texts) that characterized earlier periods when book ownership was limited — often to the Bible and devotional works — and few had ready access to books.[32]

These new readers sought, in addition to edification, entertainment and information in books. The increase in the publication of literary works, particularly novels, in the eighteenth century — that is, in the period of the first reading revolution — adumbrated what was to come. The relation between the publication of theological books and that of literature shifted in favor of the latter: in 1770, 25% of all books published were theological and 16.5% literature; in 1800, 13.5 % were theological and 21.45% were literature. Furthermore, in 1770, 4% of all books published were novels, but by 1800 that percentage had risen to 11.7%.[33] Between 1760 and 1769, 200 new novels were published in the German territories; between 1800 and 1809, the number increased elevenfold to 2,207.[34] While some novels are certainly treasured and reread, novels do not demand the intensive reading required in a religious age by the Bible.

And the hunger for literature continued to grow. Friedrich Sengle writes of the emergence of an "allgemeine Leselust" (general desire to read) that in the first half of the nineteenth century led to ever more reading circles and lending libraries and an increasing wish for entertaining literature in prose.[35] This reading public also sought information. The modern encyclopedia emerged in this period in the German territories in the form of the *Brockhaus*, which the *Encyclopædia Britannica* praised in 1848 with the words, "No work of reference has been more useful and successful, or more frequently copied, imitated, and translated, than that

known as the 'Conversations-Lexikon' of Brockhaus."[36] This era also saw
the beginning of the growth in journals and magazines (*Zeitschriften*):
from 1826 to 1927, the number of titles multiplied eighteenfold — that
is, it more than doubled every twenty-five years.[37] The annual "Taschenbücher" (pocketbooks), small-format, illustrated books containing entertaining literary selections of various kinds, likewise flourished in the first
half of the century. By furnishing these yearly publications with sentimental engravings, and, as in the case of Cotta's *Taschenbuch für Damen*
(1799–1831; Pocketbook for Ladies) and Fouqué's *Frauentaschenbuch*
(1815–31; Women's Pocketbook), even adding the word "woman" to
the title, publishers made early efforts in the first half of the nineteenth
century to cultivate an expanding class of readers, that is, women readers.[38] However, as the example that Karin A. Wurst mentions in her article on garden culture demonstrates, small-format books targeting women
were certainly not confined to literature. The *Küchentaschenbuch für
Frauenzimmer zur täglichen Wahl der Speisen für das Jahr 1796* (Kitchen
Pocketbook for Women for Selecting Daily Meals for the Year 1796), for
example, taught women about managing the kitchen.[39]

Many of the new readers were in fact female. Women's reading was
to become increasingly important to publishing as it industrialized and
sought expanded markets. Between 1865 and 1879 women's magazines,
family magazines, and *belles lettres*, for example, experienced a 202.8%
growth as a result of an increase in overall reading and women's reading
in particular.[40]

Over the course of the long nineteenth century publishers themselves
changed in character and recalibrated their relations with their authors
and their works. What had once been a sector composed largely of small
family businesses, handed down from generation to generation, that produced a limited number of titles began to be displaced by significantly
larger capitalist enterprises with responsibilities to shareholders.[41] Under
these new market conditions and in good economic times, some entre-
preneurs in the publishing industry got rich as the century wore on. In
fact, as Jäger outlines, by 1908 men involved in the publishing industry
occupied a noticeably prominent place among Germany's millionaires.[42]

The "emancipation of the writer," as Jäger and Estermann term the
transition from patronage to a market system, began to gain traction in
the late eighteenth century and made possible the profession of the writer
in the nineteenth century; yet this emancipation was perilous.[43] Christoph
Martin Wieland, they assert, was the only early-nineteenth-century writer
to achieve — albeit in a modest fashion — something akin to the status of
the modern freelance writer.[44] The ideas of intellectual property and literature as commodity were, for much of the period under scrutiny, poorly
understood; indeed, the debate over the value of books and rights to intellectual property continued into the twentieth century. Copyright was

long in acquiring its modern character, and no widely recognized international copyright laws existed until the Berne Convention of 1886.[45] Early in the eighteenth century it was in fact generally the publisher — not the author — who sought privileges from the ruling authorities to prevent the printing of pirated copies. Even the *Allgemeine Landrecht für die Preußischen Staaten* (ALS; General Law of the Land for the Prussian States) of 1794 regulated the rights of publishers and not of authors.[46] Nevertheless, according to the ALS, publishers had to seek the permission of authors to print new editions of previously published work. The most significant legislation securing authors' rights in the German territories did not, however, occur until the period of German unification: laws pertaining to written work, illustration, music, and dramatic work were passed in 1870 by the North German Confederation, and laws pertaining to graphic works and photography were passed in Imperial Germany in 1876.

Honoraria for authors varied widely over the long nineteenth century and for much of this time were not tagged to actual sales. Those who tried in the new age of the market to live by the pen struggled; many, like Theodor Storm, for example, wrote and published on the side. Jäger and Estermann note that in 1824, Goethe received from Cotta 65,000 thalers for his "Ausgabe letzter Hand" (final authoritative edition). By contrast Gottfried Keller, they point out, received for his now canonical novel *Grüner Heinrich* (1853–55; Green Henry) a total of 742 thalers for the five-year span, 1850–55, in which he worked on the novel.[47] With such disparities and uncertainties, the relations between authors and publishers could understandably be tense — in the present volume, the essays of Jeffrey L. Sammons and Mary Paddock on Heinrich Heine and Julius Campe and Frank Wedekind and Albert Langen, respectively, examine some of these sorely laden misunderstandings. Heine and Wedekind were of course not alone in thinking that they were unfairly compensated or that their publishers were making money at their expense. Writers struggling in an economy that they themselves often did not fully comprehend found many to blame for their poor income or lack of success.

The prolific freelance writer Wilhelm Raabe (1831–1910), for example, dealt with twenty-two different publishers over the course of the approximately fifty years of his writing career, was seldom satisfied with his honoraria, and thought that his publishers overcharged for his books and thus stood in the way of his success.[48] Furthermore, when the economics of publishing did not go to his liking, he blamed a reading public that he feminized.[49] Earlier in the century, the Berlin writer Willibald Alexis, who tried to earn his living from the book trade as editor, journalist, and fiction writer while speculating on the side in real estate, and who never managed to find the audience he desired, also railed against the consumer of literature, whom it suited him to imagine as female.[50] Readers were largely women, he fumed in 1844 in a letter to Friedrich Hebbel, and wanted "Niedliches, Geschmeidiges, Interessantes" (cute things, soft things, piquant things), not the sort of rough-hewn figures that he created in his historical novels.[51] The fact that two of the most commercially successful novelists in the new market economy were women presumably only confirmed the prejudices of such frustrated authors. Indeed, the anonymous reviewer for the *Deutsches Museum* of Luise Mühlbach's *Berlin und Sanssouci oder Friederich der Große und seine Freunde* (Berlin and Sanssouci or Frederick the Great and His Friends) grumbled in 1854 that whereas book dealers were complaining that the number of novel readers was declining, the number of women writing them was increasing weekly.[52]

From 1848 until her death in 1873, Luise Mühlbach — with an eye firmly trained on the need to support her daughters, two sisters-in-law, and her mother-in-law — cranked out historical novel after historical novel that met with international success, even if she could not profit from the pirated printings and unauthorized translations of her works on the other side of the Atlantic.[53] Eugenie Marlitt, who like Mühlbach managed to tap the vein of the reading public of the 1860s and '70s, famously was able to support herself and her brother's family with her serialized fiction for the family magazine *Die Gartenlaube*. Her publisher, Ernst Keil, who in part owed the success of his periodical to her popular novels, presented her with a desk in 1869 and then in 1870–71 enabled her with generous honoraria to build a towering villa in her hometown, Arnstadt.[54] "Wie überglücklich mag sich Eugenie in ihrem selbst erschaffenen Heim gefühlt haben, das sie ganz allein ihrer Feder verdankte" (how deliriously happy Eugenie must have been in the home she had earned herself and that she owed entirely to her pen), imagined Else Hofmann, who was herself trying to earn a living with her pen in 1918 in the midst of war.[55]

By the end of the nineteenth century and on into the twentieth, market segmentation and the development of niche markets were well underway and addressed by publishers in myriad ways. One such niche market targeted the "young girl" (and her parents) as a consumer of books; indeed, her leisure time and education had become a cultural preoccupation of Imperial Germany. The contributions of Jennifer Drake Askey and Jana Mikota to the present volume give a sense of this niche market and these preoccupations. But there were many more such markets and many ways of addressing the readers who constituted them and of offering them alternate forms of education, entertainment, and consumption.

While for some, reading was a collective activity — within the family, in literary circles, or at readings by authors, for example — the emergence of niche markets suggests that book reading was also becoming an ever more individual and individualistic affair, with books catering to a variety of tastes, promising the consumer erotic titillation, entertainment, self-help and self-fashioning, education, status, moral edification, information, and aesthetic pleasure. Even as the contents of books catered to a wide range of interests and tastes, their makeup, too — illustrations, covers, print, paper — appealed to different tastes, age groups, and pocketbooks. Books thus served increasingly across a broad spectrum of society as signifiers of taste, affiliation, and, to use Pierre Bourdieu's term, "distinction."[56]

The democratizing of literature and the widespread possibility of ownership of books in an age with many more books for sale was accompanied by an expanded interest in the connoisseurship of books, a connoisseurship that ranged from the display of mass-produced books in private homes to such elite cultural practices as the collection of rare books and the production of deluxe editions or art books in limited editions for purchase by subscription. As Ulrich Bach outlines below in his essay on the collector Eduard Fuchs, elite connoisseurship and the production of high-quality art books could paradoxically be tied to left-wing political agendas for educating the masses through books. On the other hand, as Völkner and Tatlock point out concerning books published by Langewiesche and Keils Nachfolger/Union Deutsche Verlagsgesellschaft respectively, mass-produced books could also strive for the appearance of quality and pretension and could thus appeal to the wish to collect of informed consumers of more modest means.

In 1867, the release from copyright of the classic literary works of German authors who had died prior to 1837 made possible the creation of legitimate cheap editions of classic authors for the masses by such publishers as Reclam and Tauchnitz. Such "classic libraries," together with reading anthologies tailored for schools, helped to create modern ideas of the literary canon — that is, of which books should be read by the German nation. The book could in fact be used in various ways to help create and reproduce that canon. In contrast to Reclam with its highly affordable editions, other publishers took on canonizing projects that catered to a well-heeled readership. For example, Gustav Könnecke's deluxe folio volume *Bilderatlas zur Geschichte der deutschen Literatur* (1887; Picture Atlas for the History of German Literature), which less than ten years later (in 1895) appeared in a second, much-expanded edition, offered a comprehensive picture book (including over 1,000 illustrations) with summary facts about German literature — beginning with Tacitus — and relying mainly on portraits of authors.[57] It is perhaps unnecessary to point out that Könnecke included few women writers in the German canon that he created with his "atlas" even though by the time he first published the volume, women were increasingly involved in the various segments of the book trade.

Along with the proliferation of newspapers and magazines, the reviewing of books expanded too, ranging from sophisticated discussions among literary cognoscenti to recommended reading in advice books to simple descriptions of fiction meant largely to attract buyers. Brockhaus's *Blätter für literarische Unterhaltung* reviewed literature for an educated middle-class readership from 1826 to 1898, and from 1848 to 1861 Freytag and Julian Schmidt reviewed books in *Die Grenzboten* to promote both a new kind of literature and a national-liberal political program. These are but two of many such journals. The broad documentation of Alfred Estermann and Peter Uwe Hohendahl's *Literaturkritik 1848–1870* and Helmut Kreuzer's recently published three-volume *Deutschsprachige Literaturkritik 1870–1914* provides a helpful overview of the spectrum of literary criticism in the key years of growth in the German publishing industry.[58] But in addition to the newspapers and magazines that were mined for these two collections, the *Journal des Luxus und der Moden* (discussed by Karin A. Wurst in this volume), advice books, family magazines like *Die Gartenlaube*, and magazines for women like *Der Bazar* (The Bazaar) also weighed in on books and reading in the nineteenth century, thus helping to shape reading cultures and the modes of consumption associated with them.

* * *

The essays in this anthology have been arranged chronologically in four thematic subdivisions. The opening set of four addresses examples of formats and modes of consumption of information and entertainment, and their roles in social formations and public discourse over the course of the long nineteenth century. The first two of these essays direct our attention to the beginning of the period under scrutiny, offering two different takes on consumption, books, and reading. Using the example of Christoph Martin Wieland's works as a point of departure, Matt Erlin examines luxury editions and their formats and the discussions surrounding them from the late eighteenth and early nineteenth centuries as they reflect taste, propriety, and, indeed, national interest. Erlin argues that such books can usefully be seen as part of the broader cultural phenomenon of conspicuous expenditure and its attendant pleasures in an emergent consumer society. While excessive consumption and luxury generally were subject to moral disapprobation, in the form of books they could in the late eighteenth and early nineteenth centuries be justified by connoisseurship; that is, the purchase of a luxury edition was legitimated by being situated within a framework "of intellectual interests and refined pleasures that enjoy[ed] wide acceptance among contemporaries."[59] Likewise, luxury editions appealed to Germans' sense of competition with other nations and could be justified as a means of attaining a cultural level equal to that of England, France, or Italy; in this sense high-quality, luxury editions supported the national interest and also contributed to canon formation.

Karin A. Wurst situates her investigation of print media in the cultural context of the garden mania of the late eighteenth and nineteenth centuries. Her discussion of Friedrich Justin Bertuch's highly successful

Journal des Luxus und der Moden reveals the active role that this monthly magazine played in fueling and shaping the mania for gardening in the late eighteenth- and early nineteenth-century German-speaking world and the patterns of consumption associated with it, a mania that in turn critically shaped class formation. Wurst demonstrates that through its articles, book reviews, illustrations, and advertisement of products the *Journal* encouraged readers to imagine gardening and home gardens as within their reach and as subject to their particular preferences and self-understanding. While the *Journal* privileged the English landscape garden over the formal French garden, it also brought into view an English-German hybrid version distinguished by its combination of beauty and utility and thus by an emphasis on fruits and vegetables, as well as flowers and ornamental shrubs and trees. With a strong appeal to the five senses, the *Journal* vividly presented gardening as a total and restorative experience that could be pursued in some fashion year round. It thus promoted distinctive self-fashioning through consumption and leisure-time activity that enabled differentiation within the middle classes.

In her study of the history of the Brockhaus *Conversations-Lexikon*, Kirsten Belgum outlines the emergence of the modern encyclopedia in nineteenth-century Germany. The modernity of the *Brockhaus* consisted of its address of a large, non-scholarly, mainstream audience and its determined and creative attempts to remain current with the rapid developments and events of the century. Even as the reference work expanded in size and won ever more readers, it also registered significant shifts in German society and politics. Comparing the edition from the 1820s with that from the 1880s, Belgum traces changes in the outlook of the encyclopedia in four key areas: 1) its understanding of German history, 2) technology and science, 3) the presentation of the contemporary world vis-à-vis German interests, and 4) the use of illustrations to produce a totalized view of the world. The thirteenth edition, she demonstrates, exhibited confidence in the path of German history and the importance of German achievements and thus endorsed the German Empire. As she points out, the Brockhaus encyclopedia did not merely serve its readers as a reservoir of knowledge, but also interpreted the world for them from a nationally biased perspective in a nationally biased context.

Lynne Tatlock examines the popular fiction of three women writers that, after its initial serialization in the family magazine *Die Gartenlaube* in the 1860s and '70s, re-circulated in the late nineteenth and early twentieth centuries in the form of illustrated collected works and thus won new generations of female readers. While a historically informed reader can discern the origins of these volumes in a period and mind-set that pre-date their re-publication, the illustrations and decorative bindings of the volumes intimated to the late nineteenth-century consumer that the stories emerged from her own present and, moreover, that the ideas of femininity, virtue, and community in them still obtained. Although these books were pilloried by contemporaries with allegiance to feminism or the avant-garde as well as by those who promoted a national canon of superior German literature, the enduring success of this domestic fiction suggests that it supported the values, dreams, and self-understanding of mainstream German women readers. These readers, who were taught that they were doing their duty to their nation by mothering and maintaining the home, could find in these books affirmation of those duties; more importantly, through reading these old-fashioned books in modern dress, they could experience domesticity as offering adventure, emotional fulfill-ment, and sexual titillation as well.

Whereas Tatlock scrutinizes editions that generally appealed to female readers, the following set of two essays focuses on girl readers and their reading socialization in Imperial Germany. In her examination of Ferdi-nand Hirt's targeting of the girl reader in the 1880s — and in the par-ticular case of *An deutschem Herd* (On the German Hearth), the series of historical novels that he commissioned from Brigitte Augusti (pseud. for Auguste Plehn) — Jennifer Drake Askey demonstrates how the book trade cultivated a niche market and at the same time affirmed domestic roles for middle-class women that contributed to the national economy. In commissioning historical novels for girls in the manner of Gustav Frey-tag's popular six-volume *Die Ahnen* (1872–80; The Ancestors), Hirt and Augusti tapped into a popular genre of the time and tailored it specifically for the young middle-class female reader. Augusti's five-volume series (1885–88) introduced the girl reader to a patriotic history that unfolded for her in affective terms. Presented with heroines with whom she could readily identify, she learned from the books of her duty to play a role in the German national project as the literal and symbolic protector of the German hearth and home. Askey explains, furthermore, how the books themselves were part of a larger marketing strategy of appealing to mid-dle-class girls, their parents, and educators. The books not only overtly addressed parents and educators in their forewords, but also served as vehicles for advertising Hirt's broader publishing program.

Hirt & Sohn numbered, as Jana Mikota notes in her study of readers for higher girls' schools in Imperial Germany, among those German pub-lishers who made a fortune in publishing schoolbooks. But Hirt was only one of many publishers engaged in this lucrative business. In her contribu-tion to this volume on book history, reading, and social formation, Mikota examines the web of forces — the publishing industry, state education pol-icy, the author-editors of reading anthologies, teachers and their schools, and publications devoted to education — that shaped the school reader (in her particular example, the many editions of Kippenberg's reader) and thus girls' reading socialization in the late nineteenth and early twentieth cen-turies. Mikota traces the shift late in the century from contents focused on moral pedagogy to historical-aesthetic contents that grounded school girls in Germany's national literature and thus also contributed to national canon formation. She points especially to the emphasis in these readers on poetry — poetry that according to the pedagogy of the time was to be memorized. With this early and regular exposure to the genre, the graduate of the higher girls' school was well prepared for the recitation and writing of poetry that permeated middle-class sociability. Moreover, unlike women educated in earlier periods, she, armed with a literary aesthetic and historical education, left school less likely to indulge in reading the inferior products of mass culture and with better chances of succeeding should she undertake writing endeavors of her own.

While each of the preceding essays pays attention to publishers and the conditions of publishing, the two essays in the section "Writers and Their Publishers" focus more tightly on the fraught relations between a writer, now considered among Germany's most important authors, and his publisher. In each case, the writer's (sometimes mistaken) apprehension of the publisher and the publishing industry made for tense relations that centered largely on money — the publisher's alleged profits at the writer's expense. In the instance of Wedekind, as Mary Paddock outlines, the desire of the writer to settle the score adversely affected his literary production.

In the case of the Hamburg publisher Julius Campe and the writer Heinrich Heine, Jeffrey L. Sammons examines a thirty-year relationship that exhibited the intimacy and tension of a "marriage." Sammons takes issue with recent studies that suggest that this association was a model business relationship between friends or one between the prototype of the modern publisher and the prototype of the modern writer —views that, Sammons believes, draw conclusions based on preconceived notions of Heine. Sammons points out that Heine had little business sense, little interest in comprehending the economics of publishing and censorship as it affected publishing, and indeed little understanding of the connection between income and work. While work-for-work Heine was one of the better paid writers of his day, his high standards and meticulous work habits prevented him from maintaining the productivity of a professional writer. Nor did he possess the savvy of the professional writer when it came to forming alliances, and he was thus unable to recognize Campe as his most important ally. Sammons stresses in his account that Heine's relationship with Campe cannot be understood in modern terms because the conditions of publishing were not yet modern; that is, author's royalties were not yet calibrated to sales, but were instead a lump sum honorarium. Furthermore, no national or international copyright existed, and there was nothing resembling a free press in the German states.

The fifteen-year relationship between the ever-irascible Frank Wedekind and his publisher, Albert Langen, also proved to be difficult, and its rancor was rooted in particular in the perceived conflict between art and commerce. Mary A. Paddock examines this infamous relationship as it worsened after the so-called *Simplicissimus* Affair of 1898. When Langen founded the satirical magazine *Simplicissimus* in 1896, Wedekind was among the first to become a regular and successful contributor. However, as Paddock outlines, Wedekind did not see himself as gaining from this publishing relationship, but rather as securing the profits of an unscrupulous publisher even as he himself neglected his dramatic work. When in 1998 Wedekind supplied the magazine with a poem mocking Emperor William II, the issue of *Simplicissimus* containing it was confiscated. In the wake of its censorship and subsequent notoriety, its circulation tripled. While Langen conducted his affairs from abroad in safety and luxury, Wedekind was tried in Germany some months later for *lèse majesté*. As Paddock explains, this incident confirmed Wedekind's belief that Langen desired to make a profit to the disadvantage of his authors, and Wedekind thereafter repeatedly sought to take revenge on Langen in his writing. In doing so, however, he in the end caused his own art to suffer. Most notably, Paddock argues, his overtly autobiographical and vindictive play *Oaha* remains, in its many revisions, among his weakest works.

The final set of three essays in this anthology examines the book in the first three decades of the twentieth century in the context of mass markets and new competition from other media. Each considers how, even in the decades that perceived a crisis of the book in Germany, books could educate the masses, could provide a "last island of freedom" in a historical moment marked by right-wing activity and the threat of censorship, or could serve as a means of mediating between mass and elite culture.[60]

Katrin Völkner examines Karl Robert Langewiesche's successful "Blaue Bücher" (Blue Books) as they were marketed, beginning in 1902, to a mass audience with the claim that they supported the generally held truth that, for the sake of the nation, Germany's masses needed to embrace the country's tradition of *Bildung*. According to this widely shared view of *Bildung*, every individual had the possibility of improving himself or herself through "reading up" and thus participating in the nation's cultural traditions. The reading of culturally sanctioned texts, furthermore, could, it was thought, render the masses less vulnerable to the influences of mass commercial culture. As mass-produced books sold at a reasonable price, the Blaue Bücher forged an alliance between mass culture and high culture. Even as they upheld such cherished bourgeois beliefs and values as originality, the autonomy of art, and the cultivation of one's personality and talents, they reflected the standardization and rationalization that characterized the mass market. As Völkner outlines, with a limited number of titles, new marketing strategies, the branding of his books, and a selection of titles that emphasized self-improvement and cultural education, Langewiesche managed to make a profit while negotiating the tensions between consumption and availability on the one hand and exclusivity and distinction on the other.

Theodore F. Rippey examines Kurt Tucholsky's *Schloss Gripsholm* (1931; Castle Gripsholm) as a response to the crisis of the book in late Weimar Germany. In this work, Rippey argues, the satirist and journalist Tucholsky's desire to break through as a *book* author and Rowohlt's desire to produce a high-grade commodity for a broad market met in lighter fare for the reading public — indeed, in a re-imagining of literary activity keyed to the changing times. *Schloss Gripsholm* commences with an almost cheerful fictional exchange between the writer Tucholsky and the editor Ernst Rowohlt in which the former ties his ability to write to appropriate compensation. The humorous opening adumbrates more serious matters. As Rippey demonstrates, Tucholsky strove for artistic and commercial success with this novel at a politically fraught historical moment when he saw the book as the medium that offered a modicum of freedom in the public sphere. He discovered in the book a capacity to heighten the awareness of the contingency of feelings, to highlight the relationship between individual sensibilities and collective corporality, and to make available new modes of experiencing the relationship between self-composing language and socially composed power. Furthermore, in writing a "summer novel," a book that a man might give his girlfriend (in the words of Tucholsky's fictive Rowohlt), Rippey explains, Tucholsky worked with some of the conventions of popular fiction, creating scenes that operate in the register of emotion and sensation and yet simultaneously invite analytical reader response.

Ulrich Bach's examination of the collecting activity of the left-wing intellectual Eduard Fuchs as it impinged on his publication of books and the cultural transmission of art, as well as on his wish to mediate between mass and elite culture in Imperial and Weimar Germany, concludes this collection of eleven essays on books and social formation in the long nineteenth century. Fuchs, who famously is discussed by Walter Benjamin in his essay "Eduard Fuchs, der Sammler and Historiker" (1937; Eduard Fuchs, the Collector and Historian), passionately collected German as well as international art objects — including the more ephemeral print art of the caricature — until the National Socialist seizure of power forced his exile. While collecting can be essentially private, individualistic, and elitist, Fuchs, who believed both in individual sexuality as the driving force of creativity and in social conditions as the basis for art, cannibalized and rearranged his own collections to create books meant to educate the masses, producing as a result seminal books on the history of material art. Indeed, Fuchs and his publisher, Albert Langen, saw his collections and the resultant books as the forefront of the "discovery" of eroticism at the beginning of the twentieth century and thus as politically significant — indeed liberating — in repressive Imperial Germany. However, as Fuchs himself well knew, in the end his books — luxurious coffee-table books — failed their broad educational purpose. Unaffordable for all but the wealthy, they were more likely to decorate bourgeois villas than to be read in proletarian kitchens. In the end Fuchs owed the commercial success of his books to the bibliophiles and not to the masses that he wished to reach.

These eleven essays, of course, cannot aspire to a comprehensive look at the complex and dense field of book history in the long nineteenth century. They do, however, spotlight multiple ways of contextualizing literary production, of examining the pressures on publishing, writing, and reading and their consequences, and they direct our attention to some of the kinds of books produced in this period for readers' edification and entertainment, to those who did things with these books, and to the (national) culture and subcultures thereby engendered, reinforced, or, indeed, undermined.

Notes

[1] Victor Hugo, *The Hunchback of Notre Dame*, The Modern Library (New York: Random House, 2002), 172–73.

[2] Lynne Tatlock, "Realist Historiography and the Historiography of Realism: Gustav Freytag's *Bilder aus der deutschen Vergangenheit*," *The German Quarterly* 63, no. 1 (1990): 59–74, esp. 63–66.

[3] I have borrowed the phrase "century of words" from the title of Daniel Moran's book on Johann Cotta, *Toward the Century of Words: Johann Cotta and the Politics of the Public Realm in Germany, 1795–1832* (Berkeley: U of California P, 1990). The coinage stems originally, as Moran notes, from a letter written by Klemens von Metternich (1808), where Metternich addresses the importance of public opinion (Moran, 1).

[4] See Theodore F. Rippey, "The Weimar Literature Industry and the Negotiations of *Schloss Gripsholm*," in the present volume. Tucholsky, "Auf dem Nachttisch," *Die Weltbühne* 25, no. 9 (1929): 337, qtd. in Ute Maack, "Warum schreibt das keiner? Kurt Tucholskys Literaturkritik," in *Kurt Tucholsky: Das literarische und publizistische Werk*, ed. Sabina Becker and Ute Maack (Darmstadt: Wissenschaftliche Buchgesellschaft, 2002), 245.

5 Gideon Reuveni, "The 'Crisis of the Book' and German Society after the First World War," *German History* 20, no. 4 (2002): 438–39.

6 Ibid., 447.

[7] See Katrin Völkner, "*Bildung* for Sale: Karl Robert Langewiesche's Blaue Bücher and the Business of 'Reading Up,'" in the present volume.

[8] Robert Darnton, "What is the History of Books," *Daedalus*, Summer 1982: 65–83. This essay has been variously anthologized and amplified; see Darnton, "Histoire du livre — Geschichte des Buchwesens: An Agenda for Comparative History," *Publishing History* 22 (1987): 35–41. Darnton returned to the essay again in 2007 in Darnton, "'What is the History of Books?' Revisited," *Modern Intellectual History* 4, no. 3 (2007): 495–508.

[9] David Finkelstein and Alistair McCleery, introduction to *The Book History Reader*, ed. Finkelstein and McCleery, 2nd ed. (London: Routledge, 2006), 8.

[10] John O. Jordan and Robert L. Patten, eds., *Literature in the Marketplace: Nineteenth-Century British Publishing and Reading Practices* (Cambridge: Cambridge UP, 1995), 11; qtd. by Finkelstein and McCleery, introduction, 8.

[11] Reinhard Wittmann, "Die bibliographische Situation für die Erforschung des literarischen Lebens im 19. Jahrhundert (1830–1880)," in *Buchmarkt und Lektüre im 18. und 19. Jahrhundert: Beiträge zum literarischen Leben 1750–1880*, Studien und Texte zur Sozialgeschichte der Literatur 6 (Tübingen: Max Niemeyer, 1982), 233.

[12] Ibid., also Rudolf Schenda, *Volk ohne Buch: Studien zur Sozialgeschichte der populären Lesestoffe 1770–1910*, Studien zur Philosophie und Literatur des neunzehnten Jahrhunderts 5 (Frankfurt am Main: Vittorio Klostermann, 1970), 28.

13 William St Clair, *The Reading Nation in the Romantic Period* (Cambridge: Cambridge UP, 2004), 3.

[14] On fiction and nationalism see Todd Kontje, *Women, the Novel, and the German Nation 1771–1871: Domestic Fiction in the Fatherland* (Cambridge: Cambridge UP, 1998) and Brent O. Peterson, *History, Fiction, and Germany: Writing the Nineteenth-Century Nation* (Detroit, MI: Wayne State UP, 2005). Both studies importantly broaden the spectrum of writers to include popular and now lesser-known authors to offer a better sense of the "actually read" and its role in cultural formations. See also Kirsten Belgum, *Popularizing the Nation: Audience, Representation, and the Production of Identity in* Die Gartenlaube, *1853–1900* (Lincoln: U of Nebraska P, 1998), 17–27.

[15] Peter Uwe Hohendahl, *Literarische Kultur im Zeitalter des Liberalismus, 1830–1870* (Munich: C. H. Beck, 1985); Franco Moretti, *Graphs, Maps, Trees: Abstract Models for a Literary History* (New York: Verso, 2005). By looking at statistics rather than by reading, Moretti suggests models for a comprehensive literary history that takes into account far more than the canon.

[16] On the conversation between literary criticism and book history, see Leah Price, "Introduction: Reading Matter," *PMLA,* special issue: *The History of the Book and the Idea of Literature* 121, no. 1 (2006): 9–16.

[17] Moran, *Toward the Century of Words*, 5 and 5n8. Moran notes that the market for books in German expanded even more rapidly than the figures suggest, because book production was not stepped up until after the end of the Seven Years' War and, furthermore, German book production increased at the same moment that the market for books in Latin collapsed.

[18] Thomas Nipperdey, *Deutsche Geschichte 1800–1866. Bürgerwelt und starker Staat* (Munich: C. H. Beck, 1983), 588.

[19] Georg Jäger and Monika Estermann, "Geschichtliche Grundlagen und Entwicklung des Buchhandels im Deutschen Reich bis 1871," in Georg Jäger, ed., *Geschichte des deutschen Buchhandels im 19. und 20. Jahrhundert. Das Kaiserreich 1871–1918* (Frankfurt am Main: Buchhändler-Vereinigung GmbH, 2001), 1/1:18. Jäger and Estermann's historical overview has been of invaluable assistance to me in writing this introduction.

[20] Reinhard Wittmann, *Geschichte des deutschen Buchhandels: Ein Überblick* (Munich: C. H. Beck, 1991), 271.

[21] Reuveni, "Crisis of the Book," 442.

[22] Claus W. Gerhardt, "Die Wirkungen drucktechnischer Neuerungen auf die Buchgestaltung im 19. Jahrhundert," in *Buchgestaltung in Deutschland 1740 bis 1890: Vorträge des dritten Jahrestreffens des Wolfenbüttler Arbeitskreises für Geschichte des Buchwesens in der Herzog August Bibliothek Wolfenbüttel, 9. bis 11. Mai 1978,* ed. Paul Raabe (Hamburg: E. Hauswedell, 1980), 150. I thank Shane Peterson for calling my attention to this source and the information contained in it. The first German rotary press was produced in Augsburg in 1872. See also Marion Janzin and Joachim Güntner, *Das Buch vom Buch: 5000 Jahre Buchgeschichte,* 3rd ed. (Hannover: Schüter, 2007), 321, and the useful overview of the industrialization of book production by Peter Neumann, "Herstellung und Buchgestaltung," in Jäger, *Geschichte des Deutschen Buchhandels im 19. und 20. Jahrhundert,* 1/1:170–96.

[23] Gerhardt, "Drucktechnische Neuerungen," 148–49.

[24] Helwig Schmidt-Glintzer, introduction to *Gebunden in der Dampfbuchbinderei: Buchbinden im Wandel des 19. Jahrhunderts,* Wolfenbüttler Schriften zur Geschichte des Buchwesens 20 (Wiesbaden: Harrassowitz, 1994), 7. In the same volume see Ernst-Peter Biesalski, "Die Entwicklung der industriellen Buchbinderei im 19. Jahrhundert," 61–98.

[25] Nipperdey, *Deutsche Geschichte,* 588. See also the essay by Belgum below on the *Brockhaus.*

[26] Heinz Sarkowski, *Das Bibliographische Institut: Verlagsgeschichte und Bibliographie, 1826–1976* (Mannheim: Bibliographisches Institut, 1976), 104 and 118, respectively. I thank Kirsten Belgum for calling my attention to this information.

[27] Jäger and Estermann, "Geschichtliche Grundlagen," 1/1:18.

[28] Ibid., 24.

[29] Gerd Schulz, "Das Klassikerjahr 1867 und die Gründung von Reclams Universal-Bibliothek," in *Reclam 100 Jahre Universal-Bibliothek: Ein Almanach* (Stuttgart: Philipp Reclam Jun., 1967), 11–28. On Langewiesche, see Katrin Völkner, "*Bildung* for Sale: Karl Robert Langewiesche's Blaue Bücher and the Business of 'Reading Up,'" in this volume.

[30] On the collected illustrated works, see Lynne Tatlock, "The Afterlife of Nineteenth-Century Popular Fiction and the German Imaginary: The Illustrated Collected Novels of E. Marlitt, Wilhelmine Heimburg, and E. Werner," in the present volume.

[31] Rudolf Schenda, "Alphabetisierung und Literarisierungsprozesse in Westeuropa im 18. und 19. Jahrhundert," in *Sozialer und kultureller Wandel in der ländlichen Welt des 18. Jahrhunderts,* ed. Ernst Hinrichs and Günter Wiegelmann, Wolfenbütteler Forschungen 19 (Wolfenbüttel: Herzog August Bibliothek, 1982), 6, qtd. by Jäger and Estermann, "Geschichtliche Grundlagen," 1/1: 21–22.

[32] Ibid., 22.

[33] Wittmann, *Geschichte des deutschen Buchhandels,* 111–13. Figures provided by Barbara Kastner, however, indicate that in 1871 theology had overtaken "schöne

Literatur" (literature including poetry, novels, shorter prose fiction, and plays) in number of titles 1,362 to 950. After some fluctuation, in 1897 the latter overtook the former permanently, and in 1913, 2,683 theological titles were published as compared with 5,319 in "schöne Literatur." See Barbara Kastner, "Statistik und Topographie des Verlagswesens," in Jäger, *Geschichte des deutschen Buchhandels im 19. und 20. Jahrhundert*, 1/2:318–21.

[34] Jäger and Estermann, "Geschichtliche Grundlagen," 1/1:18.

[35] Friedrich Sengle, *Die Formenwelt*, vol. 2 of *Biedermeierzeit* (Stuttgart: J. B. Metzler, 1972), 27.

[36] Qtd. in Sengle, *Formenwelt*, 30.

[37] Georg Jäger, "Das Zeitschriftenwesen," in Jäger, *Geschichte des deutschen Buchhandels*, 1/2:369. Jäger quotes Gerhard Menz, *Die Zeitschrift: Ihre Entwicklung und ihre Lebensbedingungen; Eine Wirtschaftsgeschichtliche Studie* (Stuttgart: Poeschel, 1928), 33.

[38] Sengle points out further that women's names are frequently featured on the title pages, as in *Libussa, Aglaja, Ceres, Hertha, Psyche*, and *Hulda* (Sengle, *Formenwelt*, 46). See Sengle, 43–55, for a concise account of this genre. The Lilly Library at Indiana University in Bloomington, Indiana, contains a collection of ca. 2,000 of these *Taschenbücher*. Matt Erlin points to the cultural disapprobation directed at the consumers of these pocketbooks, consumers understood to be female, in his contribution to the present volume, "How to Think about Luxury Editions in Late Eighteenth- and Early Nineteenth-Century Germany."

[39] Karin A. Wurst, "The Shaping of Garden Culture in the *Journal des Luxus und der Moden* (1768–1827)," in the present volume.

[40] Ilsedore Rarisch, *Industrialisierung und Literatur: Buchproduktion, Verlagswesen und Buchhandel in Deutschland im 19. Jahrhundert in ihrem statistischen Zusammenhang* (Berlin: Colloquium Verlag, 1976), 66–67. See also Jennifer Drake Askey, "A Library for Girls: Publisher Ferdinand Hirt & Sohn and the Novels of Brigitte Augusti," in the present volume.

[41] For an overview of the transformation of the book trade from family enterprises to stock companies, see Georg Jäger, "Der Verlagsbuchhandel," in Jäger, *Geschichte des deutschen Buchhandels*, 1/1:197–215.

[42] Georg Jäger, "Der Verleger und sein Unternehmen," in Jäger, *Geschichte des deutschen Buchhandels*, 1/1:223–24.

[43] Jäger and Estermann, "Geschichtliche Grundlagen," 1/1:26–38.

[44] Ibid., 27.

[45] Martin Vogel, "Recht im Buchwesen," in Jäger, *Geschichte des deutschen Buchhandels*, 1/1:134–35.

[46] Ibid., 123.

[47] Jäger and Estermann, "Geschichtliche Grundlagen," 1/1:28.

[48] Jeffrey L. Sammons, *Wilhelm Raabe: The Fiction of the Alternative Community* (Princeton, NJ: Princeton UP, 1987), 36–37.

[49] Ibid., 38.

[50] On Alexis's feminizing of the public, see Lynne Tatlock, "Gendering Fashion and Politics in the Fatherland: Willibald Alexis' 'Doppelroman' *Die Hosen des Herrn von Bredow*," in *Autoren damals und heute: Literaturgeschichtliche Beispiele veränderter Wirkungshorizonte*, ed. Gerhard P. Knapp (Amsterdam: Rodopi, 1991), 232–55.

[51] Willibald Alexis: Letter to Friedrich Hebbel, Berlin, 4 January 1844, in *Friedrich Hebbels Briefwechsel mit Freunden und berühmten Zeitgenossen*, ed. Felix Bamberg (Berlin: G. Grote, 1892), 2:354.

[52] Anon., "Luise Mühlbach. Berlin und Sanssouci oder Friedrich der Große und seine Freunde. Historischer Roman," in *Literaturkritik*, vol. 4, ed. Alfred Estermann and Peter Uwe Hohendahl (Vaduz, Liechtenstein: Topos Verlag, 1984), 4:263.

[53] The letters from Luise Mühlbach to her publisher Hermann Costenoble, edited by McClain and Kurth-Voigt, provide a revealing look at the financial situation of a freelance writer. See William H. McClain and Lieselotte E. Kurth-Voigt, eds., "Clara Mundts Briefe an Hermann Costenoble. Zu L. Mühlbachs historischen Romanen," *Archiv für Geschichte des Buchwesens* 22, no. 4/5 (1981): cols. 917–1250.

[54] Else Hofmann, *E. Marlitt: Ein Lebensbild*, ed. Fayçal Hamouda (Arnstadt: Edition Marlitt, 2005), 19, 24, respectively.

[55] Ibid., 36.

[56] Pierre Bourdieu, *La distinction: critique sociale du jugement* (Paris: Éditions de Minuit, 1979).

[57] Gustav Könnecke, *Bilderatlas zur Geschichte der deutschen Literatur* (Marburg: Ewert, 1887). The first edition covers 50 CE to 1850 and is 316 pages long. The second edition of 1895 (also published in Marburg with Ewert) was expanded to 423 pages to include authors after 1850.

[58] Estermann and Hohendahl, ed., *Literaturkritik*, and Helmut Kreuzer, ed., *Deutschsprachige Literaturkritik 1870–1914. Eine Dokumentation*, 3 vols. (Frankfurt am Main: Peter Lang, 2006).

[59] Matt Erlin, "How to Think about Luxury Editions in Late Eighteenth- and Early Nineteenth-Century Germany," in the present volume.

[60] On the book as an "island of freedom" see Rippey, "The Weimar Literature Industry," in the present volume.

I. Distinction, Affiliation, and Education in Consuming Formats

1: How to Think about Luxury Editions in Late Eighteenth- and Early Nineteenth-Century Germany

Matt Erlin

THE FUNERAL OF CHRISTOPH MARTIN WIELAND in 1813 offered a fitting tribute to one of Germany's best-loved poets. According to a detailed report published in Friedrich Schlegel's *Deutsches Museum*, the casket was put on display on January 24, and large numbers of Weimar residents, representatives "aus allen Klassen" (of all classes), came to pay their final respects. Upon arrival, they encountered what must have been an impressive and moving scene:

> Auf einer Estrade ruhte der Sarg, in welchem der Todte mit ganz unveränderten Zügen, mit jener ihm eigenen Freundlichkeit, die selbst den Ernst der Todesstunde gemildert hatte, in ein weißmus-selinenes Sterbekleid gehüllt, einen von der Hand seiner jüngsten Tochter geflochtenen Lorbeerkranz auf dem Haupte, sanft ruhete. Die blauseidene Drapperie, womit der Unterkörper bedeckt war, floß auch auf den in der Verlängerung des Sarges liegenden Deckel herab. Da lag zunächst auf einem rothatlassenen Kissen sein *Obe-ron* und sein *Musarion*. Ersterer nach der schönsten Ausgabe von Göschen, letzteres Gedicht nach der bey Herrn von Degen in Wien 1808 erschienenen wahrhaft vollendeten Prachtausgabe. . . . Ein Lorbeergeflechte umarmte diese unsterblichen Erzeugnisse seines Geistes, und unter ihnen lagen auf einem weißen Atlaskissen franzö-sische Ehrenzeichen der Legion und der St. Annenorden, zwölf Can-delabers ergossen ihr Licht auf dieß angemessene Leichenbette.[1]

The atmosphere suggested by this description is one of tasteful opulence, an opulence befitting both the gravity of the occasion and the reputation of the deceased. The anonymous author of the report makes a point of noting the rare colors and fabrics of the goods on display — the white muslin burial gown, the blue silk drapery, and the red and white decorative satin pillows. Each of these items represents a socially sanctioned instance of extravagance meant to honor the artist and attest to his stature. The same can be said of the literary works included to memorialize his artistic achievements. Given the occasion, it seems only fitting that each of these works would be in the form of an exquisite luxury edition rather than any ordinary pocketbook version. Together with the other luxury goods, these editions helped to create the atmosphere of solemn celebration that characterized the event.

This description of Wieland's funeral ceremony offers more than mere testimony to the popularity of one of Germany's first canonical authors. In its conspicuous inclusion of two literary works among a series of luxury goods, it also points to a facet of book history that has thus far received little attention from scholars. Whereas scholarship on luxury editions in Germany in this period has tended to situate them exclusively within the context of developments in printing and publishing, the funeral description suggests that we place them within the broader framework of an emerging consumer society — more specifically, within the framework of eighteenth- and early nineteenth-century debates regarding the consequences of what was perceived as a rapid expansion in luxury.

These debates exercised the quills of countless elites in the period, leading to the publication of literally hundreds of books, treatises, and journal articles on the topic. Virtually all of the major intellectuals of the Enlightenment intervened at some point in their careers: Voltaire and Rousseau in France, Mandeville, Hume, and Adam Smith in Britain, and Herder, Kant, and Georg Forster in Germany.[2] Most commentators were deeply concerned with the spread of what they considered to be excessive consumption. For them, luxury was a cancer on the national body, the destroyer of families, and a source of immorality and physical enervation for the individual. A smaller group proved more sanguine, claiming for the first time in the long history of debates on the topic that at least some degree of luxury was ultimately beneficial for both the individual and society. They emphasized luxury as a spur to industry and a healthy circulation of money, as well as its role in the refinement of manners and the propagation of good taste.[3]

Regardless of their particular position, both sets of commentators often focused on the exotic imported commodities that came to be available on an increasingly wide basis in the period — coffee, tea, and spices, as well as textiles and various other fashionable goods. The description of Wieland's funeral, however, reminds us that one of the most widely circulated luxury commodities in the period, one characterized by an extraordinary degree of product differentiation as well as highly sophisticated techniques of marketing and brand management, was produced locally. That commodity was the book.

As in the case of other "premium" goods at the time, the increased circulation of luxury editions provided a source of celebration for some and a source of consternation for others. Each of these positions, however, can be viewed as part of a more general process through which surplus consumption was being reframed, a process that entailed, among other things, an effort to re-contextualize the pursuit of sensual pleasure. In the wake of a breakdown of previously valid criteria for establishing the legitimacy of certain forms of conspicuous expenditure such as social rank (elaborate fashions and forms of material culture) or religion (feasts and festivals), individuals were forced to come up with new frameworks for understanding, limiting, and morally sanctioning such pleasures.[4] Wieland's funeral provides evidence of the emergent conception of "good" luxury even as the emphasis on tastefulness, simplicity, and restraint in the description demonstrates the fragility of such legitimacy. As a number of articles from the period make clear, funerals in particular were sometimes singled out as occasions of unnecessary extravagance, and it is probably no coincidence that the author of the article quoted above emphasized the suitability or appropriateness of Wieland's ceremony (the term used is "angemessen").[5]

In the analysis that follows, I will focus on the ways in which luxury editions in particular figured in efforts to demarcate the boundaries of acceptable extravagance, whether as instances of an allegedly dangerous excess or as laudable examples of cultivated affluence. In the process, I plan to pursue two aims: the first is to demonstrate that new insights into the history of the book during the long nineteenth century in Germany can be gained by viewing developments in publishing against the backdrop of the broader history of consumer culture; the second is to expand upon some of the recent scholarship on that history, which has tended to emphasize individual self-fashioning and class identity to the neglect of the national contexts of consumption. Before turning to these topics, however, it will be necessary to explain in greater detail just what, precisely, constituted a luxury edition at the time.

The Look of Luxury

When Wieland received the edition of *Musarion* that eventually ended up in his casket, he was duly impressed. In a letter to Karl August Böttiger of September 14, 1809, he offers the following description: "Ohne Zweifel hat Ihnen der Buchhändler Degen in Wien auch ein Exemplar seiner über alles Prächtigen u schönen Prachtausgabe meiner Musarion zugeschickt. Was sagen Sie zu diesem typographischen Wunder in einer Zeit wie die unsrige?" (No doubt the publisher Degen in Vienna has also sent you a copy of his incomparably magnificent and exquisite luxury edition of my Musarion. What do you say to this miracle of typography in times like these?)[6] (see fig. 1.1). His expression of admiration might have surprised some contemporaries. Joseph Vinzenz Degen, publisher of the edition and director of what was eventually to become the state printing press (the *k. k. Hof- und Staatsdruckerei*) in Vienna, was viewed by many

MUSARION.

VON

CHRIST. MART. WIELAND.

EIN

GEDICHT IN DREY BÜCHERN.

WIEN.

IN DER DEGENSCHEN BUCHDRUCKEREY.

1808.

Fig. 1.1. J. V. Degen's edition of *Musarion*, published with the
permission of the Herzog August Bibliothek, Wolfenbüttel.

as a somewhat shady character. These German critics, however, most likely knew nothing of his activities as a spy for the Austrian government in the 1790s.[7] Rather, they took issue with his role in the long-running *Nachdruck* (print piracy) controversy between Protestant Germany and the Habsburg Empire.

Like many of his fellow Austrian publishers, Degen was accused of distorting the market and robbing honest authors of their due through the publication of unauthorized editions.[8] In Degen's case, moreover, his alleged transgressions were inextricably linked to his luxury productions since he and his supporters claimed that the quality of these editions precluded them from charges of piracy. In a brief advertisement in the *Intelligenzblatt* of the *Annalen der Literatur und Kunst in den Österreichischen Staaten* (Annals of Literature and the Arts in the Austrian States) dated January 1804, he makes his case, claiming that those who have made such accusations need only look in the catalogue of the Leipzig book fair, "in welchem bekanntlich Nachdrücke nicht angezeigt werden" (in which, as is well known, reprints are not advertised), in order to see the error of their ways.[9] A review of three of Degen's editions that appeared a year earlier in the same journal had made the same argument. As the author puts it, "[diese Prachtauflagen] sind kein Nachdruck, sondern ein Denkmahl der Achtung der deutschen Nation, das Hr. Degen . . . einigen der ersteren Dichtern Deutschlandes errichtet hat" (These luxury editions are not reprints, but rather a monument of admiration for the German nation, which Herr Degen has erected to some of the leading poets of Germany).[10]

Not all interested parties found such claims convincing, as can be gleaned from a letter, dated September 19, 1803, sent to Goethe by Christian August Vulpius. Vulpius warns his brother-in-law of a group in southern Germany that is publishing a complete edition of Herder's works, and he goes on to explain that "ein gewisser Hr. Degen, renomirter Wiener Buchhändler" (a certain Herr Degen, renowned Viennese bookseller) plans to publish luxury editions of all the great German authors. He advises Goethe to announce his own authorized edition of his collected works so as to avoid losing his well-deserved honorarium to this "Raub Gesindel" (thieving rabble).[11]

By 1809, however, Degen's reputation appears to have improved, due in no small part to the undeniable quality of precisely the series of editions that had provoked the ire of Vulpius. What was it that made Degen's work so exemplary? Scholarship on the history of publishing in Germany has made it clear that with regard to the material aspects of the book, publishers, authors, and readers at the time focused their attention primarily on three elements: paper, typeface, and illustrations. Each of these elements also proves significant for understanding the ways in which defenses mounted in favor of such editions mirrored broader trends in an emergent consumer culture.

Good paper was hard to come by in late eighteenth-century Germany. Until the mid-nineteenth century, when the use of wood-based paper became widespread, virtually all paper was made from rags in a production process that was extremely labor-intensive. The rags had to be collected, sorted, cleaned, and transformed into the pulp that would eventually be turned into the individual sheets of paper. The scarcity of the raw material meant that publishers and printers had a difficult time maintaining adequate supplies. Some states even instituted export restrictions on rags in an effort to address the problem.[12] In the short term publishers generally found it most expedient to print editions in a variety of paper qualities and in a range of sizes, from duodecimo to royal folio. The majority of copies appeared on simple *Druckpapier* (printing paper) while a smaller number, generally including those given to the author or his friends, was printed on more costly *Schreibpapier* (writing paper), which had undergone an additional process of strengthening and smoothing in order to reduce absorbency.[13] Imported papers from Switzerland and especially Holland were considered particularly rare and desirable, to such a degree that Wieland, in the preface to an earlier, second edition of *Musarion* (1769) published by Ph. E. Reich, drew attention to the fact that Reich had secured a supply of several bales of Dutch paper for the project.[14] The Degen edition of *Musarion*, however, raised the bar yet another notch. Not only did it appear in folio format, it was also printed on what was known as *Velinpapier* (vellum), an especially strong and smooth white drawing paper, so called because of its similarity to parchment (see fig. 1.2).[15]

Paper size and quality were not merely significant for the general durability of a book, they were also closely linked to typographical aesthetics. The whitest papers permitted maximum contrast between lettering and background, thereby increasing clarity. Larger sheets allowed for larger characters and wider letter-spacing, and lower degrees of absorbency made it less likely that the letters would bleed into one another or to the other side of the page. But the most urgent typographical dilemma for luxury producers in late eighteenth-century Germany came from a different direction and introduced a number of complicating variables into the decision-making process. The burning question of the day was which typeface to use: the traditional German *Fraktur* (black letter) or the Roman-inspired *antiqua*. As Wolfgang von Ungern-Sternberg has written, this question proved to be a frequent source of controversy after 1750.[16] While Latin type had become the standard in other European countries, in Germany German letters continued to be used for the overwhelming majority of texts appearing in the vernacular.

This widespread use of *Fraktur* became a target for criticism, however, at least for those authors and publishers concerned with the reputation of German literature abroad and among readers in Germany, especially those at court, who took their cue from France and Italy.[17] An example of

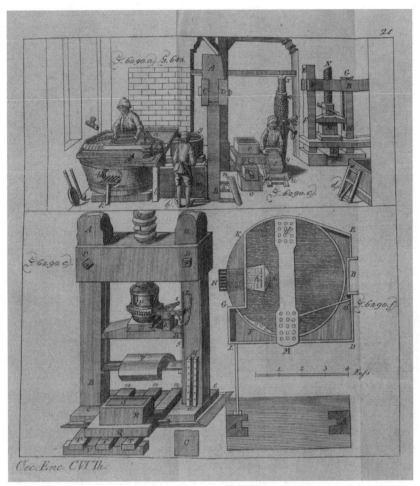

Fig. 1.2. Paper production in eighteenth-century Germany, J. G. Krünitz, *Oekonomische Encyklopädie,* vol. 106 (1807), published with the permission of the Herzog August Bibliothek, Wolfenbüttel.

the standard line of attack appears in a review of Degen's *Musarion* edition — which had been printed, of course, in *antiqua*. The author begins with a remark on the long inferior state of the printer's art in Germany. He attributes the achievement gap between Germany and other European countries in part to the fact that the latter had re-adopted "die edle reine Form der Römischen Lettern . . ., gegen die mönchisch-gothische Schnörkelei der sogenannten Deutschen" (the noble, simple form of the roman letters . . . as opposed to the monkish-gothic curlicues of the so-called German).[18] The implied contrast here between classical antiquity and the allegedly grotesque monasticism of the Middle Ages indicates that, at least among its supporters, the use of *antiqua* was viewed as part of a more general, anti-baroque endorsement of neoclassical aesthetics.

Decisions about which typeface to use, however, could not be based solely on such aesthetic considerations, because these decisions had practical economic consequences as well. Friedrich Schiller makes this clear in a letter he sent to his publisher, Crusius, in November 1799. Schiller insists here on the use of "deutsche Schrift" (German script) for the upcoming edition of his poems, because he claims to know "aus Erfahrung . . . daß man ein Buch dadurch in weit mehr Hände bringt" (from experience . . . that in this way a book ends up in many more hands).[19] As surprising as it may sound to a twenty-first-century reader, the general public simply found the German type much easier to read. In the words of H. M. Marcard, "die Hauptsache, weswegen ich für die Beybehaltung der teutschen Schrift bin, ist diese: sie ist den Augen angenehmer als die lateinische. . . . nicht dem Auge als Beurtheiler der Schönheit, sondern den Augen als Organ" (the main reason that I am in favor of the continued use of the German script is the following: it is more pleasant to the eyes than the Latin. . . . not the eye as a judge of beauty, but rather as the organ of sight).[20]

The typeface controversy is interesting for a number of reasons, not least because it provides a less familiar perspective from which to consider the interpenetration of class and aesthetics at the time and because it speaks to the topic of cultural nationalism. These facets of the debate, however, together with its various phases, have been fairly well documented.[21] For our purposes it is enough to note that around 1800, *antiqua* was the typeface of choice for the most exquisite luxury editions. Schiller himself says as much in response to Crusius's suggestion that he publish a luxury edition of his poems to accompany the regular edition. Agreeing with Crusius's own position he writes, "Lateinische Schrift ist zu einer Prachtausgabe wohl notwendig, aber sie dürfte freilich nicht gar zu klein gewählt werden" (Latin script is probably necessary for a luxury edition, but of course one must avoid choosing a typeface that is too small).[22] In the case of the Degen edition of *Musarion*, the *antiqua* characters are described by the previously mentioned reviewer as exemplary, not only in terms of "Schnitt," "Reinheit," "Gleichheit" (cut, purity, evenness), but also with regard to "die Schwärze der Schrift" (the blackness of the script). He does take issue with the occasionally uneven appearance of the umlauts and with the presence of "störende weiße Pünktchen" (irritating little white dots) in the thick lines of some characters. He also expresses some reservations about the illustrations — which brings us to the third major focus of attention in discussions of luxury editions at that time.

Illustrations constituted an important means of making a book more attractive to potential buyers, but one that had a significant impact on the price of the work. In addition, the inclusion of high-quality images, by heightening both the appeal of the work and its cost, also increased potential profit margins for the producers of cheaper, unauthorized reprints.[23] Publishers thus had to weigh carefully their decisions about how many and what kinds of illustrations to use. Some books were made available with and without illustrations, and occasionally images were offered for purchase separately.[24] The presence of any kind of visual material was noted in book reviews and advertisements, whether this material was in the form of portraits — Johannes Pezzl's *Charakteristik Joseph II* (1803; The Character of Joseph II) — landscapes — I. A. Schulte's *Ausflüge nach dem Schneeberge in Unterösterreich* (1802; Excursions to the Schneeberg in Lower Austria) — or diagrams and tables — J. Schemerl's *Ausführliche Anweisung zur Entwerfung, Erbauung und Erhaltung dauerhafter und bequemer Strassen* (1807; Detailed Instructions for the Design, Construction, and Maintenance of Durable and Comfortable Roads). With regard to works of literature, the most common illustrations at the end of the century were renderings of particular scenes from the plot.[25] In virtually all cases the images were in the form of copper-plate engravings — woodcuts were scorned by readers by this point — and both the artist of the original image as well as the engraver were frequently mentioned by name in advertisements and reviews, indicating that certain artists could increase the appeal of a book.[26]

The images in Degen's *Musarion* edition, for example, were originally drawn by the artist Karl Josef Aloys Agricola and engraved by Friedrich John. John was among the most respected engravers of his day, and he had already provided engravings for Göschen's luxury editions of the collected works of both Wieland and Klopstock.[27] In keeping with a generally restrained, neoclassical style of the *Musarion* edition, the illustrations were in this case modest in size and limited to three in number. Each appears as a headpiece at the beginning of each of the three sections of the poem and illustrates a scene from the work (see fig. 1.3).

A few examples will help to convey a sense of how these three factors — paper, typeface, and illustrations — were combined in order to achieve the remarkable degree of product differentiation that characterized the book market in this period. The milestone edition of Wieland's collected works, for example, published by G. J. Göschen in Leipzig between 1794 and 1811, appeared in four separate formats as described below:

Gr. 4 m. Kupfern auf geglättetem Velinpapier erster Sorte	250 Rtlr.
Gr. 8 m. Kupfern auf geglättetem Velinpapier erster Sorte	125 Rtlr.
Taschenformat (Kl. 8) m. Kupfern auf geglättetem Velinpapier	112 Rtlr. 12 Gr.
"Wohlfeile Ausgabe" in gewöhnlichem Format auf Druckpapier ohne Kupfer	27 Rtlr.[28]

M U S A R I O N.

ZWEYTES BUCH.

Was, beym Anubis! konnte das
Für eine Stellung seyn, in welcher Fanias
Die beiden Weisen angetroffen?
„Sie lagen doch — wir wollen bessers hoffen! —
Nicht süfsen Weines voll im Gras?" —
Diefs nicht. — „So ritten sie vielleicht auf Steckenpferden?"
Das könnte noch entschuldigt werden;
Plutarchus rühmt sogar es an Agesilas.

Fig. 1.3. Illustration from Book 2 of *Musarion*, published with the permission of the Herzog August Bibliothek, Wolfenbüttel.

A similar variety often characterized the publication of individual works, as advertisements from the *Annalen der Literatur und Kunst in den Österreichischen Staaten* make clear. A copy of an edition of Freiherr von der Lühe's two poems, *An Flora und Ceres* ("To Flora" and "Ceres"), published by Degen was available in the following formats:

In 4to, auf Velinpapier mit zwey Porträten des Verfassers, gezeich. von Kininger, und gestochen von John	10 fl[orins]
Dasselbe Werk, auf großem Velinpapier in 4to	15 fl.
Auf Velinpapier in 8vo, ohne Kupfer	3 fl.
Auf Druckpapier in 8vo	30 kr[euzers]²⁹

The fact that different currencies were used in Northern Germany, Southern Germany, and Austria renders comparisons between the two examples difficult, but it is possible to get an idea of the dramatic differences in price that characterized different editions of a given work. In the Wieland example given above, the luxury edition (known as the "Fürstenausgabe" [prince's edition]) is almost ten times as expensive as the bargain edition, and in the case of Freiherr von der Lühe, the most costly edition is thirty times as expensive as the cheapest. At the outset of plans to publish Wieland's collected works, the publisher Göschen wrote, "Jeder Kaufmannsdiener, jeder unbemittelte Student, jeder Landpfarrer, jeder mäßig besoldete Offizier soll Ihre Werke kaufen können" (Every merchant's servant, every impecunious student, every country pastor, every officer with a modest salary shall be able to buy your works).³⁰ Whether or not this was the case is extremely difficult to judge in the absence of detailed information on eighteenth-century budgets. Given that twenty-seven reichsthalers corresponded roughly to the price of two new pairs of boots in Dresden in 1764 and was slightly more than the annual rent for a simple flat in Berlin in 1793 (between eighteen and twenty-four reichsthalers), it seems that even the inexpensive edition would have constituted a major purchase for those of modest means.³¹ And it is certainly clear that the *Fürstenausgabe* would have been marketed to a very select audience.

One final aspect of the book as material commodity must be mentioned in this context — the binding. In most cases, questions related to book-binding did not figure into the discussion between authors and publishers about the formal aspects of editions of their works, because individual purchasers generally made separate arrangements with either the publisher or a bookbinder to have printed sheets bound according to their wishes and their budget. There were exceptions. Degen, for example, sometimes made his books available pre-bound, both in paper ("broschiert") and in boards ("cartonniert"), in either case "in gefärbtem Umschlage" (covered in colored paper).³² In the case of the *Wiener*

Taschenbuch für das Jahr (Vienna Pocketbook for the Year), which Degen published between 1803 and 1809, the type of binding was a key element in product differentiation. Almanacs in general relied heavily on extra-textual factors in order to increase their marketability. The 1806 edition of the *Wiener Taschenbuch*, which contained twenty-one copper-plate engravings and twenty tables "zur Bemerkung der Festtage des häuslichen Glückes und des gesellschaftlichen Lebens" (for marking the celebration days of domestic bliss and social life) was available in a gilt-edged, paper-bound version with a slipcase for seven florins, in English morocco leather for twelve, in the same morocco leather with a lock for thirteen, and in yet another version of the same with silver edging and an additional, free-standing set of illustrations for twenty florins.[33]

Geldautoren and *Bücherluxus*

The emphasis on concrete particulars in the foregoing discussion may give the impression that the production and consumption of luxury editions were a foregone conclusion in the period and that the editions themselves were accepted by all as the natural realization of the inherent potential of the printer's art. Indeed, commentators around 1800 often speak in terms that give this impression. In addition, much of the scholarship has approached the topic from this perspective, as if the exquisite works that appeared in the period embodied some sort of objective ideal that printing had been prevented from achieving until then.[34] Rather than a true explanation for the production of these editions, however, the adoption of such a perspective by late eighteenth-century advocates must be understood as a subtle means of asserting their legitimacy. Claims about the realization of aesthetic ideals constituted one of several strategies — I will turn to some of the others shortly — that were employed in the eighteenth and nineteenth centuries in order to justify the existence of what was seen as a potentially problematic luxury good. There was, after all, no shortage of commentators who viewed these editions with great suspicion. One of the more vociferous was the Swiss bookseller Johann Georg Heinzmann, whose *Über die Pest der deutschen Literatur* (On the Plague of German Literature) of 1795 decried a wide range of phenomena linked to the expansion of the literary market in the latter part of the century. A sense of his line of attack and its multifarious resonances can be gained from arguments such as the following:

> Sonst war es eine Hauptsorge des Schriftstellers, daß sein Werk correkt, und um einen ehrlichen Preis, nicht mit übertriebenem Luxus, aber doch anständig, gedruckt erschiene, damit der Preis dem Inhalt angemessen sey. Jetzt wissen unsere Autoren und Buchhändler so

wenig mehr von dieser deutschen Ehrlichkeit, daß man keine Bücher auf besser Papier und splenditer gedruckt siehet, als gerade die Schriften der Geldautoren, die mit Prangen und Scheinen ihre Leerheit decken.[35]

This alleged detachment of interior and exterior, essence and appearance, is a recurring theme in discussions of luxury editions and luxury more generally at the time.[36]

Adam Bergk, author of the popular treatise *Die Kunst, Bücher zu lesen* (1799; The Art of Reading Books), offers a variant of this concern when he argues, "Bücher sind zum Lesen, und nicht zur Ausschmückung von Zimmern bestimmt. Glänzende Einbände sind Vorlegeschlösser, die wir nicht abzureißen wagen, denn wie leicht könnte der schöne Einband beschmutzt werden! Wer daher seine Bücher zum Lesen bestimmt, muß sie nicht in prächtige Gewänder kleiden" (Books are meant to be read, not to be used to decorate the room. Brilliant bindings are like padlocks that we do not dare to tear off, for how easily we might sully the beautiful cover! Whoever thus intends that his books be read must never clothe them in magnificent robes).[37] In contrast to Heinzmann, whose primary target is the alleged greed of publishers and authors and the unscrupulous marketing of worthless books, Bergk views the problem with regard to utility. Extravagant ornamentation reduces the functionality of the book and is thus to be avoided. As with Heinzmann, however, the central question is whether the exterior exists in a harmonious relationship with the interior. While Bergk is generally a much more liberal thinker than Heinzmann, the implication of his utilitarian position is actually more radical, since there appears to be no possible justification for elaborate ornamentation, whatever the content of the work or the merit of the author. For Bergk, a luxury edition is a kind of category error, something along the lines of a non-alcoholic schnapps.

Concerns about the relationship between the interior and the exterior reappear even in the writings of those industry pioneers who did the most to encourage the production of up-market editions. In an advertisement for his opulent printing of the *New Testament* of 1803, G. J. Göschen legitimates the enterprise in terms that mirror those of Heinzmann: "Wenn typographische Pracht und Eleganz zuweilen an unbedeutende, oder wohl gar sittenverderbliche Werke verschwendet worden ist, so müssen hingegen alle Verehrer der christlichen Religion . . . mit Vergnügen und Beyfall ansehen, daß die Ehre einer typographischprächtigen Ausgabe den Urkunden der christlichen Religion widerfahre . . ." (If typographical magnificence and elegance have at times been wasted on insignificant or even immoral works, then admirers of the Christian religion must acknowledge with all the more pleasure and acclaim the fact that the founding documents of the Christian religion have been honored with a typographically magnificent edition. . . .).[38] What contents, in other words, could be more deserving of an elegant exterior than those profound and eternal truths contained in the Bible? In this instance Göschen was also participating in a long and established tradition of producing high-end Bibles for wealthy customers. The very fact that he finds it necessary to justify the undertaking, however, testifies to the existence of some unease about the matter.

One of the most telling examples of this unease comes from Wieland himself, whose initial reaction to Göschen's idea of publishing the "Fürstenausgabe" of his works reveals serious reservations about the project:

> Lachen Sie nicht über mich, liebster Göschen, — aber ich muß Ihnen meine Schwachheit, wenn es eine ist, gestehen: ein inneres Gefühl, das mir etwas mehr als bloße Bescheidenheit zu sein scheint, repugniert in mir dem Gedanken, alle meine Schriften in einer so prächtigen Ausgabe als Ihre Quart-Ausgabe sein wird, in die Welt gehen zu sehen. Es kommt mir gerade so vor, als ob ich mich zum Baron oder Grafen machen lassen sollte. Ein Autor muß wenigstens ein König seyn, um sich ohne Schamröthe eine so außerordentliche Ehre anthun zu lassen.[39]

Nothing about the context of these remarks suggests that Wieland is indulging in false modesty; rather, his comments demonstrate the extent to which estate-based categories for understanding the meaning of material possessions still exercised a powerful influence at the end of the eighteenth century. Despite the increasing proliferation of new and exotic consumer goods, in other words, there remained a strong sense of a substantive and natural link between certain forms of material culture and social rank. Even writers who advocated luxury as a means to spur individual industry and propel society toward prosperity often insisted that such luxury found its natural limit in the restraints imposed by a traditional society of orders. The rather liberal J. G. Büsch, to give just one example, asserts that the peasant must be encouraged to enjoy "die Früchte seines Fleisses" (the fruits of his industry); he goes on to make clear, however, that the affluence to which this industry gives rise must be in harmony with "seinem übrigen Zustande und Bestimmung" (his general circumstances and vocation).[40] In the example from Wieland, we can see the writer's conviction that the magnificent artifact proposed by Göschen is simply inappropriate for a middle-class author. It is worth noting in this context that Wieland does not condemn extraordinary luxury per se — as a squandering of valuable resources, for example. Rather, he reveals the degree to which, even late in the eighteenth-century, certain levels of pomp were thought to be appropriate only to the upper echelons of society.[41]

Such residual perceptions notwithstanding, it is also clear that a renegotiation of precisely this link was well underway in late eighteenth-century Europe. The challenge, as several recent studies have shown, was to rethink traditional conceptions of the relationship between people and things, to develop classifications and taxonomies that would legitimate the new intensity of surplus consumption and production. Taking our cue from the anthropologist Mary Douglas, who was one of the first to emphasize how goods are "needed for making visible and stable the categories of culture," we can understand this task in semiotic terms.[42] To the extent that the pre-existing connection between sign (forms of material culture) and referent (social rank) had become unstable or was deemed inadequate, it became necessary to re-establish some kind of semiotic order through a process of re-signification. In the terms used by Heinzmann in his attack, the task was to take what had long been viewed as "übertriebener Luxus" (exaggerated luxury) and make it "anständig" (respectable).

Legitimation Strategies

Woodruff Smith has provided a useful conceptual framework for thinking about this process. In *Consumption and the Making of Respectability* (2003) he introduces the idea of a "cultural context," which can be understood as a web of institutions, behaviors, discourses, locations, and material objects that are meaningfully linked to one another and that "make 'sense' as an ensemble to people living in a particular time and area."[43] He offers the contemporary example of the context of sports, which includes a whole range of equipment, games, and designated locations, to which one could also add various ritualistic behaviors (tailgating) as well as concepts like "soccer moms" and the purchase of certain types of folding chairs. Smith's overarching argument has to do with the way in which a selection of independent but overlapping contexts came to be subsumed as aspects of a single new context that became global in scope in the nineteenth century, that of respectability. There is much of interest in his analysis, but for our purposes the most significant aspect is his treatment of luxury. For Smith, the new, positive conceptions of luxury that emerged in the period represented so many attempts to reconcile morality with various forms of sensual pleasure. In his words, "the context of luxury is best understood as including both a set of morally problematical behaviors and the cognitive and linguistic frameworks within which people attempted to deal with the problems posed by those behaviors — but excluding solutions that called for doing without pleasant sensual experiences altogether."[44]

Smith focuses on three cognitive categories that play a key role in this effort to render sensual pleasure derived through consumption socially acceptable. The first is "taste," which provided a set of allegedly universal rules for organizing new forms of entertainment and shaping the consumption of non-essential goods. Notions of good taste, which in the eighteenth and early nineteenth centuries generally emphasized balance, order, and restraint, were of course set by social elites. Because of this and because the development of good taste allegedly required years of training and guidance, this category also had the advantage of helping to stabilize existing and emerging social hierarchies without invoking the arbitrary privilege of birth.[45]

The other two categories, "comfort" and "convenience," had a less immediate connection to social hierarchy though they functioned nonetheless as crucial elements in the evolving self-understanding of the middle class. The key point is that the idea of comfort, which appears in German writings from the period as "Bequemlichkeit" or "Gemächlichkeit," does not simply provide a neutral, descriptive label for certain kinds of pleasure, but that it functions normatively. That is to say, "comfort" becomes a designation that simultaneously categorizes and legitimates such pleasures by placing them within a cognitive context that links them to other, positively connoted activities and institutions. An evening spent smoking expensive tobacco in front of a roaring fire might be linked to such ideas as the value of friendship or the centrality of home and family.[46] The category of convenience functioned in a very similar manner, only in this case the emphasis was placed on an increase in efficiency or effectiveness and the elimination of unnecessary discomfort. In a late eighteenth-century context one might point to the new paraphernalia designed to assist the burgeoning numbers of recreational readers (lamps, desks, chairs).

Other scholars have approached the topic from a perspective similar to Smith's. Both John Crowely, writing about the British context, and Torsten Meyer, who discusses German cameralism, have addressed how the idea of comfort serves to validate the consumption of certain non-essential goods.[47] Focusing on the French context, Michael Kwass has shown how eighteenth-century thinkers like Georges Marie Butel-Dumont used Enlightenment arguments to disassociate forms of discretionary consumption from the traditional status hierarchy. By explicating the desire to consume in terms of a universal human right to the pursuit of happiness and pleasure, Dumont worked to neutralize the argument that luxury among the middle and lower classes was simply an expression of vanity and the quest for status.[48]

Though these scholars differ in a number of respects, they all demonstrate the means through which, over the course of the seventeenth and eighteenth centuries, advocates of luxury developed new cognitive categories to sanction what might have been perceived as extravagance. In the words of Smith, these categories "afforded a framework within which sensual experiences provided or suggested by commodities of bewildering variety and unprecedented availability could be enjoyed without appearing to threaten anything of significance."[49] None of these authors addresses books in any detail, but this framework of taste, comfort, and convenience nonetheless provides a good starting point for an analysis of German luxury editions in the period. At the same time, however, a consideration of these editions also reveals the need for a more nuanced approach to late eighteenth-century luxury goods, because the categories postulated by Smith and others are inadequate to capture the full range of strategies used to legitimate the production and purchase of such editions.

With good reason, much recent work on luxury has emphasized individual self-fashioning and the eighteenth-century shift away from the representative social function of consumption, which had been most powerfully embodied in early modern sumptuary laws. In many cases, this new emphasis stems from dissatisfaction with earlier scholarship on the topic, and especially the pioneering studies of Neil McKendrick, whose analyses posit competitive display and the emulation of the upper classes as the main wellspring of luxury consumption in the eighteenth century.[50] The desire for a more differentiated approach to the topic is certainly justified; however, the case of the German luxury editions suggests that we might want to revisit the categories of competition and emulation from a somewhat different direction. Discussions of these editions indicate that imitation of one's superiors was indeed a crucial aspect of contemporary consumer behavior, but in the advertisements and book reviews under consideration here, the imitative impulse appears to have been redirected away from social competition and toward national rivalry.

Before turning to the patriotic context of the production of luxury editions, however, we should note that Smith's categories do provide insight into many of the legitimation strategies used by producers and consumers of German luxury editions. To assert the need for additional nuance is not to claim that these categories lack validity in a general sense. The strategies in question are anything but monolithic, and in many instances the notions of taste and convenience (comfort less-so) figure prominently in the discussion. Declarations of the tastefulness of a particular edition appear frequently, particularly in reflections on the superiority of *antiqua* lettering over the allegedly baroque and grotesque *Fraktur*. Even a seemingly offhand reference, for example, to those "Männer von Kunstsinn und Geschmack" (men of artistic sensibility and good taste) who undertake to produce quality luxury editions gives a sense of the way in which this notion helps to construct an imagined — and rather exclusive — community of individuals with a unique capacity for aesthetic appreciation.[51]

Perhaps the most interesting facet of the discourse on taste is the frequent recourse to the closely related notion of connoisseurship as a way to justify the existence of these works. To be seen as a connoisseur is to be seen as someone for whom the purchase of a particular object is determined by a larger framework of intellectual interests and refined pleasures that enjoys wide acceptance among contemporaries. In reviews and advertisements, the target audience for these exquisite works is constructed in explicit opposition to those who are seduced by baubles and trinkets, those for whom the purchase of a luxury item represents an impulsive indulgence of purely sensual pleasures. Often the connoisseurship of the legitimate buyer is framed in terms of collecting; a review of Göschen's 1802 edition of Schiller's *Don Carlos*, for example, refers to those who will want to add the work to their "auserwählte Büchersammlung" (discriminating collection of books).[52] A discussion of editions of Ramler and Virgil makes reference to "Bibliophilen aller gebildeten Nazionen Europas" (bibliophiles from all the cultivated nations of Europe).[53] Many of Degen's most famous editions were actually marketed as part of such series as the *Collectio auctorum latinorum* (Collection of Latin Authors) or the *Sammlung deutscher Dichter* (Collection of German Poets). The idea of a collection, particularly a collection of Latin or German "classics," implies substantive knowledge and expertise on the part of its owner. It speaks to his ability to synthesize, to integrate individual elements into a coherent and meaningful whole. In this respect, it is thus seen to reflect a motivation far more respectable than the one driving the — presumably female — purchaser of gilded trivialities like the "Prachtausgäblein von Kalendarlein, Taschenbüchlein, Gedichtlein" (pretty little volumes of little calendars, little pocketbooks, little poems), which, according to one commentator, "leider! so sehr Mode geworden [sind]" (unfortunately! have become all the rage)."[54]

In other cases this expertise is couched not in terms of the content of the work but in terms of print culture itself, as knowledge of the inherent potential of the art (or science) of typography.[55] Indeed, the entire constellation of elements described in reviews of these works has as its organizing spirit a notion of technical expertise. It is this expertise that allows one to appreciate such details as the "Schönheit der Typen, genaue Beobachtung der Zwischenräume, Geradheit der Linien, Schwärze des Drucks und Weiße des Papiers" (the beauty of the type, precise monitoring of the spacing, straightness of the lines, blackness of the ink, and whiteness of the paper) and gives rise to "den Beifall aller Kenner" (the applause of all connoisseurs).[56] Such comments also point to the convergence of the idea of taste and the category of convenience, fusing the invocation of progress toward the perfection of typography with the ideas of efficiency and utility in the sense of ease of reading. The reviews of Karl August Böttiger, author, archeologist, and editor of the *Journal des Luxus und der Moden* (Journal of Luxuries and Fashion) in Weimar, offer some of the most conspicuous examples of this tendency. He repeatedly couples the decorative and the purposive, employing phrases like the "verständige Zweckmäßigkeit der Ornamente" (judicious efficacy of the ornamentation) or applauding the relatively narrow margins of a Virgil edition, despite the fact that those "verwöhnte Liebhaber der unsinnigen Papierverschwendung" (spoiled fanciers of the senseless waste of paper) would no doubt rather have it otherwise.[57]

Böttiger's model for the ideal luxury edition seems to take its cue from idealist theories of the work of art, which he combines with a healthy dose of Enlightenment utilitarianism. He describes a new edition of Valerius Wilhelm Neubeck's poetic work *Die Gesundbrunnen* (The Fountains of Health) as "eine splendide Ausgabe im größten Format . . . die durch die reinste Harmonie aller Theile zu einem schönen Ganzen und durch die sorgfältigste Präcision in der Ausführung selbst, diejenige Forderungen zu befriedigen anfängt, deren Erfüllung bis jetzt den Teutschen unmöglich schienen" (a splendid edition on a grand scale . . . which, as a result of the incomparably harmonious combination of all parts into a beautiful whole and the extraordinary precision of the execution, begins to satisfy those demands whose fulfillment has seemed impossible for the Germans up until now).[58] Taken as a whole, his comments offer a uniquely comprehensive collection of the arguments on the basis of which what had been a single, negatively charged category of luxury became differentiated into "good" and "bad" variants. Pointless excess ("Papierverschwendung") is opposed to taste and expert knowledge ("Beifall aller Kenner"), technological achievement ("sorgfältigste Präcision"), and utility or convenience ("Geradheit der Linien," "Schwärze des Drucks").

Gilding the Nation

A closer look at the rhetorical staging of these arguments, however, reveals that they also appear as part of a larger framework that presumes German inferiority in the field of publishing and celebrates each luxury edition as a step toward the achievement of parity. The foregoing quotation from Böttiger, for example, refers to the demands of high-quality publishing that Germans have been unable to meet "bis jetzt" (up until now). The review of Degen's *Musarion* edition in the *Journal des Luxus und der Moden* begins by pointing out that Germany has recently delivered "mehrere typographische Werke . . . die mit Recht mit den schönsten Arbeiten der Ausländer an die Seite gestellt werden können" (several works of typography . . . that can justifiably be placed side by side with the most exquisite productions of foreign presses).[59] Similar comments appear in virtually all of the positive reviews of these works, often with specific references to such printing houses as those of François Didot in France and Giambattista Bodoni in Italy, whose productions were considered exemplary. The publishers who undertake such editions are praised as patriots who spare no expense, "auch in dieser Hinsicht der teutschen Literatur die Schamrothe vor ihren Nachbaren zu ersparen und zu beweisen streben, daß teutschen Händen auch Werke der Eleganz entsteigen können . . ." (to strive, also in this respect, to save German literature from humiliation in the face of its neighbors and to prove that works of elegance can also arise from German hands . . .).[60]

Of course, in a general sense it is hardly surprising to find narratives of cultural competition in texts from this period. German-speaking elites from Friedrich Nicolai to Goethe had been lamenting their nation's alleged lack of cultural accomplishment since at least the 1750s, and the widespread upsurge in patriotic sentiment in the wake of the French Revolution has been well documented. Apparent in these reviews, however, is an aspect of this competition that has not been recognized, namely the interpenetration of such patriotic sentiment and the discourse on luxury production and consumption at the time. Scholars have noted the often nationalistic undertone of the debate over gothic type, but the function of patriotism in the reviews is of a somewhat different character. Whereas in the typeface controversy national pride appears as an end in itself, in the case of the luxury editions this pride is used to justify the existence of what might otherwise be seen as wholly superfluous. In other words, the use of national comparisons figures critically in the legitimation of luxury by allowing these editions to be recast as national treasures rather than personal indulgences. The legitimacy of such treasures, moreover, is all the greater in light of the fact that they represent so many attempts to measure up to a standard already established by other nations. In this instance then, one does indeed find that the principle of emulation generates motivation for consumption. Unlike other examples of imitative "conspicuous consumption," however, such emulation poses no threat to social stability. On the contrary, it helps to stabilize relations among different social classes by providing an object of identification at the national level, one that can be admired and approved by everyone, even if it can only be owned by a select few.

One way to gain a better sense of this community-building (and canon-forming) function of luxury consumption is to take commentators at their word when they refer to these editions as "ein Denkmal des teutschen Geschmacks und Kunstfleißes" (a monument to German good taste and artistic productivity) or "ein schönes Monument" (a beautiful monument).[61] Such comments suggest that rather than serving solely as a means of individual or class identity formation or an expression of individual status-seeking, these consumer objects also provided a mechanism through which surplus expenditure was linked to a sense of national pride. The object memorialized or celebrated is sometimes the art of printing as such and sometimes the author and his work. Optimally the two are combined into a seamless unity, an ideal that returns us to the connection between interior and exterior discussed previously. One reviewer expresses particular satisfaction with Degen's *Musarion* because, in his words, "Schönheit der Ausführung und Schönheit des Inhalts sich hier so glücklich verbinden" (beauty of execution and beauty of content converge here so serendipitously).[62] Though the author does not go into any detail regarding the content of

Wieland's poem, the fact that it advocates a life of modest pleasures and opposes both asceticism and mindless excess does make it a particularly felicitous choice for such an edition.

Occasionally the logic of the patriotism argument is reversed, as when J. W. von Archenholz, in his discussion of Wieland's collected works, worries that an insignificant list of subscribers might reflect a lack of appreciation for a poet who is the "Stolz seiner Nation" (pride of his nation).[63] And occasionally the importance of national identification is explicitly cast in opposition to more local patriotism, as when Böttiger points out that "jeder Teutsche, der die klassischen Nazionalwerke nicht nach der kleinen Erdscholle, die ihn hervorbrachte, mißt, wird . . . begierig seyn, [Ramlers] Gedichte in dieser vollendeten Ausgabe . . . zu besitzen" (every German who does not measure the classical works of a nation according to the little clump of earth from which he emerged will be eager to possess Ramler's poems in this exemplary edition).[64] In all cases, however, the categories of taste, comfort, and convenience are situated within the larger context of national improvement, and this larger context appears to provide one of the key frameworks through which the sensual pleasures provided by these products are accommodated to popular conceptions of morality.

Keeping such comments in mind, one can perhaps draw a parallel between these editions and the actual national monuments that proliferated in the nineteenth century, from Cologne Cathedral to the Kyffhäuser Monument. Testimonials from the period demonstrate that at least some of these volumes, in particular those produced by Degen, did take on a monument-like function in serving as sites of pilgrimage, and not only when they appeared as part of a famous author's funeral. Carl Bertuch, journalist and son of the editor of the *Journal des Luxus und der Moden*, for example, made sure to view Degen's editions while attending the Vienna Congress as a representative of the *Vereinigung der deutschen Buchhändler* (Association of German Booksellers). In his *Tagebuch vom Wiener Kongress* (Journal from the Congress of Vienna) he writes, "Degen zeigt uns vor Tisch die Prachtexemplare 1. von Lucan, 2. von Musarion, 3. Epithalama von Bondi. Sowohl Druck als Einband ganz meisterhaft. — Die Zubereitung des Pergaments als Velin ganz vorzüglich" (Before the meal, Degen showed us the luxury editions 1. of Lucan, 2. of *Musarion*, 3. *Epithalma* by Bondi. Printing and binding both magisterial. — the preparation of the parchment as vellum truly exquisite.)[65] In a similar manner, the ill-fated August von Kotzebue takes note of Degen's work in his *Erinnerungen von einer Reise aus Liefland nach Rom und Neapel* (*Reminiscences of a Journey from Livonia to Rome and Naples*), first published in 1805. While in Vienna, he writes, he makes a point of visiting "den thätigen Buchhändler Degen" (the industrious bookseller Degen). He then goes on to invoke the motif of foreign superiority, claiming that Degen's editions of Uz and Zimmermann (*Musarion* had not yet appeared at this point) "wetteifern mit denen der reichen Britten; selbst die kostbaren Einbände geben den englischen nichts nach" (compete with those of the wealthy Brits; even the costly bindings keep pace in all respects with their English counterparts).[66] In addition, some of the subscription offerings for these books operate in a manner very similar to those calls for contributions to the construction of monuments, appealing to patriotic sentiment and a sense of competition with other nations.

There are of course key differences as well. Subscribers to the luxury edition of Wieland's collected works actually took individual possession of the product. In addition, in the case of publications like this one, appeals to national pride are linked much more directly to commercial interests. Publishers generally included a page listing pre-subscribers to a work, just as public monuments often have a plaque commemorating donors, but in the case of the luxury edition this commemoration served as an additional form of advertising for the product. A prestigious list of pre-subscribers could generate additional post-publication interest in the volume.

Another context in which commentators stress the patriotic implications of consumption may help to cast the specificity of the luxury editions into greater relief. Karin Wurst has shown how the late eighteenth-century German debate about the pros and cons of a national costume reveals a shifting framework of identity construction in the period, as elites began to develop models of social solidarity that transcended the traditional corporatist social structure of the German states. In terms of the models of community around which it was organized then, this cultural debate points forward to the more explicit political nationalism of the nineteenth century. In terms of the history of consumer culture, however, the debate is essentially backward-looking, since most advocates of such costumes cast their arguments in explicit opposition to luxury, to what was seen as an unhealthy appetite for new, extravagant, and often foreign goods.[67] The perceived value of the national uniform was seen to stem from its functionality and restraint as well as from its ability to render the wearers equal. In contrast, the arguments in support of the luxury editions attempt to justify extraordinary levels of individual expenditure on highly ornate products that simultaneously establish or reinforce social hierarchies, even as they appeal to broader patriotic sentiments. In this sense the advocates of luxury editions anticipate the strategies used by late nineteenth- and early twentieth-century American advertisers who stressed consumption as a means to unify the people even as they carefully cultivated the role of goods as symbols of social distinction.[68]

Degen's editions in particular also enable us to see the entanglement of self-interest and public spirit on the production side of the equation. While his celebrated luxury editions of the poet Johann Peter Uz and the author-physician Johann Georg Zimmermann were sold on the open market to anyone who could afford them, his *Musarion* edition was never marketed at all. Instead, he offered copies as gifts to the author and a few other distinguished personalities. While Wieland's own copy was printed "auf geglättetem Velinpapier" (on pressed vellum paper), two additional copies were printed on parchment and presented to Emperor Napoleon and Tsar Alexander. There is no reason to doubt that the publisher had a genuine interest in the development of typography in Germany or in celebrating Wieland's literary achievements. His contemporaries, however, while they acknowledged his contributions, also recognized that his apparent self-sacrifice and generosity could be seen as the continuation of self-aggrandizement by other means. As Carl Bertuch explains in his previously cited *Tagebuch*, Degen demonstrated extraordinary self-sacrifice in undertaking the luxury editions, "die aber darin sich belohnte, daß er sich dem Hof geneigt machte und die Staatsdruckerei erhielt, wodurch er zum reichen Mann wurde" (which, however, in the end paid off by winning him the admiration of the court and the state printing company, as a result of which he became a rich man).[69]

Conclusion

Ultimately, whether one is considering the desire to produce or purchase these works, it proves impossible to disentangle more cold-blooded commercial calculations from patriotic sentiment or any of the other motivations that might have influenced individual decision-making. This very confusion of motives, however, provides the key to understanding how such extravagant objects acquired legitimacy in the period. The turn of the nineteenth century marks the final dissolution of what can be termed a correspondence model of consumption, which, though never all-encompassing or unassailable, posited a fixed and allegedly natural link between specific forms of expenditure and one's position in a stable social hierarchy. This model is replaced by one based on immanent coherence, where there is no absolute standard according to which "excessive" consumption can be determined.[70] As long as one can construct a meaningful and coherent narrative that attaches individual expenditure to an aim perceived as socially beneficial, any level of luxury can be made to appear justifiable. In this respect the story of German luxury editions is part of the larger eighteenth-century story — the most memorable chapter of which was written by Adam Smith — of how individual self-interest and the interests of society ultimately come to be conceived as identical.

In many ways this identification would seem to be firmly established in our own day, and there is much about contemporary consumer culture that suggests a world very different from the one in which Degen was operating. When, for example, J. K. Rowling produced seven handwritten copies of her story collection *Tales of Beedle the Bard* bound in brown morocco leather and decorated with hand-chased silver ornaments and semiprecious stones, there was certainly no public expression of concern over whether such objects constituted an unnecessary luxury. Neither, it should be pointed out, was there any attempt to pitch these editions as technical or artistic achievements. On the contrary, as her decision for a handwritten manuscript over a printed book makes clear, these copies were self-consciously anachronistic, intended to provide access to some semblance of authenticity in a thoroughly commodified society. It is true that both Degen and Rowling can be seen as tapping into the consumer's desire for singularity and uniqueness, but the former achieves this by gesturing toward the future, whereas the latter does so by gesturing toward a less commodity-saturated past or perhaps toward a fantasy world in which such objects would seem at home.

Nonetheless, it is worth noting that Rowling, like Degen, decided to give six of these copies away, albeit to friends rather than potential patrons. She also donated the proceeds ($3.98 million) from the auction of the seventh copy to the Children's Voice charity campaign. Her actions indicate that the need to establish the legitimacy of luxury has by no means disappeared, whether for producers or consumers. In the case of the latter, the context of fandom constitutes a contemporary variant of the more traditional idea of the collector, which continues to exist alongside it. In other spheres as well, narrative frameworks organized around notions of cultivation, comfort, convenience, and even — occasionally — national interest, continue to be invoked as a way to justify discretionary expenditure that might otherwise be deemed excessive. To these one can also add narrative frameworks organized around health and environmental sustainability — the legitimacy of extravagant spending on organic foods, for example, would seem to be beyond question among certain groups of consumers.

The only alternative to these contingent justificatory narratives would be a model of consumption that applies some sort of absolute standard to individual expenditure. The correspondence model discussed above offers one example of such a standard, but there are others. At the turn of the nineteenth century the German philosopher J. G. Fichte addressed the question of luxury in his treatise on trade policy, *Der geschlossene Handelsstaat* (1800; The Closed Commercial State). Fichte does not advocate an estate-based, hierarchical approach to consumption, but neither does he celebrate the desire for luxury as a spur to industry, self-improvement, and technological advancement. Instead, he argues for the equitable distribution of resources. As he puts it, "Es sollen erst alle satt werden und fest wohnen, ehe einer seine Wohnung verziert, erst alle bequem und warm gekleidet sein, eher einer sich prächtig kleidet" (Everyone should first have enough to eat and a place to live before anyone adorns his home; everyone should have warm and comfortable clothing before anyone begins to dress magnificently).[71] From our current perspective, his position seems just as irrefutable as it does antiquated and impractical. Even in 1800, as Degen's own success indicates, it is not clear that anyone was still listening.

Notes

[1] "Wielands Begräbniß," *Deutsches Museum* 3 (1813): 174. "The casket was placed on a low platform. Inside the deceased rested quietly, wrapped in a white muslin burial gown and crowned by a laurel wreath woven by his youngest daughter. His features were completely unchanged, his characteristic kindliness seemingly rendered even more gentle by the gravity of the hour of his death. The blue silk drapery that covered the lower half of his body also flowed out over the cover that lay in the extension of the casket. Resting there on a pillow of red satin were, first of all, copies of his *Oberon* and his *Musarion*, the former in the most beautiful edition published by Göschen, the latter poem in the truly faultless luxury edition that appeared with Herr von Degen in Vienna in 1808. . . . An arrangement of laurel branches surrounded these products of his immortal spirit. Beneath them, on a pillow of white satin were French badges of honor from the Legion and the Order of St. Anne; twelve candelabras cast their glow upon this fitting burial scene."

[2] For a detailed discussion of the discourse of luxury since antiquity, see Christopher Berry, *The Idea of Luxury: A Conceptual and Historical Investigation* (Cambridge: Cambridge UP, 1994).

[3] A summary and commentary can be found in the editorial introducing Friedrich Justin Bertuch's new *Journal des Luxus und der Moden* Bertuch: "Es ist so viel schon für und gegen Luxus gesagt und geschrieben, und er ist so gränzenlos und unbedingt verdammt und verteidigt worden, daß es sonderbar damit zugehen müßte, wenn nicht auch hier, wie gewöhnlich, die Wahrheit in der Mitte stehen sollte" (Friedrich Justin Bertuch und Georg Melchior Kraus, "Einleitung," *Journal der Moden,* January 1786, 4; So much has already been written, both in favor of and against luxury, and it has been so endlessly and unconditionally condemned and defended, that it would be a very curious thing if it did not turn out that in this case, as usual, the truth should lie somewhere in the middle).

[4] See Woodruff Smith, *Consumption and the Making of Respectability 1600–1800* (London: Routledge, 2003), 63–81.

[5] See for example Georg Sieveking, "Fragmente über Luxus, Bürgertugend und Bürgerwohl," *Verhandlungen und Schriften der Hamburgischen Gesellschaft zur Beförderung der Künste und nützlichen Gewerbe* 4 (1797): 171.

[6] Christoph Martin Wieland, *Wielands Briefwechsel,* ed. Siegfried Scheibe, vol. 17, pt. 1 (January 1806–September 1809) (Berlin: Akademie Verlag, 2001), 669.

[7] Werner M. Bauer, "Der Verleger und Drucker Joseph Vinzenz Degen und Johann Baptist Wallishausser und ihre Stellung in der österreichischen Literatur ihrer Zeit," in *Die Österreichische Literatur: Ihr Profil an der Wende vom 18. zum 19. Jahrhundert (1750–1830),* ed. Herbert Zeman (Graz: Akademische Druck & Verlagsanstalt, 1979), 179–203.

[8] The details of the *Nachdruck* controversy have been well documented. For a discussion that includes detailed bibliographical information on both primary and secondary sources, see Heinrich Bosse, *Autorschaft ist Werkherrschaft: Über die*

Entstehung des Urheberrechts aus dem Geist der Goethezeit (Paderborn: Schöningh, 1981).

[9] Joseph Vinzenz Degen, "Berichtigungen," *Intelligenzblatt der Annalen der Literatur und Kunst in den Österreichischen Staaten*, January 1804, 6.

[10] "Zimmermann von der Einsamkeit," *Annalen der Literatur und Kunst in den Österreichischen Staaten*, January 1803, 8.

[11] "Vulpius to Johann Wolfgang von Goethe, 19 September 1803," in *Christian August Vulpius: Eine Korrespondenz zur Kulturgeschichte der Goethezeit*, ed. Andreas Meier, vol. 1: *Brieftexte* (Berlin: Walter de Gruyter, 2003), 88.

[12] Irmgard Kräupel, "Buchausstattung," in *Lesewuth, Raubdruck und Bücherluxus: Das Buch in der* Goethezeit," ed. Jörn Görres (Düsseldorf: Goethe-Museum Düsseldorf, 1977), 152.

[13] Ibid., 149.

[14] Qtd. in Wolfgang von Ungern-Sternberg, "Schriftstelleremanzipation und Buchkultur im 18. Jahrhundert," *Jahrbuch für Internationale Germanistik* 8, no.1 (1976): 82.

[15] Johann Georg Krünitz, *Ökonomische Encyklopädie*, s.v. "Velinpapier," http://www.kruenitz1.uni-trier.de/. It should be mentioned that Degen was also famous for having renewed the art of printing on actual parchment and that two copies of his *Musarion* were printed on that material. See W. u. B., "Musarion von Wieland: Pracht-Ausgabe von Degen in Wien 1808," *Journal des Luxus und der Moden* 24 (1809): 790–93.

[16] Ungern-Sternberg, "Schriftstelleremanzipation," 83.

[17] Ibid.

[18] "Prachtausgabe der *Musarion* in Wien," *Neue Berlinische Monatsschrift*, October 1810, 235.

[19] *Schillers Werke: Nationalausgabe*, ed. Lieselotte Blumenthal and Benno von Wiese, vol. 30, *Briefwechsel: Schillers Briefe 1.11.1798–31.12.1800*, ed. Lieselotte Blumenthal (Weimar: Hermann Böhlaus Nachfolger, 1961), 120.

[20] H. M. Marcard and C[hristoph] M[artin] Wieland, "Apologie der teutschen Lettern, mit einer Antwort des Herausgebers," *Der neue Teutsche Merkur* 3 (1793): 100–101. Wieland's own position is a bit hard to determine. In his editorial response to the article he argues that the author has been too hasty in his conclusions. In a letter to Göschen dated July 15, 1799, however, he claims that the sale of his collected works has been hindered by the "verwünschten lateinischen Lettern" (accursed Latin letters), and he goes on to maintain that the German type is easier to read. Qtd. in J. G. Gruber, *C. M. Wielands Leben* (1827; repr., Hamburg: Hamburger Stiftung zur Förderung von Wissenschaft und Kultur, 1984), 287.

[21] See, e.g., Wulf D. v. Lucius, "Anmut und Würde: Zur Typographie des Klassizismus in Deutschland," in *Von Göschen bis Rowohlt: Beiträge zur Geschichte des deutschen Verlagswesens*, ed. Monika Estermann and Michael Knoche (Wiesbaden: Otto Harrassowitz, 1990), 33–61; Fritjof Luhmann, "Wandlungen der Buchgestaltung am Ende des 18. Jahrhunderts," in *Buchgestaltung in Deutschland 1740–1890*, ed.

Paul Raabe (Hamburg: Dr. Ernst Hauswedell & Co., 1980), 89–104. The topic is also discussed in the previously cited article by Ungern-Sternberg, 83–86.

[22] *Schillers Werke: Nationalausgabe*, ed. Norbert Oellers and Siegfried Seidel, vol. 40, pt. 1, *Briefwechsel: Briefe an Schiller 1.1.1803–17.5.1805*, ed. Georg Kurscheidt and Norbert Oellers, 21.

[23] Rosemary Hoffmann-Scholl, "Die Buchillustration im 18. Jahrhundert," in Raabe, *Buchgestaltung in Deutschland*, 40, 47.

[24] The *Intelligenzblatt der Annalen der Literatur und Kunst*, for example, advertises two portraits of Freyherr von der Lühe for 6 fl. if purchased separately from the edition of his poems *An Flora und Ceres* and at a discount (3 fl.) if purchased together with the work. See Degen, Book advertisement in the *Intelligenzblatt der Annalen der Literatur und Kunst in den Österreichischen Staaten*, January 1803, 20.

[25] Hoffmann-Scholl, "Die Buchillustration," 46.

[26] Ibid., 47.

[27] Dr. Constant von Wurzbach, ed., *Biographisches Lexikon des Kaiserthums Oesterreich*, vol. 10 (Vienna: Die kaiserlich-königliche Hof- und Staatsdruckerei, 1863), 238.

[28] Qtd. in Ungern-Sternberg, "Schriftstelleremanzipation," 79n.16. The formatting of the information suggests that it comes directly from an advertisement for the edition, but the citation does not provide any details in this regard.

Quarto with copperplate engravings on premium quality, smooth vellum paper	250 Rtlr.
Octavo with copperplate engravings on premium quality, smooth vellum paper	125 Rtlr.
Pocketbook format (small octavo) with copperplate engravings on premium quality, smooth vellum paper	112 Rtlr. 12 Gr.
"Budget edition" in standard format on printing paper without copperplate engravings	27 Rtlr.

[29] Degen, Book advertisement in the *Intelligenzblatt der Annalen der Literatur und Kunst in den Österreichischen Staaten*, January 1803, 20. One Florin=60 Kreuzer.

In quarto on vellum paper with two portraits of the author, drawn by Kininger and engraved by John	10 fl[orins]
The same work, on large vellum paper in quarto	15 fl.
On vellum paper in octavo, without copperplate engravings	3 fl.
On printing paper in octavo	kr[euzers]

[30] Qtd. in Ungern-Sternberg, "Schriftstelleremanzipation," 79n.16.

[31] Bernd Sprenger, *Das Geld der Deutschen: Geldgeschichte Deutschlands von den Anfängen bis zur Gegenwart* (Paderborn: Ferdinand Schöningh, 1991), 149.

32 Degen, Book advertisement in the *Intelligenzblatt der Annalen der Literatur und Kunst in den Österreichischen Staaten*, June 1804, 168.

33 Degen, Book advertisement in the *Intelligenzblatt der Annalen der Literatur und Kunst in den Österreichischen Staaten*, November 1805, 240.

34 See for example Lucius, "Anmut und Würde," esp. 41–45.

35 Johann Georg Heinzmann, *Appell an meine Nation, über die Pest der deutschen Literatur* (1795; repr., Hildesheim, Gerstenberg, 1977), 167; "previously, a primary concern of the author was to ensure that his work was printed correctly, without exaggerated luxury but nonetheless decently, and offered at an honest price that corresponded to the content. Now our authors and booksellers have forgotten this German honesty to such a degree that no books appear on better paper or are printed more splendidly than those of the greedy hacks who cloak their emptiness with showiness and flashiness."

36 Examples from the more general discussion can be found in Johann Heinrich Zedler, *Universallexikon aller Wissenschaften und Künste*, s.v. "Mode," vol. 21, 707, http://www.zedler-lexikon.de/ and in "Ueber den Luxus in Berlin," *Journal des Luxus und der Moden* 2 (1787): 411.

37 Johann Adam Bergk, *Die Kunst, Bücher zu lesen, nebst Bemerkungen über Schriften und Schriftsteller* (1799; n.p.: Zentral Antiquariat der Deutschen Demokratischen Republik, n.d.), 33.

38 Georg Joachim Göschen, "Ankündigung einer Prachtausgabe des griechischen Neuen Testamentes nach Griesbachs Recension," *Beylage zum Intelligenzblatt der Annalen der Literatur und Kunst in den Österreichischen Staaten*, January 1803, viii.

39 Qtd. in Gruber, *C. M. Wielands Leben*, bk. 7, 37; "Do not laugh at me, my dear Göschen, but I must confess to you my weakness, if that is indeed what it is: an inner feeling, which appears to me to be more than mere modesty, is repulsed at the thought of seeing all of my writings introduced to the world in such a magnificent edition as your quarto-edition will be. I feel as if I must have myself elevated to the rank of baron or count. An author would have to be at least a king to allow himself to be paid such an extraordinary honor without embarrassment."

40 Johann Georg Büsch, *Abhandlung von dem Geldumlauf in anhaltender Rücksicht auf die Staatswirtschaft und Handlung* (Hamburg and Kiel: Carl Ernst Bohm, 1780), pt. 1, 274.

41 Another assertion by Büsch demonstrates how notions of estate-based consumption were combined with emerging economic models that emphasized utility. Of the nobleman he writes, "Er muss nicht nur wol leben, er muss hoch leben, damit das ihm so reichlich zufliessende Geld wieder in Umlauf komme" (He must do more than live comfortably, he must live in a grand manner, so that the money he receives in such abundance is reintroduced into circulation). Ibid., pt. 2, 63.

42 Mary Douglas and Baron Isherwood, *The World of Goods: Towards an Anthropology of Consumption*, 2nd ed. (London: Routledge, 1996), 38.

43 Smith, *Consumption*, 13.

⁴⁴ Ibid., 67.

⁴⁵ Ibid., 81–83.

⁴⁶ Ibid., 84.

⁴⁷ John Crowley, "The Sensibility of Comfort," *The American Historical Review* 104, no. 3 (1999): 749–82; Thorsten Meyer, "Zwischen sozialer Restriktion und ökonomischer Notwendigkeit: Konsum in ökonomischen Texten der Frühen Neuzeit," in *"Luxus und Konsum" — eine historische Annäherung,* ed. Reinhold Reith and Torsten Meyer (Münster: Waxmann, 2003), 62–81.

⁴⁸ Michael Kwass, "Ordering the World of Goods: Consumer Revolution and the Classification of Objects in Eighteenth-Century France," *Representations* 82 (Spring 2003): 87–114.

⁴⁹ Smith, *Consumption*, 85.

⁵⁰ A brief discussion of McKendrick and some of the objections can be found in Don Slater, *Consumer Culture and Modernity* (Cambridge: Polity, 1997), 19–20, 148–73.

⁵¹ G[eorg] von Reinbeck, "Deutsche Typographie als Luxus betrachtet," *Journal des Luxus und der Moden* 23 (1808): 521.

⁵² "Prachtausgabe von Schillers *Don Carlos* mit Kupfern," *Journal des Luxus und der Moden* 18 (1803): 42.

⁵³ K[arl] A[ugust] Böttiger, "Zweckmäßige Prachtausgaben von Virgil und Ramler," *Der neue teutsche Merkur* 3 (1800): 303.

⁵⁴ "Thomas Abbt *vom Verdienste*," *Neue allgemeine deutsche Bibliothek* 104, no. 1 (1805): 221.

⁵⁵ The same can be said of the discussions of copper engravings, the production of which is referred to in the period as *Chalkographie.*

⁵⁶ Böttiger, "Zweckmäßige Prachtausgaben," 310, 309 respectively.

⁵⁷ Ibid., 309.

⁵⁸ Böttiger, "Neubecks *Gesundbrunnen,* eine typographische Merkwürdigkeit," *Der neue teutsche Merkur* 3 (1798): 297.

⁵⁹ "Prachtausgabe der *Musarion* in Wien," 790.

⁶⁰ "Teutsche Typographie als Luxus betrachtet," 521.

⁶¹ F. Schöll and K[arl] A[ugust] Böttiger, "Ueber den Abbé Delille und die Prachtausgabe seiner Georgika in Basel," *Der neue teutsche Merkur* 2 (1797): 239; "*Musarion* von Wieland," 790.

⁶² "Prachtausgabe der *Musarion* in Wien," 236.

⁶³ J[ohann] W[ilhelm] von Archenholz, "*Sämmtliche Werke,* by Christoph Martin Wieland," *Minerva* 2 (1795): 185.

⁶⁴ Böttiger, "Zweckmäßige Prachtausgaben," 312.

⁶⁵ Carl Bertuch, *Bertuchs Tagebuch vom Wiener Kongreß,* ed. Hermann Freiherrn v. Egloffstein (Berlin: Gebrüder Paetel, 1915), 44.

⁶⁶ August von Kotzebue, *Ausgewählte prosaische Schriften,* vol. 43 (Vienna: Ignaz Klang, 1843), 306.

[67] Karin Wurst, "Fashioning a Nation: Fashion and National Costume in Bertuch's *Journal des Luxus und der Moden*," *German Studies Review* 28, no. 2 (May 2005): 367–86.

[68] See Charles F. McGovern, *Sold American: Consumption and Citizenship, 1890–1945* (Chapel Hill: U of North Carolina P, 2006), 97–106.

[69] Bertuch, *Tagebuch*, 44.

[70] The publication of Bernhard Mandeville's *Fable of the Bees* (1723) marks a crucial moment in the emergence of this idea of relative luxury. As the author explains, "if once we depart from calling everything luxury that is not absolutely necessary to keep a man alive, then there is no luxury at all." Bernhard Mandeville, *The Fable of the Bees and Other Writings*, ed. E. J. Hundert (Indianapolis, IN: Hackett, 1997), 66.

[71] J. G. Fichte, *Ausgewählte politische Schriften*, ed. Zwi Batscha and Richard Saage (Frankfurt am Main: Suhrkamp, 1977), 79.

2: The Shaping of Garden Culture in the *Journal des Luxus und der Moden* (1786–1827)

Karin A. Wurst

A MUCH DISCUSSED CULTURAL PRACTICE in German print culture around 1800, the garden phenomenon contributed to a comprehensive and distinctly modern lifestyle. Friedrich Justin Bertuch's widely read magazine *Journal des Luxus und der Moden*[1] (The Journal of Luxuries and Fashion), illustrated by Melchior Kraus, discusses changing fashions in clothing, gardens, furniture, coaches, and other luxury goods.[2] It is in this sphere of cultural consumption and knowledge transfer, which in turn is intimately tied to the press, that the garden design as a cultural trend became popularized. Bertuch's successful career, in publishing and (cultural) entrepreneurship, embodies one version of the emerging social and economic independence of the German middle class around 1800. His role and that of his most famous publication, the periodical *Journal des Luxus und der Moden*, deserve a prominent place in the history of popular print culture and cultural knowledge transfer in Germany at that time.

By investigating Bertuch's *Journal*, this essay asks questions different from those posed in the voluminous critical literature on gardens and gardening that address the formal transition from French garden styles to the English landscape garden, the transition from an emblematic to an expressive quality, the aesthetics of the garden, or its relationship to landscape painting.[3] Instead it explores how one of the most popular and long-lived monthlies of the time framed and popularized garden discourse. We can assume that many readers were already familiar with these debates; the *Journal* popularized them further.[4] Moreover, the exploration of how the media created and shaped the domestic garden phenomenon around 1800 contributes to our understanding of the complexity and contested agency of culture at the turn of the nineteenth century. The "Gartenliteratur" phenomenon allows us to study culture as something that is constantly created in the various practices of everyday life, including consumption.[5]

Friedrich Justin Bertuch (1747–1822) was an influential publisher and a highly successful businessman. His "Landesindustrie-Comptoir," a form of for-profit co-operative, brought the products of the region's artisans together to advertise, market, and ship while also providing and purchasing the raw materials and tools needed to produce them. It thus played an important role in the creation and dissemination of material culture at the turn of the nineteenth century.[6] It is not surprising, then, that in the methodological wake of Cultural Studies, Bertuch has attracted considerable scholarly attention as publisher and editor of journalistic works for the emerging leisure reading market.[7] His fairy tales for adults and children, the *Blaue Bibliothek* (Blue Library) and the *Blaue Bibliothek für Kinder* (Blue Library for Children); his illustrated encyclopedic work for children, *Bilderbuch für Kinder* (The Picture Book for Children); the political and cultural magazine *London und Paris*; and his most popular publication, *Das Journal des Luxus und der Moden*, were widely read. He rose from service at the court of Duke Carl August as "Hofmeister" (tutor) to become the duke's financial advisor. Eventually he gained independence from the court to lead an autonomous, comfortable lifestyle and achieved social prestige in his native Weimar.

Bertuch's name has become synonymous with the kind of cultural consumption and aesthetics of everyday culture that constituted the context for the phenomenon of the garden as it was conceptualized and described in the *Journal des Luxus und der Moden*. His brand of cultural entrepreneurship enabled him not only to become a wealthy and powerful man himself, but also to create jobs and income for artisans in the *Landes-Industrie-Comptoir* and in his print shops. He employed women too, those who colored the illustrations in the *Journal* and worked in the silk flower manufacturing facility overseen by his wife.[8] Fusing theory and practice, cultural and economic development, he understood the economic power of fashionable luxury consumption to provide employment and income for local populations. His vision for economic reform combined the understanding that economic conditions (local manufacturing facilities as well as distribution centers) had to be created so that the demand for non-essential goods (luxury items), which print publications like the *Journal* fostered, could be satisfied locally and thus money would not flow abroad for the import of luxury goods. The *Journal des Luxus und der Moden*, however, created interest in and demand for aesthetic products and practices for everyday life far beyond the immediate region around Weimar. In the advertising supplement to the *Journal*, the *Intelligenzblatt*, Bertuch also conducted business by commission and mail-order.

Glimpses at the emergent concept of lifestyle governed by taste gleaned from the *Journal* provide a wide-ranging picture of the various facets of cultural life around 1800 and the self-representation of the middle class. The many aspects of everyday consumption challenge the vision of a monolithic bourgeoisie at the turn of the nineteenth century. As I argue in my book *Fabricating Pleasure: Fashion, Entertainment, and Cultural Consumerism*, it becomes clear that we are observing a middle class intently occupied with differentiating itself internally — no longer vis-à-vis the nobility — by displaying distinct tastes and lifestyles.[9]

In its forty-two volumes, some forty-thousand print pages, and 1,493 illustrations, the *Journal* (1786–1827) traces social and cultural changes and their effects and reflections from around the time of the French Revolution until the conservative reorganization of Europe after the Congress of Vienna. It was sold primarily by subscription and cost four and later (beginning in 1811) six reichstalers per year. With the subscription Bertuch included an advertising supplement, the *Intelligenzblatt*, which also served as a form of catalogue for mail-order. In the first years about 2,000 copies were printed and sold. In addition to those from the ranks of the nobility, the readership included the economic elite within the middle class (merchants and bankers), academics (physicians, lawyers, professors, and artists), and civil servants and their families. Geographically, the main distribution was in the Protestant regions in the middle and northern German states. Sales became weaker after the turn of the century when the *Journal* had to compete with new publications. By 1806 the numbers had fallen to 1,200, and by 1824 only 300 to 400 copies were sold annually, the sales no longer covering the production costs.

The *Journal* played a significant role in creating and shaping cultural practices, denoting a sense of identity for a range of middle-class readers: what they did and had and how they defined themselves. Cultural identity was by the late eighteenth century no longer automatically defined by one's family, but became the responsibility of the individual as the various strata of the middle class no longer limited their household furnishings to family heirlooms that symbolized their heritage. Magazines helped to shape taste, which, in turn, along with financial means, determined the kinds of acquisitions that adorned the home and the garden. Moreover, the information that the illustrations and descriptions of famous landscapes in the *Journal* and other print publications provided for leisure-time reading contributed to the general knowledge of landscape design.[10]

Given the prevalence of advertisements for the latest books on gardening and landscape design in the *Intelligenzblatt*, the topic must have enjoyed immense popularity, especially toward the end of the century. In 1798, for example, we find several announcements and descriptions of new garden publications, like the following one on pomology (Latin *pomum* fruit), the science associated with fruit-bearing trees. The advertisement for *Der Teutsche Obstgärtner* (The German Pomologist), is followed by one for a multi-volume reference work on flowers, *Der Geöffnete Blumengarten* (The Accessible Flower Garden), organized according to botanical classifications, with illustrations and descriptions in German and French. This notice is followed in turn by one concerning a special offer:

the highly popular (and inexpensive) *Botanik für Frauenzimmer welche keine Gelehrte sind* (Botany for Women Who Are Not Experts) was offered together with *Der Geöffnete Blumengarten* — both by the same author, Professor Batsch — at a discounted price: "Nachricht wegen Hrn. Prof. Batsch Botanik für Frauenzimmer und dessen geöffneten Blumengarten" (Notice Regarding Prof. Batsch's "Botany for Women" and his "Accessible Flower Garden"). The advertisement explains that while *Botanik* was immediately sold out, *Blumengarten* had experienced losses over the course of the subscriptions (it was obviously published in individual sections); the bundling of the more heavily illustrated and thus more expensive work (*Blumengarten*) with the more popular one was to boost sales.

A few entries later, we see in the *Journal* an announcement entitled "Litterarische Anzeige über den Erdäpfelanbau" (Literary Announcement on Potato Planting) describing the more advanced state of potato farming in England, where seventeen different varieties of potato and specifically designed plows are available for this purpose. This entry is followed by a note to the owners of gardens recommending a garden calendar ("*Gartencompagnion* oder immerwährender Gartenkalender für Herrn und Damen, worinn man angezeigt findet, was man zu jedem Monat im Blumen- Frucht- und Küchengarten als auch im Gewächshaus zu thun hat" [Vademecum or Perpetual Calendar for Gentlemen and Ladies, Showing the Tasks one has to Complete in the Flower-, Fruit-, and Kitchen Garden as well as in the Greenhouse Every Month]) and by an announcement entitled "Anzeige an Liebhaber von engl. Anlagen" (Notice for Enthusiasts of English Landscape Gardens). In addition, the *Intelligenzblatt* contains information on forestry: "Kurze practische Anweisung zum Forstwesen" (Short Practical Guide to Forestry).[11]

As these sample entries from 1798 suggest, the intended readership ranged from professional and specialized users of agricultural products, such as landowners with large forests and large-scale potato growers (who presumably were the only ones in a position to use the illustrations of the special plows as blueprints for their own), to the owners of large forested areas, to the larger amateur audience using gardening for domestic purposes and, above all, for pleasure.

The *Journal* was thus positioned between the philosophical, scientific, and economic learned discourses on the one hand, and the emerging market orientation and more populist engagement with contemporary ideas and with the objects of material culture on the other. To select the *Journal* to explore the creation of the garden phenomenon instead of the many specialized publications on gardening was to underscore that the garden phenomenon had to be seen as one of many factors in the creation of a lifestyle. Like other cultural practices discussed in the *Journal*, the shaping of the garden experience was subject to fashionable change and thus dynamic.[12]

The *Journal* propagated the *experience* of the garden and not the garden as mere object. This essay explores how the *Journal* and its advertising supplement, the *Intelligenzblatt*, in their day, sparked interest and conveyed a sense that the creation of a pleasurable garden experience could be within reach for its readership. With its reference to other books on landscape design, the *Journal* both reinforced its own message of the desirability of gardening as part of a modern lifestyle and entered into a kind of division of labor with other publications on gardening with distinct missions. With the reference to the detailed description of the *Neue Englische Garten bey Arlesheim, ohnweit Basel* (New English Garden near Arlesheim in the Vicinity of Basel) from 1786, for example, the reader can learn what constitutes innovation in garden design. The author also refers the reader to the French original, which, unlike the *Journal,* contains illustrations of the landscape garden.[13] While the Journal depicts itself in conversation with state-of-the-art knowledge — in this case on gardening — it is at the same time very clear on its own role in popularizing this knowledge and making the information useful for the more practical demands of its readership.

Thus the *Journal* not only described the large public landscape gardens as destinations for travel and inspiration but offered descriptions and recommendations for the appointment of the domestic garden, its furniture, its decorative objects, the ever-changing fashionable selections of plants, and the garden's possibilities as a site for various forms of sociability and as a realm for educating the young, for conducting amateur scientific experiments, for collecting, and for experimenting with new crops for a more sophisticated culinary experience. The forms of leisured sociability that the garden experience provided were regarded as important moments for the psychological well-being of the self.

To create the garden as an experience, the *Journal* had to capture the imagination of its readership. It did so by furnishing descriptions of visits to exemplary gardens, explanations of desirable practices, and advertisements of products, furniture, and plants, along with the visualizations of these objects in the form of illustrations. The announcement of new or improved products and objects for the enjoyment of the garden takes the form of the following example: "Zwey Englische Garten-Sitze" (Two English Garden Seats) are described as delightful gifts for garden-lovers to enjoy the arrival of spring; the announcement suggests their pleasurable use in the experience of drinking in the pleasures of spring. The entry's practical side supplies a drawing for the benches, which can easily serve as a pattern for imitation of the "leicht zu verfertigenden Garten-Kanapes" (easily built garden benches) that rest not on legs but on broad bases ("Fußschwellen"), so that they won't sink into the wet ground.[14] As in many examples, the entry emphasizes not only the practical aspect of the object, but also, very importantly, the pleasurable experience of the garden, dwelling on the opportunity to indulge, in comfort, in the sights, scents, and sounds of the new spring. The aesthetic experience is enhanced by utility and practicality that minimize the inconvenience of traditional chairs (see fig. 2.1).

As we shall see below, the descriptions in the *Journal* of garden phenomena tend toward vividly conjuring up sights, sounds, touch, and smell to stimulate the imagination of its readers, inviting them to picture themselves enjoying such surroundings. Unlike other contemporary publications that it refers to, when it evokes the experience of the garden, it does so verbally rather than with images, as we see in the examples. We are not presented with images of people enjoying the landscape; the *Journal* merely provides information as building-blocks to stimulate the desire to create the experience. The *Journal* was in fact so successful, I argue, precisely because it provided the information that allowed its readers actually to picture themselves creating this kind of experience for their own enjoyment. The illustrations thus tend to be of objects that can serve as features in establishing a garden. I also suspect that because the *Journal* was limited as to the size and quality of its images, it stayed away from depicting complex scenes to conjure up the desired sensations and feelings; instead it used language to prompt the imagination to create a vision in the reader's mind. The combination of depictions in text and image of the items for the garden or the decorative objects for the home, coupled with practical advice on how to use the objects and how to purchase them, enticed readers to imagine themselves replicating the enjoyable experiences associated with the emergent garden culture.

The *Journal* creates the garden discursively as an experiential space, one that both the imagination and the sensual body inhabit through the ambulatory experience of immersion that the garden offers, with its engagement of not only sight but also touch — the feel of hard and soft surfaces — sound, and scent as well as the experience of heat and coolness. It issues an invitation to imagine the use of this space through the occupation with plants and flowers as collections and as botanical experiments and in learning opportunities for self-improvement or playful learning for children. The varied sensory experience of the landscape, the *Journal* proposes, creates a variety of moods and emotional reactions which, in turn, are experienced as something pleasant.

In creating the multi-dimensional and multi-layered cultural phenomenon of the middle-class "garden," the *Journal* followed in the footsteps of Christian Cay Lorenz, who had significantly contributed to the garden mania in Germany. Much more than a mere change of style from the more formal French fashion in gardening to the English landscape garden, the middle-class garden was created by a complex set of new values ranging from an increased aesthetic interest in novelty, variety, experimentation, and hands-on experiences to an interest in (popular) science that sought

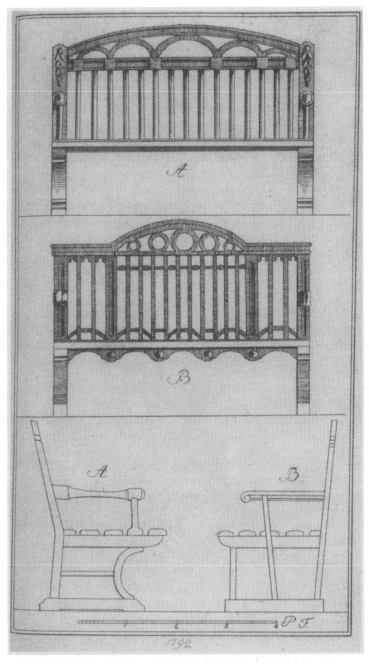

Fig. 2.1. "Englische Garten Sitze" (English Garden Seats),
Journal 1792, plate 12, published with the permission of the Thüringer
Universitäts- und Landesbibliothek, Jena.

a sense of clarity and transparency in the engagement with natural phe-nomena.[15] Of particular interest to the theoretician of the literature on gardening at the end of the eighteenth century is the creation of a multi-sensory, emotional, and intellectual experience that relies on the powers of the imagination associated with the modern garden.[16]

The English landscape garden appeals by creating a complexly layered experience that alternates between the sensations created by openness and closure, sun and shade, softness and brilliance, shades of green and flow-ers, nature and civilization. The convenience of the walkways creates plea-surable ambulatory experiences, and the benches facilitate another kind of motor-sensory interaction with the environment which, furthermore, invites contemplation. The *Journal* mentions the sounds of moving water and birdsong as auditory experiences that complement the motor-sensory and visual experience of the garden. As an article from 1790 elaborates, the variety of deliberate design choices creates various moods to be expe-rienced, moods ranging from the melancholy solitude of a leafy, shaded area to the gaiety of a brightly colored flowerbed in another part of the garden. Furthermore, the author writes,

> Die größten Schönheiten eines englischen Gartens entstehen durch ausgebreitete Ebenen und Hügel; durch glänzende Wasserspiegel und braußende Flüsse; durch silberhelle sich schlängelnde Bäche und sanfte Wasserfälle; durch düstere Hayne und einzelne Baumgruppen; durch das sanfte Grün weit ausgebreiteter Rasenteppiche und durch wilde Formen schroffen Felsen; durch wechselweise beschränkte und ausgebreitete Aussichten in fruchtbaren Fluren und nach entfernten Gebirgen; durch verschiedene an schicklichen Stellen angebrachte Gebäude, Monumente, und Brücken; durch das bunte Gemisch von mancherley Schattierungen von Grün und die Abwechslung welche die Blühten der hier aus entfernteren Ländern versammelten Bäume und Sträuche gewähren, die sich noch durch einige an schicklichen Stellen angebrachte Blumen Parthien vermehren lässt, und endlich durch den Gesang der Vögel; durch bequemere Wege, und einla-dende Ruhebänke.[17]

Here the *Journal* makes clear to the reader that one of the principles of English landscape design is the enhancement of selective features to deepen their impact. The artificiality and the technical know-how required to create the desirable effects become apparent in the design of pleasing water-features that create movement and sound, particular vistas, look-out points, and pleasing tableaux, grottos, and places for games.

The designed landscape offers the visitor a space for a kinesthetic experience, an opportunity for ambulatory motion through time and space. The visitor participates in reassembling the variety of individual and sometimes quite independent and contrasting scenes and vistas. At the same time, the variety of landscape features evokes a wealth of different sensations, emotions, and feelings. It "requires a sentimental look in which the eye moves in and around the three-dimensional space, registering incident and contrast, generating expectation, and delighting in surprise. This garden typically contains aural as well as visual stimulation, both of which serve to animate the viewer into a sequential experience of distinct sensations."[18]

Günter Oesterle and Harald Tausch argue in their study *Der imaginierte Garten* (The Imagined Garden) that the role of the imagination in the garden phenomenon is not to be underestimated.[19] While their study focuses on the role of memory in creating the garden experience, I here examine how the *Journal*, in text, image, and advertisement, stimulated the imagination of the readership to fashion garden experiences for themselves. Furthermore, while Oesterle and Tausch, quoting Carl Heinrich Heydenreich's "Originalideen über die interessantesten Gegenstände der Natur" (1793; Original Ideas about the Most Interesting Things in Nature), point to the role of the imagination (*Phantasie*) in assisting the visitor to create a *picture* of the whole constructed from the sequential vistas seen in a garden, my own focus is on the discursive creation of multi-layered emotional and multi-sensory experience of the garden as a *comprehensive experience* that in turn invites and enables readers to create such an experience for themselves.[20]

Reading almost like a supplement to the comprehensive description of 1790 quoted above, another extensive entry on creating a garden in the modern English style in Germany followed in June 1795. This article adapts the English model to create a distinctly English-German version of the landscape garden; the focus here is on fusing beauty with utility. It starts out by evoking the mood of an English landscape garden but suggests modifications that replace exotic plants with equally attractive domestic fruit- and nut-bearing shrubs and trees. After all, so the argument goes, the garden becomes even more attractive because it not only provides visual, aural, and kinesthetic pleasures, but also yields treasures for the table. The article reminds the reader of the attractive features of the landscape garden while also pointing to the desirability of more practical substitutions. True to its overarching tendency to combine the aesthetic with the greatest sense of utility for a range of cultural practices, the *Journal* goes even farther, suggesting that when readers create a landscape in the English manner in their own gardens, there is no need slavishly to imitate its use of exotic species to achieve the desired effect. Instead, the term "englisch-teutsche[r] Garten" suggests that domestic fruit-bearing shrubs and trees could be used to achieve similar or even more desirable effects:

Plan. Zu einer Englisch-Teutschen Gartenanlage mit Obstge-
büsch und Obstbäumen.
Der natürliche Hang der Menschen zur Mannigfaltigkeit und
Abwechslung, die Zufriedenheit in sich, und das Vergnügen, das
er fühlt, wenn er die Natur nachahmt und derselben getreu bleibt,
bewürkte, daß die Engländer bey Anlage und Anpflanzung ihrer
Lustgärten (oder vielmehr Landschaften, die blos zum Vergügen
bestimmt sind) den Geschmack der Chineser [*sic*] liebgewannen,
daraus das Steife des Regelmäßigen verbannt, und Sträuchen aus
den entferntesten Ländern in einer gewissen Unregelmäßigkeit, die
jedoch wieder etwas regelmäßiges in der Natur hat, für das Auge
und das Gefühl des natürlichen Schönen gefällig, einnehmend und
reitzend gemacht haben. . . . Was für einen Vorzug sollten die wil-
den Gesträuche in Anschaung ihres Grüns vor dem Gesträuche und
Bäume unserer mannigfaltigen Obstgeschlechter haben? Wie angenehm verschieden ist nicht auch das Grün derselben? Welch einen
wonnevollen Anblick gewähren nicht die Blüten unserer Mandel-
bäume, Abrikosen, Kirschen, Aepfel, Birnbäume etc. vom ersten
Frühlinge an? . . . Wenn man nicht beträchtlichen Raum hat, so
muß das Kernobst, Apfel und Birnen, auf zwergartigen Grundstäm-
men . . . veredelt seyn.[21]

Not only do domestic bushes and trees please the visual and aural
senses, but they also provide a scientific showcase for domestic pomology
and create an abundance of healthful culinary delights for a varied table.
Practical suggestions follow on how to create such an English-German
garden that contains all the useful elements of a typical domestic garden
(fruits and vegetables) yet arranges them in such a way as to evoke the
sensations of an English landscape garden. The new interest in the science
of pomology and grafting offered solutions even for the garden of modest
size in the form of dwarf varieties and other modified varieties.

Grass-covered paths in pleasing serpentine lines allow not only pleasant walks, the *Journal* explains, but also convenient access to the trees,
which often also provide shade for tables and chairs and other outdoor
amenities. "Laubhütten und Nischen" (vine-covered garden huts and
niches) provide further opportunities for shaded walks and rest as well
as additional plantings such as grapes or other climbers. To enhance the
appearance of the whole, flowers should fill the spaces, and even vegetables can be tucked here and there into the landscape without adverse
aesthetic effect. If there is the opportunity to bring water into the garden
in the form of a small creek or a pond ("lebendiges Wasser oder Bach . . .
und etwa ein Teich"), it will heighten the pleasurable effect.[22] Depending
on how the various strata of the middle class wanted to define themselves,
they could focus either more on the aesthetics or on the economic use of

the garden, or they could take more advantage of the garden as a teaching tool and a site for amateur botany.

My study distances itself from a stance of cultural politics that attacks the power of consumption as producing manipulated victims of false consciousness. The *Journal* and the reading practices of the monthly were in themselves important instances of consumption that, in turn, shaped other cultural practices. Methodologically it becomes clear that cultural practices are complex and often conflicted. I do not wish to argue, for example, that the *Journal* simply manipulated its readership to consume or that its editor exerted deliberate social control over its readership. Instead the present essay reveals the complex interrelationship that is culture in the confluence of reading practices with the coveting of desirable objects and experiences. New knowledge and inventions that made everyday life easier and more convenient produced new objects and products, which in turn frequently required new furniture to house them and new spaces to display these conveniences. The resulting changes in lifestyle led to the re-imagining of living spaces, including the exterior extension of lifestyle, the garden, during the time frame marked by the publication of the *Journal* (1786–1827).[23]

The *Journal*, as an institution that both produced and disseminated knowledge, represented a systematic practice that affected other cultural discourses such as the garden phenomenon, fashion, and luxury goods for the adornment of house and garden. In particular, the garden as a form of designed nature and an extension of the domestic interior sheds light on the experiences that shaped and were shaped by middle-class forms of domesticity and leisure. Andrea van Dülmen, in her comprehensive study on garden culture around 1800, *Das irdische Paradies: Bürgerliche Gartenkultur der Goethezeit*, describes the middle classes' love of gardens with particular attention to life in the garden, family life, and the garden as a space for introspection.[24] She correctly points out that the literature on gardening was voluminous and reflected a new identity and way of life: "Im Garten kann all das, was dem empfindsamen Menschen in Natur und Landschaft anrührt, was seinen eigensten Stimmungen entspricht, wie in einem Bild konzentriert wurden. Und damit wird der Garten zu dem idealen Ort der Selbstwahrnehmung im Spiegel der Natur" (The garden concentrates all that touches sensitive people in nature and landscape, all that corresponds with his or her most intimate moods, in one image. Thus the garden becomes the ideal space for self-perception in the mirror of nature).[25]

My own cultural analysis of the garden phenomenon, however, does not assume a "reflection" model but a constructivist understanding of cultural phenomena as discussed above.[26] Objects and practices creating a certain lifestyle significantly shape identity construction. The active relationships between producing the phenomenon of the garden in the various garden publications, the consumption of the information, and the formation of the interest and a desire to incorporate these ideas into the creation of the garden are made meaningful through representation. The meaning of the garden phenomenon is thus not fixed but remains fluid and contextualized.

The *Journal* itself reflected on its own function in producing culture in a dialogic relationship with its readers — or at least it created the fiction of entering into an exchange with its readers. They not only sent feedback but also took on the role of informants who reported on the latest trends in Europe. They participated by sharing information and thus played an active role in taste formation. In the particular case of an article on furniture, for example, the editorial voice explains that the information on furniture seemed to have attracted a lot of positive attention and therefore the *Journal* vows that it will try hard to provide increasingly more information on new, attractive, and useful furniture and thus improve taste in furniture in Germany:

> Wir haben mit Vergnügen gesehen dass dieser Artikel im Journal der Moden unsern Lesern sonderlich angenehm zu seyn scheinet. Wir werden uns daher, aufgemuntert durch den allgemeinen gütigen Beyfall, mit welchem die Leser uns beehren, auf alle Art bemühen, ihnen immer neue, schöne und nützliche Meublen zu liefern, und, so viel oder wenig wir können, zu Verbesserung und Vervollkommnung des Geschmacks, in Rücksicht auf Ameublement, in Teutschland mit beyzutragen.[27]

The *Journal* made explicitly clear, that the information it provided should be regarded as subject to readers' opinion and not as simple advocacy or endorsement of positions on taste and propriety. The readership was invited to use its critical judgment with regard to the phenomena described.

As a self-described chronicler of the times, the *Journal* was compelled to report also on those aspects of culture that it did not necessarily endorse. Here a rather obvious example proves useful. The *Journal* had reported on the case of Parisian courtesans as fashion taste-makers, and after being criticized for reporting on this unseemly topic defended itself by arguing that this phenomenon was, after all, a part of the comprehensive picture that the *Journal* as chronicle dedicated itself to painting.[28] Far from indulging in and recommending "Sittenlosigkeit und Ausschweifungen" (immorality and sensual excess) or practicing self-censorship, the *Journal* makes a case for critical reading instead of mindless consumption.[29]

Likewise, the *Journal* understands the change in taste from the French formal classicist design to the English landscape garden to be an effect of fashion that it subjects to its readers' judgment.[30] However, the

Journal explains fashion not as merely random change but as a principle that speaks to a need or desire and is able to fulfill this better than the older style or practice.

As the example below suggests, the *Journal* enumerates the advantages of the new English style, arguing that the current fashion in landscaping is superior because it requires merely an enhancement of the beauty of nature. Furthermore, because of its broad functionality, it is more practical and economical. Unlike the French heavily stylized shrubs and trees, the more natural growth in the English garden allows the vegetation to be attractive at all levels of maturity and saves cost and labor, making it more broadly affordable and achievable:

> . . . niemand wird es jetzt bezweifeln, dass der englische Geschmack, welcher bloß verschönerte Natur verlangt, das ist, die schon vorhandenen Schönheiten in ein vortheilhaftes Licht setzt, vor allen übrigen den Vorzug verdiene: erstlich weil er das Gemüth des Lustwandelenden, oder des am Teiche Ruhenden, nach den verschiedenen Aussichten in die mannigfaltigsten aber allzeit angenehmen Stimmungen versetzt, und zweytens, weil sich eine englische Gartenanlage mit jedem Jahr verschönert und durch das höhere Alter würdiger wird, da hingegen ein französischer Garten in seiner Kindheit alles in der größten Unvollkommenheit darstellet, und wenn seine schönste Periode von etwa fünfzehn Jahren geblüht hat, wieder veraltet, und nichts als ein Gemisch von verkrüppelten, halb gestorbenen Bäumen und Hecken übrig lässt. . . .[31]

Providing explanations for its fashionability such as longevity and the more modest cost of upkeep in comparison with the formal French garden, the *Journal* thus offers a rationale for imitating this style in the private domestic garden on a smaller scale.

The challenge for the reader, who might be interested in creating these effects in the much smaller domestic garden, was how to translate these same principles to the proper scale. Advice on how to accomplish this translation focuses on the clever arrangement of details so that the garden appears bigger and offers new experiences every ten feet. The *Journal* underscores the achievability of such a design in a smaller domestic environment and thus inspires and invites its readers to imagine the possibilities for their own situations. The descriptions engage readers' interest in experimentation, inviting them to take delight in *trompe l'oeil*, to make a small space seem large through careful landscape design. They allow the reader to marvel at the effect of being swept away from the cares of civilization by the seemingly natural yet carefully designed landscape garden that hides its artifice and design. A few examples of how the *Journal* suggests that this transformation could take place will make these ideas clearer.

In the small garden, the *Journal* claims, the gaze will take in the whole length of the property that is much smaller than in the English landscape garden model: "Der geringe Flächenraum läßt sich leicht übersehn, und gewährt nur einen sehr kurzen Spaziergang. Das erste muß man durch vorgezogenes Gebüsch zu verhindern suchen, und den Spaziergang muß man durch schlangenförmig gewundene Gänge zu verlängern bemüht seyn" (The small space can be easily viewed at one glance and allows only for short walks. The first [of these aspects of the smaller garden] must be compensated for by the careful placement of trees and shrubs to create smaller vignettes. Serpentine, winding paths must extend the length of the walkways to facilitate longer walks).[32]

Features are designed to create the most desirable experience and use of the space. Ordinary creeks can be turned into shady groves by creative multi-storied plantings offering shelter from the heat and thus creating an inviting resting place. If a creek allows for the diversion of water, a fashionable cold bathing site in a space with plantings to create the desirable seclusion is recommended as a healthful and attractive feature of the garden. The *Journal* suggests including bridges to allow for more varied walking experiences.[33]

The *Journal* also provides specific suggestions as to which species of trees and bushes yield the best results and provide the prettiest and most colorful effects, and invites the reader to imagine them.[34] The strategic placement of flowerbeds, the selection of flowers based on their colors, scents, and growing habits, and other helpful hints for achieving the desired special effects contribute to the achievement of a highly varied sensory impact even on the smaller scale of the middle-class domestic garden.[35] Paying attention to the color and shape, and such special qualities as scent or particularly attractive sounds when the wind rustles the leaves, the *Journal* alternates between describing both the overall concept and providing practical advice for the selection of particular species.

This comprehensive article also recommends the careful placement of a garden house, depending on the existence of a view beyond the garden and on the preferences of its owner. Again, the experience and the desired use — whether one loves the view from a second story or prefers the more immediate access to the garden house and convenient refreshments that a one-story garden house affords — decide its placement.[36] Simple al fresco meals were part of the attraction of the garden experience. Other sites for socializing are recommended, such as (vegetation-covered) seating areas ("Laubhütten," "grüne Cabinets").[37] Benches invite rest as well as enjoyment of the views. The *Journal* places emphasis not only on the functionality of an object but also on its convenience; it favors painted wooden benches over the less healthful and colder stone or grass benches.

Other articles highlight individual features of the modern garden. An article from 1789 points out, for example, that a carefully designed flower garden, the proud possession of a middle-class owner — unable to afford an English garden or even a garden in the English manner — could include some of the fanciful elements in the fashionable Chinese style contained within the English garden design as long as it was done in good taste.[38] We recall that evoking Chinese design denoted an appreciation of the irregular, of seemingly wild or untamed nature, in contrast to the symmetry of the French garden style.[39] Readers were invited to imagine the pleasant sensations and experiences that this kind of garden offers and at the same time were reassured that they too could create a garden in the English manner. This allowed less well-to-do members of the middle class to imagine their own more affordable version of the landscape garden.

In addition to the mere aesthetic and sensual experience of the garden and walks in nature, the pedagogical uses of the garden mania are mentioned: the *Intelligenzblatt* of 1804 draws attention to this aspect in its advertisement of the publication "*Spaziergänge mit meinen Zöglingen* Herausgegeben von F. A. L. Matthai. Lehrer an der Königl. Hof- und Töchterschule" (Walks with my Young Charges, edited by F. A. L. Matthai, teacher at the royal court and daughters' school) and describes the content in the following way: "Der Verfasser benutzte die Spaziergänge, welche er mit seinen Zöglingen machte, nicht nur bloß zu einer wohlthätigen Bewegung ihres Körpers, sondern zugleich als Mittel zu einer zweckmäßigen Beschäftigung ihres Geistes. Die mannichfaltigen Gegenstände der Natur . . . geben ihm Gelegenheit den Verstand und das moralische Gefühl der Kinder zu vervollkommnen" (The author used the walks with his young charges not only for the beneficial exercise of their bodies, but also as a useful occupation for their minds. The varied objects of nature . . . gave him the opportunity to perfect the intellect and the moral sense of the children).[40]

Other strata of the middle class that were more interested in enjoying botany as a hobby could focus on the articles that assisted in this pastime, such as those on pomology, botanical experiments, or the creation of new cultivars to enhance culinary variety:

> Anzeige für Gartenbesitzer, Obstliebhaber und Oekonomen: Pomologisches Theoretisch-praktisches Handwörterbuch oder alphabetisches Verzeichniß aller nöthigen Kenntnisse sowohl zur Obstkultur, Pflanzung, Veredlung, Erziehung und Pflege und Behandlung aller Sorten Obstbäume, und der ökonomischen Benutzung ihrer Früchte u.s.w., als auch zur Beurtheilung und Kenntniß der vorzüglichsten bisher bekanntesten Obstsorten aller Arten und ihrer Klassifikationen u.s.w.[41]

In a similar vein, horticultural experiments not only helped to increase the varieties of flowers but also served as a learning laboratory for children, in particular boys who learned botanical principles alongside their fathers or who engaged in the art and science of pomology ("Baumzucht") and experimented with the grafting and enhancement of fruit-trees to create new cultivars.

The popularity of gardening also coincided with the interest in a more varied and refined culinary experience on the one hand and the realization that there is economic interest in expanded fruit production. This scientific and applied aspect of gardening also led to the desire to prolong the season for growing vegetables and flowers. New techniques extended the period during which fruits and vegetables remained available. Cold frames, cellar beds, manure hotbeds, and greenhouses in turn extended the growing season. Experimenting with new crops set the stage for creating produce for a more varied and carefully planned dining experience. The increase in varieties of domestic fruits and vegetables produced by this new interest in horticulture was, furthermore, accompanied by the increasing availability of exotic spices.[42]

The growing number of advertised books on gardening is accompanied in the *Journal* by an expanding interest in cookbooks and guides to creating a varied dining experience. We find advertisements for books on meal preparation — such as the *Küchentaschenbuch für Frauenzimmer zur täglichen Wahl der Speisen für das Jahr 1796* (Kitchen Pocketbook for Women for Selecting Meals for the Year 1796) — creating variety and seasonal distinction.[43] The advertisement mentions the illustrations in the advertised books "auf denen die geschmackvollste Art, die Tafel bey feyerlichen Gastmählern zu besetzen, vorgestellt und erläutert wird. . . (in which the most tasteful way to set the table on festive occasions is introduced and explained . . .).[44] The *Küchenlexikon für Frauenzimmer* (Kitchen Reference Book for Women), likewise advertised in 1796, was also written for women who prepared meals themselves or who directly supervised their cook.[45]

The *Journal* also advertises books on regional cooking, as in the notice "Neues Hannöverisches Kochbuch" (New Cookbook with Hannover Specialities), a cookbook for "Bürgerliche Haushaltungen" (middle-class households) for "praktischen Nutzen" (practical use) instructing users on how to prepare basic dishes, soups, meats, fish, vegetables, and starches as well as desserts, and containing descriptions of the proper order of the dishes.[46] A page later the "Productenbuch für die Küche oder Anweisung für junge Mädchen und Hausfrauen, diejenigen Producte, welche in der Küche zubereitet werden, nach ihrem wahren Gehalte kennen und beurtheilen zu lernen" (Book on Products for the Kitchen and Instructions for Girls and Housewives on Gaining a Thorough Knowledge of Those Products Prepared in the Kitchen and Being Able to Evaluate Them) is announced and recommended.[47] As these examples of cookbooks show, the culinary interest resulting in a more refined and varied cuisine was accompanied by aesthetic concerns regarding attractive presentation, the proper sequencing of the courses, and the pleasing arrangement of the dishes.

Many of the cookbooks in fact focused on the aesthetic presentation of the food and the table. The display of flowers in innovative containers beautified the table. The *Journal* itself offers suggestions as to how to grace the table with flowers and depicts the appropriate bowls or containers. The following article from 1797, for example, describes the aesthetic presentation of the dessert table with its interplay of flowers, vases, flower bowls, and the dessert (see fig. 2.2):

> Die Blumen waren von jeher, und sind noch jetzt die angenehmsten Gegenstände für alle Arten von Verziehrungen. . . . Wir liefern hier einen solchen schönen Blumen-Korb, von matt lackiertem Blech, blau und weiß à la Wedgewood, aus der Fabrik des Hrn. Krause zu Braunschweig . . . durchbrochen, in welchem der Einsatz mit einem Draht-Gitter versehen steht, um Wasser oder nassen Sand hineinzuthun und Blumen hinein zu stecken. Dieser Blumen-Korb in der Mitte auf die Tafel gesetzt, und, ist die Tafel groß, noch etliche kleinere Bouquetiers von blauem Glase, Wedgwoods Steinguthe oder Porcellan, hie und da auf die Tafel vertheilt, giebt eine sehr natürliche, einfache und gefällige Dessert-Verzierung, wozu sich dann Obst und dergl. in schönen Körbchen oder Schaalen überaus gut schickt.[48]

The new more convenient containers for the display of flowers, the *Journal* maintains, enable the housewife or maid without special expertise to create an attractive arrangement and thus achieve an integrated presentation of a beautifully set and adorned table.

Furthermore, the interest in the culinary aspect of gardening is addressed by modern conveniences like the ice house, the *Journal* reports. A shady corner in the garden can become the site for a covered ice pit: "Eine Eisgrube ist, zur Abkühlung des Getränkes und zur Frischhaltung des Fleisches, Wildprets, der Butter und mehrere Speisen bey Sommerhitze, eine sehr angenehme und selbst für die menschliche Gesundheit sehr wolhtätige Sache" (An ice pit is not only a very pleasant but also a useful thing for human health, for the cooling of beverages, preservation of meat, wild game, and butter, and many dishes in the summer heat).[49] An elaborate description of its features and of how to build one and store ice in it is accompanied by an illustration that provides further aid for building it (see fig. 2.3).

Every new object or cultural practice produced a web of new inventions further contributing to a more complex and differentiated array of possibilities for the creation of distinct lifestyles. The availability of ice allowed for more options and more choices as to when to use perishable foods and extended the season of their use; it also created the desire to

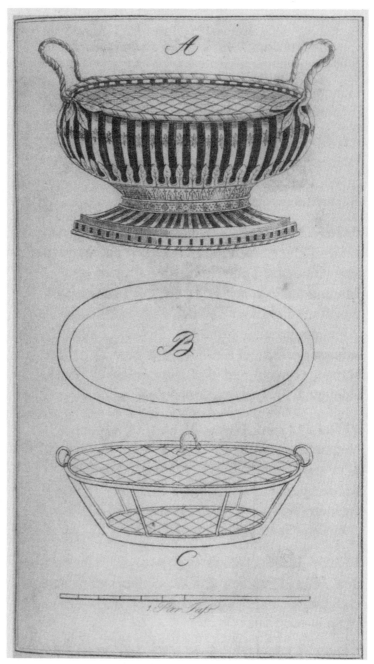

Fig. 2.2. "Ein Blumenkorb zur Tafel Verzierung" (A Flower Basket for Decorating the Table), *Journal* 1797, plate 21, published with the permission of the Thüringer Universitäts- und Landesbibliothek, Jena.

Fig. 2.3. "Anlage einer Eisgrube" (Layout for an Ice Pit),
Journal 1793, plate 27, published with the permission of the
Thüringer Universitäts- und Landesbibliothek, Jena.

have ice more conveniently stored close-by in an aesthetically integrated
ice house in the garden. Attractive containers were created to hold the ice
at the table too. The preciousness and aesthetic value of the vessels for ice
are underscored by the fact that the *Journal* depicts the bowl for ice and
matching fruit bowls in a color plate rather than in the usual black-and-
white print.

In addition, new furniture was created that permitted the convenient
and attractive use of ice in the home. Furnishings with specially built-in
boxes for ice to cool beverages grace the pages of the *Journal*, which
praises such furniture in the more modern England, as for example in
the notice "Ein Englischer Schenk-Tisch mit Eiskästen" (An English Bar-
Counter with Iceboxes):

> Die Schenke-Tische der Engländer sind so geschmackvoll und
> zweckmäßig, als ihr ganzes Ameublement. . . . In den verschlosse-
> nen 5 Schubfächern können 24 Bouteillen Wein liegen. Im Sommer
> kann man, um den Wein Frisch zu erhalten in diese Schubfächer ein-
> passende Eis-Kästen (nämlich Kasten von Bleche mit Eise versehen)
> setzen, und die Bouteillen hineinlegen.[50]

Innovative furniture became fashionable not only for the interior — the
category of "Ameublement" plays a central role in the *Journal* and its
contribution to the fashioning of bourgeois interiors — but also for outdoor use; special furniture permitted socializing and informal entertaining
in the garden. The *Journal* includes articles describing the taking of tea

and coffee in the garden and the specific furniture to make this fusion of nature and culture even more comfortable and pleasant. Specifically designed garden furniture and umbrellas allowed comfortable access to the sensual delights of the flowers while offering shade and physical comfort. The pleasures that the domesticated garden provides permit risk-free indulgence in sensual pleasures within the safety of a contained domesticated space:

> Auch sahe ich in diesem Garten einen Garten-Stuhl auf dessen Lehne ein Sonnenschirm mit etwas langer Stange steckte, und also dem Blumen-Liebhaber, der sich irgend nahe ans Blumenbeet setzte, die Flor recht genießen oder dabey lesen wollte, allenthalben einen transportablen schattigen Sitz gewährte; welche Erfindung mir sehr wohlgefallen hat.[51]

At the same time, as the *Journal* richly testifies, a wave of new fashionable indoor furniture was in turn designed for the purpose of bringing the outdoors into the house. The so-called flower tables, frequently combined with bird cages, contained designated space for the display of flower arrangements, thus bringing the joys and skills associated with flower gardening together with the interest in interior design and the beautification of living quarters. The variety of the furniture designed explicitly for the display of flowers and plants increased. Special designs accommodated long-stemmed plants; others were able to display a variety of flowers on multiple tiers; still other furniture allowed for the display of a single opulent arrangement. Furniture for flower displays was complemented with specially designed vases that facilitated easier arrangement of these treasures from the garden (see figs. 2.4 and 2.5).[52]

To display and overwinter particular flowers, a whole range of special stands and garden structures with numerous display shelves was created. The idea of an indoor garden captured the imagination of the time and became a popular practice. The indoor garden too was in part an attempt to extend the season so as to have plants and flowers available all year around as well as to use flowers as an element in interior design. For the less wealthy strata of the bourgeoisie, overwintering was most likely also a question of cost, so that the exotic or tender plants gracing the summer garden would not need to be purchased anew every year.

The *Intelligenzblatt* and other publications also began to advertise varieties of fashionable flowers.[53] Seed and bulb selections became more plentiful and varied. Those flowers with seemingly endless varieties, such as carnations, primroses, and tulips, were especially popular because they also appealed to the interest in collecting, to a delight in the varieties of the same. Flowers, like other objects, became subject to fashion. The article from 1789 describing the garden cabinet in the Chinese style confirms the most popular flowers: "Hyazinthen, Tulpen, Aurikel, Nelcken"

Fig. 2.4. "Geschmackvolle Blumenvase" (Tasteful Vase for Flowers),
Journal 1819, plate 6, published with the permission of the Thüringer
Universitäts- und Landesbibliothek, Jena.

Fig. 2.5. "Pariser Blumentisch mit Voliere" (Paris Flower Table with a Birdcage), *Journal* 1809, plate 8, published with the permission of the Thüringer Universitäts- und Landesbibliothek, Jena.

(hyacinths, tulips, primroses, carnations).[54] Publications, the *Journal* among them, advertised the latest books supporting the collecting of cultivars as a new pastime.[55] The interest in flower gardening and amateur botany also inspired an interest in documenting these fleeting treasures from the garden in drawings and paintings. Just as we find the classification and professional depiction of flowers in books on botany, we also see books on drawing with an explicit focus on flowers.[56]

Seeds were collected, classified, described, and stored in furniture especially designed for the purpose. Collecting not only extended the pleasurable occupation with the beloved plants beyond the actual growing season, but also helped to create and support a hobby of collection that in turn produced such new demands as those for special furniture and such new artifacts as collections of pressed leaves and their descriptions for friends and other flower enthusiasts.[57] Indeed, as the *Journal* testifies, the interest in collecting generated new demands for the management of the treasured varieties of plants. Special cases for storing seeds and bulbs, for displaying the varieties, and for sharing or exchange with other enthusiasts and collectors were created. Pressed leaves and flowers in these new collections in turn became models for drawing from nature or for embroidery. The domestication of the garden contributed significantly to the involvement of women in design decisions and enabled their access to collecting or flower painting as a hobby. As we saw in the case of books on amateur botany, women were explicitly included in the targeted readership.

Specialized household objects according to the latest fashion supported the creation of a more diverse lifestyle in which taste began to play a decisive role. Furthermore, as articles in the *Journal* make clear, with the addition of furniture and other decorative objects, nature was transformed into an extension of interior space. Changes in architectural tastes placed the social spaces, the library, the drawing room, and the dining room on the ground level. Doors and larger windows opened the view into the garden, and transitional spaces such as terraces and walkways provided convenient access to certain parts of the garden. As an extended domestic interior, small or large garden spaces served as important sites for spending leisure time in a pleasurable manner alone or among family and friends and as sites for more elaborate social gatherings.

The *Journal* describes the latest inventions that could support these trends of joining interior and exterior such as the so-called Belvederes, awnings made of (non-rusting) metal that were less expensive to install and maintain than wooden structures and that overall required less expensive structural architectural detail. Describing their use in Paris, the author of an article from 1786 points to the pleasure they afforded. With the help of these Belvederes, city dwellers with little opportunity to enjoy fresh air could create a shady space outside of their house where they could conveniently enjoy some small-scale gardening and access to the pleasures of nature without having to travel to the country:

> Für Leute die durch ihre Geschäfte und Lebensart in große Städte und ihre Häuser eingesperrt sind, und der freyen Land Luft fast gar nicht genießen können, muß es überaus angenehm seyn, in ihrem Hause selbst eine solche Anlage zu haben, wo sie sich wenigstens das Fantom eines Gärtchens schaffen, und wenn sie Blumisten sind, wenigstens eine Stunde des Tages, ohne beträchtlichen Zeit-Verlust unter ihren lieben Hyazinthen, Aurikeln, Nelken u.s.w. sitzen, und etwas gesündere als eingesperrte Zimmer-Luft athmen können.[58]

This article highlights convenience and efficiency, thus suggesting that even the most unlikely place — the city — allows some form of access to nature, albeit with the assistance of the latest invention in science and technology.[59] Even in a large city, human ingenuity could create a garden-like experience even if it consisted of only a few planters and flower boxes to be enjoyed in the shade of these new and robust awnings.

There are other dimensions to the garden phenomenon that go beyond the parameters of the present study, but that are nevertheless worth mentioning here. One of these is the "musealization" of nature, although it should be seen in a more comprehensive and dynamic way than that suggested by Jarrett, Rachwał, and Sławek in their study on the aesthetics of garden culture.[60] Their focus is on displayed nature that turns it into a set of collectibles — which, of course, does hold true, for example, for the collection of flower varieties. However, this individual, object-based view could also be expanded to include collecting instances created by decorative objects or special features of the garden — such as water or garden structures — and garden furniture, that is, what in essence amounts to the collection of varied experiences.

Not unlike the modern museum, which creates a pleasurable experience that allows for informal and formal learning, for socializing, for self-improvement, etc., the garden became a carefully orchestrated whole that nevertheless remained dynamic and open to change; it was both natural in the growth habits of trees and plants and the changing seasons on the one hand, and, on the other, artificial through design (new plants, new color schemes, and new objects). Expanding the web of cultural practices associated with the garden phenomenon, the *Journal* also reports on other new leisure activities such as travel and visits to flower exhibits or particularly stunning flower displays in public gardens.[61]

Even though the *Journal* mostly celebrated the modern inventions associated with gardening, it was not above warning of excesses and urging prudence. One example, mentioned above, was the recommendation to plant productive domestic fruit-trees instead of exotic bushes and trees so that the garden would be more useful. As we shall see shortly, it also warns of the dangers of the excessive use of fragrant flowers indoors, referencing the fashionable practice of "winter gardens" that enabled the wealthy to turn winter into a summer experience.[62] Indoor gardening is described as an aesthetic undertaking as well as a useful one that allows tender plants to survive the winter: the *Intelligenzblatt* announces, for example, the publication of *Der Wintergärtner oder Anweisung, die beliebtesten Modeblumen und mehrere ausländische zur Zirde der Garten dienende Gewächse ohne Treibe- und Glashäusern in Zimmern, Kellern und anderen Behältern zu überwintern* (The Indoor-Gardener or Instructions on How to Overwinter the Most Popular Flowers and Decorative Outdoor Plants without Greenhouses and Glass Structures in Rooms, Basements, and other Forms of Containers).[63]

The *Journal* sometimes evinces the tensions between its emphasis on aesthetics and its other function as an advisor in health matters and advocate for a healthy lifestyle. In an article from 1792, for example, the editor points to the dangers of excessive indoor use of fragrant flowers in closed spaces, which considers to contribute to respiratory problems and fainting, especially in vulnerable ladies. Here we find a good example of the comprehensive mixture of aesthetic, economic, health, and scientific arguments and a short reading list of scientific botanical works brought to bear on the mania for indoor flowers. The author deplores the excessive fashion of turning rooms into ever-blooming gardens and in the process importing rare and expensive bulbs and display containers. While he recognizes that this has become part of the luxury of everyday culture, well-to-do people can be prone to excess, he believes, especially the ladies who are partial to flowers as decorations for the home because of their beauty and their pleasant scent.[64] This article thus acknowledges and thereby chronicles the prevalence of this practice in the circles to which the readers of the *Journal* belonged, and also manages even to refer to the frequently criticized practice of preferring imports over domestic luxury items and the negative financial consequences — despite the fact that this point hardly pertains to the subject at hand. It also mentions the layered sensual effects of indoor gardens, the experience of the visually aesthetic quality of flowers, and their pleasant fragrance, which perfumes the indoor air.

However, rather than celebrating this phenomenon to which the *Journal* in text and image as well as in its offers to sell or import had contributed significantly, this particular article focuses on the dangers of overdoing it. Citing common experience and scientific experts to support the health warning, the author goes on to describe several experiments to support his claim, experiments that could be easily imitated. He refers, for example, to tests that show that if one places a heavily scented flower into a closed glass cylinder and then places a flame or a small animal inside, the flame goes out and the animal dies.[65] A list of alleged actual experiences reported by physicians rounds out the cautionary article.[66] As a late-Enlightenment lifestyle magazine, the *Journal* celebrated and fostered new cultural experiences while at the same time bringing scientific evidence in support of the particular practice or, as in this example, the potential dangers of manipulating and instrumentalizing nature.

The shaping of the garden experience by the *Journal* is central to the extended discourse on new and differentiated middle-class lifestyles that had significant ramifications for other areas of culture: gardening and horticulture as a hobby, collecting as a pastime, the creation of new furniture and objects to display the collected plants and flowers, interest in expanding the culinary repertoire, the use of objects from nature to inspire flower painting and embroidery, and travel to destinations such as famous landscape gardens and flower exhibits. The *Journal* played an important role in shaping the garden phenomenon by stimulating the imagination of its readers to envision themselves enjoying and being able to create such a multi-sensory and multi-layered environment, and also by offering information in text and image on objects that served as the building blocks of the desired lifestyle and by describing possible desirable experiences associated with the garden and its context. The *Journal* raised expectations about this experience: it should be dynamic insofar as it allowed for choice in and control over the creation of varied experiences and insights; it should be interactive and allow its users to touch and experiment; and it should allow all family members to learn in an enjoyable way. The garden experience was designed to accommodate social interaction with family and friends, and it contributed to the status and sense of belonging to a group, that is, a certain layer of the middle class distinguished predominantly by taste. Most importantly, the *Journal* shaped the experience of the garden by foregrounding the aspect of revitalization — the garden as a means to refresh and restore oneself in an increasingly complex modern environment.

Notes

[1] Friedrich Justin Bertuch and Georg Melchior Kraus, eds., *Journal des Luxus und der Moden* (Weimar and Gotha: Ettische Buchhandlung 1786–1827). The publication underwent several name changes: vol. 1 (1786) *Journal der Moden*; vols. 2–27 (1787–1812), *Journal des Luxus und der Moden*; vol. 28 (1813), *Journal für Luxus, Mode und Gegenstände der Kunst*; vols. 29–41 (1814–26), *Journal für Literatur, Kunst, Luxus und Mode*; vol. 42 (1827), *Journal für Literatur, Kunst und geselliges Leben*. The abbreviated title *Journal* will be used in the text regardless of these name changes.

[2] As the subject matter of the *Journal* Bertuch lists, "1) weibliche und männliche Kleidung; 2) Putz; 3) Schmuck; 4) Nippes; 5) Ameublement; 6) alle Arten von Tische- und Trinkgeschirre, als: Silber, Porzellan und Glas; 7) Equippage, sowohl

Wagen als Pferdezeug und Livrén; 8) Häuser- und Zimmer-Einrichtungen und Verzierung; 9) Gärten- und Landhäuser"; (1) female and male dress; 2) accessories; 3) decorations; 4) small porcelain figurines; 5) furniture; 6) all kinds of table- and drink-ware, for example silver, porcelain, and glass; 7) carriages, including the carriage itself as well as horse tack and uniforms; 8) house- and room-designs and decorative objects; 9) garden- and country houses); *Journal,* January 1786, 12.

3 For a summary of these discussions, see Stephen Bending, "Re-Reading the Eighteenth-Century English Landscape Garden," in *An English Arcadia: Landscape and Architecture in Britain and America,"* ed. Guilland Sutherland and Harriet Ritvo (San Marino, CA: Huntington Library, 1992), 379–99. The aesthetic qualities of especially the English landscape garden and its relationship to painting — the question of whether to compose the landscape as if it were a painting — were hotly debated; see William Gilpin, *An Essay upon Prints. Containing remarks upon the principles of Picturesque Beauty* (London, 1786). Likewise the traditional emphasis on the quasi-framed view, or the picturesque, representing "a point of view that frames nature into a series of *living tableaux,"* was contested; see, e.g., David Marshall, "The Problem of the Picturesque," *Eighteenth Century Studies,* vol. 35, no. 3 (2002): 414. The "tendency to admire natural scenery according to the principles of art, to appreciate a landscape the more it resembled a painting," which "led a certain class of people to redesign the natural scenery around them in order to reproduce the reproductions of landscape painting" is set aside here as it is well researched (Marshall, 415). Marshall notes that "Joseph Spence Pope declared: 'All gardening is landscape painting'" and, furthermore, that "in his influential treatise on gardening, William Shenstone declared: 'Landscip should contain variety enough to form a picture upon canvas; and this is not a bad test, as I think the landskip painter is the gardiner's best designer'" (Marshall, 416).

4 As Susanne Müller-Wolff notes, it is interesting that the really famous gardens in England — Stourhead, Twickenham, Rousham — are not discussed. She argues that because the *Journal* was interested in taste formation, it selected examples that illustrated the particular feature that it sought to highlight; see Susanne Müller-Wolff, "Über Englische [*sic*] Gärten, französische Landsitze und den Park bey Weimar. Die Gartenkunst im Journal des Luxus und der Moden," in *Das* Journal des Luxus und der Moden: *Kultur um 1800,* ed. Angela Borchert and Ralf Dressel (Heidelberg: Winter, 2004), 230. The extensive description of an English landscape park at the French country estate of Ermenonville alludes to the painting-landscape discourse in the comment that the visitor feels as if he had stepped into a Poussin painting: "man glaubt eine Landschaft von Pussin zu sehen" (*Journal,* April 1786, 152; one believes one is seeing a landscape by Poussin).

5 "Diese Texte formen einen Gartendiskurs, der sich durch die inhaltliche Ausrichtung seiner Textbestände definiert und Gartentheorien, praktische Fragen der Gärtnerei, Beschreibungen von Gartenanlagen und Rezensionen umfaßt" (All these texts constitute a garden discourse that is defined by the content orientation of its texts and includes theoretical works on gardening, practical horticultural questions, descriptions of gardens, and reviews of the literature on gardening); see Michael Gamper, *"Die Natur ist republikanisch": Zu den ästhetischen, anthropologischen und politischen Konzepten der deutschen Gartenliteratur im 18. Jahrhundert* (Würzburg: Königshausen & Neumann, 1998), 4.

[6] When Bertuch applied for permission for this endeavor, he quoted as the goal: "der hiesigen Landes-Industrie aufzuhelfen, geschickte Arbeiter zu bilden, ihren Wohlstand zu beförden und neue Zweige der Industrie hierher zu verpflanzen" (to help the local industry, train adept workers, promote their prosperity, and to transplant new branches of industry here), qtd. by Christina Junghanß, "'Es ist ein Unglück vor die teutschen Handwerksleute, daß sie gar keinen Unternehmungsgeist besitzen [. . .]' Bertuch als Wirtschaftsförderer," in *Friedrich Justin Bertuch (1747–1922): Verleger, Schriftsteller und Unternehmer im Klassischen Weimar*, ed. Gehard R. Kaiser and Siegfried Seifert (Tübingen: Niemeyer, 2000), 301.

[7] See, e.g., Kaiser and Seifert, *Friedrich Justin Bertuch*, and Borchert and Dressel, *Kultur um 1800*.

[8] For an overview of Bertuch's economic activities, see Reiner Flik, "Kultur-Merkantilismus? Friedrich Justin Bertuchs 'Journal des Luxus und der Moden' (1786–1827)," in Borchert and Dressel, *Kultur um 1800*, 27. Subscription rates and cost as well as geographical and social distribution are based on Flik's research.

[9] Karin Wurst, *Fabricating Pleasure: Fashion, Entertainment, and Consumption in Germany. 1780–1830* (Detroit, MI: Wayne State UP, 2005), 23–40, and also Michael Gamper, *"Die Natur ist republikanisch"*: "Im gesellschaftlichen und politischen Bereich ereigneten sich Veränderungen, die Individualitätsvorstellungen neu definierten und den Einzelnen, die Einzelne in ein neues Beziehungsfeld stellten. Die Konstituierung der bürgerlichen Kleinfamilie, die Trennung von Arbeits- und Wohnort, die Aufsplitterung in Öffentlichkeits- und Privatsphäre und der Drang bisher politisch machtloser Gruppen zu politischer Verantwortung dank neuer Legitimationstrategien sind Faktoren die zu einem Umschichtungs- und Ausdifferenzierungsprozeß gehören, der von einer stratifikatorischen zu einer funktionalen Gesellschaftsdifferenzierung führte" (7; In both the political and the social arenas changes took place that redefined the concept of individualism which placed the individual in a new social context. The creation of the new intimate nuclear family, the separation of the place of work from the living quarters, the splintering into public and private spheres, and the push by previously politically excluded groups for political responsibility thanks to new strategies of creating legitimacy for themselves are all factors in a reorganization and process of distinction that led from a stratified society to one characterized by function). Unless otherwise noted, all translations are my own.

[10] Along with gardening books and periodicals, the *Journal* facilitated the transformation of the garden from a utilitarian space to a primarily aesthetic space. Many new specialized pocketbooks and calendars, usually for a general audience, were published, for example the *Taschenkalender auf das Jahr 1798 für Natur- und Gartenfreuden. Mit Abbildungen von Hohenheim und andern Kupfern* (Pocket Garden Calendar for the Year 1798 for the Enjoyment of Nature and the Garden. With Illustrations of Hohenheim and other Engravings). The books popularized gardening methods and horticultural knowledge. They taught how to design, plan, and maintain a garden by offering information and inspiration. "How-to" advice ranged from offering an almanac and a calendar of the sequence in which the fruit species ripen to giving basic information such as how to keep rabbits away from trees and how to introduce new varieties of fruits and vegetables. At the same time, this particular publication also offered insights into the aesthetics

of design and discussed famous landscapes, i.e., the gardens of Hohenheim, thus blending concrete advice with inspirational models not unlike our contemporary lifestyle or gardening magazines.

11 "III. Der Teutsche Obstgärtner. Das 1ste Stück des Teutschen Obstgärtners 1798 ist erschienen, und enthält folgende Aufsätze: Erste Abtheilung. 1. Besondere Naturgeschichte der Geschlechter der Obstbäume; und zwar No. 5 des Pfirsichenbaums. 11. Birnen-Sorten No. 49 Die schönsten Sommer-Birn. . . . Der Jahrgang von 12 Stücken kostet bey uns in allen Kunst und Buchhandlungen, auf allen löbl. Postämtern, Adreß- und Zeitungs-Comptoirs, 6rthl. Sächs. oder 10 fl 48 kr Rheinisch" (III. The German Pomologist. The first installment of the German Pomologist 1798 has been published and contains the following essays: First Part. 1. The Particular Natural History of the Types of Fruit-trees, to wit, No. 5 of the Peach tree. 11. Pear-Types No. 49, The Finest Summer Pears. . . . With us, the year's volume of twelve installments costs 6 Saxon reichsthalers or ten Rhenish florins 48 kreuzers in all art and book shops, in all praiseworthy post offices, and newspaper bureaus.) *Journal/Intelligenzblatt* Mai 1798, XXVIII; "IV. *Der Geöffnete Blumengarten.* *Journal/Intelligenzblatt* Mai 1798, XXVIII–XXIX; "VIII. *Botanik für Frauenzimmer* welche keine Gelehrte sind," *Journal/Intelligenzblatt* Mai 1798, XXVIII–XXIX; "V."Nachricht wegen Hrn Prof. Batsch Botanik für Frauenzimmer und dessen geöffneten Blumengarten," *Journal/Intelligenzblatt* Mai 1798, XXIX–XXX. "XXXV. Litterarische Anzeige über den Erdäpfelanbau," *Journal/Intelligenzblatt* Mai 1798, LXIII; "XXXVI. An Garten-Besitzer," *Journal/Intelligenzblatt* Mai 1798, LXII-LXIII; "XXXVII. Anzeige an Liebhaber von engl. Anlagen," *Journal/Intelligenzblatt* Mai 1798, LXIII; "XXVII. Kurze practische Anweisung zum Forstwesen," *Journal/Intelligenzblatt* Mai 1798, CXXIII. In the *Intelligenzblatt*, the individual entries are numbered with Roman numerals (before the title), and the page numbers are also given in Roman numerals.

12 For a more detailed exploration of the concept of fashion, see Wurst, *Fabricating Pleasure,* 139.

13 "Von diesen romantisch schönen Anlagen, die ohngefähr eine Idee vom Chinesisch-Englischen Style in der modernen Gartenkunst geben können, ist eben das erste *Cahier* von sechs Blättern der schönen Aussichten, von Hrn. Gmelin in Handzeichnungsmanier gestochen, bey Hrn. von Mechel erschienen" (*Journal,* September 1786, 303; Recently the first Cahier of six pages of the beautifully drawing-like etchings by Mr. Gmelin appeared. They give a good impression of these romantically beautiful large-scale gardens that are an approximate representation of the Chinese English style).

14 The model gardens described were, for example, the "Park von Ermenonville," *Journal,* April 1786, 152–63; "Der neue Englische Garten bey Arlesheim ohnweit Basel," *Journal,* September 1786, 303–11; "Palais Royal zu Paris," *Journal,* November 1786, 379–94. The example of the modern garden bench is one of many objects depicted in word and image: "Zwey Englische Garten-Sitze," April 1792, 219.

15 Wurst, *Fabricating Pleasure,* 67. For a description of how the *Journal* conveyed scientific information, see Paul Ziche, "'Auf eine wohlfeile und bequeme Art einen anschaulichen Begriff von einer Wissenschaft zu geben.' Beschreibung

im 'Journal des Luxus und der Moden' in der Mechanik und Wissenschaft um 1800," in Borchert and Dressel, *Kultur um 1800,* 243–60.

[16] Günter Oesterle and Harald Tausch, eds., *Der imaginierte Garten* (Göttingen: Vandenhoeck & Ruprecht, 2001). Oesterle und Tausch note the "beabsichtigte und nachdrücklich reklamierte Mannigfaltigkeit und Verschiedenheit der in ihm dargestellten Szenen" (10; the variety by explicit design and variation within the depicted scenes).

[17] *Journal,* June 1790, 303: "The most significant beauty of the English garden is derived from its large-scale plains and hills, the glistening water of lakes and rushing rivers, the silver shimmering rivulets and soft waterfalls, from gloomy groves and clumps of trees, from the soft green of the wide carpets of lawn and the rugged shapes of steep crags, from alternatively expansive and limited views onto fertile fields and distant mountains, from various and carefully placed buildings, monuments, and bridges, from the colorful mix of the various shades of green and the diversion of the blooms of the trees and shrubs collected from distant lands and enhanced by well-placed flowerbeds, and finally from the song of the birds and the comfortable paths and inviting benches."

[18] Peter de Bolla, "The charm'd eye," in *Body and Text in the Eighteenth Century,* ed. Veronika Kelley and Dorothea von Mücke (Stanford, CA: Stanford UP, 1994), 94.

[19] "Im Zeichen der anthropologischen Wende entsteht in unterschiedlichen Disziplinen ein Veranschaulichungs- und Experimentierbedarf für 'Natur', der Hand in Hand geht mit einer durch die Implantierung der Imagination bedingten Weiterung traditioneller Memorialräume. Dem kann der formale französische Garten nur bedingt genügen" (11; With the anthropological turn we see in the various disciplines a desire for visualization and experimentation with regard to natural phenomena which accompanies an expansion of traditional spheres of memory by implanting the powers of the imagination. The French-style garden was little-suited for this).

[20] "Danach kann ein Garten nur dann 'als Werk schöner Kunst . . . angesehen werden', wenn es gelingt, die 'Phantasie' des umherwandelnden Betrachters derart zu inspirieren, dass sich in ihm die Aufeinanderfolge mannigfacher Ansichten in ein 'schöne[s] und wohlgefällige[s] Totalbild' verwandelt" (Oesterle and Tausch, *Der imaginierte Garten,* 12; A garden can only become a 'work of fine art' . . . if the imagination of the ambulatory spectator can be inspired to such a degree that it assembles the consecutive vistas into a beautiful and attractive whole).

[21] *Journal,* June 1795, 257–74: "Plan for an English-German Garden. With fruit-bushes and fruit-trees. The natural tendency of humans to desire variety and diversity, the inner contentment and the pleasure felt when they imitate nature and remain true to it, caused the English, in the design and plantings of their pleasure gardens (or to be more precise, their landscapes devoted to pleasing effects), to begin to appreciate the taste of the Chinese, who had banned all stiffness and formality from their gardens, and with the result that exotic bushes placed in irregular fashion were considered pleasing to the eye and the emotions. . . . What advantage should the exotic greenery have over the green of our domestic fruit-bearing bushes and trees? How varied are the shades of

green of the aforementioned? How pleasant is the sight of the blossoms of our almond trees, our apricot, cherry, apple, pear trees etc. from the very beginning of spring? . . . Should space be limited, one should select varieties of apples and pears grafted onto dwarf stems."

[22] Ibid., 270–73.

[23] For a more comprehensive discussion of these issues, see Daniel Miller, *Material Culture and Mass Consumption* (Oxford: Blackwell, 1987), and John Storey, *Cultural Consumption and Everyday Life* (Oxford: Oxford UP, 1999), in passim.

[24] Andrea van Dülmen, *Das irdische Paradies: Bürgerliche Gartenkultur der Goethezeit* (Cologne: Böhlau, 1999).

[25] Van Dülmen, *Das irdische Paradies*, 17.

[26] I am not primarily interested in a description of the garden phenomenon but in the discursive creation of the phenomenon in the *Journal*.

[27] *Journal*, March 1786, 135: "We saw with delight that this article in the 'Journal of Fashions' seemed to be of special interest to our readers. Encouraged by this gracious support that the readers bestow on us, we will seek to provide them as much as we can with ever new, beautiful, and useful pieces of furniture, and thus to contribute as much or as little as we can to taste formation with regard to furniture in Germany."

[28] ". . . weil auch dieser Zug zu dem großen Welt- und Sitten-Gemälde unserer Zeit, zu welchem wir als Historiker dieses Werks, Figuren, Gruppen und Farben sammeln, mit gehört" (*Journal*, March 1786, 137; . . . because this trait also belongs to the comprehensive picture of our contemporary world and customs, for which we as historians of this undertaking assemble the figures, groupings, and colors).

[29] Ibid.

[30] "So wie alles in der Welt von je dem Wechsel der Mode unterworfen war und bleiben wird, so war es auch der Geschmack in Anlage der Gärten. Der teutsche, der holländische, und der französische wechselten miteinander ab, und alle diese scheint jetzt der englische Geschmack, oder der Wunsch einen Park zu besitzen, zu verdrängen" ("Ueber Englische Garten-Anlagen auf beschränkten Plätzen,"*Journal*, June 1790, 300; Just as everything in the world has been and always will be subject to fashionable change, it is the same for the taste in garden design. The German, Dutch, and French gardens traded places and the new English taste and the desire to own a park seem to push all the aforementioned aside).

[31] Ibid., "Nobody will doubt that the English taste, which merely requires enhanced nature — that is, which places the already existing beautiful features into the proper light — deserves to be favored among all others: first because it puts the strolling visitor or the one resting by the pond in different — depending on the views — but always pleasant moods, and second because an English landscape improves with age and becomes more imposing, while the French garden is mostly imperfect in its early years, reaching its peak of beauty around its fifteenth year and declining after that, so that eventually the only thing remaining is a mix of crippled and half-dead trees and hedges."

[32] Ibid., 303–4.

[33] "Brücken und Stege in Englischen Gärten," *Journal*, August 1790, 474–76.

[34] *Journal*, June 1790, 307.

[35] Ibid., 314–16.

[36] "Das Gartenhaus erhält folglich die bequemste Stelle in der Mitte; man mag nun ein Gebäude von zwey Stockwerk lieben, oder einen Gartensaal vorziehen, der nur einige Stufen erhaben ist, weil man sich in diesem der kleinen Bedürfnüße und Erfrischungen gleich im Vorbeygehn bedienen kann, und weil die Gesellschaft im Hause und im Garten weniger getrennt ist, als wenn beyde Theile erstlich über Treppen zu einander steigen müssen" (ibid., 317; The garden house receives the most convenient spot in the middle of the garden regardless of whether people like a two-story building or prefer a one-story building that is only a few steps up because one can easily take care of one's small needs or partake of refreshments as one walks by and because visitors in the house and the garden are less separated than when they have to use stairs to mingle).

[37] Ibid., 321.

[38] "Ein Garten-Kabinet in Chinesischem Geschmacke," *Journal*, May 1789, 225.

[39] *Journal*, June 1795, 258.

[40] *Journal/Intelligenzblatt* "IX. Spaziergänge mit meinen Zöglingen" 1804, CCXXX–CCXXXI; CCXXX.

[41] *Journal/Intelligenzblatt* 1802, CLXV; "Notice to owners of gardens, fruit enthusiasts, and economists: pomological, theoretical-practical handbook or alphabetical lists of all necessary information on pomology, planting, grafting, and care and treatment of all varieties of fruit trees and of the economic use of their fruits, etc., and also for judging and understanding the best cultivars that we know so far and their kinds of classifications etc."

[42] "Both went hand in hand with an interest in cookbooks and more elaborate cuisine gracing the middle-class table. If traditional mealtimes had been simple and hurried, the larger variety of foods, its more elaborate preparation, and its presentation required a significant time investment for preparation and consumption and transformed mealtimes into social and cultural occasions for interaction and conversation"; see Wurst, *Fabricating Pleasure*, 289.

[43] "XXVI. *Küchentaschenbuch für Frauenzimmer zur täglichen Wahl der Speisen für das Jahr 1796*," Journal/Intelligenzblatt 1795, CCXLVI.

[44] Ibid.

[45] "XXIX. *Küchenlexikon für Frauenzimmer*," *Journal/Intelligenzblatt* 1796, CCXV–VI.

[46] "XIX. Neues Hannöverisches Kochbuch," *Journal/Intelligenzblatt* 1803, CCXXXIV.

[47] "XXII. Productenbuch für die Küche oder Anweisung für junge Mädchen und Hausfrauen, diejenigen Producte, welche in der Küche zubereitet werden, nach ihrem wahren Gehalte kennen und beurtheilen zu lernen," *Journal/Intelligenzblatt* 1803, CCXXXV–VI.

[48] "Ein Blumenkorb [aus lackiertem Blech] fürs Dessert und zur Zimmerverzie rung,"*Journal*, July 1797, 378–79; "Flowers are and always have been the most pleasant objects for all kinds of decorations. . . . We can deliver such a beautiful flower-basket made from matte lacquered metal, blue and white in the manner of Wedgewood, from Mr. Krause's factory in Braunschweig, with openings in which an insert with a grid is placed to hold water or wet sand for the display of flowers. If this flower-basket is placed in the middle of the table, and if the table is large, supplemented by a few smaller vases made of blue glass, Wedgewood stoneware, or porcelain here and there, you have a very natural, simple, and attractive dessert decoration, which can be nicely supplemented by small baskets or bowls with fruit."

[49] "Wohlfeile und beste Anlage einer Eisgrube in einem Garten," *Journal*, September 1793, 459.

[50] "Ein Englischer Schenk-Tisch mit Eiskästen," *Journal*, January 1793, 59; "The bar tables of the English are as tasteful and convenient as all their furniture. . . . The five lockable drawers can store twenty-four bottles of wine. In the summer one can insert ice boxes (that is metal boxes filled with ice) and place the bottles inside to keep the wine fresh."

[51] "Ein Garten-Kabinet im Chinesischen Geschmacke," *Journal*, May 1789, 226; "In this garden I also saw a garden chaise with an umbrella on a long pole attached to the armrest, which allowed the flower aficionado to get quite close to enjoy the flowerbed or to read; this invention of a portable shady seat readily available pleased me very much."

[52] "Pariser Blumentisch mit Voliere," *Journal*, March 1809, 196–97.

[53] For an extensive description of the fashionable flowers of the time, see van Dülmen, *Das irdische Paradies*, 127–31.

[54] "Ein Garten-Kabinet im Chinesischen Geschmacke," *Journal*, May 1789, 226.

[55] Van Dülmen, *Das irdische Paradies*, 267nn112 and 113.

[56] Van Dülmen, *Das irdische Paradies*, 256. See, e.g., the article "VII. Zeichen-Mahler- und Stickbuch zur Selbstbelehrung für Damen, welche sich mit diesen Künsten beschäftigen, von J. S. Netto" (Manual of Drawing, Painting, and Embroidery for Ladies Who Occupy Themselves with These Arts and Want to Teach Themselves, by J. S. Netto), *Journal/Intelligenzblatt* August 1797, CLXXIV.

[57] Van Dülmen, *Das irdische Paradies*, 94. "Die Samen mußten gereinigt, geordnet und beschriftet und nach Möglichkeit in einem eigenen Samenkabinett untergebracht werden. Für Tulpen, Hyazinthen, Ranunkeln usw. sollte man ebenfalls spezielle Kästen anschaffen, in denen man nach dem Abblühen jeder Zwiebel in einem eigenen Fach, mit einer Nummer bezeichnet und nach Farben oder Besonderheiten geordnet, aufbewahren konnte. Den 'Blumisten' bot das Anlegen von Nelken- oder Tulpenblätterkatalogen eine Möglichkeit, die Beschäftigung mit ihren Lieblingen bis in den Winter auszudehnen und sich an ihrer Pracht und Vielzahl zu erfreuen. Auf diesem Weg ließen sich auch die neuerzielten Formen und Farben festhalten und noch nach dem Flor für sich selbst und Gleichgesinnte dokumentieren: die Blumenblätter wurden kunstvoll gepresst auf Papierbögen

geklebt und beschriftet. Diese Kataloge konnten verschickt und ausgetauscht werden, in jedem Fall aber dienten sie den Blumenliebhabern dazu 'in einsamen Stunden ihre Gartenfreuden zu vermehren. Sich zu der Zeit mit ihren Lieblingen zu beschäftigen, wenn sie der Schnee bedeckt'" (The seeds had to be cleaned, organized, and labeled and then if at all possible stored in a designated seed cabinet. For tulips, hyacinths and primroses etc. one should procure designated boxes in which, after the foliage dies back, the bulbs can be stored, each in its separate compartment, labeled with numbers and organized according to color or other distinguishing characteristics. Flower enthusiasts had the opportunity to extend their occupation with their beloved flowers into the winter by creating catalogues of carnation- or tulip-petals, and to enjoy their splendor and variations. In this manner the newly created forms and colors could be captured and documented for one's own use and that of other flower enthusiasts even after the flowers were finished blooming: the petals were carefully pressed, glued on paper and labeled. Like the pages of catalogues, they could then be sent and traded; in every instance, however, they served flower enthusiasts by "increasing their enjoyment of the garden in quiet hours and enabling them to occupy themselves with their beloved flowers despite winter snows").

[58] "Ueber die Belvederes und eine neue Erfindung," *Journal*, March 1786, 119; "For those people who are tied down in the city by their businesses and lifestyle and can hardly enjoy the open air in the country, it must be quite pleasant to have a space around their house where they can create the semblance of a garden, and if they are flower enthusiasts, at least have the opportunity to sit among their beloved hyacinths, primroses, and carnations without wasting a lot of time (in travel) and to breath a bit better air than that in their (usual) closed rooms."

[59] The *Journal* article discusses the scientific breakthrough and the thorough testing of the material in some detail; ibid., 111–12.

[60] David Jarrett, Tadeus Rachwał, and Tadeaus Sławek, *Geometry, Winding Paths and the Mansions of Spirit* (Katowice: Wydawnictwo Uniwersytetu Śląskiego, 1997), 88.

[61] Van Dülmen, *Das irdische Paradies*, 118.

[62] Karl Victor von Bonstetten wrote of building a greenhouse to Friederike Brun: "Da hab' ich ein Treibhaus gebaut, wo Du im Winter unter grünen Bäumen lesen, schwatzen und spazieren kannst, da ist immer Sonne, oder Ihr heizt ein" (I built a greenhouse where you can read, chat, and walk in the wintertime, where the sun always shines, or you can heat it). Letter of Karl Victor von Bonstetten to Friederike Brun, qtd. by van Dülmen, *Das irdische Paradies*, 79.

[63] "XVII. *Der Wintergärtner* oder Anweisung, die beliebtesten Modeblumen und mehrere ausländische zur Zirde der Garten dienende Gewächse ohne Treibe- und Glashäusern in Zimmern, Kellern und anderen Behältern zu überwintern," *Journal/Intelligenzblatt* 1802, CCLVI.

[64] "Ueber den Luxus der Zimmer-Gärten," *Journal*, December 1792, 598.

[65] Ibid., 599–601.

[66] Ibid., 602–3.

3: Documenting the Zeitgeist: How the *Brockhaus* Recorded and Fashioned the World for Germans

Kirsten Belgum

W E LIVE IN AN ERA ADDICTED TO bits and bytes of news and information. The dominance today of the internet over print and even electronic media has demonstrated that immediate and convenient access to a seemingly endless reservoir of information is a priority for many. A highly popular and growing segment of this information supply consists of on-line encyclopedias, including *Wikipedia*, the free-content encyclopedia that boasts articles in over two hundred languages and more than 2.5 million entries in English alone.[1] These on-line encyclopedias are constantly in flux. Indeed, the technology of the internet allows a reader to track the daily (sometimes hourly) changes to entries in the massive *Wikipedia*.[2] Such changes often reveal contested views about specific terms and the contemporary struggle to define our society. In the case of the predecessor to these on-line reference works, the paper encyclopedia, the task of tracking changes over time requires manual paging through various editions and of course involves many fewer versions. But the changes over time in those multi-volume paper encyclopedias can also provide us with insights into the shifting views and priorities of their contemporary society. In other words, encyclopedias are repositories of historical knowledge and the shaping of meaning.

This paper focuses on a German case during the first era of popular, mainstream encyclopedias and examines the changes during a half-century in one of the most important and influential German encyclopedias, Brockhaus's *Conversations-Lexikon.* Two core questions underlie this study: first, how Brockhaus publishers chose to package and sell these documents of human knowledge to a large audience; second, what they included in that package and how. The main conclusion I have come to after sifting through two editions of this encyclopedia (the twelve-volume seventh edition from the 1820s and the sixteen-volume thirteenth edition from the 1880s) is that the recipe for success in the nineteenth century was for an encyclopedia to be *both* universal and national, that is, to keep up with the latest information about the world while also explicitly addressing the national audience and furthering a coherent story of national progress.

Since antiquity encyclopedias had been reference works that attempted to provide a comprehensive view of human knowledge; one of the earliest examples is Pliny the Elder's *Historia Naturalis* (77 CE), which contained 2,500 chapters in thirty-seven books and drew on works from five hundred authors.[3] But these ancient works and their medieval successors were generally written for and read by a very limited segment of society. The first European encyclopedias that had large publication runs of course required the printing press, but it was really only in the mid-seventeenth century that encyclopedias began to be written in national vernaculars as opposed to Latin.[4] Already in that century some encyclopedias from one country borrowed from those published in other parts of Europe. The eighteenth century brought more experimentation, such as the first truly English encyclopedia, the *Lexicon Technicum* (1704; Technical Encyclopedia) and the German *Reales Staats- und Zeitungs-Lexikon* (1704; Real State- and Newspaper-Encyclopedia). Compared to the ancient *Historia Naturalis*, both were relatively short, limited to a few volumes. More important, however, is the fact that their orientation shifted from world knowledge to relevant and up-to-date information. The English encyclopedia focused on current advances in technology while the German one aspired to give relevant political information. This is not to say that all eighteenth-century endeavors were so focused or so small. We might not be surprised to find that the first expansive (indeed, enormous) encyclopedia of the modern era was published by a German, Johann Heinrich Zedler, between 1731 and 1750. Zedler's sixty-four-volume work was so ambitious that it even engendered the fear that it "would be so comprehensive and up-to-date that no other books would be sold!"[5]

Modern encyclopedism hit its stride with the great French Enlightenment project of Diderot and D'Alembert in the 1750s to 1770s. In this era the *Encyclopédie* began not only to document the world and its history, but also to include opinions and defiantly promote new ideas, such as the assertion of inalienable human rights.[6] It also inspired similar projects. At the close of the eighteenth century there were numerous experiments in the realm of encyclopedias. While many of them faltered, one such false start ultimately led to the long and successful story of the Brockhaus encyclopedia. In 1796 Renatus Gotthelf Löbel and Christian Wilhelm Francke began a work entitled *Conversations-Lexikon mit vorzüglicher Rücksicht auf die gegenwärtigen Zeiten* (Conversational Encyclopedia with Particular Consideration of the Contemporary Period).[7] As the title suggests, this new venture was intended for a generally educated audience as a resource for polite conversation in society and, as such, it helped to inaugurate a new genre of encyclopedia. To that end it was also written in an easy conversational style.[8] Despite this novelty, Löbel and Francke's project stalled. Löbel died unexpectedly in 1799 and Francke, who worked as a lawyer, continued to edit the work alone, but between 1800 and 1808 the publication of the successive volumes became increasingly infrequent and they appeared under the imprint of three different publishers.[9] Given these delays, by 1808 the work was not quite as "contemporary" as it initially boasted. It contained, for instance, no mention of Napoleon Bonaparte. This is where our story takes a turn. At the Leipzig book fair in 1808, Friedrich Arnold Brockhaus, a relatively inexperienced German bookseller based in Amsterdam, bought this dormant encyclopedia. What may at the time have seemed like a foolish venture eventually became the publishing miracle that turned his company into a long-lasting success story and founded his family's publishing dynasty.

What was the recipe for this success? In large part it certainly required sophisticated insights into the field of publishing, including an alertness to the marketing needs of an encyclopedia and the ability to gain and maintain public confidence. The biggest challenge for the publisher of any encyclopedia is the constant battle against time. Not only does it take years to generate a modern encyclopedia, but with each passing year even a new work becomes out of date. The genius of Brockhaus thus consisted not in purchasing the dormant encyclopedia, but in keeping it as current as possible. He did this in two ways. The first was to create two supplemental volumes that would bring the already "old" work up to date by adding the momentous events of the previous fifteen years and thus convince potential customers of the current value of the work.[10] These new volumes appeared already between 1809 and 1811 under the expanded title of *Conversations-Lexicon oder kurzgefaßtes Handwörterbuch für die in der gesellschaftlichen Unterhaltung aus den Wissenschaften und Künsten vorkommenden Gegenständen mit beständiger Rücksicht auf die Ereignisse der älteren und neuern Zeit.*[11] By 1811 Brockhaus was able to sell almost the complete run of 2,000 of his acquired and expanded encyclopedia.

Even more strategically effective was Brockhaus's other plan: to begin work immediately on a second edition. The first two volumes of the revised second edition were already available in 1812, and by the fall of 1813 the first four volumes of this second edition were sold out. Rather than just finish that edition in the same size (and not be able to sell any additional complete sets due to the already limited run of the first four volumes), Brockhaus proceeded to start the third edition at the same time. Thus, in the next two years (1814–16) he began to publish a slightly revised version of volumes 1–4 (as part of the third edition) while he completed volumes 5–7 (which were thus the same for both the second and the third edition). As Brockhaus was completing volumes 8–9, he also chose to revise volume 7. He did this in part to fend off attempts by the firm A. F. Macklot in Stuttgart to reprint — that is, plagiarize — his entire work.[12] By updating volume 7 he could thus dub the entire finished project in 1819 (including the final volumes) the fourth edition. Brockhaus also soon realized that he needed to employ expert editors to contribute to the work and hired professors from the universities of Leipzig, Wittenberg, and Halle. Thus by 1819 Brockhaus had established his reputation as a skilled publisher and masterful businessman. The fifth edition of the *Conversations-Lexikon* appeared between 1818 and 1820, and the sixth edition, which Friedrich Arnold did not live to see in print, was distributed in early 1824.[13]

The attempt of Macklot as early as 1816 to print unauthorized copies of Brockhaus's *Conversations-Lexikon* shows both the popularity of this new genre and the financial benefits of selling one. Moreover, the fact that Brockhaus's company was faced with some important competitors in the 1820s (Pierer's) and 1830s (Meyer's), both of which quickly became successful in their own right, additionally indicates not only the dramatically exploding demand and thus market for encyclopedias, but also the financial attractiveness of the genre as a publishing product.[14]

One more piece of publishing history is relevant here. While today the name Brockhaus is associated primarily with the publication of the notable encyclopedia and similar reference works, in the nineteenth century the firm had a diverse publishing repertoire, including journals, German and foreign literature, and a wide array of scientific, technical, historical, theological, and even philosophical works. These journals reveal not only the diversity of topics in which Friedrich Arnold Brockhaus and his successors were interested, but also the political orientation of the firm and its owner. The first of these was the *Deutsche Blätter* (German Pages), which began to appear in the fall of 1813. This example of the political press during the Wars of Liberation provided readers with the first authentic and timely reports from the Battle of Nations at Leipzig and as a consequence quickly reached a circulation of 4,000. With the Battle of Waterloo and the Peace of Paris in late 1815 its mission was ended, and it stopped publication in the spring of 1816. But in the following years, three different periodicals in Brockhaus's publishing repertoire came under the scrutiny of the Prussian state and were either banned or censored for a time. *Isis, oder encyklopädische Zeitung von Oken* (1817–48; Isis, or the Encyclopaedic Newspaper by Oken) focused mostly on science, art, history, and literature, but also included political essays in the form of book reviews. It became a collection point for patriotic submissions from throughout Germany since it was published under the protection of the 1806–10 press freedom that prevailed in Weimar. But first Austria (which banned it immediately) and then Prussia pressured the Weimar government, which in turn made Oken choose between his editorship and his professorship (he chose the former).[15]

Another Brockhaus periodical, *Zeitgenossen: Biographien und Charakteristiken* (Contemporaries: Biographies and Charakter Sketches), included contributions about notable people active in the period 1789–1815. One such biography, which also appeared as a separate edition, Johann Friedrich Benzenberg's biography of King Frederick William III of Prussia, led to the censoring of Brockhaus's publishing house in Prussia in 1821.[16] In the publication of his journals, Brockhaus repeatedly ran into conflict with Prussian censors because he sided with the liberal voices of the Wars of Liberation and was eager to report on grand political events, even when it included unauthorized references to the Prussian king and queen.[17] In short, he was unstinting in calling for the freedom of the press. This strong liberal tradition, alongside the publisher's professional expertise, helped to shape Germany's most famous encyclopedia.

The Conversations-Lexikon: From the 1820s to the 1880s

By the mid 1820s Friedrich Arnold Brockhaus and his company had produced a highly successful, popular reference work. The numbers alone attest to this. Whereas the first edition of the *Conversations-Lexikon* sold out quickly with a run of 2,000 copies, the fifth edition (1818–20) first appeared in 12,000 copies but had to be reprinted twice, each time with 10,000 additional copies, bringing the total print run to 32,000. In the 1820s alone the firm published three distinct editions, and each appeared in several paper qualities to cater to readers of varying income levels.[18]

The success of the *Conversations-Lexikon* can be measured in sheer numbers in the subsequent decades as well.[19] The best evidence for this is the increasing size of the Brockhaus publishing firm as a whole. In 1823 Brockhaus had one hundred employees; by the end of the 1820s it employed 180 people and was the largest printer in Germany (with twelve hand presses and three rapid presses). In 1832 it added a bindery and in 1833 a stereotype foundry for producing its own stereotype plates for printing. In 1834 steam power was added to the three rapid presses.[20] By 1850 the firm had nine rapid presses, in 1872 twenty-two, in 1894 thirty, as well as a rotary press.[21] In these decades Friedrich Arnold's sons and grandsons inherited not only his firm, but also some of his political views. The liberal from the 1810s and 1820s who was willing to take on plagiarizing competitors and the censors of the Prussian state gave way to the national liberal grandson of the 1880s who was active in regional politics and elected to a seat in the Reichstag.

To get a sense of the "shape" the Brockhaus encyclopedia took, we can look at some changes between the seventh and the thirteenth editions, which lie more than fifty years apart (1827–29 and 1883–87).[22] Some of the changes that we see between these two editions of course have to do with new developments in the world. In the first place these included discoveries, exploration, the expansion of colonial interests, and innumerable technological innovations. These developments obviously would make their way into any encyclopedia that purported to be up-to-date.

But other changes between the 1820s and the 1880s that were significant for German society and culture were political in nature. A whole host of developments had taken place in the German states, many of which ultimately led to the founding of the German Empire, a unified German nation-state that most German liberals had sought for decades. This path included the creation of the German Zollverein (Tariff Union) in 1834, the Revolution of 1848, and the North German Confederation, and then ultimately the war against the French and the unification of Germany, with the exclusion of Austria, into a nation-state under Prussian dominance. While these various momentous events enter into the 1880s edition of the *Conversations-Lexikon*, there are also other, less obvious ways the consolidation of German society and a German identity is marked in the pages of this all-encompassing reference work. In other words, the encyclopedia tells us explicitly and implicitly about the changes that occurred within German society.

The problem with encyclopedias for the scholar (which is of course also their attraction for the common user as well as the historian of the book) is the vast amount of information and commensurately large number of topics they contain. Due to space constraints I will limit my discussion of the interests and perspectives of this seminal reference work to four main themes over a half century. I suggest that we can read the shifts in these topics as a kind of seismographic trace of the changes in German society. These are 1) a teleological view of German history, 2) a celebration of technology and scientific improvements that foregrounds German contributions to these domains, 3) a depiction of the contemporary world with particular emphasis on Germany's interests, and 4) the form and rhetorical presentation of a totalizing image of the world that demonstrates a confidence in the ability of this new genre to grasp and present material on a wide range of topics.

A Teleology of Germany

Over the course of fifty years (and six editions) a significant change occurred in the *Conversations-Lexikon*'s characterization of Germany, including German culture, society, and history. As a major reference work of course the *Conversations-Lexikon* covered many topics that had nothing specifically to do with Germany. These range from distant lands and historical figures from all eras to plants and animals found around the world. Not surprisingly, a greater amount of space in this German-language encyclopedia is devoted to German individuals, culture, and landscapes than to those of any one other nation or region of the world. But what differences can we see if we compare the presentation of Germany in the 1820s with that in the 1880s? First, we find a whole host of areas in which the *Conversations-Lexikon* promotes the development of Germany (as a culture, a society, and a political configuration). One of the areas in which this promotion of Germany occurs most strikingly is the encyclopedia's discussion of national geography. A sampling of notable regions reveals a common enthusiasm for the geography of Germany in both editions. Yet, the differences are clear and consistent: an emphasis in the 1820s on the romantic qualities of these areas and in the 1880s on the economic, industrial, political, even geo-political significance of these same regions.

One example of this shift can be seen in articles in both editions that present the area of the Rhine River. In keeping with the role of the Rhine as a national icon already in the early part of the century and on the basis of the tourist trade that began along the Rhine in the 1820s, both the seventh and the thirteenth editions of Brockhaus's *Conversations-Lexikon* celebrate the ancient and romantic scenery associated with this region. Both comment on "mannigfaltige Felsen- und Bergpartien und wild romantische Ansichten" (VII, 9:245; XIII, 13:662; diverse rocky and mountain areas and rustically romantic scenes).[23] However, the similarities begin to diverge here. The seventh edition describes the ability of tourists to view these vistas from the many river boats that shuttle daily between Mainz and Cologne and offer the tourist "wohlfeile und bequeme Gelegenheiten" (VII, 9:245; inexpensive and comfortable opportunities). By contrast the thirteenth edition focuses much more on commercial rather than touristic aspects of shipping: "eine vorzügliche Wichtigkeit, besonders für das westl. Deutschland, hat der R. durch die Schifffahrt" (XIII, 13:660; in shipping, the Rhine holds an exquisite importance, especially for western Germany).

In part this difference could be a function of a changing economy between the 1820s and the 1880s. But the fact that the entry in the later edition also seeks to demonstrate the long history of continuity regarding commercial uses of river navigation shows that the encyclopedia's orientation had shifted. To be sure, even the seventh edition points out that "Karl der Große ließ dieses Felsenbett zuerst für ganz kleine Schiffe fahrbar machen" (VII, 9:245; Charlemagne first had this rock bed made navigable for very small ships). But the thirteenth edition expands this historical continuity, considerably promoting modern achievement: "die preussische Regierung ließ seit 1834 die Durchfahrt, bei welcher man eine tiefe Stelle des Flußgrundes das Bingerloch nennt, durch Sprengen so vergrößern, daß dieselbe, ausser bei sehr niedrigem Wasserstande, nunmehr gefahrlos ist" (XIII, 13:661; [S]ince 1834 the Prussian government has enlarged this passage, of which a deep section of the river bottom is called the Bingen Hole, by blasting, so that it is not dangerous except at very low water levels).[24]

Finally, the latter edition devotes more space to a discussion of the military significance of the Rhine, including the "Pfahlbrücke" (pile bridge) that Julius Caesar's armies used against the Gauls, the bridges made of boats and barges in the Thirty Years' War, and army crossings during the Napoleonic wars. In a tale of historical progress that leads directly up to the present day, it concludes that these former difficulties have been recently overcome through "die großartigen Eisenbahnbrücken" (the grandiose railway bridges) at Strassbourg (Kehl), Mannheim, Main, Coblenz, Cologne, and Hamm (XIII, 13:661). In this way, even historical overviews in the later edition serve the rhetorical purpose of demonstrating Germany's emergence as a great nation and its logical path to the present.

The case of the Harz region is similar. In the seventh edition the entry on the Harz concludes with a paragraph about cultural and emotional aspects of this mountainous landscape. This paragraph includes praise for the "open" orientation of the towns, the construction of homes and churches, the types of indigenous flora (wild berries, truffles, morels) and animal husbandry (cattle, sheep, goats, horses), and the occupation of the residents (mining of silver, iron, lead, and copper). The section ends with a comment about the tourist attractions of the area: the Brocken "mit seiner Aussicht, jetzt auf seiner Spitze mit einem 130 Fuß langen, von Granitblöcken erbauten Wirthshause, nach seinem Erbauer, dem Grafen Stolberg-Wernigerode, die Friedrichshöhe gennant" (VII, 5:106; With its view, now on the summit with a 130 foot long inn, built of granite blocks, named "Frederick's Heights" after its architect, Graf Stolberg-Wernigerode).

In contrast, the thirteenth edition focuses on economics and politics (rather than anthropology, cultural life, or points of interest). It also mentions the height and location of the Brocken, but more space is devoted to listing the German states that currently have control over segments of the Harz. In particular, it discusses economic issues such as the power of the mountain streams and the usefulness of the mountain products as well as mining, metallurgy, and the mineral riches in the Harz region (XIII, 8:877). The main addition of the 1884 edition, however, is administrative and political history. One fifth of the two-page article is devoted to a political history of the region dating back to the time of Charlemagne[25] and concludes with a discussion of recent treaties between Brunswick and Prussia and the regional control of the mining industry by Prussia and Anhalt (XIII, 8:878).[26] In such articles, Brockhaus's *Conversations-Lexikon* moves from an emphasis on cultural and scenic elements to one that records both the continuity and the progress of political consolidation in Germany over time.

This teleological view of Germany also dominates the later articles on German culture. The article from the 1820s on German literature reflects self-doubt or at least insecurity about the status of a national literature: it begins with long quotations from August W. Schlegel about the lack of unity in literature and the missing connection between German nationality and the nation's literature, stating that Germany can only be considered to have a national literature under the following conditions:

> Wenn man unter Literatur einen ungeordneten Wust, ein rohes Aggregat von Büchern versteht, die kein gemeinschaftlicher Geist beseelt, unter denen nicht einmal der Zusammenhang einer einseitigen Nationalrichtung bemerkbar ist: wo die einzelnen Spuren und Andeutungen des Bessern sich unter dem unübersehbaren Gewühl von leeren und mißverstandenen Strebungen, von Verkehrtheit und Verworrenheit, von übelverkleideter Geistesarmuth und fratzenhafter anmaßender Originalitätssucht fast unmerklich verlieren. (VII, 3:173)[27]

Several pages later (after a summary of the history of German literature), the author concedes the difficulty of assessing contemporary German literature. Here, too, a sense of incompleteness regarding a core national project predominates:

> Wollen wir selbst die jüngste Zeit der deutschen Literatur schildern, so ist dies ein mißliches Unternehmen. Denn, wie bedeutend oder unbedeutend die Erscheinungen sein mögen, die sich innerhalb derselben zusammendrängen, wir haben sie ganz vor Kurzem selber mit durchlebt und stehen mehr oder weniger auch jetzt noch unter ihrem Einflusse. Weisen wir daher auf das hin, was uns als vorherrschende Richtung in dem literarischen Streben der letzten Jahre vorgekommen, so bescheiden wir uns gern, nichts zu geben, als eben unsere Ansicht, womit wir keiner fremden zu nahe zu treten gedenken. (VII, 3:180)[28]

Yet, not only does this passage acknowledge a lack of a firm historical path; it also includes extensive use of the first-person plural voice that magnifies the carefully self-reflexive stance of the author.

By contrast, the article in the thirteenth edition from the 1880s (which devotes twenty-three pages to a discussion of German literature and focuses mostly on history) asserts a clear historical trajectory within German history that has completely overcome the insecurity and hesitancy of the earlier edition. In part this change is reflected in an oblique dismissiveness of other cultures:

> Je festere Wurzeln das Christentum in dem deutschen Volke schlug und je mehr es bei ihm eine innerliche Heimat fand, wie bei keinem andern Volke, desto mehr wurde die deutsche Gesamtbildung eine wesentlich auf christl. Grundsätzen geruhende, und dieser Geist durchdrang auch die ganze deutsche Litteratur, ohne daß

es dazu speziell geistlicher Leitung und Überwachung bedurfte.
(XIII, 5:127)[29]

Above all, the suggestion of the uniqueness and originality of the German
response to historical impulses implies a cultural strength and resilience that
is lacking in other European traditions. The encyclopedia introduces each
new period or key author as part of a larger story of increasing German
strength, assertiveness, and confidence: "Lessing ist der eigentliche Befreier
des deutschen Geistes, der Chorführer der neuen Nationallitteratur" (XIII,
5:140; Lessing is the actual liberator of the German spirit, the choir director of the new national literature). Other examples include "Die gewaltige
litterarische Thätigkeit rief gegen das J. 1770 eine allgemeine Gärung der
Geister hervor, welche nicht bloß die gelehrt Gebildeten, sondern auch den
höheren Bürgerstand berührte" (141; The powerful literary activity around
the year 1770 called forth a general agitation of the minds, which touched
not only educated scholars, but also the upper middle class) and "Goethe
und Schiller haben die deutsche Litteratur in allen Teilen der Erde zu einer
geehrten erhoben" (143; Goethe and Schiller have raised German literature to an honored place in all parts of the world).

In all these passages an authoritative and objective third-person voice
leaves no room for doubt or insecurity. In keeping with this tone of
confidence, the article in the thirteenth edition also uses a wide array of
affirmative adjectives to describe the various contributors to the German
national history. Just a few of the epithets that appear in one half-page
(one column) include: *nahmhaft, schwunghaft, glänzend, sinnig, witzig,
geistreich, verdienstlich, gründlich, tiefeinschneidend, strebend, gedanken-
reich, liebenswürdig, meisterhaft* (144; famous, lively, brilliant, sensitive,
witty, ingenious, meritorious, thorough, incisive, striving, thoughtful,
pleasant, magisterial). This overwhelming array of affirmative adjectives
does not exclude a critical view of some phases of German literary production, but it assures that the overall tone of the later article invokes
greatness and, thus, progress.

The same tendency holds true for the articles on "Deutsche Kunst"
(German Art) in both editions.[30] The seventh edition suggests an
indebtedness of German culture to both preceding and neighboring
cultures. The article "Deutsche Malerkunst" (German Painting) begins
by acknowledging the dominant influence of the Romans on German
culture: "Das Eindringen der Römer an die Ufer des Rheins und der
Donau bewirkte eine große Veränderung in den Sitten der deutschen
Völker" (VII, 3:184; The incursion of the Romans as far as the banks
of the Rhine and the Danube effected a great change in the customs of
the German peoples). In contrast, the article on German art in the thirteenth edition not only uses the singular *Volk*, as opposed to the plural
notion of "die deutschen Völker" (the German peoples) that appeared

in the seventh edition, but also gives the German element a more active and decisive role in the reshaping of preceding culture, as opposed to the passive role implied in the preceding quotation: "Dem germanischen Volke war im Verein mit den romanischen Nationen eine eigenthümliche und großartige Aufgabe beschieden, die Kunstelemente der Antike in ein neues Bett überzuleiten" (XIII, 5:122; The German people in conjunction with the Romance nations faced the unique and grandiose challenge of transferring the artistic element of antiquity to a new bed.). Uniformity and singularity predominate, and again an explicitly outlined trajectory of German history precludes any deviation from the dominant story of German success.

Some social and political issues receive similar treatment. Thus, the article in the thirteenth edition on "Preßgesetze, Preßfreiheit, Preßvergehen" (Press Laws, Freedom of the Press, Press Offenses) gives much more space to the German case than to that of other nations: two of the three pages in an article on "Presse and Preßgesetzgebung" (XIII, 13:266; Press and Press Legislation), for example, deal with the situation in Germany. But in these cases a relatively progressive view of Prussian policy prior to the founding of the German Empire in 1871 emerges. Even in the case of censorship, where Hanover and Prussia are credited with pushing for liberal policy in the Congress of Vienna, i.e., after "Napoleonic Despotism" and the reaction of the Carlsbad Decrees of 1819, a clear sympathy is expressed for the oppressed "Young German" authors of the 1830s (XIII, 13:265). The list of improvements, such as the removal of restraints, provides the main focus of the section on the German Empire (XIII, 13:266). The tension here reveals the middle-class dilemma within the creation of the German nation-state between an appreciation for and support of the revolutionary power of German liberalism in the Pre-March period on the one hand and an eagerness to endorse the German Empire that Bismarck had managed to establish in 1871 on the other.

Celebrating a New Era of Science and Technology

While most of the topics mentioned above deal with German culture and politics, other domains also play a similar role in the two editions of the encyclopedia. A second element that markedly distinguishes the *Conversations-Lexikon* of the 1820s from that of the 1880s pertains to technology. From the seventh to the thirteenth edition there is a dramatic increase in the number and length of articles that pertain to science and technological innovation. To a great extent, of course, this expansion reflects the rapid changes that industrialization and scientific research brought about over the course of this intervening period in the western world as a whole. Indeed, it should not surprise us that the entry for *Eisenbahn* (Railway) in the 1820s (before any railways even exist in Germany) is only one-half page long, whereas in the 1880s it is nineteen pages long, including four full pages of illustrations, and is supplemented by an additional twenty-four pages devoted to such related entries as *Eisenbahn-abgaben* (Railway fees), *Eisenbahnunfälle* (Railway accidents), and *Eisenbahnverwaltung* (Railway administration) (XIII, 5:855–93). There are extensive entries on items from *Baumwollmaschinen* (Cotton Machines), *Dampfschifffahrt* (Steam Ship Navigation), and *Dampfmaschine* (Steam Engine) to *Lokomotiven* (Locomotives), *Transportschraube* (Transportation Propeller), and *Ventilation* (Ventilation).

While these technological advances are developments of the modern world as a whole and thus the entries often include the contributions and accomplishments of developers and industrial producers from other nations, national progress and national pride repeatedly come to the fore in this area. Thus in the 1880s *Conversations-Lexikon*, the entry for "Torpedo" is a two-page article that includes one page of illustrations. It proclaims achievements that led to national victories: "Im Deutsch-Französischen Kriege von 1870 und 1871 wurden die deutschen Flußmündungen durch solche Kontakttorpedos geschützt" (XIII, 15:761; In the Franco-Prussian war of 1870 and 1871 the mouths of German rivers were protected by such underwater mines). Or under the entry for "Uhren" (Clocks) the encyclopedia boasts that, while Switzerland is recognized as a main country for the fabrication of clocks, numerous German clock products are famous throughout the world and a significant element in international trade (especially Black Forest cuckoo-clocks). The entry goes on to describe the major clock- and watch-making trade schools in Germany only. In other words, the encyclopedia displays a particular fascination with the developments in science and technology that take place close to home and that are of domestic manufacture and use. Similarly, images of the railway, which we will examine in more detail below, while of course including English and American examples, nonetheless foreground such German cases as the Stuttgart railway station. Above all, German progress in science and technology is of greatest or most emphatic interest to the editors of the thirteenth edition of the *Conversations-Lexikon*.

The Contemporary World and German Interests

While technology and innovation constitute a significant instance of the encyclopedia's promotion of Germany within the modern world as a whole, writing in these areas is by no means the only example. Another profound way in which the contemporary matters of Germany and the world enter into the encyclopedia is more directly political and pertains to foreign interests of the German nation-state. A decided attention to contemporary events sets the thirteenth edition apart from the earlier seventh edition. Not by coincidence do some of these current events also relate to other publications of the Brockhaus firm itself. There is room for only two such examples here.

The issue of colonialism was of course more important in the 1880s than it had been in the 1820s for much of Europe. The race for colonial acquisitions and control increased over the course of the nineteenth century even for established colonial powers like England and France. And here, as well, Germany staked a claim. Even before Bismarck's famous Africa Conference of 1884–85 there were numerous private German ventures in Africa, and Bismarck himself, despite his aversion to colonial conquest, had approved the creation of German protectorates to support these existing initiatives. Thus, whereas the seventh edition has a full-page entry on the "African Society" that discusses this British organization in the 1820s for an entire page, the edition from the 1880s reduces this report to one fourth of a page, placing emphasis instead on Germany and Belgium as well as on Great Britain.

Of interest here is also how little the 1820s *Brockhaus* reported on some topics. The entire continent of Africa, for instance, received only a six-page entry. The tone of this early article is emphatic and enthusiastic with some of the descriptions bordering on the fantastical (each of the first three sentences ends in an exclamation mark): "seit Jahrtausenden schon in die Geschichte eingeführt, dennoch auch für uns noch immer, was es den Alten war, — das Reich des Wunderbaren!" (VII, 1:111; having been introduced into history thousands of years ago, yet still for us today what it always was for the ancients, — the empire of the fantastical!). It lists in amazement the strange indigenous creatures: the hippopotamus, the ostrich, and especially the camel, which it calls the "beneficent gift" of the continent (112). It also notes with indignation the slave trade which, it points out, is still considerable although "most nations of Europe have renounced it through agreements." The article remarks that recently 150,000 Africans a year had been brought to the West Indies not even counting those whom "die Nordamerikaner in ihre Südstaaten schleppten" (114; the North Americans carted off to their southern states).

By contrast, the thirteenth edition takes a comprehensive approach to the subject and — on the surface at least — a more objective tone. It is worth pointing out that the first volume of this edition (which includes all entries beginning with the letter "A," and thus also "Africa") was published in 1882, i.e., before the declaration of German protectorates in Africa. The entry on "Africa" in this edition is sixteen pages long (XIII, 1:183–99) and accompanied by an additional ten pages of plates: six on the physical geography, two on cultural artifacts, and two with images of Africans. It begins with extensive discussions of the dimensions, topography, geography, geology, flora, and fauna of the continent. A description of rivers, the variations in climate, vegetation, and the animal world makes up two full pages of the article, and six pages are devoted to so-called

"Geschichtliches und Entdeckungsreisen" (193–98; Historical Concerns and Voyages of Discovery), in other words to those sections of Africa that are of German relevance. In addition the supplemental volume 16, published in 1887, includes nine more pages on "Africa," complete with a fold-out "Übersichtskarte von Afrika" (Overview Map of Africa) measuring 18 x 23 inches and depicting the continent in extraordinary detail, with the various colonial possessions identified in color. A full-page entry is also devoted to the recent "African Conference" of Bismarck; it reports with the detail of a newspaper article. Included in the entry "Deutschland und Deutsches Reich" (Germany and the German Empire) in the supplemental volume there are two further fold-out, colorized maps depicting the "Kolonien and Schützgebiete des Deutschen Reichs" (Colonies and Protectorates of the German Empire), as well as a two-page color plate depicting twenty-four examples of "Völkertypen aus Kolonien des Deutschen Reichs" (Types of Peoples from the Colonies of the German Empire).[31] Thus, while general European colonialism is an issue of interest, German interests, even prior to official German involvement, but especially afterward, far outweigh those of other nations.

Similar to colonialism, the subject of European exploration of ancient sites allows the thirteenth edition of the *Conversations-Lexikon* to promote German conquests. A notable case is that of Heinrich Schliemann, the wealthy German businessman who chose to pursue his lifelong passion of finding the city of Troy and others where Homer's heroes battled. The seventh edition of the *Conversations-Lexikon* from the 1820s already exhibits a strong interest in Greek antiquity. Inspired by the classical revivalism of the late eighteenth century, Brockhaus's encyclopedia in the 1820s affirmed the culture of Hellenic Greece: "Das Ideal in diesen Werken ist der Sinn der Natur; der durchgreifende Charakter derselben Verkörperung des Geistigen, welche die Einbildungskraft harmonisch anregt und bewegt und das Vollendeteste der Natur gleichsam für die Ewigkeit festzuhalten strebt" (VII, 1:325; The ideal in these works is the meaning of nature; the sweeping character of that same embodiment of the spiritual that harmoniously stimulates and moves the imagination and strives to hold fast to the most perfect elements of nature for eternity). This edition includes numerous articles on such topics as "Athens" or "Herodotus." However, many others that will appear by the 1880s, such as "Acropolis" and "Mycenae," are absent.

After the excavations of Heinrich Schliemann beginning in 1871, related entries undergo some central changes that reflect his popularity and notoriety. The thirteenth edition of the *Conversations-Lexikon* thus includes not only a full-page entry on Schliemann himself, but also a two-page plate representing the sites of his discoveries and a large array of artifacts, such as buttons, rings, coins, axes, vases, and pitchers found at "Ausgrabungen von Mykenä, Orchomenos, Tiryns und Troja" (Excavations of Mycenae,

Orchomenos, Tiryns, and Troy). The entry on Schliemann explains his significance as "richly deserving in the study of antiquity," even before it lists his birthdate (XIII, 14:407). It notes his dedication to conducting these excavations with his own funds: "Auf eigene Kosten erforschte er, in Begleitung seiner Gattin, einer Griechin, seiner beständigen Mitarbeit-erin, mit durchschnittlich 150 Arbeitern von 1870 bis 1882 die Baustelle von Ilion" (407; From 1870 to 1882 he researched the site of Ilion at his own expense, in the company of his spouse, a Greek woman who was his constant assistant, and with on average 150 workers). Finally, the essay describes his achievement with an emphatic adjective "noch großartiger" (even more grand) and closes with a listing of his numerous academic hon-ors (408), in the meantime remarking that Schliemann donated many of his unearthed treasures to the German Empire and that they are housed in a special section (that bears his name) of the Museum für Völkerkunde in Berlin (407). The entry does not point out, even when listing the many publications by Schliemann about his excavations, that the Brockhaus firm was Schliemann's main publisher and that these books appeared in the same house that was printing this article.

Even more noteworthy, however, is the addition to the *Conversations-Lexikon* of some key entries that were not included in the edition from the 1820s. Thus, while Mycenae was certainly a known concept in the 1820s, it does not appear in the seventh edition, but does appear in the edition from the 1880s, including an extensive reference to the materials found by Schliemann's excavation there. Likewise, the entry on "Troja" (Troy) in the thirteenth edition includes the additional claim that the presumed location of the ancient city "hat neuerdings eine bedeutsame Stütze erhalten durch die Resultate der Nachgrabungen, welche H. Schliemann (s.d.) auf der Stätte des histor. Ilion, dem Hügel Hissarlik in den J. 1871–82 veranstaltete" (XIII, 15:859; has recently received a significant sup-port through the results of the excavations which H. Schliemann (*qv*) has conducted at the site of the histor[ical]. Ilion, the hill of Hissarlik in the years 1871–82). In other words, the interest in Greek antiquity is now linked both to the contribution of a German entrepreneur and, indirectly, to the publishing firm itself.

One other example also demonstrates the involvement of the Brockhaus encyclopedia in promoting other works from the publishing house. Henry Stanley was the American adventurer and traveler who took up the chal-lenge in 1871 of finding the British missionary Dr. Livingstone, who had gone missing in Central Africa. The Brockhaus company in the 1880s had a vested interest in both men and their works; it had acquired the autho-rized permission to publish a German translation of Stanley's story of his rescue of Livingstone, *Through the Dark Continent* (1878). The brothers, Eduard and Rudolf (both sons of Heinrich Brockhaus and grandsons of the firm's founder, Friedrich Arnold), took a particular interest in getting their firm access to something special from Stanley. They approached his publisher to procure a special introduction by him to German readers of the German edition of his book about the Congo. In 1885 the publisher granted their wishes with a letter to the Brockhaus firm that was printed in facsimile form and included (along with a German translation of it) as the foreword to the German edition. Heinrich Eduard Brockhaus's history of the family publishing company, which appeared on the occasion of the hundredth anniversary of the firm's founding, boasts of the contact that his father and uncle had to the famous Stanley as well as to Schliemann.[32]

Totalizing Image(s) of the World

The ambition of the Brockhaus firm to expand its encyclopedic repertoire and offer an even more comprehensive view of the world became apparent in the 1840s. In this decade the firm acquired the *Allgemeine Enzyklopädie der Wissenschaften und Künste* (Universal Encyclopaedia of Sciences and Arts), the seemingly endless encyclopedia known as "Ersch and Gruber" for short after the two initial editors, Johann Samuel Ersch and Johann Gottfried Gruber.[33] However, the enormity of the project, which had proven to be a challenge to its original publisher, Friedrich Gleditsch, who died in 1831, overwhelmed the Brockhaus firm as well. The second section (which covered the letters H-N) was stopped in 1855 with the completion of its thirty-first part (only up to the entry "Ligatur"). By the death in 1877 of the new editor, Prof. Hermann Brockhaus, a scholar of oriental languages and the younger brother of Friedrich and Heinrich, the project as a whole was languishing. Beginning in 1882 another twelve parts of the third and final section (covering O-Z) appeared, but by 1889 the work (at over 160 volumes) was stopped, far from the end of the alphabet, with the entry "Phyxios."[34]

In the meantime, however, the more compact *Conversations-Lexikon* continued to thrive, albeit in a slightly expanded format. It grew steadily but modestly from twelve volumes in the 1820s and '30s (the seventh and eighth editions) to fifteen volumes in the 1840s and '70s (from the ninth through the twelfth editions).[35] The 1880s brought two significant changes in the physical appearance of the *Conversations-Lexikon*. The first was the layout of the individual pages. Through the twelfth edition the encyclopedia had the same single-column layout that it had had from the beginning. This changed dramatically in the 1880s with double columns on each page and a significantly smaller typeface to accommodate more words and also more entries per page. The second major change in the appearance of the *Conversations-Lexikon* was the inclusion beginning in the 1880s of a large number of illustrations. The cost of including illustrations was moderated by the fact that the Brockhaus firm had already added an institute for the in-house production and printing of illustrations in the 1840s.[36]

The Brockhaus firm had explored the use of illustrations as early as the 1830s. This occurred first in its *Bilder-Conversations-Lexikon* (Illustrated Conversational Encyclopedia) that was less comprehensive (four volumes) but did not do as well as the larger *Conversations-Lexikon*.[37] In the late 1840s the firm published a new illustrated work entitled *Bilder-Atlas zum Conversations-Lexikon: Ikonographische Enzyklopädie der Wissenschaften und Künste* (Illustrated Atlas to the Conversational Encyclopedia: Iconographic Encyclopedia of the Sciences and Arts).[38] Consisting of eight volumes of illustrations in plates and two volumes of accompanying text, this work was sold as a supplement to the *Conversations-Lexikon* and was reprinted in 1869–74.[39] But by the 1880s the firm chose to integrate these images directly into the encyclopedia itself, the firm's most popular publication. They appeared in two forms: 1) individual figures imbedded in the text of entries and 2) single and double-page plates of figures that were inserted close to the relevant entries. As such they reveal a new approach to providing a totalizing view of the world.

Already in the *Ikonographische Enzyklopädie* we see a use of visual images in a comprehensive yet detailed manner. These tightly packed illustrations (engravings) provide not only the big picture, but also its many parts and details. In a manner that was familiar from other contemporary print genres, such as the family magazine and the weekly illustrated magazines, these images often show a view of an object from a perspective that provides more detail and overview than would be possible from any one physical vantage point. One example is the aerial-view city maps of European capitals such as Paris, London, Vienna, and Amsterdam that appear side-by-side in the two large volumes of plates in the *Ikonographische Enzyklopädie*.[40] By the 1880s the emphasis on the presentation of German cities is much more pronounced, and these overviews are embedded in the entries themselves.[41] These are often accompanied by the image of a notable site of that same city: thus for Cologne the *Conversations-Lexikon* includes both a map and a full-page illustration of the Cologne Cathedral. This latter picture shows an impossibly complete image of the cathedral, from a vantage point at least three stories higher than any of the surrounding buildings, a location that would not have been accessible to any contemporary residents of Cologne (see fig. 3.1). The often idealized perspectives presented by artists of such engravings are thus frequently more tendentious than the "factual" photographs which they are attempting to approximate. These drawings can not only generate physically non-existent views, but, through the process of isolation and concentration, they can leave out elements or objects that might otherwise interrupt a complete and coherent view of something (such as the full-face perspective presented here of the Cologne Cathedral including both of its towers).

KÖLNER DOM.

Der Kölner Dom.

Brockhaus' Conversations-Lexikon. 13. Aufl.   Zu Artikel : Kölner Dom.

Fig. 3.1. Cologne Cathedral. *Brockhaus' Conversations-Lexikon: allgemeine deutsche Real-Encyklopädie*, 13th ed., vol. 10 (Leipzig: F. A. Brockhaus, 1882–87), plate following page 420.

Another example of how the Brockhaus firm was increasingly interested in not only showing a comprehensive, totalizing view of the world, but in presenting its readers, first and foremost, with images of Germany and its achievements is the case of technology. If we compare only the images of the railroad that appear in the *Ikonographische Encyklopädie* of the 1840s and 1850s (see fig. 3.2) with those that appear embedded in articles from the thirteenth edition of the *Conversations-Lexikon* (see fig. 3.3), we see a notable difference. Both sets of illustrations are detailed

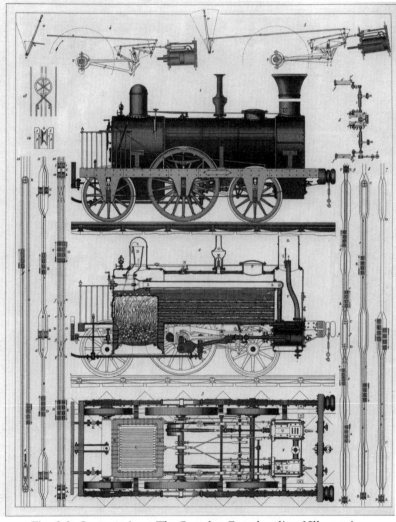

Fig. 3.2. Locomotives. *The Complete Encyclopedia of Illustration*
(New York: Park Lane, 1979), 542.

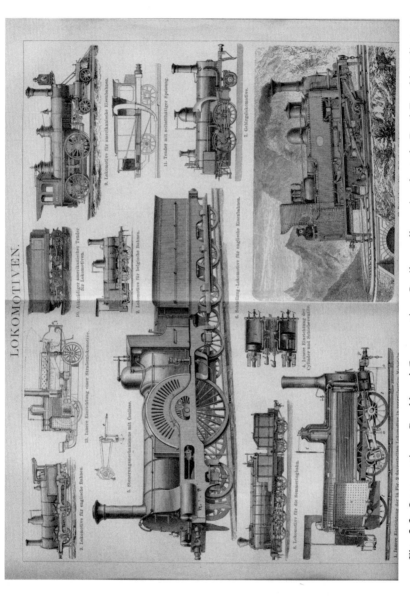

Fig. 3.3. Locomotives. *Brockhaus' Conversations-Lexikon: allgemeine deutsche Real-Encyklopädie,* 13th ed., vol. 11 (Leipzig: F. A. Brockhaus, 1882–87), plate following p. 156.

and meticulously drawn in terms of proportions and minutiae. Yet the earlier plates from the *Ikonographische Enzyklopädie* present the reader with densely packed figures that show many cross-sections, cut-aways, and flat views with numerous dimensions included. The later images in the thirteenth edition of the *Conversations-Lexikon* (some embedded in the articles and others in accompanying plates) show some of these perspectives, but also more external views of locomotives, cars, bridges, and tunnels in a more integrated perspective that suggests the three-dimensionality of the objects; even the sample segments of rails and tracks are depicted at an angle, in parallel projection, not from a flat, top-down perspective. In addition, more of the objects related to the railway industry are shown in the context of an outdoor setting, not in isolation. Finally, the later images in the *Conversations-Lexikon* from the 1880s are less about the technical details and the inner workings of the locomotives, tracks, tunnels, embankments, wagons, and bridges, and more about giving the viewer a coherent, recognizable, and complete external view.

To cite one last example of the innovations in viewing the world that illustrations brought to the *Conversations-Lexikon* in the 1880s, we turn to some of those entries that reveal an astonishingly passionate exception to the general attempt to remain dispassionate in the presentation of the world. Two instances will suffice to demonstrate the national fervor that crept into the otherwise relatively objective depictions of the Brockhaus encyclopedia in the second decade after the founding of the German Empire. The first is Leipzig, one of the many German cities that the encyclopedia presented to its readers. Here we do not just see the city and its environs in the year 1885, as the caption of the topographical map boldly states; instead this black-and-white map includes numerous blue and red boxes (either in outline or fully colored-in) that represent, as the key at the bottom of the map informs us, a scenario from seventy-two years earlier, in the morning and afternoon of 18 October 1813, during the Battle of Nations at Leipzig, where the allied armies resoundingly defeated the French armies of Napoleon (see fig. 3.4). In this way a contemporary map is made into a historical narrative and reminder of past greatness (XIII, 10:927). Similarly, the victory of the Prussian and allied forces over the French in 1870 at Sedan is discussed in the context of a smaller map of this French city. In this instance, the story in the entry connects the map and the many small surrounding towns and valleys that are included on it to the narrative about the German victory.

A second, and rather odd example, amounts simply to a fascination with technology that dominates the depiction of history and literature. To be sure, the reason for an entry on Götz von Berlichingen in a German encyclopedia has first and foremost to do with his role as a nobleman who supported the Reformation (including the Peasants' War of 1525). Yet in this instance, after a detailed discussion of his various military and

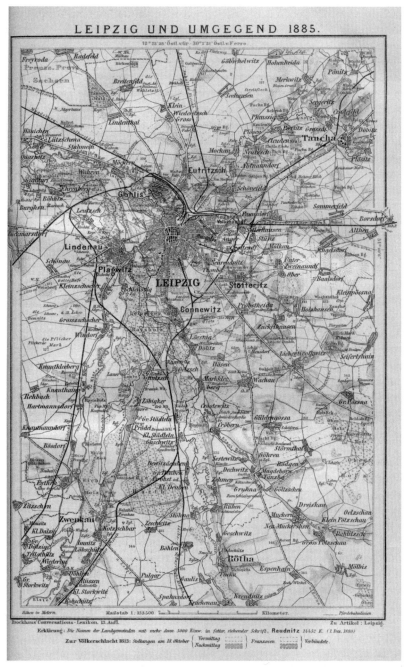

Fig. 3.4. Leipzig and environs. *Brockhaus' Conversations-Lexikon: allgemeine deutsche Real-Encyklopädie*, 13th ed., vol. 10 (Leipzig: F. A. Brockhaus, 1882–87), plate following page 926.

political roles and his exemplary behavior even under self-enforced house arrest for eleven years, the article veers in a completely different direction, namely a detailed discussion of Berlichingen's famous "iron hand" (see fig. 3.5). This discussion includes an illustration with eight distinct figures that show the mechanical hand from diverse angles and cross-sections. And almost more surprising than the image are the meticulously presented descriptions of how each spring, cog, and lever within the hand and fingers operates. Indeed, this obsession with the mechanical specifics takes up as much space as the biography of the historical man himself (XIII, 2:833–35). This case of national ingenuity and creativity (although the creator is not named) is given much more space than the brief reference to Goethe's iconic play about Berlichingen.

Conclusion

By the mid 1820s Friedrich Arnold Brockhaus and his successors had constructed a German model of delivering useful knowledge to a German readership that was 1) popular and 2) financially successful and that 3) appealed to a mainstream, middle-class audience. In the 1880s that was still the case. Indeed, the popularity, financial success, and mainstream appeal of the encyclopedia, judging from the size of the later editions alone, was considerable. The later edition also continued to demonstrate the commitment of its editors and publisher to a liberal political position; however, it also reveals a noticeable and significant change in its structure and message. The *Conversations-Lexikon* from the 1880s exudes not only a clear interest in affirming the German nation and the recently founded and unified German nation-state, but it also communicates a self-assurance and confidence about the path of Germany through history that can be read as a ringing endorsement of the German Empire. In addition, it provides a more complete and totalizing picture of the world and, most importantly, of German achievements in that world. And this is true not only because of the incorporation of illustrations such as pictures and maps, but also because of the nation-affirming manner in which they are deployed.

Beginning in the nineteenth century, the encyclopedia experienced not only rapid expansion and a highly successful role as a good financial investment for publishers; it also became a popular and influential genre that presented a coherent portrait of the world for the growing middle-class readership.[42] Just as this genre expanded and reached an ever-larger audience, so too the developments of the modern era, particularly for Germany, seemed to occur at an increasing rate. The *Conversations-Lexikon*, which accompanied and recorded this change, therefore is a fascinating document of the priorities of an age, as well as the manner in which the age chose to portray the world.

trat er, als zwischen Rupert von der Pfalz und Albrecht V. von Bayern=München der landshuter Successionskrieg ausbrach, zu Albrechts Partei. In diesem Kampfe verlor er bei der Belagerung von Landshut die rechte Hand, die künstlich durch eine eiserne (s. unten) ersetzt wurde. Als durch Kaiser Maximilian I. 1495 der Ewige Landfriede zu Stande gekommen war, zog sich B. auf sein Schloß zurück. Trotzdem geriet er bei dem unruhigen Geiste der damaligen Zeit mit seinen Nachbarn, den Reichsstädten am Neckar und den Burgrittern am Kocher, auch jetzt wieder in immer sich erneuernde Händel und Fehden, in denen er stets ebenso viel Tapferkeit als ritterlichen Biedersinn zeigte. B. stand 1519 dem Herzog Ulrich von Württemberg gegen den Schwäbischen Bund bei und verteidigte Möckmühl.

Urteil gefällt, der Ge[ ] entlassen, nachdem er v[ ] Schloß Hornberg gleichf[ ] zu sein. Er sollte die [ ] mehr ein Pferd besteig[ ] Schlosse zubringen, sich [ ] nisses halber rächen, a[ ] brauchen, im Falle b[ ] bingungen aber sich zu ei[ ] anheischig machen. Zud[ ] gefügten Schadens Ma[ ] thuung leisten. Viele [ ] sich mit Hab und Gut f[ ] So lebte nun Götz von [ ] erst nach Auflösung des [ ] gnadigt. Kaiser Karl V[ ] Ritter auf, [ ] serl. Fahnen [ ] tan Soliman [ ] auch einige [ ] ger, darunte[ ] die Ehre wett [ ] rung zu käm [ ] zog er mit de[ ] Franz I. nach [ ] in der Cham[ ] bis Château=[ ] Friedens von [ ] zog er sich a[ ] wo er seine [ ] verbrachte. [ ] Obschon er [ ] war, wurde [ ] Familie im [ ] Schönthal bei [ ] nes Denkmal [ ] ihm selbst ve[ ] erst von Pist[ ] dem sehr oft [ ] treues Gemäl [ ] ten jener Pe[ ] Goethe entna [ ] seinem «Göt[ ] der histor. W[ ]

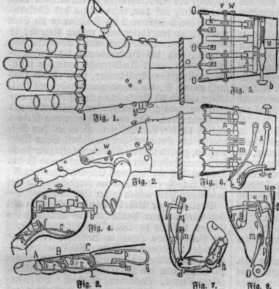

Fig. 1. Fig. 5. Fig. 2. Fig. 6. Fig. 4. Fig. 3. Fig. 7. Fig. 8.

Nach tapferster Gegenwehr bedingte er sich freien Abzug, der ihm auch zugesagt wurde. Allein verräterischerweise wurde er überfallen, gefangen genommen und nach Heilbronn geschleppt, und erst 1522, nach Ausstellung einer Urfehde und Bezahlung eines Lösegeldes, erhielt er seine Freiheit zurück. Auch am großen Bauernkriege 1525 nahm [ ]

Die erwähnte eisern[ ] Jagstfeld gezeigt. Sie i[ ] bung in Fig. 1 von inne[ ] gesehen dargestellt. Der [ ] gende Bewegungen: Die [ ] Aufstützen oder mit Hilf[ ]

Fig. 3.5. Götz von Berlichingen's hand. *Brockhaus' Conversations-Lexikon: allgemeine deutsche Real-Encyklopädie*, 13th ed., vol. 2 (Leipzig: F. A. Brockhaus, 1882–87), 834.

Encyclopedias are by definition repositories of knowledge, but they are (like all texts) also readable as documents of language and of the implications and shades of meaning that come with linguistic — and, increasingly, with visual — choices. In addition to serving as a source of information, an encyclopedia also documents a zeitgeist, a way of seeing the world and interpreting it for a contemporary and national readership. By comparing how one publishing company's flagship encyclopedia presented the same topics in a different light at different historical moments, this study has shown the ways in which even a sober and ostensibly objective reference work such as the encyclopedia is shaped by its historical context. In the case of the *Conversations-Lexikon*, we see not only the new historical events that transpired between the 1820s and the 1880s, but also the evolution of the national story from one of insecurity and unclarity to a confident tale that at times spoke in retrospect of a predictable and even inevitable positive trajectory of the German nation. We can thus read this non-fictional product of the publishing industry not only as the story of how Brockhaus's initially liberal agenda was transformed into a positivistic, universalist view of the larger German role in the world, but also, and more generally, as a record of the evolving process of nation-building and the place of textual discourse in it.

Notes

[1] This information is according to *Wikipedia*'s homepage: http://www.wikipedia.org/ (accessed 28 August 2008).

[2] To do this in *Wikipedia* entries, one goes to the "history" tab above the beginning of an article and selects from a list of all changes that have been made to the article over the years.

[3] As Robert Collison points out, "this vast work, comprising some 2,500 chapters in 37 books, could never have been designed for continuous reading." The compiler, Pliny the Elder (Gaius Plinius Secundus, 23–79 CE) was not expert in any field, but rather an anthologist. He drew on works of five hundred authors from many countries. He was, "with a remarkable instinct for arranging things in an orderly fashion," like many other encyclopedists an administrator "accustomed to seeing the world in terms of divisions and sub-divisions." See Robert Collison, *Encyclopaedias: Their History Throughout the Ages* (New York: Hafner Publishing Co., 1966), 25.

[4] Indeed Collison mentions some early exceptions to this such as Latini's encyclopedia in French written for the cultivated upper classes in Italy (63–65) and a few from the sixteenth and seventeenth centuries, works often translated from other comprehensive and summarizing works (86–89).

[5] Collison, *Encyclopaedias*, 104. By that time encyclopedias were generally arranged alphabetically rather than through a classificatory system based on disciplines or fields of knowledge.

[6] *Encylopédie I*, ed. Alain Pons (Paris: Flammarion, 1986), 257.

[7] Although the title of this encyclopedia underwent some changes in the course of the nineteenth century (see note 13), for the sake of simplicity I will refer to all editions of it by the short name: *Conversations-Lexikon*.

[8] Anja zum Hingst, *Die Geschichte des Großen Brockhaus: Vom Conversationslexikon zur Enzyklopädie, mit einem Geleitwort von A. G. Swierk* (Wiesbaden: Harrassowitz Verlag, 1995), 23–25.

[9] Roland Schäfer, "Die Frühgeschichte des Großen Brockhaus," *Leipziger Jahrbuch zur Buchgeschichte* 3 (1993): 69–84.

[10] It is difficult to reconstruct whether these supplemental volumes were Francke's or Brockhaus's idea. Francke created them. See Heinrich Eduard Brockhaus, *Die Firma Friedrich Arnold Brockhaus von der Begründung bis zum hundertjährigen Jubiläum, 1805–1905* (Leipzig: F. A. Brockhaus, 1905), 24.

[11] An approximation of this title in English would be "Conversational Encyclopedia or Succinct Concise Dictionary for those Items from Science and the Arts that Appear in Social Conversation, with Particular Consideration of Events from Older and More Recent Times." See zum Hingst, *Geschichte des Großen Brockhaus*, 93, and Anton Ernst Oskar Piltz, "Zur Geschichte und Bibliographie der encyklopaedischen Literatur insbesondere des *Conversations-Lexicon*," in *F. A. Brockhaus in Leipzig, Vollständiges Verzeichnis der von der Firma F. A. Brockhaus in Leipzig seit ihrer Gründung durch Friedrich Arnold Brockhaus im Jahre 1805 bis zu dessen hundertjährigem Geburtstage im Jahre 1872 verlegten Werke. In chronologischer Folge mit biographischen und literarhistorischen Notizen* (Leipzig: F. A. Brockhaus, 1872–75), xxxiii–xl.

[12] Brockhaus, *Firma F. A. Brockhaus*, 25.

[13] It was only with the fifth edition that Brockhaus added the term "Encyklopädie" that was to stick with the work for most of the nineteenth century. From the fifth to the eleventh editions the work was entitled *Allgemeine deutsche Real-Encyklopädie fur die gebildeten Stände: Conversations-Lexicon* (i.e., from 1820 to 1868, with the spelling shifting to "Lexikon" in 1827); see Piltz, "Geschichte und Bibliographie," xxxviii–xlviii. With the twelfth edition (in 1879) the order of the titles was reversed to *Conversations-Lexikon: Allgemeine deutsche Real-Encyklopädie* until the latter title was dropped altogether in the fourteenth edition in 1895; see zum Hingst, *Geschichte des Großen Brockhaus*, 94–97.

[14] Pierer's encyclopedia starts in 1826; the first edition of Meyer's encyclopedia is published from 1839 to 1852 in forty-six volumes, with six supplemental volumes appearing between 1853 and 1855.

[15] Brockhaus, *Firma F. A. Brockhaus*, 32.

[16] Nonetheless, this periodical appeared (with four and later eight numbers published each year) until 1841. Brockhaus, *Firma F. A. Brockhaus*, 33.

[17] Beginning in fall 1818 Brockhaus published *Hermes oder kritisches Jahrbuch der Literatur* with the intention of reviewing the newest and most important cultural developments in Germany, similar to the *Edinburgh Review* and the London *Quarterly Review*. With the implementation of the restrictive Carlsbad Decrees of September 1819, however, "Brockhaus beschloß nämlich, die Zeitschrift

nunmehr auch zum literarischen Mittelpunkte des Kampfes für Preßfreiheit und konstitutionelle Staatsformen zu machen" (Brockhaus decided, namely, to make the magazine from this point on into the literary center of the struggle for the freedom of the press and constitutional state forms). Caution led him to locate the place of printing and publication officially in Amsterdam, to retain apparently only the "Commission," and to call himself the "Eigenthümer und Redacteur" (owner and editor); see Brockhaus, *Firma F. A. Brockhaus*, 35. Another Brockhaus periodical, the *Literarisches Wochenblatt*, was banned in Prussia in August 1820 due to a passage in a French diplomatic report relating to the Prussian king and queen. An appeal to the state chancellor, Hardenberg, achieved nothing, and it was only readmitted under a new title after repeated negotiations with Minister von Schuckmann. This periodical was banned again in late 1825 after the death of Friedrich Arnold Brockhaus and again only re-permitted in 1826 under a new title, *Blätter für literarische Unterhaltung*, which was published until 1898; see Brockhaus, *Firma F. A. Brockhaus*, 36–37.

[18] According to Piltz the ten volumes of the fourth edition cost twelve thalers, fifteen Neugroschen, if published using *printing paper*, eighteen thalers and 22.5 Neugroschen on *writing paper*, but forty thalers for "fine median vellum paper." The sixth edition (1824) appeared with five different types and qualities of paper. But the seventh and later editions appear again in only three paper qualities. The cost of the seventh edition (according to the quality of paper) was fifteen, twenty or thirty-six thalers; the eleventh edition in 1865 cost twenty-five thalers (assembled in sets), twenty-nine (bound in linen), thirty (bound half in leather), thirty-seven (on vellum paper and assembled in sets), and forty-five (on vellum paper and bound half in leather), respectively (Piltz, "Geschichte und Bibliographie," xli–xlvi).

[19] Johann Goldfriedrich, *Geschichte des Deutschen Buchhandels vom Beginn der Fremdherrschaft bis zur Reform des Börsenvereins im neuen Deutschen Reiche, 1805–1889* (Leipzig: Verlag des Börsenvereins der Deutschen Buchhändler, 1913), 202–3.

[20] Goldfriedrich, *Geschichte des Deutschen Buchhandels*, 203.

[21] Brockhaus, *Firma F. A. Brockhaus*, 299.

[22] While some historians of the book (and some internal studies by the Brockhaus firm itself) have traced the story of Brockhaus and the development of its famous encyclopedia over the last two hundred years (see Brockhaus, zum Hingst, and Piltz), to date no one has conducted a detailed content and stylistic analysis of the work's approach to mediating the world to German readers. For a history of the Brockhaus firm in the twentieth century see Arthur Hübscher, *Hundertfünfzig Jahre F. A. Brockhaus, 1805–1955* (Wiesbaden: F. A. Brockhaus, 1955), 207–294 and Thomas Keiderling, *F. A. Brockhaus, 1905–2005. Band 2 der Festschrift F. A. Brockhaus 1805–2005* (Leipzig/Mannheim: F. A. Brockhaus, 2005).

[23] All passages from the two editions of the *Conversations-Lexikon* will be cited listing first the edition number in roman numerals followed by the relevant volume and page numbers. Thus "VII, 9:245" refers to *Allgemeine deutsche Real-Encyklopädie für die gebildeten Stände: Conversations-Lexikon*, 7th ed., vol. 9 (Leipzig: F. A. Brockhaus, 1827), 245; and "XIII, 13:662" refers to *Brockhaus' Conversations-Lexikon: allgemeine deutsche Real-Encyklopädie*, 13th ed., vol. 13

(Leipzig: F. A. Brockhaus, 1882–87), 662. All translations of passages from both editions are my own.

[24] It is also important to note that the seventh edition contains an additional entry on "Rheinschifffahrt und -Handel" (Rhine Shipping and Trade) that is seventeen pages long and seems to have been inspired extensively by one document, the "1815 Wiener Congreßschifffahrtsacte" (VII, 9:252; 1815 Ship Travel Act of the Congress of Vienna) and the Negotiations of the Central Commission that followed it. Much like the entries in Ersch and Gruber's later *Allgemeine Enzyklopädie der Wissenschaften und Künste* (discussed below), this entry consists mostly of an extensive summary of minute details, such as an entire page of the kinds of goods transported in which regions (VII, 9:266–67), and even quotes regional commissars at length from special protocols (260). This entire article is so specific to the first half of the 1820s that it disappears completely by the 1880 edition.

[25] "Auf dem Unterharz bildeten sich nach und nach mehrere dynastische Territorien" (XIII, 8:878; in the lower Harz several dynastic territories gradually developed).

[26] "Doch trat infolge eines 1874 geschlossenen Vertages Braunschweig seine Hoheitsrechte in diesem Gebiet an Preußen ab" (indeed, Brunswick transferred its sovereign rights in this area to Prussia in the wake of a treaty concluded in 1874).

[27] "If one understands literature to be a disordered mess, a rough aggregate of books that is not enlivened by a communal spirit, and among which not even the connections of a unified national direction can be noticed; where the individual traces and hints of something better are almost imperceptibly lost among the melee of empty and misunderstood strivings, of mistakes and confusion, of poorly disguised spiritual poverty and grotesque, arrogant addiction to originality."

[28] "If we want to depict the most recent era of German literature, then this is an unfortunate enterprise. No matter how significant or insignificant the events may be that clustered within this period, we have recently lived through it ourselves and still stand more or less under its influence. Thus, if we point to that which seems to us to be the dominant direction in the literary striving of recent years, then we make do with offering nothing more than our own opinion, whereby we do not presume to approximate that of another."

[29] "The deeper the roots of Christianity took hold in the German people and the more it found a home with the same, unlike with any other people, the more the complete constitution of the Germans rested essentially on Christian principles, and this spirit also infused all of German literature without requiring any special spiritual leadership or surveillance."

[30] "Deutsche Malerkunst" (German Painting) VII, 3:184–88; "Deutsche Kunst" (German Art) XIII, 5:122–26.

[31] All of these maps and plates are located between pages 264 and 265 in volume 16 of the thirteenth edition.

[32] Heinrich Brockhaus boasts of the close ties the Brockhaus firm and family had to Schliemann: "er weilte oft in Leipzig bei seinem Verleger, und Dr. Eduard Brockhaus besuchte ihn 1884 in Athen, sowie bei seinen Ausgrabungen in Tiryus" (Brockhaus, *Firma F. A. Brockhaus*, 326; he often spent time in Leipzig at his publishers, and Dr. Eduard Brockhaus visited him in 1884 in Athens as well

as at his excavations in Tiryus). He further notes with regard to Stanley that business contact had to be made through Stanley's English publisher, but of the firm he writes: "[sie] stand . . . mit ihm [Stanley] doch in angenehmen Beziehungen, und er erfüllte gern ihren Wunsch, für die deutschen Leser ein Vorwort zu seinem Werke über den Kongo zu schreiben" (329; [it] stood in a pleasant relationship to him [Stanley], and he gladly fulfilled its wish that he draft a preface for German readers of his work about the Congo).

[33] *Allgemeine Enzyklopädie der Wissenschaften und Künste,* ed. Johann Samuel Ersch and Johann Gottfried Gruber (Leipzig: Gleditsch [later Brockhaus], 1832–89).

[34] The end result of this goal of completeness was very uneven. For example, much of the fifty-five-page article on Karoline von Günderrode consists of long passages excerpted from Günderrode's letters and works, as well as from the letters of Wilhelmine Günderrode and long quotations from a variety of sources on Günderrode's death, including Bettina von Arnim's treatment of it (Ersch and Gruber, 97:167–231). In other words, what appears as an encyclopedia entry is in effect a full-fledged biography. Nine of the twenty-five pages of the entry on "Faust" consist of a plot summary of the oldest Faust book (Ersch and Gruber, 41–42:93–118). In effect such instances of extensive quotation and summary simply served to increase the size of the massive encyclopedia.

[35] See Piltz, "Geschichte und Bibliographie," xliii–xlvi. The change in the political situation of Germany in 1870–71 made a new edition necessary, resulting in the twelfth edition that appeared 1875–79. It also contained fifteen volumes, but the extent of the entire work grew from 900 to 964 sheets; see Brockhaus, *Firma F. A. Brockhaus,* 303–4.

[36] zum Hingst, *Geschichte des Großen Brockhaus,* 145. Other encyclopedias before this time did include illustrations, but in full plates of woodcuts (such as those of Diderot and D'Alembert's *Encylopédie*) and at substantial cost. The early *Encyclopædia Britannica* also had illustrations.

[37] zum Hingst, *Geschichte des Großen Brockhaus,* 145.

[38] The version available to me is a twentieth-century reprint of the American publication of this *Ikonographische Enzyklopädie* which appeared as the *Iconographic Encyclopædia of Science, Literature, and Art,* published by R. Garrigue in New York in 1851; see *The Complete Encyclopedia of Illustration* (New York: Park Lane, 1979).

[39] Brockhaus, *Firma F. A. Brockhaus,* 304.

[40] Most of the cities are capitals: London, Paris, Constantinople, St. Petersburg, Warsaw, Berlin, Vienna, Lisbon, Naples, Rome, Milan, Madrid, Saragossa, Barcelona, Copenhagen, Stockholm, Antwerp, Amsterdam, Livorno, Ancona, Modena, and Florence.

[41] In one volume alone (vol. 10) there are topographical maps of the following cities: Kassel, Koblenz, Köln, Königgrätz (battlefield), Königsberg, Leipzig (and the following non-German cities, "Kairo," "Kalkutta," "Kanton," "Kapstadt," "Kashmir," "Konstantinopel" and "Kopenhagen"). This volume also includes a two-page color topographical map of the regions of Kärnten, Krain, Salzburg, Steiermark, Tirol, und Vorarlberg.

[42] Collison, *Encyclopaedias,* 10.

4: The Afterlife of Nineteenth-Century Popular Fiction and the German Imaginary: The Illustrated Collected Novels of E. Marlitt, W. Heimburg, and E. Werner

Lynne Tatlock

A NY STUDY OF THE CONSEQUENCES of the reading of the past ought to consider the print which was actually read," William St Clair asserts in *The Reading Nation in the Romantic Period*, and "not some modern selection, whether that selection is derived from judgments of canon or from other modern criteria."[1] As St Clair demonstrates in this meticulously researched work, tracing print and "understanding how certain texts came to be made available in printed form to certain constituencies of buyers and readers" can aid us in writing a history of reading as it affects cultural formations (7). Patterns of reading depend on the availability and the affordability of books. St Clair points out, for example, that for a brief period in late eighteenth-century England, the release of older books from copyright meant that an old canon of books was newly accessible to publishers for reprinting (122–23).[2] Moreover, he asserts generally of reading: "although new texts were being written, circulated, and read during all periods of the past, most of the reading that has historically occurred has been of older texts that were accorded value after they were first written and that continued to be copied for new readers by whatever technology was available" (433–34).

Book history in the nineteenth-century German-speaking world exhibits analogous developments. For example, the release in 1867 from copyright of works by authors who had died by 1837 gave rise to, among other things, Reclam's *Universalbibliothek*, which invited a broader audience to re/read the classics of the Age of Goethe in cheap editions.[3] I am not, however, interested here in the reading of reprinted and reedited versions of what were or came to be the canonical literary texts of high (national) culture, but instead in the reprinting and re-editing, and thus enduring and belated reading in Imperial Germany, of popular fiction and, in particular, popular fiction by women, a quasi-mimetic fiction that reproduced domestic values as romance.

The fiction of three nineteenth-century German women writers — E. Marlitt (pseud. of Eugenie John, 1825–87), Wilhelmine Heimburg (pseud. of Bertha Behrens, 1848–1912), and E. Werner (pseud. of Elisabeth Bürstenbinder, 1838–1918) will serve as a case in point.[4] Hardly the ephemera that one might expect them to be, the novels and novellas of these three women authors continued to sell well and to be widely read for decades after their initial appearance as serialized fiction in the family magazine *Die Gartenlaube* in the 1860s, '70s, and '80s. They continued to be republished and read after the collapse of Imperial Germany and even after the Second World War — indeed, in the present day.[5] Up to the end of the nineteenth century, advice books too recommended some of these works alongside literature by now canonical male authors.[6] As must-read books of popular literature, these books in some sense once formed their own canon.

The re-publication of these novels in the late 1880s, 1890s, and early 1900s as collected illustrated editions speaks to the continuity and disjuncture between the contents of the actually read and contemporary political, social, and cultural conditions and trends. The content and worldviews of these novels tend not to reflect the aggressive jingoistic culture of late-century Germany under the reign of William II in which the books were reprinted, even when they bear traces of that imperial culture.[7] Nor do the plots and values of these novels have a strong affinity to the modernism of that period or to the vigorous questioning of gender norms of the late nineteenth century and the early twentieth century by such women writers as Gabriele Reuter, Helene Böhlau, Hedwig Dohm, and the Austrian writers Lou Andreas-Salomé and Rosa Mayreder. Nor do they participate in the gritty and belated naturalism of a Clara Viebig.[8] Instead these women's novels originate in a vaguely national liberal ideal with roots in the period preceding the founding of the empire forged with iron and blood.

With their emphasis on delayed gratification, self-possession, and duty, they foreground family romance in the German provinces and affective communities, where femininity grounded in a sentimental domesticity appears to matter deeply and where it is assiduously cultivated and validated. Indeed, the books valorize the alleged "feminine" ability to read the human heart and to ferret out stories even in the most unprepossessing domestic situations. *Aus dem Leben meiner alten Freundin* (1878; From the Life of my Elderly Woman Friend), the first volume of Heimburg's collected novels and stories, asserts, for example, the ability of the female narrator to recognize, despite her husband's skepticism, that even an "old maid" has an interesting story to tell.[9]

The following examination of the illustrated collected works of Marlitt, Werner, and Heimburg aims to provide insight into what was actually purchased and read in Imperial Germany. Even if out of step with many aspects of contemporary reality, precisely the imagined Germany produced in these novels and novellas fed, as we shall see, into German nationalism and national identity in this period as this nationalism and national identity were expressed in and helped to form gender. In these novels a "German imaginary" at home in the province and the family and ostensibly ruled by women and sentiment persisted in late nineteenth- and early twentieth-century German women's reading.

Forgotten Reading

While a considerable body of scholarship on the *Gartenlaube* now exists, with the exception of Marlitt's novels, the afterlife of *Gartenlaube* serialized fiction from the 1860s and 1870s remains largely unexamined.[10] It was long easy for literary historians to ignore or dismiss Marlitt, Heimburg, and Werner, given the hostility directed at them and others like them by early twentieth-century critics across the political and cultural spectrum — by the male forgers of the new German national canon, by proponents of an avant-garde art that eschewed the sentimentality of the bourgeois nineteenth century, and by feminists who hoped to refashion ideas about women and their social roles.

In the view of a skeptical German professor writing in 1905, "To none of these [women] authors of the seventies . . . belongs the distinction of having contributed to the permanent fund of literature the first book of lasting worth."[11] In that same year, the Austrian feminist Rosa Mayreder pilloried such popular reading in her famous essay on "family literature," beginning with the forceful opening assertion, "Niemals noch ist die herrschende Vorstellung vom Weibe, das 'Ideal' des Weibes so sehr versimpelt gewesen wie im 19. Jahrhundert." (To date the reigning idea of woman, the "Ideal" of woman, has never been as silly as in the nineteenth century.)[12] Pointing an accusing finger in particular at the literature favored by the *Familienblatt* (family magazine), Mayreder criticizes the generic conventions that require among other things a happy ending, a lack of complexity in the plots and consequently in the demands these books make on readers, and a dearth of serious problems concerning the relationship between the sexes. The cultural critic Ernst von Wollzogen likewise fulminates in *Das literarische Echo* in 1907 against the bad taste of contemporary readers of family magazines, whom he characterizes as silly girls, women, and old people. He expresses disappointment generally that the *Gartenlaube* has lost sight of its original national liberal mission as a result of the bad literature published there.[13] Forgetting that Marlitt in particular had participated in that mission and was in part responsible for the magazine's successful communication thereof, he grumbles in this essay that Marlitt, Heimburg, and Werner put their indelible stamp on the *Gartenlaube* and that subsequently all the editors of family magazines took these novels as their touchstone because they guaranteed customer satisfaction.[14]

Yet even if Heller, Mayreder, Wollzogen, and many others had cause to eschew these novels and their old-fashioned worldview, we should recall that the turn-of-the-century German-speaking world was fraught with inconsistency and most obviously on the subject of women's roles and rights. It was by no means clear — even to some would-be feminists — how to imagine a radically different future for women. Nor was it clear what risks women might actually run in trying to change social arrangements. In 1902 the *Gartenlaube* touted its own long-time support of emancipatory movements in what now seem confused terms:

> Schon seit langem hatte die "Gartenlaube" teilgenommen an der Bewegung, deren Ziel es ist, den Frauen geistige und materielle Selbständigkeit erringen zu helfen. 1871 erschien ein erster Aufsatz über die Bestrebungen des "Allgemeinen Deutschen Frauenvereins" mit den Portraits von Auguste Schmidt und Luise Otto-Peters; in den folgenden Jahrzehnten hat dann R. Artaria (Rosalie Braun) über die positiven Fortschritte auf diesem Gebiete treulich Bericht erstattet, während sie andererseits in den Familienbildern "Das erste Jahr im neuen Haushalt" und "Der Zeitgeist im Hausstande" über das große Pflichtengebiet der Hausfrauen und Mütter in den Großstädten unserer Tage sich so gut unterrichtet erwies.[15]

Although claiming to support the advancement of women, the magazine remained mired in the prevailing ideologies of the century that believed in separate spheres and gender-specific tasks for men and women, spheres and tasks underpinned by biologistic notions of gender. Like many contemporaries, the *Gartenlaube* could imagine women's independence only in a narrow sense.[16]

In 1895 — to name a further example — Gabriele Reuter had unmasked the hypocrisies in the socialization and education of middle-class women in her bestselling novel *Aus guter Familie* (From a Good Family), specifically mentioning Elise Polko's books as prescribed for girls to read "during the day" in the 1860s and 1870s at boarding school as opposed to more risqué reading at night. Yet the past persisted. Polko's *Unsere Pilgerfahrt von der Kinderstube bis zum eigenen Herd* (Our Pilgrimage from the Nursery to Our Own Hearth) appeared yet again in 1909, having gone through nine editions since its original publication in 1862.[17] Women's life, Polko (1822–99) once again (and now posthumously) told her readers in 1909, should consist of marrying and rearing children, although "die Mutterschaft ist und bleibt ein Martyrium, selbst

in den glücklichsten Fällen" (motherhood is and always will be a martyrdom, even in the happiest cases).[18]

The Marketing, Packaging, and Consumption
of the Illustrated Collected Works

As the unflattering essays of Heller, Mayreder, and Wollzogen make
abundantly clear, the works of Marlitt, Werner, and Heimburg endured
well into the first decade of the twentieth century as beloved reading. Following their original serialization in the *Gartenlaube*, they were published
as books and then as collected works. Their popularity led their publisher
in the late 1880s and '90s and early in the new century, furthermore, to
publish the collected works of each author in attractive illustrated editions. It is these illustrated collected works that will interest us here.

The republishing of the stories and novels of Marlitt, Heimburg,
and Werner as collected illustrated editions began in 1888, between the
deaths of the two emperors, William I and Frederick III, and under new
leadership at the Keil Verlag, the enterprising Kröner brothers who had
purchased the company in 1884 from Ernst Keil's widow.[19] Yet even if
1888 marked the end of an era in the life of the Second Empire with the
ascent of William II to the throne, which would soon bring about the
retirement of Bismarck in 1890, the *Gartenlaube* and its new publisher
strove on at least some fronts for continuity, particularly, as we shall see,
in its continued publication of the kind of fiction to which it owed its
success in earlier decades. With regard to the politics of gender, this very
continuity reinforced the magazine's more conservative political turn in
the 1880s and '90s after the death of its founder.[20] I will return below to
the implications of belated reading of *Gartenlaube*-fiction.

Marlitt had died the year before, in 1887, and her posthumous novel,
Das Eulenhaus (The Owl House), completed by Heimburg, was running
serially in the *Gartenlaube*. At the same time the magazine began advertising a new illustrated complete edition of Marlitt's works, "welche voll-
ständig in ca. 70 Lieferungen zum Preise von je 40 pf. (alle 14 Tage eine
Lieferung) im durchschnittlichen Umfang von 3 Druckbogen erscheinen
wird" (which will appear complete in approximately seventy installments
for the price of forty pfennigs apiece [an installment every fourteen days]
on average in the amount of three gatherings [i.e., in the octavo format,
forty-eight pages]).[21] Beginning with *Das Geheimnis der alten Mamsell*
(The Old Mamselle's Secret), the illustrated collected works promised for
eighty pfennigs a month to fill the leisure hours of younger generations
who might not yet know all of Marlitt's novels. Optionally, eager readers
could order the ten novels bound for three marks, or "elegant gebunden" (elegantly bound) for four.[22] At three or four marks, each bound

volume sold for approximately the same as 500 grams of cacao powder (3 marks), 500 grams of extra-fine pekoe tea (5 marks), or three 500-gram cans of salmon (3 at 1.20 marks each = 3.60 marks) — as advertised in the *Gartenlaube*.[23] These were not cheap editions — volumes in Reclam's *Universalbibliothek* sold by comparison for twenty pfennigs as late as 1912 — but they were affordable by the same readers who consumed cacao, tea, and canned salmon.[24] The tenth novel in the series appeared in 1890; the second edition would soon follow in 1891.[25]

While it has been repeatedly asserted that in the 1860s and '70s Marlitt's novels were read by both male and female readers of the *Gartenlaube*, the collected works, in their packaging and advertising, overtly target female readers, as I shall outline below.[26] Furthermore, even as the publisher implicitly insists on continuity in undertaking a new edition of these books, the mention in the advertisement of readers from younger generations suggests the need for effort in capturing the attention of a public ignorant of the charms of this domestic fiction from an earlier era.

In 1890, near year's end, the *Gartenlaube* began advertising, in addition to Marlitt's collected works, the illustrated *Gesammelte Romane und Novellen* (Collected Novels and Novellas) of W. Heimburg, available in seventy-five installments at forty pfennigs apiece.[27] A blurb for these novels declares that the publishing house is meeting the demand of readers "ihre Schriften in würdiger Ausstattung gesammelt als bleibenden Hausschatz zu besitzen" (to have her writings collected in a form worthy of them as an enduring family treasure).[28] The illustrations, the advertisement assures potential buyers, have been carefully reproduced from the originals using modern techniques of reproduction.[29] Furthermore, in 1894 the *Gartenlaube* could inform readers of the publication of the second edition of the collected works, so well had the first edition sold, and in 1896 the magazine began promoting the five-volume "new series" of Heimburg's novels.[30] In 1904 it announced a third five-volume illustrated series of Heimburg's novels.[31]

The success of the collected works of Marlitt and Heimburg must have persuaded the publisher to undertake a third such project. In 1893 the *Gartenlaube* began advertising the forthcoming illustrated collected works of E. Werner.[32] The advertising supplement inserted into the thirty-eighth issue of 1893 asserts that Werner's stories defy the ever-changing tastes of these fast-paced ("schnelllebig") times with their ability to maintain favor with readers over decades. Furthermore, their perennial popularity, the advertisement points out, must be an indication of their lasting value.[33] As if doubly to affirm their lasting cultural worth, the advertisement notes that they have been printed on good, long-lasting ("haltbar") paper.[34]

Like Marlitt's collected novels, the ten volumes of this illustrated series could be purchased as a handsome set for thirty marks or, if in a "feiner englischer Leinwand-Truhe" (chest of fine English [starch-filled] linen), for forty marks. The whole set could be paid for in installments as necessary.[35] Like Heimburg's and Marlitt's collected illustrated works, this too was a successful venture, and in 1901, the publisher announced a new six-volume series of Werner's more recent novels.[36] By 1905 the publisher had returned approximately fifty novels and novellas to circulation in the attractive formats of the illustrated collected works and was able to advertise all of them in anticipation of the Christmas rush.[37]

Consumers had the option of buying the collected works of these three authors with highly embellished, colorful book covers that visibly marked them as belonging to a unique series. Advertisements from the period repeatedly display them with their easily recognizable covers as collectables that fit nicely into a handsome linen box (*Leinwandtruhe*) sized to hold the entire set (see fig. 4.1). If the covers themselves held the potential for decorating the home, the box took on the aspect of the jewel case, treasure chest, or memory box, where the books could be delicately cherished, contributing to what we might call sentimental commodity fetishism.

As Janice Radway asserts of popular books in the American context, such elaborate packaging encourages book buyers and book owners to "invest material forms exchanged on the market with certain naturally occurring inherent properties."[38] An article published ca. twenty-five years later in the American magazine *Good Housekeeping* — and cited by Radway — aptly characterizes the meanings of these late nineteenth-century German collections as well. The American magazine writer notes that the very bindings of certain books "hint repose, the welcome quiet hour in this rushing world of ours. Moreover, books are full of suggestion. . . . They are essentially feminine, too."[39] While, as mass-produced objects, the collected works of Marlitt, Werner, and Heimburg are precisely *not* auratic in Walter Benjamin's sense, their striking covers nevertheless encouraged buyers and owners to see them as authentic and enduring.

Mass-produced by the Leipziger Buchbinderei-A.G. vormals Gustav Fritzsche, the decorative glossy linen covers of these three sets of collected works were durable and telegraphed substance.[40] In fact, resistant to impregnation by glue, these starch-filled cloth covers remain in good shape to this day. They are printed in multiple colors through the process of chromolithography with the book title hot-stamped with gold foil on the spine and front cover. When these books are displayed spine-out on a shelf or front-cover-up on a table, a shelf, or in a box, the gold stamping underlines their appearance of richness, thus lending their owner an air of prosperity and solidity, or rather, the decorative covers mirror for the owner herself a secure social and economic standing and her own special self.

The covers link the novels to contemporary tastes in design of the late nineteenth century, decorative styles that in response to new technology and mass production valorized (the look of) hand-made objects.

Fig. 4.1. Advertisement for E. Werner's Collected Illustrated Works, E. Marlitt, *Die Frau mit den Karfunkelsteinen*, vol. 6 of *E. Marlitt's gesammelte Romane und Novellen*. 2nd ed. (Leipzig: Ernst Keil's Nachfolger, n.d.), back page. Author Copy. Reproduced by Shelby Carpenter.

The ornamental covers of the Marlitt series evidence the influence of the English Arts and Crafts movement in the mode of William Morris (see fig. 4.2). The black, turquoise, cream, and grayish-green vegetal design applied to the light-brown cloth of the covers vaguely recalls tapestry work. Although art nouveau had yet to have its full impact in Germany when the Werner series began to appear in 1893, the saturated blue

Fig. 4.2. Cover, E. Marlitt, *Die Frau mit den Karfunkelsteinen*, vol. 6 of
E. Marlitt's gesammelte Romane und Novellen, 2nd ed. (Leipzig: Ernst Keil's
Nachfolger, n.d.). Author's copy. Reproduced by Shelby Carpenter.

covers of this series with their red, green, tan, and cream design display an affinity to that international trend, the design conventions of art nouveau here having a more angular and symmetrical look (see fig. 4.3). A present-day German used-book seller describes a Werner-novel as having a cover "mit floraler Jugendstilillustration" (with floral decoration in the manner of art nouveau).[41] Finally, the sky-blue covers for the Heimburg series show the influence of yet another prominent trend of the times: Japonisme (see fig. 4.4). This influence can be identified in the delicately rendered sprays of pink cherry blossoms and the golden fan in the lower left-hand corner of the front cover.[42] With their affinities to the contemporary designs of English Arts and Crafts, art nouveau, and Japonisme respectively, the covers for the collected works of Marlitt, Werner, and Heimburg in their time promoted these mass-produced books as objects modern in their sensibility and eternal in their values.

The charm of these illustrated editions consists as well in their abundant illustrations, images that are supplied as plates or interspersed with text on the page. An invitation to subscribe to Marlitt's collected works touts the skilled execution of the illustrations: "Die Illustrationen der neuen Ausgabe haben wir einer Anzahl der tüchtigsten Künstler übertragen und ebenso für musterhafte Ausführung der Bilder in Holzschnitt und Zinkographie, für guten Druck und eleganteste Ausstattung gesorgt" (We commissioned a number of our most capable artists with the illustrations for the new edition and likewise took care to have the pictures executed in exemplary fashion in woodcuts and zincography, saw to it that the print was good and that [the books were] most elegantly outfitted).[43] Subsequent advertisements likewise emphasize especially the qualifications of the artists and the artistry of their illustrations. At the same time, the advertisements also tout these "beautifully executed" illustrations as produced by modern, industrial techniques, stressing again their modernity and progressiveness as consumable objects.

In a given volume one can sometimes find examples of several different techniques, including especially the use of photo-engraved zinc plates that enable the printing of many copies without a reduction in quality. While some of the illustrations are reproductions of drawings, the books also display liberal use of the photographic halftone, frequently used in mass publications like magazines and newspapers, which allows for a fuller tonal range using only one color of ink. In keeping with the nostalgic vaguely Arts and Crafts look of the covers, on the other hand, book chapters often begin with an allusion to the illuminated manuscript consisting of an enlarged decorative first letter of the first word in the opening sentence, sometimes surrounded by a picture or additional decoration (see fig. 4.5).[44]

The pictures that illustrate the plots of the respective books tend, however, toward mimesis rather than decoration and do not display the stylized floral borders and medievalist illustration found, for example, in

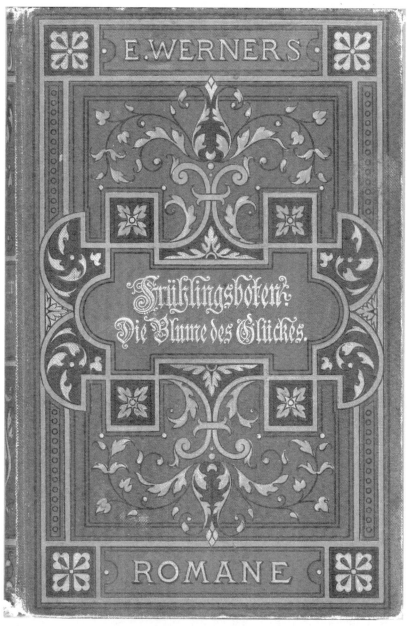

Fig. 4.3. Cover, E. Werner, *Frühlingsboten: Die Blume des Glücks*, vol. 4 of *E. Werner's gesammelte Romane und Novellen*. Illustrierte Ausgabe (Stuttgart: Union Deutsche Verlagsgesellschaft, n.d.). Author's copy. Reproduced by Shelby Carpenter.

Fig. 4.4. Cover, W. Heimburg. *Lumpenmüllers Lieschen*, vol. 2 of
W. Heimburg's gesammelte Romane und Novellen. 2nd ed. (Leipzig: Ernst
Keil's Nachfolger, n.d.). Author's copy. Reproduced by Shelby Carpenter.

as Meer lag tiefblau im Sonnenglanz, aber es ruhte nicht in träumender Stille. Unaufhörlich hoben sich weiße Schaumkronen empor und sanken wieder zusammen, und das Wogen und Branden der See einte sich mit dem Rauschen des Windes, der durch die Strandwälder hinzog. Die beiden Boote, die mit vollen Segeln der schleswig-holsteinschen Küste zueilten, hatten eine nicht ganz unbedenkliche Fahrt, denn die Wellen gingen hoch, und der Wind blies scharf von Norden, aber das Steuer schien bei beiden Fahrzeugen in sicheren Händen zu liegen, denn sie hielten unentwegt die Richtung fest und wandten sich endlich dem Herrenhause zu, das mit seiner breiten steinernen Terrasse und seinem hohen spitzen Ziegeldache aus den Laubmassen eines jetzt schon herbstlich gelichteten Parkes hervorblickte.

Es war ein altes, mächtiges Gebäude, das noch die Spuren ehemaliger Befestigung zeigte, freilich ohne mittelalterliche Pracht und Romantik. Schlicht und prunklos standen die altersgrauen Mauern da, aber sie schauten so trotzig in das Meer hinaus, als wollten sie ihm und seinen Stürmen zurufen: Kommt nur heran!

An einem der Fenster des ersten Stockwerkes stand ein Knabe von etwa fünfzehn Jahren, ein schlanker hübscher Junge, und blickte mit gespannter Aufmerksamkeit in die See hinaus. Jetzt wandte er sich in das Zimmer zurück und rief:

Fig. 4.5. Opening page of E. Werner's *Heimatklang* with elaborate first letter. In vol. 6 of *E. Werners gesammelte Romane und Novellen. Illustierte Ausgabe* (Leipzig: Ernst Keil's Nachfolger, n.d.). Reproduced by Perry Trolard.

William Morris's Kelmscott Press (founded 1891) and its international imitators. Nevertheless, in their ostensibly mimetic depiction of characters and events, the artists made choices about fashion that mask the historical origins of the novels. As we shall discuss in greater detail below, the illustrations for the most part do not portray female characters in the voluminous skirts supported by the crinolines and bustles of the 1860s and early 1870s — that is, the specific epoch in which many of these books were written or the epoch in which they overtly take place — but in the styles of the times in which the illustrations were created, the late 1880s and 1890s. By eschewing the costume of history and sometimes even ignoring fashions explicitly named in the novels, the illustrations forego nostalgia for a by-gone era.[45] Instead they intimate that the world of the novels is not lost and persists to the present day.[46] Marlitt, for example, set her *Im Schillingshof* (In the Schillingscourt; serialized 1879, published in the illustrated collected works in 1889) explicitly in the 1860s; she named specific dates, attached her plot to the American Civil War, and concluded with German unification in 1871.[47] The women in Wilhelm Claudius's illustrations, however, wear the fashions of the late 1880s. Likewise, in *Vineta*, volume 8 of Werner's collected novels and novellas, which overtly takes place during the Polish Revolution of 1863–64, Claudius depicts the women wearing the styles of the mid-1890s.[48]

With the milieux of their illustrations thus visibly contemporary with late-century readers' own world, the volumes in the illustrated editions treated their readers to trans-historical domestic romance, a universalizing view of women's sphere as static and determined by family values. At the same time, these romances provided women with a good read and a pleasurable (if false) simulacrum of influence and power. As we shall see, the power and importance attributed to women within this narrow world also encourage readers to forget the very limitations placed on that world.

Reading Out of Season

A six-part series of articles on its own history published by the *Gartenlaube* in 1902, speaks of Marlitt, Werner, and Heimburg as if referring to a mode of reading and writing that belongs to a past irrevocably separated from the present. Marlitt, Werner, and Heimburg, the author asserts, lent the *Gartenlaube* its character in *previous* decades.[49] Yet in that same year, the magazine not only advertised a second series of Werner's novels as available at a reasonable subscription price, but also carried a serialization of Werner's latest novel, *Runen* (Runes). In several forms, then, the past to which the books allegedly belonged endured in the present.

Writing in 1905 on German women writers, the above-mentioned German professor, Otto Heller, appears to respond precisely to this persistence of the past when he laments that "Americans owe their supposed knowledge of the German woman" to this literature.[50] Reacting to the lasting success of German novels by women, Heller forgets that many of the novels he detests were in fact written as long as thirty years earlier, hence their untimeliness: "the 'liberalism' of the women novelists," he grumbles, "shows itself in their incessant war upon prejudices, but they select either such prejudices as no longer prevail, or those which it is safe enough to fight. . . ."[51] While more recent scholarship on Marlitt, in particular, makes a good case for her liberalism in her own time, the assertion in 1905 of a German-born scholar with an academic career in the United States that many popular women's novels struggle against "such prejudices as no longer prevail" merits consideration; indeed, his complaint points to the fact that after their initial success in the years of serialization in magazines, novels are subsequently read and enjoyed out of season.[52]

The novels of Marlitt, Werner, and Heimburg are most certainly based in the circumscribed world of 1860s and 1870s domesticity and, moreover, tend to be set in the German regions and not the booming late-century capital city, Berlin — or for that matter any large city. Of course many late-nineteenth and early twentieth-century readers (particularly the adolescent girl and the young, unmarried middle-class woman) still lived in tightly circumscribed circumstances and presumably could not only recognize the milieux of the novels as akin to their own, but also appreciate novels that within those narrowly confined conditions provided a breadth of affective experience that their real-life situations did not.[53] Yet even readers who did not live in those precise circumstances could read these stories with pleasure.

In focusing on a provincial domestic world shaped by middle-class values, a world that in this fiction is ruled by sentiment but often threatened by social arrangements that favor the aristocracy, the novels depict social hierarchy as it is *felt*. Feeling can gloss over historical particularity. As long as readers can find an empathetic point of entry into the world of the novel, that world does not necessarily have to be keyed to the specifics of present-day social reality for readers to enjoy the novel; that is, if the story is reasonably convincing within the parameters it sets for itself, readers do not have to care about the historically particular social message or "the prejudices that no longer prevail" to experience the delicious pleasure of romance. As Ruth-Ellen Boetcher Joeres points out, for example, concerning late twentieth-century reading of *Die zweite Frau* (1874; The Second Wife), Marlitt's "current audience may have somewhat different expectations when reading her than did her *Gartenlaube* audience — romance now surpasses edification — but her popularity remains intact."[54] Even for the avid romance novel reader of 2010, the no-longer extant aristocracy of many of these novels potentially stands in for any kind of privilege or advantage or obstacle to the union of hero and heroine and thus does not necessarily present a barrier to the reader's entering the story empathetically.

What then were the contents and implicit messages of these aggressively marketed and attractively packaged novels? Three examples, one novel from the collected works of each of the three authors, will serve in the following to illustrate the contents between the ornamental covers and the domestic and national values thereby projected and affirmed — a little out of season — while delighting the reader with a romance of delayed gratification.

Desire in the German Province: E. Marlitt's Goldelse (1866/1890)

When in the 1880s Auguste Wachler rewrote and carefully bowdlerized Marlitt's perennially bestselling *Goldelse* (Gold Elsie) as the diminutive and cloyingly pious *Goldelschen* (Little Gold Elsie) for young women between the ages of twelve and fifteen, she felt compelled to explain on the opening page that the novel was not set in modern times. After all, enormous changes had taken place in the interim, among other things the forging of an empire:

> Zu der Zeit freilich, in welcher unsere Geschichte beginnt, war diese Stadt noch nicht zu der ehrenvollen Würde, die Residenz eines deutschen Kaisers zu sein, erhoben; aber auch damals schon war Berlin, wovon, wie ihr alle schon wissen werdet, hier die Rede ist, eine große und bedeutende Stadt und zumal angesehen als die Hauptstadt des preußischen Staates, dem Sitz seines Königs und dessen nächsten Angehörigen.[55]

Immediately after this patriotic introduction the story begins, as in the original, on a cold December evening but is explicitly described, unlike the original, as taking place "zu Anfang der fünfziger Jahre des laufenden Jahrhunderts" (at the beginning of the '50s of the current century).[56] Nevertheless, although Wachler specifies the timeframe of the story as a decade earlier than when *Goldelse* first appeared in the *Gartenlaube* in 1866, the accompanying illustrations by Werner Zehme signal by means of contemporary styles the timeframe of the 1880s.

Unlike this rewritten (and often reprinted) version for young girls, Marlitt's *Goldelse* contains no such historicizing introduction in its many late nineteenth-century editions and reprints. Thus when in 1890 *Goldelse*, illustrated by Wilhelm Claudius, appeared as volume 8 of the collected works, nothing about the book overtly signaled its origins in the era preceding German unification.[57] Like those in *Goldelschen*, Claudius's illustrations pay no nostalgic tribute to the crinolines of the 1850s and '60s but instead feature the bustles, skirts, and bodices of the late 1880s, *Goldelse* thus presenting itself as a contemporary story.[58]

The plot of *Goldelse* contains many characteristic features of Marlitt's fiction and would have been familiar to readers who had read the first seven volumes of the series. A feisty young woman finds her way in a provincial, domestic world threatened by moral turpitude, social injustice, and bigotry. Aristocratic ancestral pride becomes a particular source of contention as the heroine studiously avoids it on her own behalf (she is descended from an ancient family on her mother's side and, as it later turns out, also on her father's side) and (mistakenly) attributes it to Herr von Walde, the man whom she will eventually marry. As is also not uncommon in Marlitt's plots, a household in disarray because of the autocratic rule of a woman with the wrong values plays a central role. The narrator describes the petty tyrannies and prejudices of the domestic sphere in excruciating detail as the heroine, Elisabeth Ferber, aka Goldelse, repeatedly becomes the target of the bile of the religious bigot and snob Baroness von Lessen, who holds sway over her wealthy invalid cousin, Helene von Walde.

While Marlitt's plots certainly teach virtue and insist on social justice, they are also structured, as Kirsten Belgum has argued, around female desire.[59] In this respect too, *Goldelse* is no exception. In a striking scene Elisabeth, who some pages earlier has declared that she cannot imagine "wie man einen fremden Menschen lieber haben kann als die eigenen Eltern" (*Goldelse*, 100; "how . . . anyone [can] love a stranger better than father and mother" [Wister, 100]) experiences a sexual awakening beneath the cool eye of the dark and melancholy male protagonist.[60] A gifted pianist, Elisabeth performs with the full knowledge and enjoyment of her musical talent. Yet this time something is different:

> Heute aber mischte sich etwas in die Töne, was sie nicht begreifen konnte; es hatte durchaus keine eigene Stimme; sie hätte es um keinen Preis verfolgen und erfassen können, denn es flog nur wie ein neuer, unbekannter Hauch über die Tonwellen. Es war ihr, als wandelten Schmerz und Freude nicht mehr nebeneinander, sondern flössen in eins zusammen. (*Goldelse*, 124)[61]

The narrator employs euphemistic language, but language that is clear enough to anyone familiar with romance. Readers unable to pick up on this first cue, on the other hand, will inevitably do so later in the story, for the narrative will ramp up the sexual tension over the ensuing pages.

Even as readers vicariously experience Elisabeth's sexual awakening, they can also discern early on that this young woman, unbeknownst to herself, wields power over a considerably older man, the thirty-seven-year-old Baron von Walde, by virtue of her charm, beauty, talent, virtue, and intellect. The narrative also signals unspoken and barely suppressed male desire for the heroine through Baron von Walde's unexplained moodiness and unmotivated gruffness toward Elisabeth. While Elisabeth remains willfully blind to all of these indicators, the romance reader is not encouraged to be equally blind but instead to relish von Walde's growing yet unstated attraction to the heroine.

One of the pleasures of reading Marlitt's novels consists in the invitation to read the developing passion of hero and heroine for one another between the lines — an ability that becomes more refined the more one reads the genre of romance. Readers in fact have a clearer sense of what the heroine is feeling and how she is affecting the male protagonist than does the heroine herself. The happy ending is thus for some readers perhaps not nearly so exciting as the progress toward it, though few would read such a romance novel if the happy ending were not guaranteed to begin with.

In *Goldelse* the union of hero and heroine provides resolution on many levels: even as it marks the triumph over "Angeberei, und Bosheit und Heuchelei" (*Goldelse*, 136; "servility, malice and hypocrisy" [Wister, 138]) — Marlitt's central message — it also depicts the blissful fulfillment of desire, symbolized — again euphemistically — by the baby Elisabeth holds in her arms in the summation on the final page. In the end Elisabeth has achieved her heart's desire; Baroness von Lessen and her deceitful son, Hollfeld, have been banished from the Baron's estate; Herr von Walde has lost his melancholy air; and the province has yielded up its darkest secrets of obsessive passion and social injustice to be restored to its better self.[62]

In addition to structuring a plot around the fulfillment of the longings of the heroine, Marlitt strengthens her case against the privileges of birth by foregrounding the unequal, selfish sexual power that immoral aristocratic men have over women. The story's chief villain, Hollfeld, tries to cheat the aristocratic invalid Helene von Walde out of her money by mercilessly exploiting her feelings for him. Furthermore, he takes advantage of the serving girl Bertha and then deserts her, leaving her to descend into insanity, and finally he twice tries to ravish Elisabeth when she rebuffs his advances.

As if the social meaning of Hollfeld's villainous sexuality were not clear enough, Marlitt adds the backstory of a nobleman who captured a gypsy girl and kept her prisoner in his castle until she died giving birth to his son — the Ferbers are descended from this son. Although the narrator somewhat glosses over the gypsy origins, it is clear enough that their significance persists into the present: rejecting their newfound nobility and thus the obsessive ancestor who imprisoned the object of his desire, the Ferbers maintain a love for freedom and healthy self-pride that, the text implies, they may have inherited from their exotic female ancestor. Somewhat surprisingly, moreover, Marlitt does not punish mad Bertha for her attempt to murder Elisabeth out of jealousy. As if to repair the social inequality that licenses men to do what they please with women, the author does not kill off Bertha, but instead allows her to recover from her madness and to emigrate to America with a "braver junger Mann" (*Goldelse*, 328; "fine young fellow" [Wister, 337]) from her own social class who loves her.[63]

However, even as she titillates her readers and allows her heroine some adventure and freedom, Marlitt also reaffirms the tight boundaries of woman's sphere. In a characteristic narrative turn, Elisabeth physically prevents an embittered gamekeeper from murdering Herr von Walde. Immediately after she has pulled back the arm of the would-be assassin "mit aller Kraft" (*Goldelse*, 183; "with all the strength of which she was capable" [Wister, 188]), the narrator reassures readers that her feminine nature reasserts itself (". . . nachdem die Gefahr vorüber, machte die weibliche Natur ihr Recht geltend," 184; ". . . the danger was past, and her feminine nature was reasserting itself" [Wister 188]) and she trembles violently, a blissful smile on her face now that she has saved the man she loves. Thus selfless love — as the refined affective sphere in which women allegedly wield power and authority — reclaims its rights over women's agency.

Elisabeth Werner's Franco-Prussian War as Family Romance: *Ein Held der Feder* (1871/1895)

Advertisements for the Werner series promise potential buyers and readers that, in contrast to Marlitt, who reads women's hearts, Werner's exciting and suspenseful ("spannend aufgebaut") novels will lead the reader by the hand into the "laute Welt des Ringens und Schaffens, in der nicht nur Menschen sondern auch Geistesströmungen miteinander streiten" (the noisy world of struggling and achieving, in which not only people but also the trends of the times struggle with one another). Werner, this daughter of Berlin, the advertisements claim, "hatte das brausende Wehen des Zeitgeistes vernommen und ihn wohl begriffen" (had perceived the roaring wind of the spirit of the times and ably captured it). But then, the advertisement does not forget the sentimental vein to which the books overtly appeal; the blurb does go on to explain that Werner portrays the struggle with women's hearts and that she narrates with womanly warmth.[64]

The "noisy world of struggling and achieving" likely alludes to the tendency of Werner's novels to focus on male protagonists' accession to their manly place in the social and political order. This attention to male characters, however, renders the novels no less appealing to a female readership. Indeed they overtly address nineteenth-century women readers by attaching the struggles of the protagonist for his rightful place to his love for the heroine of the story, a heroine whom Werner also typically paints with strong colors and who in the end does her part to affirm the hero's

Fig. 4.6. Illustration of the heroine in 1890s fashions, E. Werner,
Ein Held der Feder, vol. 6 of *E. Werners gesammelte Romane und
Novellen: Illustrierte Ausgabe* (Leipzig: Ernst Keil's Nachfolger, n.d.),
216. Reproduced by Perry Trolard.

manhood. While making readers privy to action-based plots, Werner's novels steer a steady course toward a happy marriage, based in desire and highly gendered ideas of virtue and duty. Marriage, writes Werner at the conclusion of *Vineta* (serialized in the *Gartenlaube* in 1874; vol. 8 of the collected works), is the "innigste Band . . . das zwei Menschen vereinigen kann" (most intimate and ardent bond that can unite two people).[65] The adjective "innigst" in its double sense of intimate and ardent perfectly captures the domestic happiness that stands at the center of Werner's plots. Precisely these marriages, furthermore, secure the long-term stability of the social and political order.[66] As we shall see, *Held der Feder* (Hero of the Pen), the example of Werner's work to be examined more closely here, is no exception.

Held der Feder does offer readers a bit of vicarious adventure. Its heroine journeys from the United States to the Rhineland only to find herself in a region at war with France. Serialized in the *Gartenlaube* in 1871 just after the conclusion of the Franco-Prussian War and the proclamation of the German Empire, *Held der Feder*, as a novel about the immediate past, shares in the heady celebration of German unification. It narrates a story in which a naturalized American heroine finds her way back to her German roots and the land of her birth and also recovers her femininity even as the German male protagonist transforms from a professor to a heroic officer in the "band of brothers" that fought the French in 1870–71.

When *Ein Held der Feder* reappeared in 1895, bound together with *Heimatklang* (translated into American English both as *Home Sounds* and *The Spell of Home*), as volume 6 of Werner's ten-volume illustrated collected works, the events portrayed therein belonged not to the present, but to a then much-revered and annually commemorated history.[67] Yet in the illustrations by René Reinicke und Th. Rocholl, the heroine sports the unmistakable gigot or elongated puff sleeves, square shoulders, and circular hems of the mid-1890s and not the full skirts with crinolette and the "short bunchy puff at the back" and pagoda sleeve of the early 1870s that would have linked the tale overtly to a historical period marked by a specific style (see fig. 4.6).[68] Furthermore, the decorative cover, as described above, linked the novel to contemporary taste. A story set in the Franco-Prussian War a quarter of a century earlier was thus marketed as a book for a reader who might like to think of herself as fashionably modern even as her reading matter, and indeed the stuff of her dreams, was not. In a book so overtly linked to a particular historical moment — in both its origins and its content — the visual attenuation of that historical moment is, from the vantage of 2010, striking.

Werner's headstrong and pragmatic Jane Forest has been raised by her German parents in America. Lacking any feeling for the land in which she was born, she nevertheless promises her father to return to Germany in search of her long-lost brother. Although she plans to make an expedient marriage with an American, Henry Alison, whose feelings toward her initially appear to be as cool as hers toward him, she ultimately loses her heart to a German professor, Walther Fernow, whom she meets after a carriage accident on her way to B[onn]. The title pertains to this professor who, so Jane wishes to believe (even as she is undeniably attracted to him), is all talk and no action.

In the name of family integrity, Werner allows her heroine a series of adventures, but also subjects her to the dilemmas of propriety. Jane's search for her brother not only takes her across the ocean but leads her behind enemy lines where she tries to find out whether Professor Fernow, now the heroic Lieutenant Fernow, is in fact her brother, When he declares his love for her, she, believing that he is her brother, avers that she could never be his even if she were released from her promise to Mr. Alison. Yet when she subsequently learns that her beloved Walter Fernow is not her brother, she continues to struggle with the problem of improperly breaking off an engagement. While the story could tempt readers to believe that Jane's sacred word has authority on account of her status as a moral subject, that authority resides in social convention that supports male prerogative. Mr. Alison, as a man, has the power. He can force her against her will since she has made a solemn promise to him.

Six months later, after the war has been won, the narrator recounts in chapter 31, which is entitled "The Balance of Power" in the American translation (Shaw, 148), how Jane remains trapped by her pledge. Rather than break her word, she asks only how Mr. Alison can demand that she marry him when he knows that she loves Fernow. The balance of power tips in her favor only when she at last conforms to her womanly role, submissively appealing to Mr. Alison as the woman he loves. "Jane war sich jetzt ihrer Macht bewußt, sie ließ sich nicht mehr schrecken" (*Held*, 207; "Jane was now conscious of her power; she felt no further fear" [Shaw, 156]), the narrator notes. She falls to her knees and begs, and Mr. Alison releases her.

Werner concludes her story with springtime on the Rhine. Jane has become Johanna — that is, she has given up her American upbringing for life in a newly united Germany. She will now use her American dollars, as Mr. Atkins, her long-time friend and business advisor, dolefully predicts, to support the career of her heroic future husband, who will likely become Germany's next celebrated national poet (*Held*, 214). Readers have the satisfaction of knowing that in the German Fernow, Jane has at last found a partner who has fully recognized her charm. Werner thus makes clear in her happy ending how gender and nationality are to be construed and enforced in the new empire; twenty-four years later in the new illustrated and handsomely bound edition, only the costumes have changed.

The German National Family: Wilhelmine Heimburg's *Lumpenmüllers Lieschen* (1878/1891)

In 1891, the perennially popular *Lumpenmüllers Lieschen* (translated in Great Britain as *Lizzie of the Mill* and in the United States as both *Lottie of the Mill* and *A Maiden's Choice*) appeared between Japonesque covers as volume 2 of Heimberg's ten-volume *Romane und Novellen.*[69] Thirteen years had passed since the novel had first been serialized in 1878 in the *Gartenlaube.*[70] Germany meanwhile had witnessed the passing of two emperors and entered a brash new era. As was the case with the two previous examples, the illustrator, R. Wehle, studiously avoided reproducing the cuirass bodice and the tight, relatively straight swathed skirts common in the late 1870s when the book first appeared, and instead clothed the characters in the contemporary fashions of the early 1890s.

Lumpenmüllers Lieschen, however, contains little historical specification to begin with, and this lack of specification glosses over the disjuncture of text and image that an alert reader might perceive in the previous two examples. Set in a nameless German province, the novel explores relations between the impoverished aristocratic family, the von Derenbergs, in the decaying castle on the hill and the wealthy family that owns the paper mill in the village. Although a factory might bespeak modern times, the narrator repeatedly points out that the mill has existed for several generations.[71] Even the visit of the shallow and supercilious aristocratic Blanche to the castle fails to provide opportunity to specify the novel to a historical period. Her beautiful clothes are noted on several occasions, but in terms too vague (the narrator mentions only the color and the materials) to connect them to a particular fashion trend from a particular historical moment.

The novel primarily explores the overcoming of class prejudice and barriers to marriage between a male aristocrat and a bourgeois woman, yet from the start the text configures these barriers as largely arbitrary and imagined. They are the prejudices still harbored by the von Derenbergs' grandmother and not in the end by the grandchildren (even if the hero, Army, falls under the grandmother's sway for a significant time in the novel). If the grandmother's age did not suffice to signal to the reader that such barriers are crumbling, her nationality makes their untimeliness and inappropriateness crystal clear: she is Italian. The narrator repeatedly stresses that this Italian woman has no sympathy for the German sentimentality that facilitates the crossing of class barriers. It turns out, moreover, that even in the backstory — a parallel love story from two generations ago — this same outsider is at fault: but for the scheming of the prejudice-ridden Italian grandmother (then at the height of her beauty and power), a marriage between the mill and the castle would have taken place decades earlier. In the end the novel expels the grandmother from the affective community that is re-affirmed by a marriage between childhood playmates, the aristocratic grandson and the daughter of the wealthy paper mill owner. The grandmother voluntarily joins Blanche as her traveling companion, thus committing herself to an unstable and suspect life of roaming in the great watering holes of Europe.

In imagining an unconstrained affiliation between mill and castle — but for the machinations of the prejudiced Italian woman — *Lumpenmüllers Lieschen* shares in the national liberal ethos of her more famous contemporary Gustav Freytag. In his *Die Ahnen* (1872–80) Freytag seeks to demonstrate with a thousand years of history that the modern-day, middle-class Königs — the telos of German national history — are descended from real kings (Germanic chieftains) via centuries of intermarriage among petty nobility, free peasants, and townspeople.[72] Class barriers have broken down, according to Freytag, ultimately in favor of a middle class that is synonymous with the nation.

Heimburg's vision is less clear than Freytag's, but we do learn of the protagonist Army's fascination with his female ancestor's eyes. Only late in the novel does Army realize that the ancestor resembles not his aristocratic cousin Blanche but the bourgeois Lieschen: that is, his ancestor and Lieschen share the same eyes. The novel does not explore the implications of this similarity — merely uses it to explain Army's ultimate love for Lieschen — yet suggests thereby that the bourgeois woman and the aristocratic man actually do belong to a single family of sorts. The novel intimates in fact that aristocratic prejudice persists largely in the cities where, present in greater numbers, the aristocracy are caught up in their own exclusive social whirl. In the sedate countryside aristocrats are thrown back on their own family and the locals, of whatever class they may be. In the intimacy of the province there exists an extended family that crosses barriers; that family is constituted by love, and moreover, it is German.

Unlike *Die Ahnen* or Freytag's earlier bestseller, *Soll und Haben* (1855; Debit and Credit), Heimburg's *Lumpenmüllers Lieschen* in the end offers an ambiguous picture of the power and significance of the middle class. Rather than glorifying the middle class per se, the novel concludes with the prospect of restoring the aristocratic von Derenbergs — with the expulsion of the dangerous foreign woman and with a new male head solidly in place — to something of their former splendor. Army must learn how to manage his recovered estate and the von Derenberg family will be reinvigorated not merely with bourgeois money, but also with bourgeois cheerfulness and good health, and of course — a woman's love.

Conclusion

To what extent then might the availability and wide reading of the approximately fifty novels and novellas re-published by Keils Nachfolger/Union

Deutsche Verlagsgesellschaft in the late nineteenth and early twentieth centuries have shaped or at the very least reinforced cultural formations in Imperial Germany? Nancy R. Reagin's recent study of domesticity and national identity in Germany 1870–1945, *Sweeping the German Nation,* provides insight into the cultivation of domesticity in late-century Germany that helps to bring into focus how these popular novels might have supported and embellished gender ideologies of the period.[73]

Relying on Pierre Bourdieu's understanding of habitus, Reagin identifies and examines what she calls a "habitus of domesticity" in Imperial Germany. As the "set of dispositions, assumptions, values, and norms that are internalized through socialization (usually at the subconscious level) and strongly influence how people act and feel," this habitus of domesticity, she argues, significantly determined women's lives in this era.[74] She demonstrates how prescriptions for household management and women's choices for housekeeping within those narrow prescriptions both contributed to class formation and undergirded a German national identity based in middle-class values. Her study, however, does not include women's reading of domestic fiction. Yet by dint of addressing the imagination and emotions, precisely such reading can play a critical role, though not necessarily a straightforward one, in the socialization of its readers — on both a conscious and a subconscious level.

As we have seen, the novels of Heimburg, Werner, and Marlitt do indeed reproduce a "habitus of domesticity," yet they add a dimension to the habitus that Reagin describes, a dimension centered not merely in virtue but also in emotion, desire, and permissible pleasure. Even as these collected illustrated editions, at the time of their publication, encouraged their readers to read domestic fiction of decades earlier as contemporary, they purveyed and underpinned a sentimental transhistorical domesticity that in turn supported a German national imaginary shaped by middle-class values, idealization of the family, and limited social roles for women.

Reading domestic romance is of course not the same as "keeping house" in Reagin's sense. The popularity of the novels of Marlitt, Werner, and Heimburg suggests that the very woman whose nation told her to "keep house" and who, as Reagin demonstrates, proudly did keep house in Imperial Germany, imbued this domestic life via reading with desire, sentiment, and choice, thus making it eminently hospitable. Indeed, the widespread reading of the illustrated collected editions examined here suggests that some of these women readers dreamed, aided by Marlitt, Werner, and Heimburg, that inhabiting the domestic sphere was more than the merely instrumental "sweeping the nation."

A Maiden's Choice, the title of the American translation of *Lumpenmüllers Lieschen,* supports precisely the notion that within the sentimentalized domestic sphere women can accede to agency. Likewise, invoking and calling into question the well-worn image of oak and ivy, Marlitt's Elisabeth Ferber declared in 1866 and would continue to declare upon each subsequent reading on into the twentieth century, "Ich habe von jeher das abgenutzte Bild vom Epheu und der Eiche nicht leiden mögen und werde es am allerwenigsten an mir wahr machen" (*Goldelse*, 63; "I never could endure the trite image of the ivy and the oak, and shall most certainly not illustrate it in my own person" [Wister, 62]). The gifted Elisabeth — perhaps like her readers — thought it important to assert herself and thus to participate actively in the making of her miniaturized world. And indeed she could do so and yet never risk foregoing a happy ending.

Notes

I thank Perry Trolard and Shelby Carpenter for generating the scans used to illustrate this essay.

[1] William St Clair, *The Reading Nation in the Romantic Period* (Cambridge: Cambridge UP, 2004), 3. Subsequent references to this work are cited in parentheses in the body of the text.

[2] The Statute of Anne (1710) formalized copyright as coming into "existence with the act of composition by the author" (St Clair, 91). That right could in turn be ceded by the author to a publisher. In 1774, the House of Lords put limits on copyright by declaring perpetual copyright unlawful in both England and Scotland (St Clair, 110–11), thus reducing the copyright period to the copyright provided for by the Statute of Anne (fourteen years from first publication). Beginning with the copyright act of 1808, a series of acts began to lengthen the copyright period (St Clair, 120–21). For St Clair's account of the new opportunities thereby created for publishers, see chapter 7, "The Old Canon" (122–39).

[3] Gerd Schulz, "Das Klassikerjahr 1867 und die Gründung von Reclams Universal-Bibliothek," in *Reclam 100 Jahre Universal-Bibliothek: Ein Almanach* (Stuttgart: Philipp Reclam Jun., 1967), 11–28.

[4] Urszula Bonter lists Heimburg's date of birth as 1848, not 1850, the date that appears in most lexica. Urszula Bonter, *Der Populärroman in der Nachfolge von E. Marlitt: Wilhelmine Heimburg, Valeska Gräfin Bethusy-Huc, Eufemia von Adlersfeld-Ballestrem* (Würzburg: Königshausen & Neumann, 2005), 74.

[5] In 2006, Marlitt's *Das Geheimnis der alten Mamsell*, for example, was republished as an audio cassette: E. Marlitt, *Das Geheimnis der alten Mamsell*, ed. Volker Neuhaus, read by Maria Wolf, Grandes Dames, Delta Audio CD (2006). The Grandes Dames series also includes perennial romance novel favorites Barbara Cartland and Georgette Heyer. On the reading of Marlitt's *Die zweite Frau* in the twentieth century, see Ruth-Ellen Boetcher Joeres, "*Die zweite Frau*, Popular Culture, and the Analytical Categories of Gender and Class," chapter 6 in *Respectability and Deviance: Nineteenth-Century German Women Writers and the Ambiguity of Representation* (Chicago: U of Chicago P, 1998), 219–55, esp. 246–55. In 2009, Projekte-Verlag offered new facsimile editions at reasonable prices of Elisabeth Werner's *Wege des Schicksals* (22 Euros), *Vineta* (22.50 Euros),

and *Erzählungen* (22.50 Euros). http://www.projekte-verlag.de/csc_articles.php (accessed 9 January 2009). Even Heimburg's *Lumpenmüllers Lieschen* was republished as a book as late as 1974 in Fischer's "Schmöker Kabinett," which advertises itself as "Lesehits der guten alten Zeit" (hit books from the good old days): Wilhelmine Heimburg, *Lumpenmüllers Lieschen. Das Schmöker Kabinett*, ed. and afterword Michael Koser (Frankfurt am Main: Fischer, 1974). All three authors remain widely available in both German and English in secondhand book shops as can be determined by consulting such online vendors as abebooks.com.

[6] See, e.g., Ludwig Hamann, *Der Umgang mit Büchern und die Selbstkultur* (Leipzig: Ludwig Hamann, 1898), 55, who recommends Marlitt's *Goldelse* under "Erzählungen, Romane und Humoresken"; H. Groß, "Lektüre," in *Der Hausschatz: Ein Freund und Ratgeber für die Frauenwelt; Unter Mitwirkung hervorragender Männer und Frauen*, ed. Anny Wothe (Oranienburg: Freihof, 1886), 103, where E. Marlitt and E. Werner are both recommended to women readers; Elise Polko, *Unsere Pilgerfahrt von der Kinderstube bis zum eignen Herd: Lose Blätter*, 8th ed., with 8 illustrations by Eugen Klimsch (Leipzig: C. F. Amelungs Verlag, 1886), 81, where Heimburg's stories and Marlitt's novels are recommended reading among other books "welche die allgemeine Ausbildung bezwecken, oder ein besonderes Interesse für das weibliche Gemüt haben" (that aim at general education or are of special interest to the female heart); and Elise Polko, "Versuch einer Liste der Schöpfungen moderner Autoren zur Gründung einer Frauen-Hausbibliothek" [1890], in *Bildung und Kultur bürgerlicher Frauen 1850–1918*, ed. Günter Häntzschel, Studien und Texte zur Sozialgeschichte der Literatur 15 (Tübingen: Niemeyer, 1986), 435–46, where several novels by Heimburg and Marlitt are recommended, including *Lumpenmüllers Lieschen* and *Goldelse* (439 and 442, respectively). I thank Jana Mikota for calling my attention to Groß and Häntzschel, and I am grateful to Katrin Völkner for recommending Hamann.

[7] See, e.g., Todd Kontje's examination of discourses of emigration and empire in Marlitt's domestic fiction. Todd Kontje, "Marlitt's World: Domestic Fiction in an Age of Empire," *German Quarterly* 77, no. 4 (2004): 408–26. Kontje argues of Marlitt's oeuvre that it sends mixed messages, both exhibiting complicity in aspects of the imperialist and nationalist thinking of the day and presenting critically some of the ideological props of empire.

[8] In 1910, the article on German literature in the 11th edition of the *Encyclopædia Britannica* names Böhlau, Reuter, and Viebig, along with Ricarda Huch, as the authors of "some of the best fiction of the most recent period." (*Encyclopædia Britannica*, 11th ed., s.v. "German Literature.) These for the most part untranslated women thus numbered among the authors who were to constitute Germany's reputation on the international scene of *belles lettres*, even as Marlitt, Werner, and Heimburg were multiply translated and widely read abroad.

[9] See the scene between husband and wife in which the narrator declares her intention of getting to know her elderly neighbor only to have her husband express concern that this "old maid" will bore her. Wilhelmine Heimburg, *Aus dem Leben meiner alten Freundin*, vol. 1 of *W. Heimburg's gesammelte Romane und Novellen* (Leipzig: Ernst Keil's Nachfolger, n.d.), 13–14. This book was variously translated into English as *The Story of a Clergyman's Daughter; or, Reminiscences from the Life of My Old Friend* (1889), and *The Pastor's Daughter* (1890).

"My Old Friend" takes German "alt" in the original title for the sense of "old friend," whereas it may simply refer to the elderly character's age which allows the telling of a story from many years earlier.

[10] One important exception is Bonter's *Der Populärroman in der Nachfolge von E. Marlitt*.

[11] Otto Heller, "Women Writers of the Nineteenth Century," in *Studies in Modern German Literature* (Boston: Ginn & Co., 1905), 258.

[12] Rosa Mayreder, "Familienliteratur," *Das literarische Echo* 8 (1905), col. 411. My translation. All subsequent translations are my own unless otherwise indicated. Mayreder's essay offers a convincing critique of women's reading; however, she greatly overstates her case when she declares, for example, that divorce is a forbidden topic or that the novels of family magazines never deal with marriage and instead only with courtship. Consider Marlitt's *Im Schillingshof*, which can reach a happy ending only by means of a divorce. See Lynne Tatlock, "Eine amerikanische Baumwollprinzessin in Thüringen: Transnationale Liebe, Familie und die deutsche Nation in E. Marlitts *Im Schillingshof* (1879)," in *Amerika und die deutschsprachige Literatur nach 1849. Migration — kultureller Austausch — frühe Globalisierung*, ed. Christof Hamann, Ute Gerhard, and Walter Grünzweig (Bielefeld: transcript, 2008), 105–25. Likewise Marlitt's *Die zweite Frau* announces its treatment of re-marriage on its very title page. On this novel, see Joeres, *Respectability and Deviance*, 219–55.

[13] Ernst von Wollzogen, "Das Familienblatt und die Literatur," *Das literarische Echo* 9 (1907): cols.177–85.

[14] Ibid., col. 183. The *Gartenlaube* had five years earlier written its own history, reminding its readers of the liberal sentiments of Marlitt's novels: "Damals, als diese ersten Romane der Marlitt erschienen, waren sie der poetische Ausdruck einer sich vollziehenden Annäherung zwischen Adel und Bürgertum, zwischen Fürst und Volk im Zeichen der liberalen Ideen." ("Zur Geschichte der Gartenlaube," *Gartenlaube*, no. 8 [1902]: 137; Back then when Marlitt's first novels appeared, they were the poetic expression of a rapprochement between nobility and bourgeoisie, between prince and people, that was taking place under the sign of liberal ideas). All citations of the *Gartenlaube* are by year, issue number, and page number. The *Gartenlaube* is paginated sequentially throughout each year.

[15] "The *Gartenlaube* had long participated in the movement whose goal it is to achieve for women intellectual and material independence. In 1871, the first essay on the efforts of the *Allgemeine Frauenverein* appeared with portraits of Auguste Schmidt and Luise Otto-Peters; in the following years R. Artaria (Rosalie Braun) faithfully reported on the positive progress in this area, while she on the other hand showed herself in her family portraits, 'The First Year in the New Household' and 'The Spirit of the Times in the Home,' to be well-informed about the great sphere of duty of housewives and mothers in the metropolises of our times." "Zur Geschichte der *Gartenlaube*," no. 52 (1902): 900.

[16] For a critical examination of the treatment of women's work in the *Gartenlaube* and the reproduction of gender ideology in the magazine from its inception to ca. 1900, see Ulla Wischermann, *Frauenarbeit und Presse: Frauenarbeit und*

Frauenbewegung in der deutschen illustrierten Presse des 19. Jahrhunderts (Munich: Sauer, 1983), 40–71, 106–47.

[17] The title page of the revised edition of 1909 gives an idea of its circulation: "64. Tausend" (64 thousand). Elise Polko, *Unsere Pilgerfahrt von der Kinderstube bis zum eigenen Herd: Lose Blätter*, rev. by L. Devrient (Leipzig: C. F. Amelung, 1909).

[18] Polko, *Unsere Pilgerfahrt* (1909), 276. In this shortened version, however, the general recommendations for reading German literature have been eliminated (see note 6 above) and the text defers instead to the "literarischen Ratgeber des Kunstwart" (70; the literary advice in the [magazine the] *Kunstwart* [Curator]).

[19] Dieter Barth, "Das Familienblatt — ein Phänomen der Unterhaltungspresse des 19. Jahrhunderts. Beispiele zur Gründungs- und Verlagsgeschichte," *Archiv für Geschichte des Buchwesens* 15 (1975): cols. 121–316. According to Barth, when the Kröner Publishing House, which had purchased Ernst Keils Nachfolger in 1884, became the Union Deutsche Verlagsgesellschaft in January of 1890, the finances of Ernst Keils Nachfolger were attached to the new joint-stock company. In 1898 Keil was transformed into a company with limited liability and sold to the Union Deutsche Verlagsgesellschaft, which continued to run the company as "Ernst Keils Nachfolger G.m.b.H." (col.199 and col. 199n.222). Barth summarizes the complicated history of Ernst Keils Nachfolger (1884–1906) in cols. 194–204. The collected works of Marlitt, Werner, and Heimburg were published both under the name Union Deutsche Verlagsgesellschaft and under the designation Keils Nachfolger. For a profile of the Union Deutsche Verlagsgesellschaft, see Otto Brunken, Bettina Hurrelmann, Maria Michels-Kohlhage, and Gisela Wilkending, *Handbuch zur Kinder- und Jugendliteratur: Von 1850 bis 1900* (Stuttgart: J. B. Metzler, 2008), cols. 916–20.

[20] Belgum discusses the turn to a more conservative national politics as epitomized in the increased interest in and positive image of colonialism in the fourth decade of the existence of the *Gartenlaube* in *Popularizing the Nation: Audience, Representation, and the Production of Identity in* Die Gartenlaube, *1853–1900* (Lincoln: U of Nebraska P, 1988), 142–82. On the increasing conservatism of the *Gartenlaube* 1880–1914, see also Heidemarie Gruppe, *"Volk" zwischen Politik und Idylle in der "Gartenlaube" 1853–1914*, Europäische Hochschulschriften, Series 19, no. 2 (Bern: Herbert Lang, 1976), 72–102. On the politics of the *Gartenlaube* in this period, see also, Peter Gay, "Experiment in Denial: a Reading of the *Gartenlaube* in the Year 1890," in *Traditions of Experiment from the Enlightenment to the Present*, ed. Nancy Kaiser and David E. Wellbery (Ann Arbor: U of Michigan P, 1992), 147–64. Gay remarks in particular on the absence in the *Gartenlaube* of engagement with the burning political questions of the year 1890. William II's controversial firing of Bismarck, for example, is reported as if Bismarck had resigned voluntarily (Gay, 151–52). As the title of his article indicates, Gay characterizes the *Gartenlaube* as in denial as it remains "faithful to the digestible didactic program it had outlined over thirty-five years before" (153). According to Gay, however, "The muffled tones and anodyne attitudes of 1890 [were] something relatively new" (160). He understands this denial not as complacency, but as a mechanism for coping with a deeply felt need for reassurance about the precarious state of things.

21 Advertisement, *Die Gartenlaube*, no. 19 (1888): 324.

22 Advertisement, *Die Gartenlaube*, no. 24 (1888): 405.

23 See the prices listed for these items by the "Waaren-Versand-Magazin von C. H. Waldow (Hamburg)." The advertisement promotes these items as "gute Waare zu billigem Preise" (good wares at a cheap price) in the advertising insert in *Die Gartenlaube*, no. 43 (1889). In this period individual issues of the *Gartenlaube* sold for 1.60 marks.

24 Georg Jäger, "Reclams Universal-Bibliothek bis zum Ersten Weltkrieg: Erfolgs-faktoren der Programmpolitik," in *Reclam 125 Jahre Universalbibliothek: Ein Almanach* (Stuttgart: Philipp Reclam Jun., 1967), table, 33, and also 34.

25 Advertisement, *Die Gartenlaube*, no. 35 (1891): 596. The advertisement announces that the second edition is "beginning to appear."

26 See, e.g., Belgum, *Popularizing the Nation*, 132. Belgum points out, however, that from the beginning the novels privilege a woman's perspective (133).

27 Advertisement, *Die Gartenlaube*, no. 49 (1890): 840.

28 "Prospekt," Advertising insert, *Die Gartenlaube*, no. 45 (1890): recto.

29 Ibid., verso.

30 "Prospekt," Advertising insert, *Die Gartenlaube*, no. 36 (1894): recto, and "Prospekt," Advertising insert, *Die Gartenlaube*, no. 34 (1896).

31 Advertisement, *Die Gartenlaube*, no. 47 (1904): 860.

32 "Blätter und Blüthen," *Die Gartenlaube*, no. 40 (1893): 687. The tenth volume in the collection did not put in an appearance until 1896. See the announcement of its recent publication in *Die Gartenlaube*, no. 45 (1896): 772.

33 "E. Werners Gesammelte Romane und Novellen," Advertising insert in *Die Gartenlaube*, no. 38 (1893): recto.

34 "E. Werners Gesammelte Romane und Novellen," Advertising insert in *Die Gartenlaube*, no. 38 (1893): verso.

35 "E. Werners Gesammelte Romane und Novellen. Illustrierte Ausgabe," advertisement, in E. Marlitt, *Die Frau mit den Karfunkelsteinen*, 2nd ed., vol. 6 of *E. Marlitt's gesammelte Romane und Novellen* (Leipzig: Ernst Keil's Nachfolger, n.d.), last page.

36 "Prospekt," Advertising insert, *Die Gartenlaube* (1901). The insert is not bound sequentially in the copy of this volume to which I had access, and so it is not possible for me to stipulate which issue it accompanied. An announcement of the forthcoming series follows in 1902; *Die Gartenlaube*, no. 14 (1902): 252.

37 Advertisement, *2. Beilage zu "Die Gartenlaube," Die Gartenlaube*, no. 47 (1905). This advertisement lists all forty-six books appearing in the illustrated collected editions of Marlitt, Heimburg, and Werner.

38 Janice A. Radway, *A Feeling for Books: The Book-of-the-Month Club, Literary Taste, and Middle-Class Desire* (Chapel Hill: U of North Carolina P, 1997), 148.

39 Radway, *A Feeling for Books*, 147.

40 On bindings mass-produced by Gustav Fritzsche's firm in Leipzig, see Helma Schaefer, "Leipziger Verlagseinbände des 19. Jahrhunderts als Gegenstand einbandkundlicher Forschung," in *Das Gewand des Buches: Historische Bucheinbände*

aus den Beständen der Universitätsbibliothek Leipzig und des Deutschen Buch- und Schriftmuseums der Deutschen Bücherei Leipzig (Leipzig: Universitätsbibliothek, 2003), 147–58.

[41] Listed by the Mephisto-Antiquariat in Paderborn under http://www.abebooks. com/servlet/SearchResults?an=Werner%2C+Elisabeth&bsi=60&x=66&y=11& prevpage=2 (accessed 8 January 2009), under abebooks.com. Eduard Grosse's review of the designs of the Leipziger Buchbinderei makes clear that the press was eclectic in the designs it offered. Grosse, who advocates the new designs of the "Jungen" — that is, Jugendstil — praises the press in 1898 for its new designs in that mode. Unfortunately the designs for the collected works of Marlitt, Heimburg, and Werner are not among those that he examines in this essay. See Eduard Grosse, "Deutsche Bucheinbände der Neuzeit," *Papier-Zeitung,* 1898; (Reprint, Leipzig: Leipziger Buchbinderei-Actiengesellschaft, 1898). Gustav Fritzsche's own account of his firm marks 1878 as an important turning point for cover design. In 1878 he went to the World's Fair in Paris where he saw "die hervorragenden Kunstarbeiten französischer und englischer Buchbinder" (the outstanding art works of French and English bookbinders). Thereafter he determined to ensure that his own products matched the artistic level of the articles he had seen at the fair. See Gustav Fritzsche, *Seinen Gönnern, Freunden und Mitarbeitern aus Anlaß seines 25jährigen Geschäftsjubiläums am 4. März 1889 gewidmet* (n.p.: n.p., 1898), 19.

[42] I thank my colleague Ken Botnik in Fine Arts at Washington University for helping me to identify the trends that influenced these design covers and for explaining the process of bookmaking with concrete examples in his studio.

[43] *Die Gartenlaube,* no. 19 (1888): 324.

[44] For a variety of types of decorative first letters as chapter openings, see in addition to fig. 5, E. Marlitt, *Im Schillingshof,* vol. 4 of *E. Marlitt's gesammelte Romane und Novellen,* 2nd ed. (Stuttgart: Union Deutsche Verlagsgesellschaft, n.d.), 5, 14, 61, 95.

[45] See, e.g., *Goldelse,* where Marlitt writes of the "Rauschen selbst der umfangreichsten, elegantesten Krinolinen" (rustle of the most flowing and elegant crinoline) and of costumes worn over crinolines). E. Marlitt, *Goldelse,* illust. W. Claudius, vol. 8 of *E. Marlitt's gesammelte Romane und Novellen,* 2nd ed. (Leipzig: Ernst Keil's Nachfolger, n.d.), 92–93. Further references to this edition will be contained in the body of the text, cited as *Goldelse.* Conscious of changing fashion, Annis Lee Wister, the first American translator, added to the above description "abundant crinoline, *which was then the fashion*" (my italics), thus historicizing the text. All English translations of this text are from Annis Lee Wister, trans., *Gold Elsie,* by E. Marlitt, 1868 (Philadelphia, PA: Lippincott & Co, 1869), here 91 and 93 respectively. Further references to this translation will appear in the text as "Wister." On Wister as translator of Marlitt, see Lynne Tatlock, "Domesticated Romance and Capitalist Enterprise: Annis Lee Wister's Americanization of German Fiction," in *German Culture in Nineteenth-Century America: Reception, Adaptation, Transformation,* ed. Lynne Tatlock and Matt Erlin (Rochester, NY: Camden House, 2005), 153–82. The illustrations for *Das Geheimnis der alten Mamsell* (first serialized 1867) in the first volume of the illustrated editions constitute an exception, however. Here the artist, C. Koch, evokes the world in which

the novel originated, with the bonnets, shawls, mantillas, and crinolines of the early 1860s. See E. Marlitt, *Das Geheimnis der alten Mamsell,* vol. 1 of *E. Marlitt's gesammelte Romane und Novellen* (Leipzig: Ernst Keil's Nachfolger, n.d.).

[46] Of course for still later readers of these illustrated collected works, the stories are, by virtue of the illustrations, forever visibly fossilized in the late 1880s, 1890s, and the first few years of the new century, when the illustrations were created and the collected works first appeared; again, this is not the historical period in which the novels were written or in which they overtly take place. The disjuncture between illustration and text, of course, may not have been immediately obvious to the casual late nineteenth-century reader, the time of the novels registering simply as vaguely past but accessible through the imagination of romance. Later twentieth-century editions of these books omit these illustrations and thus avoid historical specificity, or rather the problem of visible datedness. On the subject of the cover illustration of a new and revised edition of *Die zweite Frau* (1991), see Joeres, *Respectability and Deviance,* 251–54. Joeres astutely sees the ahistorical cover art as a turn "toward gendered essentialism and away from any historical subtleties concerning gender or class" (254).

[47] For an announcement of the recent publication of *Im Schillingshof,* see Advertisement, *Die Gartenlaube,* no. 21 (1889): 356.

[48] E. Werner, *Vineta,* vol. 8 of *E. Werners gesammelte Romane und Novellen. Illustrierte Ausgabe* (Leipzig: Ernst Keil's Nachfolger, n.d.). See the illustrations throughout the novel of women in the hugely puffed sleeves and skirts that flare at the hem typical of the mid-1890s.

[49] "Zur Geschichte der *Gartenlaube,*" 137, 900.

[50] Heller, "Women Writers of the Nineteenth Century," 236. Heller was in part reacting in the American context to the fact that the novels of Marlitt, Heimburg, and Werner were so widely available in American English translation.

[51] Heller, "Women Writers of the Nineteenth Century," 254.

[52] Joeres, *Respectability and Deviance,* 29–31, 219–55; Kirsten Belgum, "E. Marlitt: Narratives of Virtuous Desire," in *A Companion to German Realism 1848–1900,* ed. Todd Kontje (Rochester, NY: Camden House, 2002), 259–82; Todd Kontje, "Eugenie Marlitt: the Art of Liberal Compromise," chapter 6 in *Women, the Novel, and the German Nation 1771–1871* (Cambridge: Cambridge UP, 1998), 183–201. Reviewing Marlitt's novelistic production before 1871, Kontje admits that the author's political messages are somewhat mixed, but he also emphatically points out that Marlitt falls out of favor with literary pundits in the 1880s due to changing historical circumstances (200). He maintains as well that her writing has received too much publicity "of the wrong sort," which has obscured the "cultural work" of her fiction (200).

[53] The impact of Gabriele Reuter's *Aus guter Familie* (1895) in and of itself suggests how little the situation of the middle-class girl had been questioned, or indeed been deemed worthy of critical attention. For information on the impact of this novel, see Lynne Tatlock, introd. to *From a Good Family,* by Gabriele Reuter, trans. Lynne Tatlock (Rochester, NY: Camden House, 1999), ix–x, xiii.

[54] Joeres, *Respectability and Deviance,* 254.

55 "Admittedly in the time in which our story begins this city had not yet been elevated to the residence of a German emperor, but already back then Berlin — all of you already know that this is what we're talking about here — was a large and important city and especially respected as the capital of the Prussian State, the seat of its king and the closest members of his family"; Auguste Wachler, *Goldelschen nach E. Marlitts Erzählung "Goldelse" für die weibliche Jugend von 12–15 Jahren*, 6th ed. (Berlin: Hermann J. Meidinger, n.d.), 1. I have been unable to determine the exact date of publication of *Goldelschen*; the earliest edition is listed in library catalogues as 188-, that is, with the last digit missing. I thank Lorie Vanchena for calling my attention to this book.

56 Ibid., 2.

57 The recent publication of the volume is announced in *Die Gartenlaube*, no. 24 (1890): 408. In 1897 a new printing of the more expensive deluxe edition ("Prachtausgabe mit Goldschnitt"; deluxe edition with gilt edge) of *Goldelse* appeared with the set of illustrations made for the novel in the early 1870s by the well-known illustrator Paul Thumann. The *Gartenlaube* advertises it for 10 marks 50 pfennigs (Advertising insert, *Die Gartenlaube*, no. 15 [1897]). Unlike the cheaper illustrated collected editions, the deluxe edition provided the more refined luxury of historical nostalgia with these older illustrations.

58 The often-reprinted deluxe edition of 1871 with illustrations by Thumann, however, features historicized clothing. In keeping with the original serialization date of *Goldelse*, Thumann takes care to reproduce the fashions of the early to mid-'60s — and not the distinct styles of the early 1870s when he presumably created the drawings. See E. Marlitt, *Goldelse. Illustrirt von Paul Thumann* (Leipzig: Ernst Keil, 1871).

59 See Belgum, "Narratives of Virtuous Desire," and, on *Goldelse* in particular, see Belgum, *Popularizing the Nation*, 133–36, where she identifies the female gaze as the most important location in the narrative of female desire (135–36).

60 Elisabeth herself, adhering to the surface narrative of virtue, insists rather that she has been in love with him "seit ich . . . in deine zürnenden Augen sah, seit ich deine Stimme gehört hatte, wie sie menschliche Grausamkeit und Härte unerbittlich richtete" (319; "when I saw in your angry eyes, and heard in the tones of your voice, how you detested cruelty and injustice!" [Wister, 328]).

61 ". . . something blended with the tones that she could not herself comprehend; she could not possibly pursue and analyze it, for it breathed almost imperceptibly across the waves of sound. It seemed as though joy and woe no longer moved side by side, but melted together into one" (Wister, 124). Readers familiar with part 11, chapter 3, of Thomas Mann's *Buddenbrooks* (1901) may recall the erotic description of Hanno Buddenbrook at the piano and thus be reminded of the proximity of the popular to the celebrated works of the literary canon.

62 The restoration of the province is reflected in part in the final description of the renovated castle Gnadeck. The renovated house is a favorite feature of Marlitt's domestic fiction and also figures prominently, for example, in *Im Schillingshof*. See Tatlock, "Eine amerikanische Baumwollprinzessin in Thüringen," 123; on the significance of the interior in Marlitt's *Im Hause des Kommerzienrats*, see Kirsten Belgum, "Critique of the Parvenu Interior: Friedrich Spielhagen and

Eugenie Marlitt," chapter 4 in *Interior Meaning: Design of the Bourgeois Home in the Realist Novel*, German Life and Civilization 9 (New York: Peter Lang, 1992), 103–27.

[63] It is not mere coincidence that Marlitt's madwoman bears the same name as Charlotte Brontë's madwoman in *Jane Eyre* (1847; first translated into German 1848).

[64] E. Marlitt, *Goldelse*, vol. 8 of *E. Marlitt's Gesammelte Werke* (Stuttgart: Union deutsche Verlagsgesellschaft, 1890), back advertising pages. The identical advertisement for the Werner series recurs repeatedly in volumes from both the Heimburg and the Marlitt series.

[65] Werner, *Vineta*, 362.

[66] Among Werner's collected novels and novellas the long wished-for happy marriage coincides, for example, with 1) restoration of good relations between the manor and the peasants (*Gebannt und erlöst*), 2) the overcoming of national animosity between Poles and Germans and the restoration of neglected estates on the Polish border (*Vineta*), and 3) the overcoming of a workers' rebellion and the restoration of good worker-owner relations (*Freie Bahn* and *Glück auf!*).

[67] An advertisement in *Die Gartenlaube* for the collected works announces that volume 6 has just appeared; *Die Gartenlaube*, no. 24 (1895): 408.

[68] I have been greatly aided in my descriptions of nineteenth-century fashion by C. Willett Cunnington, *English Women's Clothing in the Nineteenth Century* (New York: Dover Publications, Inc., 1990). The description of the early 1870s skirt as a "short bunch puff at the back" is Cunnington's (258). *Heimatklang*, which is bound together with *Held*, presents a similar instance of the making present of Germany's historical past by means of the fashions depicted in the illustrations. A story of a man who with the help of a good woman recovers his German roots, *Heimatklang* takes place in Schleswig-Holstein during the Danish-Prussian War of 1864. With two exceptions, the illustrations in the book depict Nora and Eva, the two central female characters, in fashions keyed to the year in which the book was published in the collected illustrated works, namely the year 1895: on p. 231 we see a woman in a crinoline and mantilla with pagoda sleeves, fashions of the 1860s; on p. 260 Nora and Eva appear in the fashionable hoop skirts of the 1860s only to reappear elsewhere in the novel in the fashions of the 1890s. We can only speculate as to the reason for the inconsistency. It may lie simply in the fact that the illustrations were supplied by two different illustrators. In any case, despite the two historically accurate illustrations, the force of the majority of the illustrations is, as in the case of *Held der Feder*, to evoke a transhistorical present for the reader of 1895. See E. Werner, *Ein Held der Feder, Heimatklang*, illus. René Reinicke and Th. Rocholl, vol. 6 of *E. Werner's gesammelte Romane und Novellen. Illustrierte Ausgabe* (Leipzig: Ernst Keil's Nachfolger, n.d.). All subsequent references to this volume will appear parenthetically in the body of the text as *Held* with the pertinent page numbers. Translations of quotations are from the following American translation and are subsequently cited as Shaw: E. Werner, *Hero of the Pen*, trans. Frances A. Shaw (New York: R. Worthington, 1880).

[69] The *Gartenlaube* announces the publication of *Lumpenmüllers Lieschen* in the collected works in issue no. 26 (1891): 448.

[70] *Die Gartenlaube*, nos. 40–52 (1878). See Alfred Estermann, *Die Gartenlaube* (1853–1880 [-1944]), vol. 3, bk. 1 of *Inhaltsanalytische Bibliographien deutscher Kulturzeitschriften des 19. Jahhunderts* (Munich: K. G. Saur, 1995), 199.

[71] In the afterword to Fischer's 1974 edition of *Lumpenmüllers Lieschen*, Michael Koser points out that the treatment of the paper mill in the novel presents early capitalism as an idyll in which social and economic disparities are bridged by personal bonds ("individuelle Verbindung"). He observes, furthermore, that the male aristocratic protagonist succumbs to the bourgeois idyll in the province that is made possible by capital. See Koser, Afterword, *Lumpenmüllers Lieschen*, 247–48.

[72] The novel elsewhere signals Heimburg's reading of Freytag's perennially best-selling *Soll und Haben* (1855), where a character speaks of family affairs as "ein wahrhaftes Chaos . . . Juden, Mäkler" (in a perfect chaos — Jews, money-lenders), with mortgage upon mortgage. See W. Heimburg, *Lumpenmüllers Lieschen*, illust. R. Wehle, vol. 2 of *W. Heimburg's gesammelte Romane und Novellen*, 2nd ed. (Leipzig: Ernst Keil's Nachfolger, n.d.), 133, and W. Heimburg, *A Maiden's Choice* (New York: R. F. Fenno & Company, 1899), 148. On Freytag's *Die Ahnen* as a sentimental saga of class and nation, see Lynne Tatlock, "'In the Heart of the Heart of the Country': Regional Histories as National History in Gustav Freytag's *Die Ahnen* (1872–80)," in *A Companion to German Realism (1848–1900)*, ed. Todd Kontje (Rochester, NY: Camden House, 2002), 85–108.

[73] See also Jennifer Drake Askey's essay in the present volume for information on the socialization of girls with regard to gender roles and national identity and affiliation.

[74] Nancy R. Reagin, *Sweeping the German Nation: Domesticity and National Identity in Germany, 1870–1945* (Cambridge: Cambridge UP), 2.

II. Niche Markets, Reading Socialization, and Gender: Girls as Consumers of Literature, Nation, and Canon

5: A Library for Girls: Publisher Ferdinand Hirt & Sohn and the Novels of Brigitte Augusti

Jennifer Drake Askey

THE COVER OF THE SECOND EDITION of Brigitte Augusti's *Die Erben von Scharfeneck* (1888; The Heirs of Scharfeneck) consists of a tableau of what can be termed the national domestic (fig. 5.1). In the center of the tableau stands a mother wearing a dark shawl, indicating mourning, with her hand on the head of her son, a young soldier, to whom she is giving her blessing. The soldier wears a saber at his side and holds a helmet bearing a skull and crossbones, a marker of the dedication of his life to death for his country. In the background another soldier in the same early nineteenth-century uniform sits on his horse and blows into a regimental bugle, calling the young soldier away from his mother, his little dog, and his home, and into battle. This farewell is framed by additional images that embed the domestic scene within the context of the nineteenth-century discourses on nationalism and gender. The bust of Queen Luise, Prussia's queen from 1797 to 1810 and a figure of central importance to the novel, hovers above mother and son. The queen is framed in turn by two cherubs, and her position in the "heavens" of the book cover accurately reflects her status as a secular saint in nationalist German histories. Beneath the parting scene is the author's name, framed by two Iron Crosses, which add an additional martial flair to the cover.

Queen Luise's presence on the cover of *Die Erben von Scharfeneck* sanctifies both the domestic sacrifice depicted here and the general call to national sacrifice that permeated national discourse at the time of the book's publication. The deceased queen blesses the mother's sacrifice of her son and the young man's willingness to sacrifice his own life. Upon reading the novel, the reader will realize that this dedication to Luise is, indeed, the central point of the book. Her blessing of the mother and son does not represent any particular scene in the book but rather conveys the publisher's eagerness to frame the contents of the book within the larger context of war and sacrifice. These constitute the destiny of the German people, the image suggests, and the suffering of the women

Fig. 5.1. Cover, *Die Erben von Scharfeneck*, 1888 (Ferdinand Hirt & Sohn, Leipzig). Courtesy of and reproduced by Jennifer Askey.

on the home front is just as nationally significant as the physical sacrifice of life on the battlefield.

Die Erben von Scharfeneck was the final volume in a series commissioned by Leipzig publisher Ferdinand Hirt & Sohn from Brigitte Augusti, and each of the five novels in the series is concerned to a degree with crafting a national story pertinent to the lives of young women. By depicting Queen Luise as the guardian angel of Prussian families on the cover of this final volume, the publisher asserts the symbolic importance of girls and women for the reader's understanding of Germany's cultural and historical significance.

Ferdinand Hirt & Sohn and the Commission to Augusti

Ferdinand Hirt & Sohn commissioned Brigitte Augusti (pseud. for Auguste Plehn [1839–1930]) to write *An deutschem Herd* (On the German Hearth) in the 1880s. The series is consciously modeled on the historical fiction of Gustav Freytag, but foregrounds the lives of German girls and young women.[1] In the publisher's foreword to the thirteenth edition of volume one, *Edelfalk und Waldvöglein* (Noble Falcon and Bird of the Woods), Hirt & Sohn explains its desire to create literature for young people in the manner of Gustav Freytag:

> Der große Gedanke, der Freytags *Ahnen* zugrunde lag: ferne Zeiten deutscher Vergangenheit lebendig zu machen, trockene Zahlen und tote Namen mit Fleisch und Blut zu bekleiden — gab uns die Anregung, ähnliches auf bescheidnerem Gebiet zu versuchen und die Jahrhunderte deutscher Geschichte vom Mittelalter bis zur Neuzeit für Gemüt und Verständnis der Jugend dichterisch zu gestalten.[2]

At the same time as Hirt & Sohn commissioned Augusti to write *An deutschem Herd* for girls, it also asked Oskar Höcker to write a similar series for boys. His four-volume series, *Das Ahnenschloß* (1879–81; The Ancestral Castle), covered the same historical ground as Augusti's series and focused on the adventures of young male protagonists.[3]

As these commissions reveal, the publishing house Hirt & Sohn was interested in capitalizing on the popularity of historical novels in the second half of the nineteenth century as well as in creating, perpetuating, and profiting from a gendered national reading market. The German book market expanded rapidly in the 1860s, '70s, and '80s, accompanied by increased market segmentation and differentiation. In this growing market, the portion devoted to youth literature grew to embrace diversion and entertainment, in addition to the more established pedagogical and didactic fare.[4] In this essay I will look closely at *An deutschem Herd* and explore its contextualization and presentation to young women and their educators by the publishing house. By focusing on one publisher's strategy for creating books for young people and a key example of a series it promoted, I will illuminate the intersection of nationalism, pedagogy, and the book trade in the late nineteenth century.

Since Augusti's commission was to re-create the success of Freytag's *Die Ahnen* (The Ancestors) for a young female readership, a brief overview of this historical novel is in order. Published 1872–80, *Die Ahnen* consists of six volumes that follow the fates and fortunes of various members of the far-flung König family, charting the development of a German national consciousness from the era of the Germanic tribes to the middle of the nineteenth century. Beginning with *Ingo* and *Ingraban*, *Die Ahnen* chronicles the embourgeoisement of German political and economic authority. As in his *Bilder aus der deutschen Vergangenheit* (1859–66; Pictures from the German Past), out of which *Die Ahnen* grew, Freytag focuses less on the lives and deeds of the regents of German-speaking lands and more on the stories of average Germans.

Importantly, again as with *Bilder*, *Die Ahnen* is made up of emotional stories, authentic in their assumed closeness to the lives of common Germans through the centuries, and in general Freytag's works were seen by many as especially appropriate for the burgeoning ranks of female readers. The historian Heinrich von Treitschke declared *Bilder* "eines der seltenen Geschichtswerke, welche von Frauen verstanden und mit Freude gelesen werden können" (one of the rare historical works that women can read and understand).[5] The affective, emotional nature of Freytag's narrative of German cultural history was thought by educators and scholars to be comprehensible to women and suited to their emotional understanding of the world.

The affective nature of the German national community as posited and supported by Freytag in *Bilder* cannot be overstated. Thomas Nipperdey, writing about *Die Ahnen*, has asserted that Freytag was less interested in the rise of the German state and its military might than in the development of the German people toward national consciousness.[6] The *Volk* becomes the subject of national history. As Lynne Tatlock has written, furthermore, *Die Ahnen* showcases not militaristic Prussia, but *affective, emotional* Prussia, a place where horizontal national bonds are formed through shared language, shared history, and shared literature. Tatlock asserts that national consciousness in *Die Ahnen* is "paradoxically, by means of the act of reading, both private and shared."[7] To phrase that differently, *Die Ahnen* as a novel features characters whose bonds with the national community are personal and emotional and experienced through the particularity of their station and their locality. By means of reading these stories of personal national sentiment, the late-nineteenth-century German reader can begin to sense her own feelings of belonging to a shared national community. Thus the affective model of German national consciousness is reinforced and supported through the act of reading. While Tatlock emphasizes the emotional and affective nature of Freytag's national narratives and directs our attention to the "feminine" qualities of both *Bilder* and *Die Ahnen*, Celia Applegate, in an essay on Freytag, emphasizes another salient point about his position in the nineteenth-century pantheon of both historians and fiction writers. She asserts that Freytag, along with folklorist Wilhelm Heinrich Riehl, was the leader of a "pack of pedagogues, pedants, and earnest patriots" in the ranks of "secondary school teachers, amateurs, archivists, antiquarians, and writers of historical fiction and popular history" who were engaged in mythmaking and national invention in the late nineteenth century.[8] She asserts that, while historians (and, I would add, literary scholars) are familiar with German nineteenth-century history as written by the Prussian school, with its "admiration for the victors" and nation-state teleology, we know much less about the popular proliferation of national myths at the level of the non-academic consumer of literature. Freytag's brand of middle-class national sentiment proliferated through his journalistic work as well as through cultural historical and literary works such as *Bilder* and *Die Ahnen;* it existed outside of academic historiography but enjoyed much broader popularity, as Augusti's commission from Hirt & Sohn attests. Applegate maintains that Freytag, in writing *Bilder* and *Die Ahnen*, was committed to education and enlightenment as the best path for Germans to follow to learn and know themselves.[9] His books, "bequeme Hausfreunde" (pleasant family friends) written for the edification and entertainment of the middle class, aimed to promote a cultural nationalism through which all Germans could feel themselves united.[10]

The affective affinity that Freytag's historical novels created between his readers, their region and class within the German community, and the emerging nation-state parallels the pedagogical directives for girls' schools to teach German history not through dates and battles, but instead via biographies of notable Germans and historical sketches of domestic life in Germany at different points in history. A curriculum guide for girls' schools published in 1888 states,

> Durch den glücklichen Umstand, daß die Geschichte unseres engeren Vaterlandes durchgängig zusammenfällt mit der Machtentfaltung eines einzigen edlen Herrscherhauses, dessen sämtliche Glieder sich mit den Schicksalen des von ihnen beherrschten Volkes eng und persönlich verbunden halten, vereinigen sich hier von selbst die Lebensbilder einer Reihe . . . Landesfürsten zu einer nahezu geschlossenen Darstellung der Geschichte des Landes selbst.[11]

In textbooks for girls' schools, biographies of Prussian kings and queens appeared next to vignettes from Freytag's works, nationalist poetry by such authors as Theodor Körner, and correspondence by such luminaries as Goethe — or Goethe's mother. Thus, German history in girls' schools was at its very core cultural rather than military history.[12]

Augusti takes up this challenge in her own writing of German domestic and cultural history in *An deutschem Herd*. Like Freytag she does not narrate the lives of kings and rulers (although such figures are more present in her works than in Freytag's), but draws portraits of the lives of middle-class, Protestant Germans and their experience of war, economic transformation, and changing social expectations. In doing so, the novels in *An deutschem Herd* draw girls into an emotional connection with their fellow citizens, their nation, and its history.

While Freytag drew together disparate regions of Germany in a literary communion of national sensibility, Augusti's *An deutschem Herd* encouraged young women to view themselves — as individuals and as a group — as crucial participants in the progress of German civilization. By following the girls and women of the Maltheim and Fiedler families through five centuries, the young female reader of these novels observes what was commonly referred to in pedagogical literature as the *Kulturarbeit* (here in the sense of cultural contributions) of girls and women: their contributions to the triumph of Christianity (*Edelfalk und Waldvöglein*), to the development of the middle class and its attendant respectability and piety that characterized the merchants of Germany (*Im Banne der freien Reichsstadt* [1886; Under the Banner of the Free Imperial City]), and the differentiation of Germany as a cultural, linguistic, and religious space vis-à-vis Austria and France (*Das Pfarrhaus zu Tannenrode* [1887; The Parsonage in Tannenrode] and *Die letzten Maltheims* [1888; The Last Maltheims]). In each of these novels young women do not so much move the action forward as provide a static representation of Germanness to which the narrative can continually refer. The girls and women in these novels are pious, focused on the well-being of their family, self-sacrificing, and eager to better themselves — in short, regardless of the era Augusti depicts in *An deutschem Herd*, the female protagonists display the characteristics held in highest regard by the nineteenth-century middle class.

By writing historical novels that also present a female-centered narrative of German political and social history, Augusti deviates somewhat from the model provided by Freytag's *Ahnen*. Whereas Freytag appears most interested in narrating the development of Germany's middle class and the role of the German family in the national polity, Augusti anchors her tales in the domestic and emotional lives of her female characters. Her interest in the bourgeoisie is primarily an interest in the lives of middle-class girls and women as they reconcile their domestic responsibilities with their desires and ambitions against the backdrop of political and military reality. The location of her stories largely within the domestic world of women and girls may also explain the more obvious connections between the families in the earlier volumes of the series and their descendants in the final stories. Whereas Freytag's *Ahnen* does not explicitly connect the generations in his tale to one another genealogically, Augusti's series crafts a more cohesive story of the Maltheim and Fiedler families. By covering a narrower time frame than Freytag — the Renaissance to the nineteenth century — Augusti's narrative presents more of a family saga. Children introduced in one volume are frequently found as parents or grandparents in the next. A small ring given to a girl as a remembrance of her soldier father becomes a family token and is passed through generations of the intermarried families, signifying fidelity and honor. This romantic touch (the ring has a blue flower on one side) is one of many in the series, where private romances and domestic life take center stage. Augusti's blurring of the lines between novels of adolescent development (*Entwicklungsromane*), with their romantic plot lines and empathetic figures, and historical novels sets her apart from many of her contemporaries who were writing for girls.[13]

Hirt & Sohn's commission to Augusti reflects the growing importance of the female reading market in the last half of the nineteenth century. Women represented a large portion of the explosion in the German reading public during this era. Women's magazines and family magazines, together with *belles lettres*, made up the category of *Volksschriften* in the catalogs of nineteenth-century publishing houses. This category alone experienced greater than 200% growth between 1865 and 1879 as a result of an increase in overall literacy and women's reading activity in particular.[14] In publishing popular literature of a national, historical nature for girls, Hirt & Sohn surely hoped to cultivate an ever younger female reading demographic, whose national-liberal or, increasingly, nationalist parents would be inclined to amass a library specifically for their daughters. *Mädchenliteratur* — popular literature written specifically for middle-class girls — resembled in many ways (plot, empathetic heroine, domestic values, culture of self-abasement for love and duty) the large assortment of popular literature for women in the *Kaiserreich* and could serve as preparation for engagement as a reader in that literary marketplace.[15]

As publishers of school textbooks as well as popular fiction for young people, the Hirt & Sohn publishing house could capitalize on mutually reinforcing narratives of German history that not only explained to girls the history of their nation, but also the role that providence saw for them in the national community. The goal of this correlation between the narrative of German national development in schoolbooks and its representation in popular literature was to develop a national(ized) reader community of culturally and historically informed young women. And although Hirt & Sohn relied on Freytag's national-liberal brand of historical fiction as a template for commercial success, their catalog reflected an increasingly nationalist and militaristic emphasis in the years following

1871.[16] The emphasis in Augusti's series (and Höcker's, for that matter) on the Protestant side in the Thirty Years' War, on the justifications for animosity toward the so-called historical enemy, France, as well as on the personal qualities of Prussia's ruling family reflect a conservative, Protestant, Prussian-centered view of divinely ordained German greatness.

That this intentionality can be ascribed to the publishers as well as to the authors is clear from the act of commissioning itself. Nineteenth-century publishers took an active role in many of the books bearing their imprint. Rarisch writes of the "Vermittlerrolle des Verlegers" (mediating role of the publisher), and Georg Jäger, in *Geschichte des deutschen Buchhandels*, relates that Hirt & Sohn took a very active editorial role, with Ferdinand Hirt himself seen as "geistiger Mitschöpfer" (intellectual co-creator) of many of his house's most popular titles.[17] By working together with teachers and other educators, the publishing house determined the parameters of creative expression for its authors, especially those authors whose livelihoods depended on high volume and/or commissions like the one given to Augusti. Russell Berman writes of the market constraints under which authors worked during the development of the modern book trade in Germany in the nineteenth century and remarks, "despite some counter-tendencies (including the promise of aesthetic autonomy), literary production becomes subject to the dictates of capitalist production, gradually after the middle of the 18th century and explosively in the late 19th century."[18] While none of the correspondence between Brigitte Augusti and her publisher has survived, the books themselves, as well as their framing, packaging, and marketing by Hirt & Sohn demonstrate the degree to which the publishing house itself sought to create literature that served the captive market represented by the readers of their school textbooks and other pedagogical works.[19]

Hirt & Sohn, along with the publishing house Velhagen & Klasing in Bielefeld, enjoyed a virtual monopoly in the schoolbook market in the mid-to-late nineteenth century.[20] Hirt & Sohn's *Volksschule* offerings were singular in their differentiation and segmentation as well as their success. They offered textbooks specially edited for small schools in "einfachen Verhältnissen" (modest circumstances); for schools with Lutheran student populations, with Roman Catholic students, and with "mixed" student bodies; and within each of those types of schools, readers for at least three different grade levels.[21] Book catalogs of the era classified youth literature like Augusti's *An deutschem Herd* not as *belles lettres*, but as pedagogy, making the inclusion of youth literature in Hirt & Sohn's portfolio an obvious choice. Youth literature supplemented and complemented the publisher's main pedagogical offerings by shoring up the nationally oriented, gendered, and class-conscious window on German culture and history advocated by the education ministry in Prussia and followed in schools. The young women who constituted Hirt & Sohn's readership were engaged in the process of national self-betterment and could be expected to constitute a predictable market segment for such educational and entertaining titles in Hirt & Sohn's catalog as *Vater Carlets Pflegekind* (1891; Father Carlets Foster Child), translated from the French (*La fille des Carilès*, by Joséphine Colomb) by Clementine Helm; *Kunstbetrachtung* (1910; Art Appreciation) by Wilhelm Waetzoldt; and *Im Wechsel der Tage: Unsere Jahreszeiten im Schmuck von Kunst und Dichtung. Eine Auswahl aus den Werken unserer besten vaterländischen Dichter* (1890; As the Days Change: Our Seasons Adorned by Art and Poetry. Selections from the Works of our Greatest Patriotic Poets), by Adolf Brennecke.[22]

Brigitte Augusti's *An deutschem Herd*

An deutschem Herd covers German cultural history from the traveling bards of the Middle Ages to Queen Luise and the victory of Prussia and its allies over Napoleon's forces in the early nineteenth century. Throughout the series Augusti highlights the common bond that Germans feel for their national community across time and across space, and in doing so assumes the well-developed bonds of national feeling that Freytag's work endeavors to create and justify. For example, in the third volume of her series, *Das Pfarrhaus zu Tannenrode*, which tells the story of the Fiedler and Maltheim families during the Thirty Years' War, Augusti contrasts the German cities of Magdeburg, Augsburg, Leipzig, and Nuremberg with the Austrian cities of Vienna and Prague. Each German city and town along the way suffers both the same fear and the same sense of loyalty to and love for its particular corner of Germany. Because of this shared fear and loyalty, the geographically dispersed characters are drawn together in the minds and hearts of the readers. Protestants in the small village of Tannenrode pray and fear for the fate of Magdeburg; the fall of Magdeburg to Austrian General Tilly is followed directly by the description of the fate of Leipzig.

In this manner, Augusti's series mirrors the aspirations of Freytag's own: she depicts individual German families in disparate locations all experiencing the same sense of attachment and belonging to a national community. The shared experience of feeling oneself to be German draws this community together both in the narrative itself and in the mind of the reader. In chapter 7 the characters in Leipzig hear that Magdeburg has fallen, and chapter 8 begins with a description of the siege of Magdeburg as seen through the eyes of school children. Augusti's narrative strategy thus resembles the "gloss on the word *meanwhile*" of which Benedict Anderson writes.[23] Collective history — the collective myth of belonging for people who do not "organically" belong together — is presented here as the history of shared threat and shared suffering. Additionally, the Protestant lands around Leipzig and Magdeburg are fundamentally contrasted with Vienna and Prague and Roman Catholic Austria in a way that defines "German" as narrowly as the *Kleindeutsch* solution of 1848.[24]

Histories of German children's literature in the nineteenth century place Brigitte Augusti's historical novels in a category unto themselves. Hermann Köster's *Geschichte der deutschen Jugendliteratur* (1927) proclaims Augusti's works, alongside those of Johanna Spyri and Ottilie Wildermuth, superior to mere *Backfischliteratur* (literature for teenage girls), given Augusti's concentration on historical subject material and factual research.[25] The recently published *Handbuch zur Kinder- und Jugendliteratur* maintains that her melding of historical fiction with the traditionally feminine coming-of-age story made her unique among writers of fiction for girls.[26] There, Gisela Wilkending contends that Augusti's cultural-historical novels provided opportunities to narrate autonomous female agency, especially during those times when men were away for crusades, war, or trade.[27] While the centrality of girls' and women's lives to Augusti's series remains unquestionable, this focus on women's activity does not in fact represent a radical alternative to more conservative visions of girls and women in *Backfischliteratur*, for example, or other traditional genres of literature for girls.

True to Augusti's commission, *An deutschem Herd* shows the wife and daughter of the burgher and the lower nobleman seen in Freytag's pages, but she places them in a fully realized domestic setting, where their independent activity — such as that of Frau Fiedler in *Die Erben von Scharfeneck* — can involve running an estate or household. More importantly, the internal struggles and hopes and loves of these girls and women take center stage. Augusti's historical subject matter dictates that while the female characters do not or cannot *carry* the plot forward (because, after all, they are not going to war, or to the university, or away on business), their emotional struggles, romantic entanglements, and family dramas provide the drama and suspense of the volumes, as well as reveal the essential lesson of the histories (in Höcker's *Ahnenschloß*, for example, there is by contrast more fighting and "action"). Her work provides models for female behavior that demonstrate how a woman's circumscribed life within the domestic sphere contributed to the health and cohesion of the nation.

Gabriele Fiedler, the protagonist in *Die Erben von Scharfeneck*, which is set in the era of Queen Luise and the Wars of Liberation, can serve as an illustration of the national significance of domestic femininity in Augusti's work. Gabriele serves Queen Luise as a lady-in-waiting, and her interactions with the queen function as a primer for the behavior of middle-class girls and women. As a girl she flirted with a French nobleman on the run from the Terror, but as she grows up and into her awareness of her role as the symbolic representative of the German home and family — a role her mother plays to perfection — Gabriele rejects her fascination with the Frenchman and his country. She tells the count upon meeting him years later,

> Einst wäre es Ihnen nicht schwer geworden, das unerfahrene Kind für sich zu gewinnen, aber damals wollten Sie nur das vermeintliche, reiche Erbe erwerben; das thörichte, kleine Herz galt Ihnen nichts. Jetzt liegt zwischen dem Günstling des Kaisers Napoleon und der Freundin der Königin Luise eine Kluft, die durch nichts auszufüllen ist; nie könnte ich daran denken, dem Feinde meines Vaterlandes meine Hand zu reichen.[28]

Gabriele has learned the importance of her role as a symbolic protector of the German hearth and home. Her domestic activities, whether in service of the queen or her mother, indicate her commitment to her nation and its cultural vision.

Lenore in *Das Pfarrhaus zu Tannenrode* learns a similar lesson. In this novel of the Thirty Years' War, Lenore must learn to deal with the absence of her father, an officer in the army. Augusti's narrative acknowledges the sacrifice Lenore is making and places her own reaction to the temporary loss of her father in the context of a girl's symbolic role in the family as the bearer of sunshine and good cheer.

> War das junge Mädchen auch im Laufe dieses Jahres viel ernster und stiller geworden, war auch der alte sprudelnde Übermut gedämpft durch manche trübe Erfahrung, vor allem durch das völlige Schweigen ihres Vaters, so verbreitete ihre natürliche Lebhaftigkeit, die Frische ihrer Empfindungen doch immer einen Strahl von Wärme und Sonnenschein um sie her.[29]

The young women reading Lenore's tale learned that they were expected to sacrifice their own happiness in service of the greater good of the nation. This sacrifice, however, must be given cheerfully and earnestly, much as a soldier would go off to war with both joy and trepidation in his heart.

Augusti's heroines, regardless of the century in which they lived, embody the feminine ideal that was both created and fueled by the consumption of didactic fiction and schoolbooks for young women. Their stories also reproduce a central conceit of Freytag's novels: the notion that Germany is a country united by books, by literature and schooling, and by knowledge of a common past. Through the act of reading about these fictional girls and their domestic and romantic lives, the readers of *An deutschem Herd* experience themselves as part of the continuity of German girls and women over time and the community of German girls across space. The historical narrative and its consistent focus on the qualities and duties of German women through the centuries support the broader mission of the publishing house by subtly showing that by reading about the German past — through books and literature, that is — a young woman learns who she is and what role she is to fulfill in her nineteenth-century context.

Hirt & Sohn's Catalog: A World of Education and Entertainment

Ferdinand Hirt & Sohn's expansion into the market of entertaining literature for girls and young women reveals the profitability of the combination of nationalism and pedagogy, duty and entertainment. The publishing house displayed a particular interest in young female readers and capitalized on its solid footing in the schoolbook market to create historical and domestic narratives for girls that reflected the prevailing nationalist sentiment in the imperial era.[30] The expansion also coincided with a growing commitment to public education for girls beyond grade school.[31] Ferdinand Hirt had been a *Sortimentsbuchhändler* and *Verleger* (bookseller and publisher) in Breslau, dividing his attention between the two endeavors, since the 1830s. In the 1860s he made the decision to focus on publishing for the school and youth market, and his son Arnold opened up a second office, Ferdinand Hirt & Sohn, in Leipzig. The decision to concentrate on publishing rather than *Sortiment* (retail books) was part of a general trend in the book industry.[32] Additionally, Hirt & Sohn now focused on *Jugendliteratur* and school textbooks, letting earlier experiments in *Kinderliteratur* fall by the wayside.[33]

By endeavoring to create versions of Freytag's *Ahnen* for German girls and boys, Hirt & Sohn aimed to emulate the critical and financial success of Freytag's series. As Royal Gettmann observes in his study of the British publishing industry in the Victorian era, publishers were in general attracted to manuscripts and projects similar to works already enjoying commercial success.[34] Freytag's works certainly fell into this category. By commissioning a series for girls and young women and a separate series for boys, Hirt & Sohn was also participating in the wider European publishing trend of differentiating and segmenting markets along class and gender lines. Jason Pierce writes that by the 1870s British periodicals differentiated their reading audience by addressing boys and girls separately, rather than "children" all together.[35] Wilkending remarks, furthermore, that the youth literature market in the 1860s was no longer focused solely on *Erziehung* (schooling), but also on *Unterhaltung* (entertainment). In this vein publishers sought to entertain boys and girls separately by providing them with stories tailored to their class and gender.[36] From the earliest advertising materials put out by the Leipzig branch, Hirt & Sohn designated its titles with such markers as: "Für Mädchen von 6 bis 10

Jahren" (for girls between six and ten), "Für Mädchen von 10 bis 14 Jahren" (for girls between ten and fourteen), "Für Mädchen von 12 bis 15 Jahren" (for girls between twelve and fifteen), "Für Kinder von 10 bis 14 Jahren" (for children between ten and fourteen), "Für die Jugend" (for youth), and "Für die reifere Jugend" (for older youth).[37] Hirt & Sohn's catalog of books for youth, as well as the proliferation of such gender-segregated periodical publications as Thekla von Gumpert's *Das Töchteralbum* (Album for Daughters) and *Herzblättchens Zeitvertreib* (Little Sweetheart's Diversions), and the popular *Backfisch* genre (for girls on the cusp of marriageability but with no idea of how to behave as a lady), popularized by Clementine Helm, provide evidence of successful gender segmentation in the youth literature market in Germany during the second half of the nineteenth century.[38]

The numbers for sales included in the *Geschichte des deutschen Buchhandels im 19. und 20. Jahrhundert* demonstrate that Hirt & Sohn enjoyed tremendous success in the German school textbook market.[39] Emil Wohlfarth, writing in 1926, commented that Ferdinand Hirt enjoyed a certain amount of good fortune in his publishing business due to his childhood friendship with the future *Kultusminister* (Minister of Culture) Heinrich von Mühler and his association with *Regierungs- und Schulrat* Bock (Privy and School Councilor), who also wrote school textbooks.[40] In addition to the perennial pedagogical favorite, Ernst von Seydlitz's *Geographie* (Geography), Hirt & Sohn published German readers, English vocabulary books, and historical texts for *Volksschulen, Mädchenschulen,* and *Bürgerschulen* (public primary schools, girls' schools, and public secondary schools for boys).[41] Pedagogical guidelines and sample curricula for Prussia's *Mädchen- und Töchterschulen* (girls' and daughters' schools) emphasized just the sort of emotional historical narrative for girls' learning in which Freytag specialized and which Augusti sought to recreate. Publishing popular youth literature that narrated women's and girls' lives in Germany within the nationalist context of the curriculum guidelines guaranteed Hirt & Sohn a receptive audience.

A publishing house like Hirt & Sohn had several options at its disposal for advertising its books to the target market of middle-class girls. The books themselves served as vehicles for advertising. The volumes in the series *An deutschem Herd* were bound and lavishly illustrated, thus alerting prospective buyers and readers to the quality of the product and its contents. Detailed and attractive bindings projected the image of the pre-industrial, custom-bound libraries of earlier eras and suggested that the book at hand was not a mass-produced commodity.[42] Hirt & Sohn placed particular value on the outward appearance, bindings, and illustrations of its youth literature volumes. In particular its books were characterized by original woodcuts by such well-known artists as Hugo

Bürkner and Ferdinand Koska that were produced in the in-house printing facilities.[43]

The illustrations on the front cover and inside the book depict central historical events treated in the book surrounded by a stamped and gilt border. Augusti's series in particular boasts elegant cover art which, in addition to appealing to the class-consciousness of the purchaser with a gilt and stamped binding, addressed the reading girl directly by displaying the centrality of girls to the story, the pedestal on which these girls were placed, and potentially the excitement they might experience in these pages. The *Prachtausgaben* (deluxe editions) of *An deutschem Herd* were likely purchased by adults for young women to read and display on their shelves. The presence of these books on a girl's shelves showed visitors in the family home that she was a proper young lady who not only took care to educate and edify herself in her leisure time, but was sensitive to her representational role in the family economy — or at least a girl whose parents wished her to appear so.

Furthermore, Hirt & Sohn specifically addressed parents and educators themselves in Augusti's books. In the foreword to the 1889 printing of *Die Erben von Scharfeneck*, the publisher writes,

> Als wesentlichen Zweck dieser neuen Schriften Brigitte Augustis hatten wir unsere Absicht bezeichnet: der süßlichen und ebenso reichlich, als oft zweck- und planlos aufschließenden Mädchenliteratur eine wesentliche Vertiefung durch einen weitangelegten kulturgeschichtlichen Hintergrund zu geben, und einsichtige Eltern und Erzieher um die Förderung unseres Unternehmens gebeten.[44]

In these lines, the publishing house conveys its desire to pique and retain the interest and support of parents and educators who bought or recommended this book. As with the decorative bindings, the advertisements in the back pages of the volumes of *An deutschem Herd* address both the purchasers and the readers of these books.

The modeling on Freytag's series and the degree of historical accuracy to which Augusti's series aspired indicate the importance that Hirt & Sohn placed on winning the minds and pocketbooks of parents and educators. In the publisher's foreword to many volumes of Augusti's series as well as in author notes within the novels themselves, care is taken to demonstrate a semi-scholarly adherence to source material and historical accuracy. Freytag's work is openly cited as a source and inspiration, and Augusti herself notes when she must deviate from the accurate historical record in order better to accommodate the flow of her fictional narrative. She remarks, for example, in *Das Pfarrhaus zu Tannenrode* that she includes Harsdörffer's seventeenth-century literary society the "Blumenorden, oder die Gesellschaft der Pegnitzschäfer" (Order of the Flowers, or the Society of the Pegnitz Shepherds) several decades too early in her narrative when she describes a literary circle in which one of her characters is involved.[45] In keeping with the overall pedagogical priorities of the publishing house, Augusti's work positions itself as both entertaining and historically accurate. Additionally, parents and other purchasers of the books could be certain that Hirt's leisure reading titles for girls would be politically conservative and nationally minded.

, In the back pages of each volume of *An deutschem Herd* there are as many as ten pages of advertisements for other Hirt & Sohn titles. Augusti's *An fremdem Herd* (On the Foreign Hearth), a novel series in which foreign lands and customs form the centerpiece, finds mention here as well as works by Clementine Helm and schoolbooks, such as French and English grammar books (see figs. 5.2 and 5.3). The number of these pages alone provides an indication of the success of the advertising strategy of the publishing house and the resulting sales of youth literature, as well as nonfiction educational books suitable for young people. By virtue of the framing provided by the publishing house — the attractive cover and gilt edges, the foreword, and the advertisements for "analogous" books in the back pages — Augusti's *An deutschem Herd* belongs to a literary and pedagogical universe that views Germany as central to European civilization and girls and women as symbolically crucial to the cultural and economic success of the middle class.

The books advertised in the back pages of Augusti's historical novels cohere around Germany as the center of experience and relevance for girls and around the importance of a girl's role within the home as representative of her family's station and commitment to national ideals. Such travel literature as that describing the adventures of Lady Annie Brassey by Anna Helm —"Die in vielen Auflagen vorliegenden Schriften der kürzlich auf hoher See verstorbenen kühnen Weltumseglerin Lady Brassey haben durch die inhaltliche Gediegenheit, wie auch die vornehme Ausstattung allenthalben in den gebildeten Familien beste Aufnahme gefunden" (Available in multiple editions, the writings of the intrepid world traveler Lady Brassey, who recently died on the high seas, have found universal acceptance among educated families, due to the high quality of their content, as well as their elegant appearance),[46] or *Samoafahrten: Reisen in Kaiser Wilhelms-Land und Englisch-Neu-Guinea* (1888; Samoan Journey: Travels to Emperor-Wilhelms-Land and British New Guinea), by Otto Finsch, which was advertised in the back pages of the 1889 printing of *Die Erben von Scharfeneck*, continued the national narrative set forth in Augusti's books by providing the contrast necessary to see Germany as a distinct nation, separate from other cultural entities in Europe and the world and significant in its achievements.

If *An deutschem Herd* taught young women how to see themselves, in their circumscribed domestic lives, as participating in a larger national whole, the above titles and *An fremdem Herd* showed readers how that

Fig. 5.2. Richly illustrated books for young girls, advertisements.
In *Die Erben von Scharfeneck*, 1888. (Ferdinand Hirt & Sohn, Leipzig)
250. Courtesy of and reproduced by Jennifer Askey.

national whole differed from the exotic world outside Germany.[47] Other
books advertised by Hirt & Sohn reinforce the image of civilized Germany
vis-à-vis the rest of the world — for example Ferdinand Hirt's *Geographische
Bildertafeln* (Geographic Illustrations), Julius Pederzani-Weber's *Der Ein-
siedler von Sankt Michael: Erlebnisse eines Deutschen an der Nordwestküste
von Amerika* (1895; The Hermit of St. Michael: Experiences of a German

Fig. 5.3. Books for young children, language lesson books, advertisements. In *Die Erben von Scharfeneck*, 1888. (Ferdinand Hirt & Sohn, Leipzig) 252. Courtesy of and reproduced by Jennifer Askey.

on the Northwest Coast of America), and *Kynstudt: Die Siege der Helden der Marienburg über die Heiden des Ostens* (1888; Kynstudt: The Victories of the Heroes of Marienburg over the Heathens of the East). Given that Hirt & Sohn published the oft-reprinted geography text by Ernst von Seydlitz, it comes as no surprise that many of its literary offerings required knowledge of the physical space of the world as well as reflected Germany's centrality to that space.

Conclusion: A Publisher as Creator of a National Reading Community

The schoolbooks in Hirt & Sohn's catalog represent the wisdom of the day on the subject of educating young women, which saw the domestic activities of young, middle-class women as *constituting* their national involvement. By demonstrating their adherence to supposedly age-old German feminine ideals, young middle-class women of the nineteenth century could participate in the affective bonds of national community because they recognized themselves, their own experiences, and their communities' values in the stories. By experiencing herself as one young woman among the many who read and experienced Germany through the literary and pedagogical offerings of the publishing house Hirt & Sohn and by seeing her small, domestic environment reflected and reinforced in an equally small world of literary offerings provided by the same publisher, the young reader was encouraged to accept the truth and totality of the world in which she lived and the national cultural principles that appeared to guide it.

Thora Goldschmidt's *Bildertafeln für den Unterricht im Englischen* (Illustrations for English Lessons), advertised in the back of Augusti's novels, illustrates this point well. The book advertisement shows a well-appointed, middle-class kitchen full of the latest domestic technology and states that the facing page includes language exercises that, one imagines, helped German girls picture their counterparts in England as very similar to themselves and reinforced the importance and even glamour of the woman's domestic role (see fig. 5.4). The reader sees a woman — labeled number 10, "a cook" — from behind as she stands at the stove and peers into a stock pot. Thus the reader is positioned as the mistress of a not-insignificant dominion with both moral and material authority. She is married and has children. She is the domestic head of a household large enough to merit the kitchen pictured here, with its sink and stove and gas oven, and manages a staff whom she must train, pay, and reward. The purchasing and administering of the housewares and foodstuffs destined for the kitchen indicate her commercial power — her domestic activity has economic consequences for her family and the nation — and the necessity

THE KITCHEN.

1. The kitchen-range, a cooking-stove.
2. The oven.
3. The kitchen-hatchet.
4. A pair of tongs.
5. The sauce-pan.
6. A kettle.
7. The flat iron.
8. The pot.
9. The lid, the lid of the pot.
10. A cook.
11. The sieve.
12. A frying-pan.
13. A tea-cloth; a duster.
14. The kitchen-knife, the meat-knife.
15. The dust-pan.
16. A broom.
17. The gas-burner, the gas-bracket.
18. A scoop.
19. A dish-cloth.
20. The water-pipe.
21. The tap.
22. The sink.
23. The dust-pail; an ash-bucket.
24. A tub, a washing-tub.
25. An egg-cup.
26. An egg.
27. A fish-slice; a skimmer.
28. A funnel.
29. The chopper.
30. The rolling-pin.
31. The paste-board; the chopping-board.
32. A mortar.
33. The pestle.
34. A basin, a bowl.
35. The plate-rack, the dresser.
36. A meat-plate.
37. A soup-plate.
38. A jar.
39. A market-basket.
40. The handle.
41. A grater, a nutmeg grater.
42. A mould.
43. The kitchen-table, the dresser.
44. The chopping-block.
45. A clothes-basket.
46. The ironing-board.

Fig. 5.4. For foreign language instruction, English kitchen terms, advertisement. In *Das Pfarrhaus zu Tannenrode*, 1910. (Ferdinand Hirt & Sohn, Leipzig), 232. Courtesy of and reproduced by Jennifer Askey.

of her selflessness and concern for the comfort of others. The long list of kitchen items presented on this single page, forty-six in all, also serves as a type of psychological carrot for the girls reading educational fiction. This domestic empire, the Hirt & Sohn advertising vehicle suggests, awaits the young lady who has successfully integrated the expectations of her nation and social class into her vision of her life and future.

Regardless of the royal friendships and proximity to history-in-the-making presented in Augusti's books, her readers could expect a life of unrelenting domesticity — at least if they sought approval in the eyes of their educators, parents, and clergy. The fifth edition of Goldschmidt's English book illustrates the range of female pupils' future lives in its table of contents. While the book includes information on the body, diseases, and the Royal Navy, it begins with illustrations and exercises on "The School-Room," "The Sitting-Room," "The Dining-Room," "The Bed-Room," and "The Kitchen," tracing the trajectory of a schoolgirl's life from her present position at a school desk to the moment when she, too, will have a kitchen and sitting room to manage and appoint.[48]

If the books on her shelves were to provide any indication of who she was and who she might become, then leisure reading titles and schoolbooks could signal her role as representative of her class and her nation, for they represented not only knowledge the girls were to possess, but also demarcated the parameters of their sphere of activity. As such, Hirt & Sohn's pedagogically and nationally minded catalog both created and served a gendered, nationalized reading market of young women. By mutually reinforcing texts and contexts, the publisher crafted a thoroughly German and middle-class world in which girls and women functioned as guarantors of cultural continuity and cohesion across space and time.

The purchase and consumption of these books also helped constitute the reading girls as members of a gender and class — for they were reading literature appropriate to their age and station — and as a market for pedagogical material and didactic fiction. The girls who read *An deutschem Herd* also read Hirt & Sohn's English language textbooks and geography primers in school. They learned about their place as women in Germany and Germany's place in the world through the act of reading and the consumption of literature within the larger context of didactic fiction. Hirt & Sohn's project to adapt Freytag's popular *Ahnen* twice — once for boys and once for girls — evidences a desire to create and support a gendered market for nationalist youth literature.

The publishing and advertising model pursued by Hirt & Sohn also helped structure the literary field in which authors like Augusti — with or without a commission from the publisher — had to operate. The commissioning of *An deutschem Herd* from Augusti — and *Das Ahnenschloß* from Höcker — reflected the publishing house's vast catalog of conservative, nationally minded pedagogical works. These school textbooks adhered to the Prussian educational ministry's guidelines for school curricula and glorified German culture over France; placed German culture in a central, civilizing role within European history; and lifted bourgeois women onto a pedestal, from which remove they could not only execute their domestic responsibilities, but also symbolize the respectability, piety, and commitment to self-betterment that were the hallmarks of nationally minded Germans in the second half of the nineteenth century.

Notes

[1] Brigitte Augusti, *An deutschem Herd: Kulturgeschichtliche Erzählungen aus alter und neuer Zeit mit besonderer Berücksichtigung des Lebens der deutschen Frauen* (Leipzig: Ferdinand Hirt & Sohn, 1885–88), vol. 1: *Edelfalk und Waldvöglein* (1885); vol. 2: *Im Banne der Freien Reichsstadt* (1886); vol. 3: *Das Pfarrhaus zu Tannenrode* (1887); vol. 4: *Die letzten Maltheims* (1888); vol. 5: *Die Erben von Scharfeneck* (1888). I am working with the 10th edition of vols. 1–4 (1910) and the 13th edition of vol. 5 (1913).

[2] "The great thought at the root of Freytag's *Ahnen* — to make the distant German past come to life, to clothe dry numbers and deceased names with flesh and blood — prompted us to attempt something similar on a more modest level and to present the centuries of German history from the Middle Ages to the recent past in a form appropriate to the temperament and comprehension of youth"; "Vorbemerkung der Verlagsbuchhandlung," in Brigitte Augusti, *Edelfalk und Waldvöglein: Kulturgeschichtliche Erzählung aus dem dreizehnten Jahrhundert* (Leipzig: Ferdinand Hirt & Sohn, 1912), 5. All translations are my own, unless otherwise indicated.

[3] Oskar Höcker, *Das Ahnenschloß: Kulturgeschichtliche Erzählungen für die reifere Jugend* (Leipzig: Ferdinand Hirt & Sohn, 1879–81), vol. 1: *Der Erbe des Pfeiferkönigs* (1879); vol. 2: *In heimlichem Bunde* (1879); vol. 3: *Zwei Riesen der Garde* (1880); vol. 4: *Deutsche Treue, welsche Tücke* (1881). I am working with the 2nd edition of vol. 1 (1885), the 3rd edition of vols. 2 and 3 (1894), and the 8th edition of vol. 4 (1901).

[4] Gisela Wilkending, "Die Kommerzialiseriung der Jugendliteratur und die Jugendschriftenbewegung um 1900," in *Schund und Schönheit: Populäre Kultur um 1900*, ed. Kaspar Maase and Wolfgang Kaschuba (Cologne: Böhlau, 2001), 223.

[5] Qtd. in Lynne Tatlock, "Regional Histories as National History: Gustav Freytag's *Bilder aus der deutschen Vergangenheit* (1859–67)," in *Searching for Common Ground: Diskurse zur deutschen Identität 1750–1871*, ed. Nicholas Vazsonyi (Cologne: Böhlau, 2000), 167.

[6] See Lynne Tatlock, "'In the Heart of the Heart of the Country': Regional Histories as National History in Gustav Freytag's *Die Ahnen* (1872–80)," in *A Companion to German Realism, 1848–1900*, ed. Todd Kontje (Rochester, NY: Camden House, 2002), 88–89.

[7] Tatlock, "'In the Heart of the Heart of the Country,'" 103.

[8] Celia Applegate, "The Mediated Nation: Regions, Readers, and the German Past," in *Saxony in German History: Culture, Society, and Politics, 1830–1933*, ed. James Retallack (Ann Arbor: U of Michigan P, 2000), 38.

[9] Ibid., 47.

[10] Tatlock, "Regional Histories as National History," 161.

[11] "By virtue of the happy circumstance that the history of our particular fatherland generally coincides with the coming to power of one single, noble ruling family, all of whose members feel themselves to be closely and personally bound to the destinies of the people ruled by them, biographies of a series of rulers mesh automatically into a nearly seamless depiction of the history of the country itself"; Preußischer Verein für öffentliche höhere Mädchenschulen, *Allgemeiner Lehrplan für vollentwickelte höhere Mädchenschulen* (Leipzig: G. G. Teubner, 1888), 28.

[12] See also *Deutsches Lesebuch für höhere Mädchenschulen. 8. Teil. 2. Klasse. Ausgabe für Brandenburg*, ed. G. Porger and Eleonore Lemp (Bielefeld: Velhagen & Klasing, 1909), and *Deutsches Lesebuch*, ed. J. C. Paldamus, *Ausgabe D., 3. Teil*, rev. Karl Rehorn (Frankfurt am Main: Moritz Diesterweg, 1903).

[13] Otto Brunken et al., *Handbuch zur Kinder- und Jugendliteratur: Von 1850 bis 1900* (Stuttgart: J. B. Metzler, 2008), 551.

[14] Ilsedore Rarisch, *Industrialisierung und Literatur: Buchproduktion, Verlagswesen und Buchhandel in Deutschland im 19. Jahrhundert in ihrem statistischen Zusammenhang* (Berlin: Colloquium Verlag, 1976), 66–67.

[15] Wilkending, "Kommerzialisierung der Jugendliteratur," 224.

[16] Brunken et al., *Handbuch zur Kinder- und Jugendliteratur*, 611.

[17] Rarisch, *Industrialisierung und Literatur*, 77, and Georg Jäger, "Der Schulbuchverlag," in *Das Kaiserreich 1871–1918: Geschichte des deutschen Buchhandels im 19. und 20. Jahrhundert*, ed. Georg Jäger (Frankfurt am Main: MVB, 2003), 1/2:87.

[18] Russel Berman, "Writing for the Book Industry. The Writer under Organized Capitalism," *New German Critique* 29 (1983): 41.

[19] On Hirt and schoolbooks, see Jana Mikota, "For the Love of Words and Works: Tailoring the Reader for Higher Girls' Schools in Late Nineteenth-Century Germany," in the present volume.

[20] Jäger, "Der Schulbuchverlag," 85.

[21] Ibid., 68.

[22] All of these titles are advertised in the back pages of all five volumes of the 1910 edition of *An deutschem Herd*.

[23] Benedict Anderson, *Imagined Community: Reflections on the Origins and Spread of Nationalism* (London: Verso, 1991).

[24] Augusti, Brigitte, *Das Pfarrhaus zu Tannenrode* (Leipzig: Ferdinand Hirt & Sohn, 1887), 88–92.

[25] Hermann Köster, *Geschichte der deutschen Jugendliteratur*, ed. Walter Scherf, 4th ed. (Braunschweig: Westermann, 1927; Munich-Pullach: Verlag Dokumentation, 1971), 321.

[26] Brunken et al., *Handbuch zur Kinder- und Jugendliteratur*, 35, 559.

[27] Ibid., 571.

[28] "Once upon a time it would not have been difficult for you to win the heart of the inexperienced child, but back then you were only interested in her rumored inheritance — her silly little heart meant nothing to you. Now, however, a huge, unbridgeable gulf lies between you — the favorite of the Emperor Napoleon — and me — a friend to Queen Luise. I could never consider giving my hand to the enemy of my country"; Brigitte Augusti, *Die Erben von Scharfeneck*, vol. 5 of *An deutschem Herd: Kulturgeschichtliche Erzählungen aus alter und neuer Zeit. Mit besonderer Berücksichtigung des Lebens der deutschen Frauen. Für das reifere Mädchenalter* (Leipzig: Ferdinand Hirt & Sohn, 1889), 150.

[29] "Although the young girl had become quieter and more serious during the past year, and although her old effervescent spirit had been dampened by unpleasant experiences — such as the complete silence from her father — there still radiated a ray of warmth and sunshine from her natural liveliness and the freshness of her feelings"; Brigitte Augusti, *Das Pfarrhause zu Tannenrode*, vol. 3 of *An deutschem Herd: Kulturgeschichtliche Erzählungen aus alter und neuer Zeit. Mit besonderer Berücksichtigung des Lebens der deutschen Frauen. Für das reifere Mädchenalter* (Leipzig: Ferdinand Hirt & Sohn, 1889), 107.

[30] Brunken et al., *Handbuch zur Kinder- und Jugendliteratur*, 615.

[31] See James Albisetti, *Schooling German Girls and Women: Secondary and Higher Education in the Nineteenth Century* (Princeton, NJ: Princeton UP, 1988) and Jennifer Askey, "Reading as Women, Reading as Patriots: Nationalism, Popular Literature, and Girls' Education in Wilhelminian Germany" (PhD diss., Washington University in St. Louis, 2003).

[32] Berman, "Writing for the Book Industry," 43.

[33] Brunken et al., *Handbuch zur Kinder- und Jugendliteratur*, 615.

[34] Royal A. Gettmann, "The Author and the Publisher's Reader," *Modern Language Quarterly* 8, no. 4 (1947): 469.

[35] Jason Pierce, "The Belle Lettrist and the People's Publisher; or, The Context of *Treasure Island's* First-Form Publication," *Victorian Periodicals Review* 31, no. 4 (Winter 1998): 360.

[36] Wilkending, "Kommerzialisierung der Jugendliteratur," 230–31.

[37] Brunken et al., *Handbuch zur Kinder- und Jugendliteratur*, 615.

[38] Thekla von Gumpert, *Das Töchteralbum* (Gloglau: Flemming, 1855–1930); Clementine Helm, *Backfischchens Leiden und Freuden* (Bielefeld: Velhagen & Klasing, 1863).

[39] Jäger, "Der Schulbuchverlag," 68.

[40] Emil Wohlfarth, "Ferdinand Hirt" (Vortrag gehalten im Auftrage der Schlesischen Gesellschaft zur Förderung der buchhändlerischen Fachbildung am 18. November 1926 im Saal des Städt. Schulmuseums in Breslau), *Mitteilungen des Provinzial-Vereins der schlesischen Buchhändler in Breslau* 5, no. 12 (1926).

[41] *Ernst von Sedlitzsche Geographie. In 4 Ausgaben. C: Größere Schul-Geographie*, 21st ed. (Breslau: Ferdinand Hirt, 1892). I am working with the 13th printing of this popular textbook.

[42] Wilkending, "Kommerzialisierung der Jugendliteratur," 224.

[43] Brunken et al., *Handbuch zur Kinder- und Jugendliteratur*, 612.

[44] "We had declared as our intention for the central purpose of this new work by Brigitte Augusti to deepen significantly the treacly, and equally copious, purposeless, and aimless girls' literature available by providing a broadly based cultural-historical background and by asking observant parents and educators for their support for our project"; Augusti, *Die Erben von Scharfeneck*, v.

[45] Augusti, *Das Pfarrhaus zu Tannenrode*, 135.

[46] Ferdinand Hirt & Sohn published the German translation of Annie A. Brassey, *Sunshine and Storm in the East, or, Cruises to Cyprus and Constantinople* (London: Longmans, Green, & Co, 1880) as *Sonnenschein und Sturm im Osten: Seefahrten und Wanderungen vom Hyde-Park zum Goldenen Horn, mit besonderer Berücksichtigung Konstantinopels, seines Volkslebens, des Hofes, des Harems u. a. m. Für dt. Leser, vorzüglich Frauen*, trans. Anna Helm (Leipzig: Ferdinand Hirt & Sohn, 1881). Hirt & Sohn also published *Eine Segelfahrt um die Welt an Bord der Jacht "Sunbeam"* (1880; translation of *A Voyage in the Sunbeam, our Home on the Ocean for Eleven Months* [1878]); *Eine Familienreise von 14.000 Meilen in die Tropen und durch die Regionen der Passate* (1885; translation of *In the Trades, the Tropics and the 'Roaring Forties'* [1885]); and *Annie Brasseys letzte Fahrt an Bord des Sunbeams* (1889; translation of *The Last Voyage to India and Australia in the 'Sunbeam'* [1889]).

[47] Brigitte Augusti, *An fremdem Herd: Bunte Bilder aus der Nähe und Ferne mit besonderer Berücksichtigung des häuslichen Lebens in verschiedenen Ländern* (Leipzig: Ferdinand Hirt & Sohn, 1890–93), vol. 1: *Gertruds Wanderjahre* (1890; Gertrud's Journey Years); vol. 2: *Zwillingsschwestern* (1891; Twin Sisters); vol. 3 *Unter Palmen* (1893; Beneath Palm Trees); vol. 4: *Jenseits des Weltmeers* (1893; On the Other Side of the Great Ocean).

[48] Thora Goldschmidt, *Bildertafeln für den Unterricht im Englischen*, 5th ed. (Leipzig: Ferdinand Hirt & Sohn, 1913).

6: For the Love of Words and Works: Tailoring the Reader for Higher Girls' Schools in Late Nineteenth-Century Germany

Jana Mikota

[A]uch für das Lesebuch . . . gilt das Wort, daß das Beste, was der deutsche Unterricht der Schülerin ins Leben mitgeben kann, eine verständnisvolle Liebe zu Worten und Werken unserer Muttersprache ist.

— Karl Wacker, *Deutsches Lesebuch für katholische höhere Mädchenschulen,* 1897[1]

Viel schädlicher ist es aber, unserer Ansicht nach, gar keinen Geschmack am Lesen zu haben. . . .

— Louise Otto-Peters, *Der Genius des Hauses,* 1869[2]

TODAY READERS ARE, as Harro Müller-Michaels formulates it, a "Leitmedium des Unterrichts" (principal means of instruction).[3] They serve the teaching of literature, determining what is read through, for example, the themes emphasized and the choice and nature of the excerpts included from literary works. In the nineteenth century readers likewise played an important role in the literary education of German middle-class girls. Intended for use in school as well as for reading outside of school, these readers were meant to introduce girls to the "right" reading and to accompany them after their schooldays as "reading teachers." The editors hoped that their books would have an enduring effect. Schoolteacher and editor of readers Karl Wacker (1859–1933) emphasizes, for example, in his *Deutsche Lesebuch für katholische höhere Mädchenschulen* (1897; German Reader for Catholic Higher Girls' Schools):

Wurde schon beim zweiten Bande die Hoffnung geäußert, das Buch möge den Schülerinnen auch über die Schuljahre hinaus lieb und wert bleiben, so hat bei der Herausgabe des dritten Bandes diese Hoffnung bestimmend mitgewirkt. Nicht ein Hilfsmittel lediglich

für die Schule möchte dieser dritte Band werden, sondern durch
vielseitige Anregung und durch nachhaltigere Einwirkung auf Geist
und Gemüt den Schülerinnen einen wertvollen Besitz für das Leben
sichern und ihnen noch lange ein wohl befreundetes, genußreiches
Buch bleiben.[4]

Here Wacker points not merely to the significance of German instruction
in girls' schools, that is, the place where the reader is actually put to use,
but also the importance of the reader itself.

At the end of the nineteenth and in the early twentieth century, readers were employed above all in the lower and middle forms and were usually structured so that the readings built upon one another from year to
year in preparation for the upper levels where German instruction was
based largely on the reading of complete, separately published works.
Although instruction in the upper grades relied largely on such texts, even
in these classes the teachers either did not want to or could not forego
readers completely. They were viewed as "sehr wichtige Ergänzungsmit-
tel" (very important supplementary material) and could and — so it was
thought — should be used in the upper grades.[5] In 1897 Wacker formu-
lated the rationale for their employment in these classes in the foreword
to his reader, pointing out that in the upper form too the aim was to cultivate in female pupils a "verständnisvolle Liebe zu Worten und Werken
unserer Muttersprache" (appreciative love of the words and works of our
mother tongue).[6]

The reader was indeed to function as a companion to and teacher
of reading. The forewords in these books emphasize the literary education that the female pupils will receive, that is, the readers aim to
shape girls' literary taste. Literary education was, moreover, important because beginning mid-century, middle-class women assumed
ever more the role of teachers of reading within their families, raising
their children to be habitual readers.[7] Indeed, we see this stepped-
up role for mothers repeatedly in the advice literature from the second half of the nineteenth century. Here women are recognized as
readers themselves, and their function as educators within the family
is legitimated: "Eine würdige Erzieherin, am Besten eine tugendhafte
Mutter, muss die Lectüre junger Mädchen nach ihren Anlagen und
Neigungen wählen," Elise Hohenhausen (1789–1857) told her readers in 1854. "Wo der Verstand vorherrschend ist, strebe man danach,
das Gemüth zu bilden; wo das Gemüth vorherrscht, wähle man Ver-
standeslectüre" (A worthy teacher, preferably a virtuous mother, must
select reading material for young girls according to their talents and
inclinations. When the head dominates, then one should strive to cultivate the heart. When the heart dominates, one should select readings

that appeal to the head.)[8] Mothers were encouraged in these advice books to do their duty to instruct their children.[9]

The concept of the reader emerged in the sixteenth century and indicated "Unterrichtsbücher, die der Vermittlung von Lesen und Lesetechniken dienten" (textbooks that served to impart reading and techniques of reading).[10] The nineteenth-century reader for girls' schools was, however, more than a mere collection of texts that girls were to use to practice their reading. Readers fulfilled a variety of functions, the most important of these being cultural, pedagogical, and social. Furthermore, these anthologies served to socialize pupils *as* readers. Readers offered female pupils a selection from the reservoir of cultural knowledge that transmitted certain social norms and values and thus facilitated the identification of reading girls with their social group; that is, with the aid of the reader the girls acquired knowledge of their particular "Kulturgemeinschaft" (cultural community).[11] Readers in turn helped to constitute that cultural community through their formation of a literary canon of sorts for the school setting.

In higher girls' schools of the nineteenth and early twentieth centuries, German was one of the most important academic subjects, constituting together with religion and history the center of girls' education. Latin and Greek, that is, the subjects with the greatest numbers of hours of instruction in higher boys' schools, were, by contrast, not central to girls' education. Readers served as the most important means of teaching literature in German classes in the lower and middle grades and are thus doubly relevant for a history of late nineteenth- and early-twentieth-century reading socialization: in addition to their teaching of literature, their conception and the selection and presentation of readings in them are critical factors for reconstructing the reading socialization of girls in this period.

This essay will present selected readers from the nineteenth century, highlighting the importance of the reader in general for girls' literary education in this period. In employing the concept "Lesesozialisation" (reading socialization), it relies on the research of the literary scholar Bettina Hurrelmann in this area.[12] Reading socialization — simply put — concerns the way a child becomes a habitual reader of literature. Research in the area of reading socialization examines, among other things, the influence of venues like family, school, or peer group on children's reading behaviors. In analyzing readers, the present article focuses on reading socialization in school settings of middle-class girls in the nineteenth century. A sustained focus on the school venue, which to date has been largely neglected, can ultimately provide insight into late-century cultural formations as they are expressed in gender and indeed into the growing presence of women in the literary marketplace in the early twentieth century.[13]

Nineteenth-century readers were of course significantly shaped both by schools themselves and by publishers. Readers, which were closely connected to the modernizing of the school system, therefore document the changes in girls' schools in the nineteenth century. The Prussian reforms of girls' schools of 1894 and 1908 bracket the most important period for revision of girls' readers in Imperial Germany. From 1894 on there was a state-mandated curriculum for all higher girls' schools. However, even with the new regulations of 1894, girls had no possibility of acquiring the *Hochschulreife* (school-leaving certificate that permits admission to the university). Not until the major reforms of 1908 were girls allowed admission to the *Abitur* (school-leaving examination), and not until then did they thus have the possibility of attending the university. Readers of course responded to these changes. The *Deutsches Lesebuch für höhere Mädchenschulen* (German Reader for Higher Girls' Schools) edited by August Kippenberg (1830–89) will serve below to illustrate some of the changes that occurred in the late nineteenth and early twentieth centuries. As we shall see, a closer look at the editions of this reader reveals that reading selections were repeatedly modified and that the structure of the reader was altered in response to changing times.

Readers appeared in publishing houses that specialized in schoolbooks, and these publishers of course also influenced their makeup. As a rule, the publication of readers was firmly controlled by the state, and the market for schoolbooks itself was subject to strict regulation. However, it appears that readers for girls' schools were not subject to the same kinds of strict controls applied to those for boys' schools. Thus, we can conjecture that the less strict control of schoolbooks allowed the publishers greater freedom that in turn had a significant and, as we will see, sometimes even positive influence on the selection of texts.

The further question arises as to the effects of these readers on the girls who read them. Shifts in the contents of the readers and the teaching of reading in the schools coincide with the entry of women in significantly greater numbers into the literary marketplace; that is, not until women began to receive German instruction that included literary historical and literary aesthetic perspectives did they have the educational basis to develop as writers of literature.[14] While this question of course cannot be answered within the confines of this essay, the following analysis of readers may nevertheless serve to provide the impetus for a fresh look at the importance of girls' education to women's writing and to late-century cultural formations in general.

Schoolbook Publishers and State Control of their Readers

The publication of readers for use in the schools was subject to specific rules in the nineteenth century. Readers for higher as well as for lower schools had to be evaluated and approved by the pertinent ministerial authority. As a result of this control, schoolbooks varied "nicht nur nach Schultypen, Stufen oder Klassen . . ., sondern [mussten] auch nach den Staaten des Deutschen Reiches, in Preußen auch nach Provinzen und Regierungsbezirken, in getrennten Ausgaben hergestellt werden" (not only according to type of school, level or grade . . . but also [had to be] produced in separate editions according to the states of the German Empire, and in Prussia, also according to the province and the administrative district).[15] There was close cooperation between teachers, ministries, and publishers, or, put differently, textbook publishers were distinguished by their proximity to the state, which meant complying with the goal of schools at that time, namely, as Georg Jäger formulates it, "die Nachkommen nach obrigkeitlich gesetzten Normen und Werten zu sozialisieren" (ibid.; to socialize the next generations according to norms and values determined by the authorities).

In Prussia, from October 23, 1817, on, instructional materials that were used and revised for use in higher boys' schools were subject to approval by the pertinent ministry. Elementary and secondary schools as well as private schools were supervised by the provincial governments (ibid.). Teacher conferences made recommendations for new books for high schools, and school inspectors could recommend new books for lower schools. The provincial school boards or the provincial governments had to write recommendations and present them to the ministry. The ministers or other government officials determined then whether the reader could be adopted or not. The *Centralblatt für die gesamte Unterrichtsverwaltung in Preußen* (The Central Paper for the Entire Administration of Instruction in Prussia) is one of the publications that document how this process looked and which instructional materials were authorized for higher boys' schools.

Readers for Prussian girls' schools were technically also subject to the decrees of 1817. It is therefore somewhat strange that not until the mid-1870s were readers for higher girls' schools even discussed in the *Centralblatt* and that, furthermore, not until then was supervision of them demanded there. In 1875, Adalbert Falk (1827–1900), Prussian Education Minister, complained about the widespread failure to observe the pertinent regulations involving textbook adoption in girls' schools:

> Die auf meine Verfügung vom 14. März d. J: . . . eingegangenen Berichte über die im Unterrichtsgebrauche der Volks- und Mittelschulen, sowie der höheren Mädchenschulen befindlichen Lesebücher haben ergeben, daß bei der Einführung derselben die bezüglichen Bestimmungen der Instruction für die königlichen Consistorien, bezw. Provinzial-Schulcollegien, vom 23. October 1817, §. 7. Nr. 4 und die in Gemäßheit derselben erlassenen allgemeinen Verfügungen nicht überall beachtet worden sind.[16]

The question as to the extent to which the readers that had been adopted in girls' schools actually had received official approval remains open. In fact it appears that teachers at higher girls' schools had not consistently adhered to the decrees of 1817.[17] The *Centralblatt* does not in any case provide any specific information on this subject. Only the above-cited complaint of the minister indicates some kind of abuse on the part of girls' schools. We do, however, have evidence of private as well as municipal girls' schools, for example in Bremen, requesting permission to use a particular reader. The woman teacher H. Habenicht, who taught at the higher girls' school of Marie Roselius in Bremen, wrote the following in 1886 to a certain Senator Ehmek in order to gain permission to use the reader of August Kippenberg:

> Da das in meiner Schule bisher gebrauchte Lesebuch von Lücker & Nacke in einigen Teilen den berechtigten Anforderungen für den Unterricht im Deutschen nicht entspricht, so hegte ich schon lange den Wunsch, ein anderes an seiner Stelle einzuführen. In dem neuerdings von Herrn A. Kippenberg herausgegebenen Lesebuch nun ist nach meinem Urteile und dem meines Kollegiums ein allen berechtigten Ansprüchen der höheren Mädchenschule genügender Ersatz geboten, eine Ansicht, die in dem einmütigen Urteile der einschlägigen pädagogischen Presse ihre Bestätigung findet. Auch sind in der Einführung desselben bereits namhafte auswärtige höhere Mädchenschulen vorangegangen. Ich erlaube mir daher die Bitte an die hochlöbliche Schulcommission des Senats, die Einführung des genannten Lesebuchs in meine gestatten zu wollen.[18]

In this letter, Habenicht indicates that Kippenberg's reader, which will be examined below, has already been adopted in schools outside of Bremen. Her letter makes clear that women teachers themselves sought permission to use certain readers. Habenicht justifies her petition here with a criticism of the current reader as well as with reference to reviews in the pedagogical press. Kippenberg meets her requirements, she asserts. Her letter indicates as well that readers were discussed in the various schools. Habenicht's reference to the pedagogical press also deserves notice, for, while the *Centralblatt* largely ignored readers for higher girls' schools, there were in fact references to them in periodicals that focused on women teachers and their pupils, namely in periodicals like *Die Lehrerin* (1883–1924; The Woman Teacher), the main publication for the interests of female teachers and instructors at all levels in Germany and abroad.

However, not until after the decrees of 18 August 1908 did readers for girls' schools come under greater supervision by government officials, thus giving rise to the demand that they be submitted for regular inspection. In 1909 the Prussian government official Regierungskommissar Schwarzkopff demanded greater controls on behalf of the Ministerium der geistlichen, Unterrichts- und Medizinalangelegenheiten (Ministry for Religious, Instructional, and Medicinal Affairs): "Zugleich ordne ich hiermit an, daß bezüglich der Einführung von Lehrbüchern in den Unterrichtsgebrauch bei den höheren Mädchenschulen und den weiter führenden Bildungsanstalten für die weibliche Jugend die gleichen Bestimmungen zur Anwendung gebracht werden, welche die höheren Lehranstalten für die männliche Jugend ergangen sind" (I also hereby decree that regarding the adoption of readers for use in instruction in higher girls' schools and in the institutions devoted to the further education of young women the same stipulations apply that were passed for the institutions of higher education for young men).[19]

In 1909 the *Centralblatt* remarked in the same vein concerning the oversight of textbooks in girls' schools that it had been resolved that readers for higher girls' schools would be collected and that their adoption in schools would be supervised. Additionally schools had to assemble an inventory of adopted schoolbooks. These inventories were supposed to be sent in "nach dem 1. November jedes Jahres an die Auskunftstelle für Lehrbücher des höheren Unterrichtswesens in Schöneberg-Berlin, Grunewaldstraße Nr. 6/7" (every year after the first of November to the Bureau for Readers Used in Higher Instruction in Schöneberg Berlin, Grunewald Street 6/7).[20] In short, supervision and a more strict control of instructional materials used in higher girls' schools did not set in until after 1908. In the nineteenth century, by contrast, readers were hardly regulated at all, and teachers in girls' school enjoyed greater freedom of choice. As mentioned above, it is worth considering then to what extent the editors of readers themselves also took greater liberties in the selection of readings and thus, for example, were open to including contemporary literature.[21]

An inventory of the schoolbooks that were published for use at higher girls' schools between 1 April 1913 and 14 July 1914 provides a sense of the schoolbooks that were eventually state approved. The following excerpt from this inventory includes only those works that in those years were for the first time authorized by the Ministerium der geistlichen-, Unterrichts- und Medizinalangelegenheiten. All of these readers were, as annual school reports from the period indicate, better known by the names of the editors than by their rather bland and uniform titles.

Table 1. Books Approved for the First Time for Girls' Schools
between 1 April 1913 and 14 July 1914[22]

Editor	Reader	Vols.	Place and Publisher
Joh. Hendtmann	*Deutsches Lesebuch, für den Unterricht in der Literaturkunde ausgewählt und herausg. Für den Gebrauch an Lyzeen und Studienanstalten,* bearb. v. E. Keller (German Reader for Instruction in Literature, Selected and Edited for Use in Girls' Secondary Schools, rev. by E. Keller)	3 Pts	
Muff & Dammann	*Deutsches Lesebuch für höhere Mädchenschulen* bearb. v. E. Borkowsky, H. Brinker & L. Korodi (German Reader for Higher Girls' Schools, rev. by E. Borkowsky, H. Brinker, & L. Korodi)	6 Vols.	Berlin: Grote
Plümer, Haupt & Bachmann	*Deutsches Lesebuch für höhere Mädchenschulen.* Neu bearb. v. K. Leimbach, Kl. Bojunga, A. Lentz, W. Tesdorpf (German Reader for Higher Girls' Schools, newly rev. by K. Leimbach, Kl. Bojungs, A. Lentz, W. Tesdorpf)	8 Pts.	
K[arl] Wacker	*Deutsches Lesebuch für Lyzeen und höhere Mädchenschulen.* Unter Mitwirkung v. M. Münch, El. Heinsberger, Cl. Fischer und M. Ignatia Breme bearb. (German Reader for Secondary Schools and Higher Girls' Schools. Rev. with the Assistance of M. Münch, El. Heinsberger, Cl. Fischer, and M. Ignatia Breme)	Edition A: 8 Vols. Edition B: 3 Vols.	Münster: Schöningh

The title pages of these four textbooks make it clear that they have all been revised in response to the school reforms, although a look at their tables of contents reveals that they are by no means uniform in their reading selections.

Some publishers achieved monopolies in the schoolbook market sector. The Ferdinand Hirt publishing house, for example, numbered, along with Velhagen & Klasing, among the most important publishers of schoolbooks in the nineteenth and early twentieth centuries. Hirt published not only readers, but also new and revised editions of geography textbooks by Ernst von Seydlitz, which in 1895 sold one million copies. As Gisela Wilkending notes, revised versions of these textbooks are still used today in German schools.[23] Eduard Bock's *Deutsches Lesebuch* (1871–ca. 1908; German Reader) also numbered among Hirt's successful publications for schools.

A review of Hirt's products makes clear that he did not simply publish readers but schoolbooks in general and that these belonged to a carefully structured marketing strategy that targeted schools.[24] His publishing house offered instructional materials for nearly all kinds of schools. Furthermore, he supplied separate commentaries for individual books to help lighten the load of the teachers. By 1890 Hirt had established a presence in 1,535 schools with thirty-six different textbooks and thus had become one of the most successful schoolbook publishers in Prussia.[25]

Readers for Girls' Schools in the Nineteenth Century

In the first two thirds of the nineteenth century there was a plethora of readers aimed at a female audience. These included readers with such titles as *Lesebuch für die weibliche Jugend* (1841; Reader for Female Youth), *Der Mädchenspiegel: Ein Lesebuch für Mädchen von reiferem Alter* (1829; Mirror for Girls: A Reader for Mature Girls), *Des Mägdleins Dichterwald* (1862; The Little Maiden's Forest of Poets), and *Der Mädchenfreund: Ein Lehr- und Lesebuch für Mädchenschulen* (1807; The Girl's Friend: A Textbook and Reader for Girls' Schools). A closer look at *Der Mädchenfreund* can serve here to illustrate the general character of these earlier readers.

The year-long set of readings in *Der Mädchenfreund* is oriented to girls' moral upbringing. Along with stories like "Das hoffnungsvolle Mädchen" (The Hopeful Girl) or "Die aufrichtigen Mädchen" (The Honest Girls) that demonstrate model behaviors, the reader contains tales of foolhardy, disobedient, and frivolous girls. In the foreword the editor, Bartholomäus Bacher (1773–1827), stresses that "der Mädchenfreund dazu bestimmt [wäre], daß er den Lehrern und Lehrerinnen Veranlassung geben möge, wie sie von der so wichtigen und vielfachen Bestimmung, und von den mannigfaltigen Geschäften des weiblichen Geschlechtes recht oft und recht viel mit Nutzen reden sollen" (the *Girl's Friend* is intended to provide male and female teachers with the occasion to speak quite often and quite a lot and to good effect about the very important and many roles and manifold tasks of the female sex).[26]

Bacher's *Mädchenfreund* adheres to the basic model of Friedrich Eberhard von Rochow's (1734–1805) *Der Kinderfreund* (1776; The Children's Friend). Like Rochow, Bacher set his stories within the experiential horizon of children. The active figures are girls and the situations are based in a bourgeois milieu, that is, a realm that the girl readers knew. The titles of the individual selections highlight a gender-specific education that corresponds in approach to that in literature for children and youth generally in the first half of the nineteenth century. Its exempla are meant both for beginning readers and for older girls. They treat everyday occurrences in girls' lives or criticize childish misbehavior. They consist of fictional, hortative short prose pieces that are supposed to model virtuous living for their readers and to present vicious behavior as a deterrent. Individual virtues such as industry, orderliness, moderation, and thrift are highlighted. The structures of the stories resemble one another: the identification of the protagonist, the narration of the exemplary incident, and the recounting of its outcome and its consequences for the protagonist. Patterns of narration of course vary somewhat: the stories may contrast virtues and vices or they may directly address the girl reader. The following anecdote, "Das dienstfertige Mädchen" (The Girl Who Was Eager to Serve), exemplifies the kinds of stories found in Bacher's reader:

> Marie spielte einst mit vielen Kindern auf der Straße. Da kam ein fremder Mann, und fragte sie freundlich nach dem Wege, den er nehmen müsse, um nach dem nächsten Dorfe zu kommen. Marie trat sogleich hervor, und sagte zu dem Manne: "Ich will Dir den Weg bis zum Dorfe hinaus zeigen, wo Du hernach nicht mehr irre gehen kannst." Sie gieng hierauf mit dem Fremden fort, und wies ihm von ferne die Gegend, wo das nächste Dorf lag. Der Reisende bedankte sich höflich, und wollte dem guten Kinde für seine Mühe ein Trinkgeld geben. Aber Marie nahm nichts, und sagte: "Es hat mich gefreut, daß ich Dir habe einen Gefallen erzeigen können. Lebe wohl, und reise glücklich!" Ein gutes, altes Mütterchen gieng in die Kirche. Es war Winter, und glatt gefroren: es fiel, und konnte nicht wieder allein aufstehen. Liese, ein anderes Mädchen von zwölf Jahren, gieng vorbey, und wurde von dem alten Mütterchen um Beystand angerufen. "Ja," sagte sie, "wenn Ihr mir einen Groschen geben wollet, so will ich Euch wohl helfen." Sie half ihm auch wirklich nicht eher, als bis ihr die alte Frau einen Groschen zu geben versprochen hatte. Pfui der garstigen Habsucht![27]

A moral highlights the lesson at the end of the story. In this manner girls were taught virtues necessary to their future social roles as women. Like Bacher's reader, earlier readers are divided up thematically with the moral and ethical education of the girls in the foreground and with careful attention to their "künftige Bestimmung" (future roles) as wife, housewife, and mother. The catalogue of themes is supposed to serve the girls as a kind of practical self-help (*Lebenshilfe*). It should be noted here, however, that this kind of reader was not conceived only for a female readership, but for boys as well.[28] While Bacher's reader and others like it served pedagogical purposes and also helped to socialize girls as readers, they did not introduce them to the world of literature. Readers like Bacher's in the tradition of Rochow had, however, largely disappeared from use in girls' schools by the last decades of the nineteenth century; meanwhile, in the 1870s the discussion of girls' education began to heat up and girls' schools began to change.

In the last third of the nineteenth century the literary education of girls generally acquired much greater importance, assuming a central place in German instruction. In contrast to earlier readers, the readers conceived in these years introduced girls to (national) literature and were oriented toward literary history and genre. However, the personal virtues that had been emphasized in Bacher's reader and others like it did not disappear entirely from readers; instead the editors emphasized these virtues in their forewords. Lorenz Kellner asserts, for example, in the *Deutsches Lese- und Bildungsbuch für höhere Schulen* (1895; German Reader and Textbook for Higher Schools): "Was die Wahl der Lesestücke anlangt, so war es mein Hauptaugenmerk, aufs sorgfältigste alles zu vermeiden, was Sitte und Glauben gefährden und die Phantasie der Jugend, insbesondere der weiblichen, auf Abwege führen könnte" (Regarding the selection of readings, it was my main intention most carefully to avoid anything that could endanger morality and faith and that could lead youthful imagination — especially that of girls — astray).[29] The editor's remarks provide evidence as to how readings were selected. It was not only their literary aesthetic qualities that mattered, but also their address to gender. Kellner thus points to some of the ways by which a reading canon was formed through school readers.

It was not only girls' schools, however, that underwent changes in this period; the Gymnasium, that is, the boys' school, was also much discussed, and here too German instruction in particular acquired ever greater importance at the end of the nineteenth century. At a conference on schools in December 1890, Emperor William II advocated better German instruction in Gymnasia, emphasizing the importance of reading German literature. Indeed, in 1890 Gymnasia for the first time presented a detailed canon of readings. My research to date indicates that this canon startlingly corresponds with the books generally read in girls' schools.[30]

Like those for boys' schools, the readers for girls' schools include works by Goethe (1749–1832), Schiller (1759–1805), and Uhland (1787–1862), for example. And in girls' readers too, poems by poets of the Wars of Liberation Ernst Moritz Arndt (1769–1860) and Theodor Körner (1791–1813) acquired greater importance in the last third of the nineteenth century.

In the last third of the nineteenth century and in the early twentieth century, readers used in girls' schools usually consisted of multiple volumes; they were explicitly conceived for the setting and purpose of higher girls' schools and, furthermore, displayed regional differences. Additionally, publishers provided supplementary handbooks with explanations for individual reading selections, literary histories, and reference works to accompany their readers. In the appendixes of the readers themselves, the editors often supplied biographical sketches of the authors whose works were included in the reader. These biographical sketches deserve attention in their own right because they too represent a kind of selection: not only did the editors have to choose from among a given author's works, limitations of space meant that they were able to present only a certain amount of information on each author. On the subject of Theodor Fontane (1819–98), for example, Kippenberg's *Deutsches Lesebuch für höhere Mädchenschulen* (1907; German Reader for Higher Girls' Schools) reports,

> Fontane, Theodor, geb. 1819 zu Neu-Ruppin, war ursprünglich Apotheker, widmete sich später ganz der Literatur. Ein längerer Aufenthalt in England und Schottland gab ihm reiche Anregung zu Balladendichtung (Nr. 107). Seine Schilderungen und geschichtlichen Darstellungen ("Wanderungen durch die Mark," Nr. 69, "Der deutsche Krieg von 1866," "Der Krieg gegen Frankreich"), in denen sich Selbstgeschautes und Selbsterlebtes widerspiegeln, zeichnen sich durch große Anschaulichkeit und warmes patriotisches Empfinden' aus. Vielgelesen sind auch seine feinsinnigen Novellen. † 1898.[31]

Among the many omissions in this bibliographical note, we remark in particular the absence of the titles of his novels, especially that of his now best-known novel, *Effie Briest.* Here the emphasis is instead on his nonfiction, journalistic publications, and ballads. The reader itself includes a selection from the fourth volume of Fontane's *Wanderungen durch die Mark Brandenburg* (1882; Walking Tours through the Mark Brandenburg) titled "Im Spreewald" (In the Spree Forest) and the ballad "Archibald Douglas."

It is interesting in this context to compare how women writers are presented in such biographical notes in the appendixes. Often the reader supplies there only the date of birth and death. There are, however, some longer entries. Kippenberg wrote concerning Agnes Franz (1794–1843), for example:

Franz, Agnes (1794–1843), die Tochter eines Regierungsrates in der Provinz Schlesien, erlebte in ihrer Kindheit viel Trauriges: sie verlor ihren Vater sehr früh und fiel im 13. Jahre so unglücklich, daß sie lebenslang kränklich blieb. Ihre geistigen Anlagen entfalteten sich aber um so schöner: der Verkehr mit der Natur regte sie zu ihren ersten Dichtungen an (s. Teil IV, Nr. 8). Ihr Leben ist später, obwohl sie selber in dürftigen Verhältnissen lebte, in aufopfernder Liebe für ihre Familie und für weitere Kreise verflossen. Sie nahm nach dem Tode ihrer Schwester deren Kinder zu sich und gründete im Vertrauen auf Gottes Beistand in Breslau wie schon früher in Wesel für arme Mädchen eine Arbeitsschule, als deren Vorsteherin sie starb. Ihre Gedichte und ihre sinnigen Erzählungen und anmutigen Märchen (s. Teil IV, Nr. 48) haben viel Anklang gefunden.[32]

Whereas Fontane is presented rather drily to readers and his career as an author is traced, Agnes Franz is introduced emotionally through her familial situation. Her "aufopfernde Liebe" (self-sacrificing love) is especially emphasized. Here we find both direct and indirect gender assignment. In the case of Fontane the entry sketches the outside world — it highlights his travels and their influence on his writing. The sketch of the world of Agnes Franz focuses, by contrast, more sharply on the domestic sphere. The entry nevertheless also presents the difficulties that women had in the first half of the nineteenth century. Since Franz not only lost her father, the provider in the (middle-class) family, but was also in poor health, which surely reduced her chances of marrying, she had to earn her own living and worked as a teacher and headmistress. The sketches evaluate Fontane and Franz's writing with such highly gendered words as "feinsinnig" (sensitive) and "anmutig" (charming) respectively, thereby justifying their inclusion in a reader meant particularly for girls.

In the last third of the nineteenth century, the selection of texts within a given reader expanded. Some of these readings provided girls with an introduction to the history of the German people, for example, readings from Gustav Freytag's (1816–95) popular history, *Bilder aus der deutschen Vergangenheit* (1859–67; Pictures from the German Past). Another set of texts connected German instruction to local history or geography. Notably works by such women writers as Marie von Ebner-Eschenbach (1830–1916) and the poet Lulu von Strauß-Torney (1873–1956) also appear among the reading selections in girls' readers. A comparative look at the tables of contents of these readers quickly reveals that the selection of texts was constantly being altered, revised, expanded, or reduced — that is, authors were included and then again omitted, etc. The types of texts changed as well. In all of these respects the readers actively participated in the process of canon-building.

Most of the male editors of readers were involved in some fashion with girls' schools, usually as teachers or principals. Some of the editors, such as Christian Fürchtegott Muff (1841–1911) and F[riedrich] Ch[ristian] Paldamus (1823–73), had previously edited books for boys' schools. Often they created teachers' instructional aids to accompany the readers or wrote literary histories for use in schools, and thus in various ways influenced the process of canon-building in the school venue. The participation of women teachers in the production of readers increased after 1908. In fact, after 1908 readers that had appeared before that date and that had been edited by men began to be edited by women as well. The overt employment of women as co-editors appears to have functioned in part to legitimate the books for use in a female sphere. Before 1908 women were not identified on the title page as editors or co-editors.

August Kippenberg's *Deutsches Lesebuch für höhere Mädchenschulen,* Part 6

Published in many editions, Kippenberg's reader numbered among the most important readers of the late nineteenth century. The above-cited letter from H. Habenicht to the Bremen senator is but one of many documents confirming the long-time presence and influence that Kippenberg's reader had. My examination of annual school reports from around 1900 likewise documents the increased frequency of adoption of this reader in higher girls' schools in the province of Westphalia. Given its many editions and widespread use, Kippenberg's reader serves as a particularly representative and telling example of the shifts in German instruction in girls' schools. In the following I will describe the sixth part, which was used in the seventh grade in higher girls' schools and thus aimed at girls between twelve and thirteen years old.

A new edition of the sixth volume resulted from the reforms of 1894. As the foreword to the fourth edition of this volume remarks, "Die neuen Bestimmungen über das höhere Mädchenschulwesen im preußischen Staate vom 31. Mai 1894 haben Veranlassung gegeben zu dieser neuen Ausgabe des 6. Teils des Lesebuchs von A. Kippenberg" (The new regulations concerning higher girls' schools in the Prussian state of 31 May 1894 provided the occasion for this new edition of the sixth part of the reader of A. Kippenberg).[33]

In keeping with the prescriptions of the educational reforms, the first five parts of this reader already contained "eine reiche Auswahl deutscher Märchen, Sagen und Kinderlieder, sowie eine große Reihe von Schilderungen deutschen Landes und Volkes und von Bildern tüchtigen sittlichen Lebens" (a rich selection of German fairy tales, myths, and children's songs as well as a series of descriptions of the German country and people and of pictures of sound moral life) and thus corresponded to the regulations.[34] The sixth volume, which prepared pupils for the upper form, had, however, to be revised; in particular, it added epic poetry from Middle High German — *Das Nibelungenlied* and *Gudrun*, for example.[35] However, the book did not provide the Middle High German originals; the girls read modern German translations of them.

As mentioned above, the editors of readers offered readings and literary histories in separate volumes. August Kippenberg likewise published for the upper classes a *Handbuch der deutschen Literatur* (25th unrevised edition, 1912; Handbook of German Literature) as well as *Deutsche Gedichte für die Oberstufe der Lyzeen und höheren Mädchenschulen* (14th ed., 1910; German Poems for the Upper Level of Girls' Secondary Schools and Higher Girls' Schools).

The six volumes of the Kippenberg reader, along with two supplementary volumes, were published from 1885 to 1930 in many editions.[36] While the first edition was titled *Lesebuch für höhere Töchterschulen* (Reader for Higher Daughters' Schools), the title was later changed to *Lesebuch für höhere Mädchenschulen* (Reader for Higher Girls' Schools). Kippenberg notes in the foreword of the second edition (1887) that he had to change the title of his reader because "der Name höhere Töchterschule aber für manche einen Beiklang hat, der an gewisse Schwächen früherer Zeiten erinnert, und offenbar auch im Schwinden begriffen ist, während andrerseits das Wort höhere Mädchenschule wohl nirgends einem Bedenken begegnen wird, so ist von der zweiten Auflage an dieser letztere Titel gewählt worden" (the name higher daughters' school has a certain association that for some recalls certain weaknesses from earlier times, and since it is obviously also becoming ever less used and inasmuch as, on the other hand, the term higher girls' school will probably nowhere encounter any reservations, this term has therefore been chosen for the title of the second edition).[37] Even after the death of Kippenberg in 1889 the reader continued to appear under his name. His son, Hermann August, also played a role in editing the series of readers, as did apparently also August's wife; not until after 1908, however, did Johanne Kippenberg (1842–1925), appear as a co-editor on the title page.

The Structure of Kippenberg's Reader

The forewords and tables of contents strikingly document on the paratextual level the changes in the various editions of Kippenberg's reader. They enable us to trace the process of canonization realized through readers and to review the readings that were offered to and imposed upon girls in the schools where the reader was used. Both serve furthermore as an introduction to the question of reading socialization in that period. Let us turn first to the forewords.

Like the forewords in other readers from this era, those of the various volumes of Kippenberg's reader inform readers about the background of the book, talk about the discussions surrounding the selection of readings, identify alterations in the structure of the reader, and thus make it possible to reconstruct the editors' principles. The editors discuss readings they have previously chosen and do not hesitate to evaluate them, using adjectives like "hervorragend" (outstanding), "veraltet" (outmoded), and "weniger hervorragend" (less outstanding).[38] At the same time the forewords make clear that the reader is not merely to be used in German class, but instead that the editors have seen to it that "der Forderung gerecht wurde . . . einen Vereinigungspunkt für die verschiedenen Unterrichtsgebiete zu bilden" (the demand that they constitute a point of unification for the various areas of instruction has been met).[39] The intended use in other areas of instruction explains why readings from subject areas like geography and history have been included.

The editors — the forewords demonstrate this as well — have their girl reader firmly in mind. As the introduction to *Handbuch der deutschen Literatur* (1912; Handbook of German Literature) notes, "Bei der Auswahl der Verfasser hat uns in erster Linie der Gesichtspunkt geleitet, den heranwachsenden Mädchen die Dichter nahezubringen, aus deren Schöpfung sie auch später Förderung für ihr inneres Leben und wahren Genuß gewinnen können" (Our selection of authors was undertaken primarily from the point of view of familiarizing a rising generation of girls with the poets from whose creative activity they can later gain something with which to cultivate their inner life and also experience true enjoyment).[40] These words stress girls' literary aesthetic education. In school, they are thus supposed to get to know those poets who will later be useful to them and whose work they will enjoy. In other words, the readers and thus German instruction are to familiarize girls with a kind of writing that will protect them from trashy literature. The editors apparently hoped that if girls became acquainted first with "good" and "valuable" literature, they would no longer have the desire to read trash. In any case, we see here clearly the kind of influence these books aspired to have on girls' reading socialization.

Changes in the readers, as the forewords repeatedly note, are based on feedback from male and female colleagues. Most notably, the forewords in Kippenberg's reader document the flexibility in choice of text. The foreword to the new edition of 1899 of the sixth part of Kippenberg's reader, for example, identifies the following changes:

Für die Neubearbeitung des 6. Teils des Deutschen Lesebuchs von A. Kippenberg haben sich folgende Änderungen als notwendig erwiesen, damit sich dieser Teil dem Aufbau des ganzen Werkes, das in seinen fünf vorhergehenden Teilen eine wesentliche Umgestaltung

erfahren hat, vollkommen einfüge. 1. Einige Prosastücke sind ausgeschieden und haben ihren Platz, weil mehr dahingehörend, in Teil
5 gefunden. 2. Etwa zehn Prosastücke aus verschiedenen Gebieten
sind durch solche ersetzt worden, die uns noch besser den Forderungen der preußischen Bestimmungen zu entsprechen schienen. 3. Der
reichen Auswahl von Gedichten, welche dieser Teil schon enthielt,
sind noch einige sangbare Lieder hinzugefügt, so daß der Lieder-
kanon der vorhergehenden Teile, der in der Sammlung "Deutsche
Gedichte" seinen Abschluß findet, hier vervollständigt wird.[41]

This quotation from the edition that was published immediately after
the first important reforms of girls' schools of 1894 reveals how editors
reacted to these reforms. The foreword emphasizes here that the entire
series of the reader has been modified and that some readings had to be
integrated into the earlier grades; in short, the Prussian stipulations have
been observed and put into practice. Furthermore, this foreword contains
the first reference to a canon of poetry that has been included as a separate section in the reader. I will return to this canon below.

In 1911 the foreword to the thirty-first edition of the reader in turn
takes up the regulations for higher girls' schools of 1908. According to
the editors, the first volumes of the reader supply a critical foundation for
later instruction in literature in the last two grades of the upper form. By
contrast to the earlier grades, the seventh school year — that is, the first
grade of the upper form — the foreword indicates, devotes more attention to historical developments. Indeed, the last three volumes of Kippenberg's reader are oriented to history, whereby the recent past — that
is, German life approximately since unification — becomes ever more the
focus and ultimately dominates the reader: "Den Darstellungen aus dem
Leben der früheren Zeit folgt die Einführung in das Gegenwartsleben
nach seinen verschiedenen Richtungen in Natur und Menschheit, um
zurückzuleiten in den engsten Kreis des Familienlebens" (An introduction to contemporary life in all its different tendencies in nature and in
humanity follows the presentation of life from earlier times in order to
lead [readers] back to the intimate circle of family life).[42]

The editors aim to develop in the girls in the upper classes an awareness of history, both literary and general. Under the category "Aus ver-
gangenen Tagen" (From Times Past) the reader includes, for example,
readings by Gustav Freytag such as "Germanischer Wanderzug" (Germanic Migration) or "Eine deutsche Stadt um das Jahr 1300" (A German
City around the Year 1300) from his above-mentioned popular history. In
all, the historical section contains fifty-one readings. It is then followed by
a section titled "Aus unsern Tagen" (From our Times) with eighty-nine
readings. "From our Times" signifies the inclusion of a group of readings that address the present day or the more recent past. Here we find

authors like Fontane represented by the above-mentioned reading "Im Spreewald," Ferdinand Freiligrath (1810–76) with the poem "Die Auswanderer" (The Emigrants), and Annette von Droste-Hülshoff (1797–1848) with the poem "Knabe im Moor" (Boy in the Fen). This section, however, also includes living authors such as the Austrian Peter Rosegger (1843–1918) with the story "Etwas vom alten Meister" (Something from the Old Master), which was excerpted from his autobiographical *Waldheimat: Erzählungen aus der Jugendzeit* (1877; Forest Home: Stories from My Youth).

Kippenberg's reader clearly exhibits the late-century changes that generally occurred in readers. While in readers like Bacher's *Mädchenfreund* divisions according to genre played no role, Kippenberg's reader is organized in part according to genre. Like such readers for boys' schools as Jakob Hopf and Karl Paulsiek's *Lesebuch für höhere Lehranstalten* (Reader for Institutions of Higher Learning), the Kippenberg reader therefore distinguishes between poetry and prose. Yet the editors also recognized the usefulness of overarching themes. These themes differ, however, from those of earlier readers. They focus not on moral and religious truths, but instead on nature study, history and such aspects of modern German life as patriotism. The readers justify the new organization and new contents in their forewords. In 1911, in the introduction to the sixth part, for example, the editors, wrote the following concerning the use of overarching themes, along with attention to genre, to deepen the intellectual engagement of the girls:

> In dem vorliegenden 6. Teil des Lesebuches, für das 7. Schuljahr, den Beginn der Oberstufe, bestimmt, ist wie bisher die Verbindung von Prosa und Poesie beibehalten. . . . Dadurch, daß hier, wie auf den früheren Stufen, eine Reihe inhaltlich verwandter Stücke zu einer Gedankeneinheit verbunden sind, wird ein Auseinanderfallen des Stoffes vermieden, dagegen eine größere Vertiefung erreicht und ein erhöhtes Interesse in den Schülerinnen erweckt.[43]

It is important to note here the claim that the selection of the various readings has not occurred willy-nilly but rather, as the editors formulate it, has been undertaken in order to combine readings to achieve "Gedankeneinheit" (thematic unity). The selections are united thematically, even as they are also grouped together in subchapters according to genre, as, for example, in the case of the ballads of Uhland, Schiller, and Goethe or the stories of Rosegger. In this, Kippenberg's reader differs from Bacher's *Mädchenfreund*, which does not undertake such divisions. Kippenberg's organization of readers according to genre offered the teacher the chance to discuss formal literary matters. The editors also showed themselves here to believe in the importance of providing their female pupils with insight into German literature and awakening their interest in it. Given the critical role of literary education, this foreword directly addresses reading socialization, as do others; above all, the girls' interests are to be directed toward specific literary works. Furthermore, the foreword makes it clear that the editors intended the reader to continue to serve the girls as a reading teacher after their school days.

The tables of contents are also revealing. In the edition of 1898, the sixth part of Kippenberg's reader contains two tables of contents: Table of Contents A is divided into five sections with thematic as well as generic labels; Table of Contents B employs only generic rubrics and undertakes to distinguish between prose and poetry. Prose is further subdivided into belletristic texts on the one hand, and non-fiction, academic texts on the other. Poetry is subdivided into lyric and epic poetry, the former section containing forty selections and the latter thirty-four. Lyric poetry is further subdivided into two categories: songs with religious content and songs with profane content. Here profane songs dominate with thirty-four entries as opposed to six religious songs. The seventy-four poems listed in the table of contents significantly overshadow the fifty-seven prose readings.

Prose is represented by belletristic literature with nine readings and non-fiction, academic texts with thirty-eight selections. The latter include readings like Schiller's "Der Herzog Alba bei einem Frühstück" (The Duke of Alba at a Breakfast), taken from "Der Herzog Alba bei einem Frühstück auf dem Schlosse zu Rudolstadt, im Jahr 1547" (1788; The Duke of Alba at a Breakfast at the Castle of Rudolstadt in the Year 1547), and "Mädchenerziehung u. Frauenbildung im Mittelalter" (The Education of Girls and Women in the Middle Ages), excerpted from *Die deutschen Frauen im Mittelalter* (1851; German Women in the Middle Ages), by Karl Weinhold (1823–1901).

The reader exhibits marked stability across a critical period of German history, remaining nearly identical in structure and categories from 1898 to 1922, with poetry dominating. Over the course of their school years, girls were exposed to a wide range of poetry that they had to learn by heart. In German instruction it was not, however, simply a matter of interpreting and reciting poems, but also of engaging with poetry on an emotional level. This engagement with poems fed into a quotidian discourse that took the form of sentimental conversations in middle-class salons or in the intimacy of the family. Having familiarity with a large repertoire of poetry, the girls had the possibility of reciting (or rewriting) these poems for family occasions or of reciting them later for their own children. Poetry, we can conclude from these readers, belonged to the German cultural heritage at this time and was not to be discounted or forgotten as it sometimes came to be in later decades. Indeed, schools' annual reports mention that girls recited poetry at school festivals and that poetry dominated German classes.

Despite the overall stability of structure in Kippenberg's reader, after 1908 the thematic divisions in the sixth volume did change, as did the selection of authors. The chapter on religious-moral life, present in editions of the reader before 1908, disappeared, for example, although some of the readings from that section were retained. Table 2 reveals the changes in the thematic divisions that took place in the edition of 1910/11 in the wake of the Prussian Girls' School Reforms of 1908. The rubrics "Religious-Moral Life," "Historical Matters," "Geography and Astronomy," and "Nature and the Enjoyment Thereof" have been omitted and replaced by new and different categories whose contents are oriented to the recent past. Table 2 also shows how the number of selections expanded in Kippenberg's reader between 1898 and 1911.

Table 2. Summary of the Number of Readings under Each Category in Table of Contents A, Kippenberg, *Deutsches Lesebuch*, edition A, part 6 (7th school year)

1898 (120 readings in all)	1911 (142 readings in all)
I. Religiös-sittliches Leben (Religious-Moral Life) 30 readings	A. Aus vergangenen Tagen (From Times Past) 52 readings
II. Sagen und Balladen (Myths and Ballads) 13 readings	B. Aus unsern Tagen (From Our Times) 90 readings
III. Geschichtliches (Historical Matters) (41 readings)	I. Land und Leute (Land and People) 26 reading
IV. Erd- und Himmelskunde (Geography and Astronomy) 17 readings	II. Naturleben (Nature) 18 readings
V. Natur und Naturgenuß (Nature and the Enjoyment Thereof) 19 Readings	III. Menschenleben (Portraits) 45 readings

Table 3 summarizes the changes in the rubrics and the number of readings in Table of Contents B. As table 3 indicates, the division between prose and poetry was retained after 1908, and poetry continued to dominate the selections with ninety-one entries. The reader notably included more ballads and myths after 1908; these two genres were, after all, specifically mentioned in the reforms. We will return to the importance of ballads below. Some sections have been shortened and others expanded. Under the rubric "epische Dichtung" (epic poetry) we find that twenty-two poems have been omitted, for example, Goethe's "Johanna Sebus"; twenty-eight new poems have, however, been added. As we can also see from table 3, entries with religious content are no longer specially marked as such. While the section on prose remains more or less the same in

Table 3. Table of Contents B, Kippenberg, *Deutsches Lesebuch*, edition A, part 6 (7th school year)

1898 (120 readings total)	1911 (142 readings total)
I. Poesie (Poetry) 74 Readings	I. Poesie (Poetry) 91 Readings
A. *Lyrische Dichtungen* (Lyrical Poetry) 40 Readings	A. *Lyrische Dichtungen* (Lyrical Poetry) 48 Readings
1. Lieder religiösen Inhalts (Songs with Religious Content) 6 Readings	
2. Weltliche Lieder (Profane Songs) 34 Readings	
B. *Epische Dichtungen* (Epic Poetry) 34 Readings	B. *Epische Dichtungen* (Epic Poetry) 43 Readings
1. Poetische Erzählungen und Parabeln; Idyllen (Poetic Stories and Parables, Idylls) 16 Readings	1. Balladen und Sagen (Ballads and Myths) 29 Readings
2. Sagen und Balladen (Myths and Ballads) 12 Readings	2. Poetische Erzählungen (Poetic Stories) 9 Readings
3. Legenden (Legends) 1 Reading	3. Parabeln und Sprüche (Parables and Proverbs) 5 Readings
4. Fabeln (Fables) 1 Reading	
5. Didaktisches (Didactic Readings) 4 Readings	
II. Prosa (Prose) 46 Readings	**II. Prosa (Prose) 51 Readings**
A. *Schöne Literatur* (Belles Lettres) 9 Readings	A. *Schöne Literatur* (Belles Lettres) 11 Readings
1. Erzählungen, Parabeln und Fabeln (Stories, Parables, Fables) 6 Readings	1. Erzählungen (Stories) 9 Readings
2. Sagen und Märchen (Myths and Fairy Tales) 3 Readings	2. Briefe (Letters) 1 Reading
	3. Parabeln (Parables) 1 Reading
B. *Wissenschaftliche Litteratur* (Non-Ficton, Academic Literature) 37 Readings	B. *Wissenschaftliche Literatur* (Non-Fiction, Academic Literature) 40 Readings
1. Geschichtliche Begebenheiten und Charakterbilder (Historical Events and Portraits) 21 Readings	1. Sage und Geschichte (Myths and History) 22 Readings
2. Erd- und Himmelskunde (Geography and Astonomy) 8 Readings	2. Erdkunde (Geography) 11 Readings
3. Naturkunde (Nature Study) 8 Readings	3. Naturkunde (Nature Study) 7 Readings

number of readings, the reader renames the subsection heads and adds the new category of "Letters."

It is striking too that nineteenth-century authors were better represented in later editions, with selections by, for example, Theodor Storm (1817–88), Gottfried Keller (1819–90), and Conrad Ferdinand Meyer (1825–98). More women writers also appear in the sixth part; alongside the now canonical woman author Droste-Hülshoff, Kippenberg included the lesser-known poet Agnes Miegel (1879–1964). Both women were represented by poems, the former by the above-mentioned "Der Knabe im Moor" and the latter by "König Manfred" (King Manfred) and "Henning Schindekopf."[44]

Canons of Poetry

The reforms of 1894 introduced an important instructional requirement that affected Kippenberg's and other readers. After the passage of the regulations of 31 May 1894, readers were supposed to include a canon of poems and songs that were to be memorized in the middle and upper forms. In fact the regulations of 1894 do not list specific poems to be memorized; they only stipulate the importance of memorizing poetry: "Erlernung und Vortrag einer Auswahl von Gedichten nach einem für die Schule festzusetzenden Kanon mit kurzen Notizen über die Verfasser" (The memorization and recitation of a selection of poetry from a canon determined by the school with short notes on the authors.)[45] The selection of these poems was supposed to correspond to the "Hauptlesestoff" (main reading material).[46] The only authors actually named were Goethe, Schiller, and Uhland, so it is hardly surprising that these authors were well represented in readers. Goethe and Schiller headed the literary canon in the nineteenth century and selections from their works were already well established as reading material in the schools.

A comparison of Kippenberg's poetry canon with that of a second reader, Wacker's *Deutsches Lesebuch* (1897), with which this discussion of readers opened, will bring into sharper focus the choices that the editors of Kippenberg's reader made for their canon. And to state what will shortly become obvious: the variations also demonstrate that in the late nineteenth and early twentieth century there was in fact not a prescribed set of poems for girls' schools.

The introduction to the edition of Kippenberg's reader of 1900 describes the principle of text selection with respect to the new requirement of a canon. The reader, the foreword explains, limited itself to a "mäßige Anzahl der besten Stücke . . ., die wert sind, ein Teil des geistigen Lebensgutes der Schülerin zu werden" (moderate number of the best pieces that deserve to become an enduring part of the schoolgirl's intellectual life).[47] Gender, too, played a role in the selection of texts, as the editor explains: "Die gewählten Gedichte dürfen dem weiblichen Anschauungs- und Empfindungskreise nicht fern liegen und der gedächtnismäßigen Aneignung nicht allzugroße Schwierigkeiten bieten" (The selected poems should not be foreign to the feminine perceptual and emotional sphere and should not be difficult to memorize).[48] Yet despite the gender-specific prescription of the reforms of 1894 to which the foreword alludes here, a preliminary analysis of the selections in the poetry canon reveals that quite a variety of poems was included and that they did not in fact always obviously correspond to the girls' presumed "perceptual and emotional sphere"; indeed, some of them appear, for example, to have been chosen for their national themes and thus their patriotic content. With their allusions to military conflict they seem removed from what was then considered woman's sphere.

In the canon included in the sixth part, the Kippenberg reader separated poems from (folk)songs, including only the poems to be learned in the second and third grades, that is, by girls of thirteen or fourteen. This canon contains twenty-four poems and fourteen songs (see table 4). Uhland heads the list with six poems, followed by Schiller with five and Goethe and Chamisso with three each.

The table shows that ballads dominated the poetry canon, and indeed ballads remain a standard feature of German instruction to this day. German instruction, in combination with music instruction, was to make the canon of songs available to girls as well as to boys. The knowledge of poems and songs was to secure for girls a part in German cultural life. Learning these poems by heart was therefore of central importance to this mission.[50]

Women poets were not represented in the canon, and thus we must assume that the editors did not consider them relevant to a canon for girls' schools. Again, with respect to content the titles of the poems included do not appear to be particularly oriented to the girls' gender, despite the statement in the foreword that they should be.

A look at Karl Wacker's reader from the same period reveals a familiar yet somewhat different selection. The poetry canon in Wacker's reader was predictably dominated by Goethe, Uhland, and Schiller. Like Kippenberg's canon, it included poems that arose from the Wars of Liberation and the opposition to Napoleon early in the nineteenth century, poems by the so-called "freedom poets" Arndt and Körner, presumably in support of the nationalism of the late nineteenth century. Wacker's canon also does not include a single woman writer. But there are notable differences as well.

There are only ten selections in common between the canons in these two readers: Emanuel Geibel (1815–84), "Gudruns Klage" (Gudrun's Lament); Goethe, "Der Sänger" (The Singer); Uhland, "Des Sängers Fluch" (The Curse of the Singer); Uhland, "Das Glück von Edenhall"

Table 4. The Canon of Poetry in Kippenberg's Reader Arranged Alphabetically by Author (1900)[49]

Grade 3, Seventh School Year	Grade 2, Eighth School Year
Poems	Poems
Arndt, "Deutscher Trost"	Chamisso, "Das Schloß Boncourt"
Chamisso, "Die alte Waschfrau"	Freiligrath, "Die Trompete von Bionville"
Freiligrath, "Die Auswanderer"	Geibel, "Hoffnung"
Geibel, "Friedrich Rotbart"	Geibel, "Ostermorgen"
Geibel, "Gudruns Klage"	Goethe, "Der Fischer"
Goethe, "Der Sänger"	Schiller, "Das Lied von der Glocke"
Körner, "Abschied vom Leben"	Schiller, "Das Siegesfest"
Schenkendorf, "Muttersprache"	Schiller, "Der Graf von Habsburg"
Schiller, "Der Taucher"	Schiller, "Die Kraniche des Ibykus"
Uhland, "Des Sängers Fluch"	Uhland, "Das Glück von Edenhall"
Uhland, "Die Kapelle"	Uhland, "Das Schloß am Meere"
Uhland, "Schäfers Sonntagslied"	
Songs	Songs
Chamisso, "Es geht bei gedämpfter Trommel Klang"	Arndt, "Was ist des Deutschen Vaterland?"
Goethe, "Über allen Gipfeln ist Ruh"	Eichendorff, "In einem kühlen Grunde"
Körner, "Was glänzt dort vom Walde"	Eichendorff, "O Thäler weit, o Höhen"
Mosen, "Zu Mantua in Banden"	Thiersch, "Ich bin ein Preuße"
Roquette, "Noch ist die blühende, goldene Zeit"	"Zu Straßburg auf der Schanz," Folk Song from *Des Knaben Wunderhorn*
Rückert, "Aus der Jugendzeit"	
Schenkendorf, "Freiheit, die ich meine"	
Schneckenburger, "Es braust ein Ruf wie Donnerhall"	
Uhland, "Es zogen drei Burschen wohl über den Rhein"	

Table 5. The Canon of Poetry in Wacker's Reader Arranged Alphabetically by Author (1902)[51]

Grade 3, Seventh School Year	Grade 2, 8th School Year
Arndt, "Der feste Mann"	Chamisso, "Die alte Waschfrau"
Bürger, "Das Lied vom braven Manne"	Eichendorff, "Abschied"
Geibel, "Gudruns Klage"	Fouqué, "Trost"
Goethe, "Der Sänger"	Freiligrath, "O lieb', solang du lieben kannst"
Goethe, "Erlkönig"	Geibel, "Ostermorgen"
Körner, "Aufruf"	Goethe, "Der Schatzgräber"
Lenau, "Der Postillon"	Goethe, "Johanna Sebus"
Reinick, "Im Vaterland"	Schiller, "Das Lied von der Glocke"
Schenkendorf, "Auf den Tod der Königin Luise"	Schiller, "Der Graf von Habsburg"
Schenkendorf, "Frühlingsgruß an das Vaterland"	Schiller, "Der Kampf mit dem Drachen"
Sturm, "Nimm Christum in dein Lebensschiff"	Schiller, "Der Taucher"
Trojan, "Der Hauszauber"	Schiller, "Die Kraniche des Ibykus"
Uhland, "Das Glück von Edenhall"	Schiller, "Die Macht des Gesanges"
Uhland, "Des Sängers Fluch"	"Zu Straßburg auf der Schanz," Folk Song

(The Luck of Edenhall); Geibel, "Ostermorgen" (Easter Morning); Adelbert von Chamisso (1781–1838), "Die alte Waschfrau" (The Old Washerwoman); Schiller, "Das Lied von der Glocke" (The Song of the Bell); Schiller, "Die Kraniche des Ibykus" (The Cranes of Ibycus); Schiller, "Der Taucher" (The Diver); and Schiller, "Der Graf von Habsburg" (The Count of Habsburg). Furthermore, the two editors reversed the respective levels for Chamisso's "Die alte Waschfrau," Schiller's "Der Taucher" and "Der Graf von Habsburg," and Uhland's "Das Glück von Edenhall." These variations provide a good indication that the editors were at liberty to shape the canon of poems and (folk)songs according to their own judgment. Thus, the fact that a canon of poems to be memorized was included in every reader did not mean that all schoolgirls were familiar with a single canon.

Fourteen years later, by contrast, the regulations of 1908 did not address the question of the canon as a separate issue, that is, there was no prescription for a separate chapter in readers as there had been previously. After 1908 Kippenberg's reader, apparently responding to changed regulations, no longer included a canon of poems to be memorized, but instead a canon "von sangbaren Volksliedern" (of singable folksongs).[52] The poems that were formerly in the canon did not, however, disappear from the reader, but simply became a component part of it; that is, they were interspersed among the other readings, and there was no special reference to them as belonging to a poetry canon for memorization. The volume *Deutsche Gedichte für die Oberstufe höherer Mädchenschulen* (German Poems for the Upper Form of Higher Girls' Schools), which was revised after 1908 by, among others, Johanne Kippenberg, also omitted a separate canon in its later editions. The intention of conforming to the newest regulations by excluding the canon was explained as follows in the introduction: "Bei der vorliegenden Neubearbeitung haben wir, veranlaßt durch die neuen preußischen Bestimmungen für das höhere Mädchenschulwesen, im Anschluß an diese den bisherigen Gedichtkanon ausgeschieden. Dadurch ist Raum gewonnen für Berücksichtigung der früheren Dichtungen, besonders der beiden Blütezeiten unsrer Literatur. . . . Die Dichtungen des 19. Jahrhunderts aber nehmen wie bisher den größeren Teil des Buches ein" (The present revised version has omitted the customary canon of poems in keeping with the new Prussian regulations for higher girls' schools. We have thereby gained space in which to consider earlier literature, especially the two golden ages of our literature. . . . However, the literature of the nineteenth century will take up the larger part of the book as it always has.)[53] The editors considered the first golden age of German literature to be from 1100 to 1300 and the second to encompass the age of Goethe and Schiller. With the space gained by the omission of the canon, this poetry collection was able to include more authors from the last third of the nineteenth century and from the first decade of the twentieth century. Authors such as Fontane and Felix Dahn (1834–1912) thus won a place in *Deutsche Gedichte*; at the same time, selections by older authors such as Arndt and Körner appeared much less often after 1908.

Conclusion

In this introduction to nineteenth-century German readers for higher girls' schools I have attempted to provide a sense of the structure and contents of these books and of the influence that they were intended to have on the pupils who read them. The readers, published beginning approximately in 1870, aimed to facilitate a familiarity with German literature, and they therefore provided an introduction to literary genres and literary history. While earlier readers such as Bacher's *Mädchenfreund* offered exemplary stories and prepared girls for their future roles as mother, housewife, and spouse, readers changed over the course of the nineteenth century to become in the last third ever more a girl's reading teacher. In their forewords, as I have outlined above, the editors of these late-century readers discussed the literary quality of the selected readings as well as the goal of cultivating the literary taste of girl pupils.

As we have seen, readers constituted critical instances of reading socialization in the school setting. The large number of poems and songs that girls had to learn in school, for example, gives a good sense of the fact that the girls were receiving a literary education of sorts. As mentioned above, poems were recited within the sphere of the family as one aspect of sociability; as a result of their German instruction, girls had a large number of poems at their disposal. This kind of reading socialization in school also most certainly aided women later on when they taught their own children poems and thus functioned in the home as reading teachers.

The changes in the widely used Kippenberg reader vividly document a new orientation in German instruction for girls at the turn of the century. The editors took seriously the mandate to provide girls with a literary education in keeping with the educational reforms that occurred in this period. Readers like Kippenberg's aimed to cultivate the girls' taste by introducing them to good literature and thus protect them from ubiquitously available mass-produced literature that the editors considered trash.

The forewords to these readers also exhibit important features of the process of literary canon formation; that is, they show how the texts were selected for the school setting. The aspects that we have seen in the readers reviewed in the present article include the following: 1) the selection was keyed to the age of the girls — later editions omitted some of the readings on account of the difficulty of understanding them, and even after 1908 the question of what could be demanded of girls remained important for the choice of reading material; 2) since after 1908 the forewords evidenced ever greater concern with the new regulations, the editors of readers were obviously taking them into consideration and thereby losing some of the leeway they had once had in the choice of readings; 3) the ability to use the readings in other subjects played an important role in the selection of texts; 4) the personal preferences of the editors influenced the choice of texts, as did, furthermore, 5) discussions and criticisms of teachers and colleagues.

In sum, the reader played a central role in girls' literary education, and we can reasonably postulate long-term effects on the pupils who read and learned from them. Indeed, the introduction of readers in the late nineteenth and early twentieth centuries with the stated goals of providing girls with an education in literature coincided with the entrance of ever more German women into the literary marketplace, suggesting that the introduction of a literary aesthetic and historical education conspired with other social advancements to transform women from good readers into good writers as well. After 1900 the number of women writers increased markedly, and by the 1920s some of these women actually received acclaim from the critical literary establishment. This was a generation that had not so much learned how to be good girls through their school reading, but who had been introduced to a wide range of the authors then considered to be German literature's best.

— Translated by Lynne Tatlock

Notes

This article was translated by Lynne Tatlock. I thank her cordially for the translation of my work, as well as for making it possible to present my research to an English-speaking public. I am also grateful to Faruk Pašić for his careful checking and formatting of the notes.

[1] "It is also true of the reader . . . that the best thing that German instruction can give the female pupil to take with her after she leaves school is an appreciative love of the words and works of our mother tongue." K[arl] Wacker, *Deutsches Lesebuch für katholische höhere Mädchenschulen. Unter Mitwirkung praktischer Schulmänner herausgegeben. Dritter Teil. Oberstufe. Ausgabe für das Königreich Preußen* (Münster: Heinrich Schöningh, 1897), iii.

[2] "It is, however, much more harmful in our view not to have any liking for reading. . . ." Louise Otto-Peters, *Der Genius des Hauses: Eine Gabe für Mädchen und Frauen* (Pest: Hartleben, 1869), 113.

[3] Harro Müller-Michaels, "Konzepte und Kanon in Lesebüchern nach 1945," in *Das Lesebuch: Zur Theorie und Praxis des Lesebuchs im Deutschunterricht*, ed. Swantje Ehlers (Baltmannsweiler: Schneider Verlag Hohengehren, 2003), 6. On school readers, see also Gisela Teistler, ed., *Bestandskatalog der deutschen Schulbücher im Georg-Eckert-Institut erschienen bis 1945. Teil 1: Lese- und Realienbücher, einschließlich Fibeln* (Hannover: Hannsche Buchhandlung, 1997).

[4] "If with the second volume the hope was expressed that the book would remain beloved by and valuable to pupils beyond their school days, then this hope was a determining factor in the editing of the third volume. This third volume aims to be an aid not merely for school but, by providing varied inspiration and lasting influence on (girls') hearts and minds, means to secure for them a valuable possession for life and to continue to be a friendly companion and enjoyable book for them." See Wacker, *Deutsches Lesebuch für katholische höhere Mädchenschulen*, v.

[5] Ibid., iii.

[6] Ibid.

[7] See Bettina Hurrelmann, Susanne Becker, and Irmgard Nickel-Bacon, *Lesekindheiten: Familie und Lesesozialisation im historischen Wandel* (Weinheim: Juventa, 2006).

[8] Elise [Friederike Felicitas] von Hohenhausen, *Die Jungfrau und ihre Zukunft in unserer Zeit, oder mütterlicher Rath einer Pensionsvorsteherin an ihre scheidenden Zöglinge über ihren Eintritt in die Welt* (Weimar: Voigt, 1854), 57–58.

[9] See Hurrelmann et al., *Lesekindheiten*, 117–25.

[10] Swantje Ehlers, *Der Umgang mit dem Lesebuch: Analyse — Kategorien — Arbeitsstrategien* (Baltmannsweiler: Schneider Verlag Hohengehren, 2003), 3.

[11] Ibid., 9.

[12] Bettina Hurrelmann, "Lesesozialisation," in *Sozialisation — Lebenslauf — Biografie*, ed. Imbke Behnken and Jana Mikota (Weinheim: Juventa, 2009).

[13] James C. Albisetti's *Schooling German Girls and Women: Secondary and Higher Education in the Nineteenth Century* (Princeton, NJ: U of Princeton P, 1988) remains the standard work on German girls' education in this period.

[14] See Günter Häntzschel, "'Für fromme, reine und stille Seelen': Literarischer Markt und 'weibliche' Kultur im 19. Jahrhundert," in *Deutsche Literatur von Frauen*, ed. Gisela Brinker-Gabler (Munich: Beck, 1988), 2:119–28. According to Häntzschel, Pataky's *Lexikon deutscher Frauen der Feder* lists 5,000 women writers in 1898. By comparison, there are only 500 listed in 1825 (Häntzschel, 119).

[15] Georg Jäger, "Der Schulbuchverlag," in *Das Kaiserreich 1871–1918. Geschichte des deutschen Buchhandels im 19. und 20. Jahrhundert*, ed. Georg Jäger (Frankfurt am Main: MVB, 2003), 1/2:62.

[16] "The reports that were turned in on March 14 of this year on the readers that are being used in classroom instruction in primary and middle schools as well as in higher girls' schools have revealed that in the adoption of these same readers the pertinent instructional regulations for the royal boards or the provincial school boards of 23 October 1817 §. 7. No. 4 and the general dispositions of these in keeping with these regulations have not everywhere been observed"; see "Lesebücher für Volks-, Mittel- und höhere Mädchen-Schulen," *Centralblatt für die gesamte Unterrichtsverwaltung in Preußen* 17, no. 2 (1875): 105.

[17] A discussion of the quality of readers for higher girls' schools took place in pedagogical journals like *Die Lehrerin*.

[18] "On account of the fact that the reader by Lücker & Nacke, the reader currently used in my school, in some respects does not meet the requirements of German instruction, I have long had the wish to replace it. In my judgment and in that of my faculty, Mr. A. Kippenberg's reader offers a replacement that fulfills all legitimate requirements of the higher girls' school; this judgment is confirmed in the unanimous judgment of the pertinent pedagogical press. Furthermore, well-known higher girls' schools outside of Bremen have already adopted it. I therefore take the liberty of requesting that the praiseworthy school commission of the senate permit the adoption of said reader in mine." On this subject, see the literary remains of August and Johanne Kippenberg, Bremer Staatsarchiv. StaB, B VI 10 (51) 5.

[19] "Höhere Mädchenschulen. Lehrbücher für den Unterrichtsgebrauch bei den höheren Mädchenschulen und den weiter führenden Bildungsanstalten für die weibliche Jugend," *Centralblatt für die gesamte Unterrichtsverwaltung in Preußen* 51, no. 3 (1909): 332.

[20] "Höhere Lehranstalten für die weibliche Jugend. Verzeichnis der an den höheren Mädchenschulen und weiter führenden Bildungsanstalten für die weibliche Jugend gebrauchten Lehrbücher," *Centralblatt für die gesamte Unterrichtsverwaltung in Preußen* 51, no. 11 (1909): 773–74.

[21] It should be noted here that even with greater regulation of readers, teachers still had some flexibility as to which selections they actually treated in their classes. Curricula referred only to the genres to be treated — e.g., fairy tales, myths, children's songs.

[22] "Verzeichnis der vom 1. April 1913 bis zum 14. Juli 1914 für den Gebrauch an höheren Lehranstalten endgültig genehmigten Schulbücher: [D. Allgemeine Angelegenheiten der Unterrichtsanstalten]," *Centralblatt für die gesamte Unterrichtsverwaltung in Preußen* 56, no. 9 (1914): 573–87.

[23] Gisela Wilkending, "Erzählende Literatur," in *Handbuch zur Kinder- und Jugendliteratur: Von 1850 bis 1900,* ed. Otto Brunken, Bettina Hurrelmann, Maria Michels-Kohlhage, and Gisela Wilkending (Stuttgart: Metzler, 2008), col. 612.

[24] For an account of Hirt's pedagogical program, see Jennifer Drake Askey, "A Library for Girls: Publisher Ferdinand Hirt & Sohn and the Novels of Brigitte Augusti," in the present volume.

[25] See Jäger, "Der Schulbuchverlag," 79.

[26] B[artholomäus] Bacher, *Der Mädchenfreund: Ein Lehr- und Lesebuch für Mädchenschulen. Erster Theil* (Munich, 1807; repr., Frankfurt am Main: Insel Verlag, 1977).

[27] "One day Marie was playing out in the street with many children. Along came a stranger and asked them in a friendly manner how to get to the next village."

Marie immediately went up to the man and said, "I'll be glad to show you the way out of the village so then you can't possibly lose your way." Thereupon she went off with the stranger and showed him from afar the area where the next village lay.

The traveler thanked her politely and wanted to give the good child a tip for her trouble. But Marie didn't take anything and said, "I was glad to be able to do you a kindness. Farewell and have a good journey."

A kind old granny was going to church. It was winter and slippery. She fell down and could not get up again by herself.

Liese, another girl who was twelve years old, was passing by. The granny called upon her for assistance. "Yes," she said, "if you'll give me a penny then I'll be glad to help you." And indeed she did not help her until the old lady had promised to give her a penny.

Fie on that nasty greediness!" (Bacher, *Mädchenfreund,* 14–15).

[28] With around 3,000 titles in the Cologne database of Aleki (Arbeitstelle für Leseforschung und Kinder- und Jugendmedien), the literature of moral education and the cultivation of the heart constitutes the largest generic group. See Otto Brunken, "Überblick," in *Handbuch zur Kinder- und Jugendliteratur: Von 1800 bis 1850,* ed. Otto Brunken, Bettina Hurrelmann, and Klaus-Ulrich Pech (Stuttgart: J. B. Metzler, 1998), col. 285.

[29] L[orenz] Kellner, *Deutsches Lese- und Bildungsbuch für höhere Schulen, insbesondere die oberen Klassen höherer Töchterschulen und weiblicher Erziehungsanstalten* (Freiburg im Breisgau: Herdersche Verlagshandlung, 1895), iii.

[30] On this subject, see *Verhandlungen über Fragen des höheren Unterrichts: Berlin, 4. bis 17. Dezember 1890, im Auftrage des Ministers der geistlichen, Unterrichts- und Medizinal-Angelegenheiten* (Berlin: Hertz, 1891).

[31] "Fontane, Theodor, b. 1819 in Neu-Ruppin, was originally an apothecary; later he devoted himself entirely to literature. An extended stay in England and Scotland inspired him to write ballads (No. 107). His sketches and historical pieces ("Walking Tours through the Mark," No. 69, "The German War of 1866," "The War against France"), which reflect what he himself saw and experienced, are distinguished by their great vividness and by a warm, patriotic sensibility. His sensitive novels are also widely read. d. 1898." A[ugust] Kippenberg, *Deutsches Lesebuch für höhere Mädchenschulen. Ausgabe A*, pt. 7 (Hannover: Norddeutsche Verlagsanstalt, 1907), 317.

[32] "Franz, Agnes (1794–1843), the daughter of a privy councilor in the province of Silesia, experienced a great deal of sadness in her childhood. She lost her father very early and at age twelve had such a bad fall that she remained in poor health for her entire life. But her intellectual talents developed all the more beautifully. Her contact with nature inspired her first poems (see pt. IV, no. 8). Later on, although she herself lived in near-poverty, she lovingly sacrificed herself for her family and for other circles. Upon the death of her sister, she took in her children. Trusting in God's help, she founded an industrial school for poor girls in Breslau as she had earlier in Wesel. She was serving as its headmistress when she died. Her poems and her thoughtful stories and charming fairy tales (see pt. IV, no. 48) resonated with the reading public"; see A[ugust] Kippenberg, *Deutsches Lesebuch für höhere Mädchenschulen. Ausgabe A*, pt. 6 (Hannover: Norddeutsche Verlags-anstalt, 1900), 276–77.

[33] A[ugust] Kippenberg, *Deutsches Lesebuch für höhere Mädchenschulen, Ausgabe A*, pt. 6 (Hannover: Norddeutsche Verlagsanstalt 1898), iii.

[34] A[ugust] Kippenberg, *Deutsches Lesebuch für höhere Mädchenschulen. Ausgabe B*, pt. 4 (Hannover: Norddeutsche Verlagsanstalt, 1895), n.p.

[35] Kippenberg, *Deutsches Lesebuch, Ausgabe A*, pt. 6 (1898), iii.

[36] It is difficult to determine exactly how many editions the reader actually went through since the titles of the parts changed over the years and the editions with new titles started over, beginning once again with edition 1. By 1913, for example, parts of the reader had already appeared in a 76th printing.

[37] Quoted by Georg Bessell, *100 Jahre Kippenberg-Schule 1859–1959* (Bremen: Illing Lüken, 1959), 27.

[38] See Kippenberg, *Deutsches Lesebuch. Ausgabe A*, pt. 7 (1907), n.p.

[39] A[ugust] Kippenberg, J[ohanne] Kippenberg, and H[ermann] Jantzen, *Deutsches Lesebuch für höhere Mädchenschulen. Ausgabe A*, pt. 6 (Hannover: Norddeutsche Verlagsanstalt, 1911), 4.

[40] A[ugust] Kippenberg, *Handbuch der deutschen Literatur. Unter Mitwirkung von H[ermann] Jantzen, neubearbeitet von J[ohanne] Kippenberg und A[ugust] Kippenberg*, 25th ed. (Hannover: Norddeutsche Verlagsanstalt, 1912), 5.

[41] "The following changes proved to be necessary for the revision of part 6 of A. Kippenberg's reader so that this part would fit into the structure of the

entire work, which in its five preceding parts has already experienced a substantial reshaping. 1) Some prose pieces have been eliminated and have found their place, since they fit better there, in part 5. 2) About ten prose pieces from various fields have been replaced by selections that appear to us to correspond better to the Prussian regulations. 3) A few songs that can be sung have been added to the rich selection of poems that this part already contains so that the song canon of the previous parts, which finds its conclusion in the anthology "German Poems," is completed here"; see A[ugust] Kippenberg, Introduction (1899) in *Deutsches Lesebuch für höhere Mädchenschulen. Ausgabe A*, pt. 7 (Hannover: Norddeutsche Verlagsanstalt, 1903), n.p.

[42] A. Kippenberg, et al., *Deutsches Lesebuch. Ausgabe A*, pt. 6 (1911), 3.

[43] "In the present sixth part of the reader for the seventh school year, the beginning of the upper form, the combination of prose and poetry has been retained. By uniting a series of pieces to form a thematic unity related in content, as was done in the earlier grades, we have prevented the material from falling apart and instead achieved greater depth and have awakened heightened interest in the female students"; ibid.

[44] Additional women writers whom I have found in the various editions of all of the volumes of Kippenberg's reader and who are largely represented by poems include Marie von Ebner-Eschenbach, Ricarda Huch (1864–1947), Lulu von Strauß-Torney, Agnes Franz (1794–1843), and Jenny Hirsch (1829–1902). Johanne Kippenberg herself was a regular contributor; she published under her maiden name, Johanne Koch, selections such as "Die weibliche Handarbeit" (Feminine Needlework). Gertrud Storm (1865–1936), the daughter of Theodor Storm, also was regularly included with the selection "Weihnachten bei Theodor Storm" (Christmas with Theodor Storm), for example.

[45] "Neuordnung des höheren Mädchenschulwesens," in *Centralblatt für die gesamte Unterrichtsverwaltung in Preußen* 36, no. 7 (1894): 462.

[46] Ibid., 463.

[47] Kippenberg, *Deutsches Lesebuch. Ausgabe A*, pt. 6 (1900), 269.

[48] Ibid.

[49] Ibid.

[50] On the subject of the instruction of poetry, see Hermann Korte, "Lyrik im Unterricht," in *Grundzüge der Literaturdidaktik*, 4th ed., ed. Klaus-Michael Bogdal and Hermann Korte (Munich: dtv, 2006), 203–16.

[51] Karl Wacker, "Kanon der auf der Mittel- und Oberstufe auswendig zu lernenden Gedichte; Oberstufe," in *Deutsches Lesebuch für katholische höhere Mädchenschulen* (Münster: Heinrich Schöningh, 1902), xxi–xxiii.

[52] A. Kippenberg, et al., *Deutsches Lesebuch. Ausgabe A*, pt. 6 (1911), 12.

[53] A[ugust] Kippenberg, *Deutsche Gedichte für die Oberstufe höherer Mädchenschulen* (Hannover: Norddeutsche Verlagsanstalt, 1910), n.p.

III. Writers and Their Publishers

7: Thinking Clearly about the Marriage of Heinrich Heine and His Publisher, Julius Campe

Jeffrey L. Sammons

THE MOST REMARKABLE THING about the relationship of Heinrich Heine and his publisher, Julius Campe, is that for thirty years it survived, if sometimes just barely, the language they used to one another that, at times, with other men in other circumstances, would have ended a relationship forever. It was less a business partnership or a friendship than a marriage, an observation both of them had occasion to make. Campe was the one to suggest the notion, in 1837: "gebe der Himmel, daß wir in unserer Literarischen Ehe über die Hauptsachen stets einig bleiben mögen, das ist für beide Theile das Ehrenwertheste" (may the heavens grant that in our literary marriage we always remain in accord about the main things, that is the most honorable course for both of us).[1] He reiterated it two years later: "wie kann ich annehmen, daß wir uns entzweien sollten, ernstlicher entzweien sollten, wo unsere Interessen von jeher so eng — wie zwischen Frau und Mann — verbunden waren!" (how can I accept that we should break up, seriously break up, when our interests have always been so closely bound together as with man and wife!); and again, two years after that: "Wir beide dürfen über alles sprechen, was uns gegenseitig angeht, etwa wie Frau und Mann" (we can always speak about everything we care about with one another, like man and wife); and finally much later, in 1854: "In der Ehe wird geschmollt, wenn einer der beiden die natürlichen Gränzen überschritten. Dasselbe findet in der literarischen Ehe, in der wir beiden uns befinden, ebenfalls statt. Dieser Zustand ist nicht angenehm. Machen wir denselben durch einen reellen Friedensschluß ein Ende. Ich bin dazu gern bereit und biete Ihnen meine Hand, und bitte mir die Ihrige zu reichen" (There is pouting in marriage when one of the couple oversteps the natural boundaries. The same thing also happens in the literary marriage in which we both find ourselves. This situation is not pleasant. Let us make an end of it with a genuine peace accord. I am gladly ready to do so and offer you my hand and ask that you give me yours).[2] At an early date he developed the habit of speaking of Heine's works as their children.[3] Heine finally picked up the cue: "ich [glaube] dennoch im thörigten Herzen gar nicht an der Möglichkeit einer Ehescheidung von Ihnen" (I don't believe at all in my foolish heart in the possibility of a divorce from you), but the fault lies only with Campe: "Bloß Ihr Nergeln, Ihr Schmollen, Brummen, kurz der eheliche Unfriede" (merely your carping, your pouting, grumbling, in short the marital discord).[4] Marriage will be defined for the purpose here as a negotiated incompatibility.

Julius Campe was born in Braunschweig in 1792, where he grew up as an orphan but in a family with useful connections; he was a nephew of the widely known Enlightenment writer Joachim Heinrich Campe (1746–1818), and his family tree shows him related in the course of time along a web of marriages to the publishing families of Vieweg, Westermann, Brockhaus, and Reclam. An older half-brother became associated by marriage with one Benjamin Gottlob Hoffmann in Hamburg, after whose death in 1818 the Hoffmann of the publishing house of Hoffmann und Campe was a name only.[5] Julius worked as a book-selling apprentice, then served as a volunteer in the war against Napoleon, after which he toured Italy for two years. He took over the firm in 1823 and, though more moderate than radical himself, began to build it into the most important publisher of progressive and oppositional literature in Germany. Fearless and indomitable, he battled the increasingly oppressive censorship for decades with legendary ingenuity: he bound radical works with conservative ones, he put imaginary printers and places of publication on title pages, he smuggled books in bales of commodities. He risked arrest and shutdown, experiencing both. He worked fifteen hours a day, seven days a week.

Clearly this was the publisher for a writer like Heine; their partnership seems in retrospect to have been virtually inevitable. Young Heine was having difficulty finding a footing on the literary market. He had published some poetry and essays in local papers, one small volume of poetry in 1821 and another along with two stillborn tragedies in 1823, and his first major work of prose fiction, *Die Harzreise* (The Harz Journey), in early 1826. The publication of *Die Harzreise* had been beset with difficulties caused by the unreliability of others; he was clearly in need of a capable and understanding publisher. He seems to have met Campe in his bookshop at the end of January 1826 and found in him, at first, a congenial and receptive spirit. Campe declared himself ready to bring out a volume of *Reisebilder* (Travel Pictures) containing the authentic text of *Die Harzreise*; he was even willing to pay something for it. He agreed also to publish a volume of Heine's poems to date, though he did not offer anything for that and did not want Heine to spend too much time on it; Heine later induced him to pay something for it. Campe's acquisition of the *Buch der Lieder* (Book of Songs) for next to nothing was to turn out to be one of the great publishing coups of all time and has sometimes been taken as an egregious example of the rapacious capitalist exploiting the helpless artist. In fact, neither man saw the transaction in that light at the time. Heine thought, as he repeatedly and wrongly supposed, that his lyrical period was at an end. Campe understandably regarded verse as a drug on the market; there was an ocean of verse; everyone wrote it, from schoolchildren to government ministers and even the king of Bavaria. It was the potential of Heine's innovative prose, fusing essay and fiction, that both found exciting. Neither could foresee at the time that the *Buch der Lieder* would become the most widely read and, through its song settings, *heard* book of German poetry in the world, and, indeed, it was to be a good ten years before this triumph began to emerge.

Naturally this relationship of author and publisher has been much studied.[6] The topic, however, like almost everything having to do with Heine, is affected by his peculiar place in the literary scholarship of our time, in some ways outside of and separate from the customary norms and procedures of scholarly inquiry. A few words may be inserted here about how that came about. For a couple of decades after the Second World War Heine was not a particularly lively topic. Sometimes this relative silence has been ascribed to residual antisemitism or the resistance of the Adenauer restoration to his revolutionary message, but I do not believe this is the case. Up until around the turn of the century Heine throve in Germany and internationally. From the 1860s until the Weimar Republic nearly forty collected editions of his works were published and there were many translations, not least into English. He was systematically attacked by antisemites, but the politically quite feeble, though noisy, antisemitic movement[7] had little effect on his larger reputation unless the antisemites were able to join forces with the ruling powers. It is not always remembered that in the squabble over erecting a Heine monument, originally intended for Düsseldorf and eventually erected in the Bronx in 1899, Düsseldorf was not to blame. The project was supported by the mayor and the city government, the local press, and public opinion; only when a minority of opponents mobilized the Prussian government against it did it have to be withdrawn.[8] A Heine monument was erected in Frankfurt in 1913 despite an extraordinarily intense antisemitic campaign against it.[9]

It is true that this popularity did not extend to Heine's political and socially critical writings but was largely focused on the *Reisebilder* and the poems, especially those that had become famous in the *Lieder* settings, and this was to contribute to the decline of his reputation in the Modernist era, for Heine's verse, often simplistically understood, did not pass muster in the era of the great Modernist leap forward in German poetry; it could not be set beside the work of Stefan George, Hugo von Hofmannsthal, or Rainer Maria Rilke. It is well known that the immensely prestigious Austrian cultural critic Karl Kraus mounted a ferocious campaign against

Heine's poetry and prose as polluters of style in the German language.[10] It is significant that a number of those who campaigned against Heine's reputation were, like Kraus, Jewish, such as Robert Neumann, who in 1927 wrote in the newspaper of the German-Jewish community that most of Heine's poetry was of a tastelessness no longer bearable today and that especially the Jewish community should refrain from praising him.[11] It was this devaluation of his poetry among the tastemakers that still affected his lower profile into the 1960s. The revival of his reputation was not owing to a revaluation of the poetry, at least not at first.

The modern epoch of Heine study is dated from 1962, the year of the first *Heine-Jahrbuch* (Heine Yearbook). However, the beginnings were fairly quiet, with scholarly studies and plans for a cooperative East and West German complete critical edition, which turned out not to be feasible; the endeavor split into east and west versions. But soon the German student movement supervened, which required an alternative to conventional literary history: oppositional, socio-political, persecuted, and revolutionary. Who better to fill this role than the exiled, censored, banned, neglected Heine, relentless opponent of German nationalism, critic of Goethe, friend of Marx, intermediator with the French, partisan of revolution, militant intellectual? By 1972, the year of the 175th birthday conference, the model was intact: shouting in the lecture hall; marching in the streets, especially in connection with the demand to name the new university of Düsseldorf after Heine; a satirical cabaret making fun of Heine's *Lieder* while foregrounding his political texts in the tones of Kurt Weill and Lotte Lenya.[12] Since then there has been a vast and serious era of scholarship: two great critical editions, the western one now completed, and many elaborate biographical and interpretive studies. More has been learned about Heine in the last fifty years than was known in the previous century and a half. But the political theater, though it has had a tendency to evolve into the carnivalesque, endures; it is not unusual for drummers to march down streets in memory of the French drummer from *Das Buch Le Grand* (The Book of Le Grand). At the two-hundredth birthday celebration in 1997, one could read Heine texts on banners fluttering from flagpoles and hear them recited by exotically dressed actors and actresses wandering through the *son-et-lumière* exhibit; it was possible to obtain the Heine umbrella, the Heine watch, the Heine notepad, the Heine chocolate medallions and tortes, the miniature Heine medal, the ten-mark commemorative coin, the postage stamp, the tee-shirts with a choice of two inscriptions, and the Heine eau de toilette.[13] Following the perpetual calendar of birth and death anniversaries every twenty-five years respectively, conferences and celebrations are held world-wide, generating an expanding library of printed material.

Thus Heine comes to be an idiosyncratic figure as an object of research and study. For one thing, he is virtually immune from criticism, for to criticize him would be reactionary, antisemitic — worse: *bourgeois* — perhaps even disrespectful of the self-understanding the German cultural elite has achieved in our time, for which Heine plays an iconic role similar to that of Goethe in the past. His evaluations of himself are taken at face value; if he stated, "ich war ein braver Soldat im Befreyungskriege der Menschheit" (I was a good soldier in mankind's struggle for emancipation),[14] then that is what he remains for us. His, as one might think, interesting ambivalences in matters of revolution and democracy are of no interest, for ambivalence is a bourgeois-liberal device for evading revolutionary and radical imperatives. Embarrassing episodes in his life are not discussed, for example, the evidence that he mediated bribes to journalists from the composer Giacomo Meyerbeer to insure positive reviews, and then, when he had a quarrel with Meyerbeer, attempted to blackmail him. The one study of this matter is almost never mentioned.[15]

As with Marx, Heine's enemies have no rights; only his voice is heard. So thoroughly is he allowed to occupy the discourse that the effect has been to hinder understanding of the dissidents and democratic activists of the time, toward most of whom he was contemptuous. Until relatively recently, this effect had been most noticeable in the devaluation of Ludwig Börne, a genuine democrat.[16] Heine is not permitted to hold any opinion incompatible with today's progressive views. Because he declared himself to be a cosmopolitan and because to be cosmopolitan is a virtue today, that is what he is for us, despite disdainful comments about the British, the Americans, the Poles, the Danes, the Dutch, the Belgians, even from time to time the French.[17] He must have been an enemy of the bourgeois king of the French, Louis-Philippe, so that his complex counterpoint of criticism of and sympathy for the king remained unanalyzed until recently;[18] the documentary evidence that he was perceived in France not as a revolutionary but as a supporter of constitutional monarchy and that on the political spectrum of the newspapers was most positively treated by the relatively conservative ones supportive of Louis-Philippe's government goes unremarked.[19] For several years he received a secret pension from that government, which, when it was revealed in the Revolution of 1848, caused acute embarrassment to him, not to speak of today's acolytes.[20]

Here are some admittedly extreme examples of how this works. When Heine, in the French preface to *Lutezia*, predicts that the communists would destroy art and poesy, he does not mean the communists; he means the bourgeoisie. That is the ironic joke on the reader.[21] Although Heine repeatedly, publicly and privately, insisted that he was a monarchist, not a republican, a monarchist Heine is of no use to us, so it must be shown that these utterances are ironic and mean the opposite, and that Heine was a republican through and through, correctly perceiving that the republic was France's essence, even though a French republic was not to emerge for forty years.[22] Similarly, although Heine several times denied he was an atheist and at the end of his life notoriously declared a submission to, if not exactly a belief in God, a model figure of inspiration for us today cannot be permitted even residual religious beliefs, so it becomes necessary to show that, whatever he may have said about it himself, he was a committed, unwavering atheist from beginning to end.[23]

As has been the case with the discourse about Heine generally in our time, the relationship with Julius Campe can be adjusted to fit patterns that have been imposed on him to serve present purposes, even in conscientious and competent studies such as the recent publication of a selection of the correspondence between Heine and Campe edited by Gerhard Höhn and Christian Liedtke.[24] I very much regret speaking critically about such accomplished scholars. Höhn is the author of the indispensable *Heine-Handbuch*, now in its third edition;[25] Liedtke has emerged as one of the most comprehensive of today's middle generation of Heine scholars and is an editor of the *Heine-Jahrbuch*.[26] I have personal obligations to both. This volume is not an extreme example but a typical one; much in it is substantial and observant, making it all the more significant that such competent observers should nevertheless misunderstand aspects of the relationship that emerge clearly from the documents before them as an indication of the force that ulterior presupposition can exert on the Heine discourse. Among the conventional but questionable assertions found here are that "ein Prototyp des modernen Unternehmers traf auf einen Prototyp des modernen Berufsschriftstellers" (a prototype of the modern entrepreneur encountered a prototype of the modern professional writer); indeed, that Heine was a pioneering professional writer; that he and Campe were "zu Freunden gewordenen Geschäftspartner" (business partners who had become friends), whose friendship rescued the relationship when it nearly foundered; and that Campe was a "frühkapitalistischer Verleger" (early capitalist publisher; Höhn/Liedtke, 9, 25). To bring some clarity into these matters I will briefly address three points: Heine's attitude toward the business of publishing; the character of the marriage of Heine and Campe; and, a specific point, the reason for Campe's three-year suspension of their correspondence beginning in 1848.

As we know, the efforts to make a businessman of young Heine failed ignominiously, not, it would seem, owing to incapacity but to radical lack of interest. The long and the short of it was pretty much compressed in a late comment on his father's project of apprenticing him to merchants in Frankfurt: "ich lernte bey dieser Gelegenheit wie man einen Wechsel ausstellt und wie Muskatnüsse aussehen" (I learned on this occasion how to draw up a bill of exchange and what nutmegs look like).[27] He held a paying position for only six months of his life, the co-editorship of Baron Cotta's *Neue allgemeine politische Annalen* (New General Political Annals) in 1828.

Another young writer in his circumstances might have thought himself fortunate to obtain a footing in Cotta's prestigious publishing conglomerate, but Heine treated the opportunity lightly and abandoned it easily. It has seemed to me that he never made any clear connection between income and work. There is no evidence that he had any understanding of how his Uncle Salomon had become so wealthy. All he knew was that the boorish uncle had the money and the poetic nephew in service to all mankind did not, and that this was an unjust distribution. He seems to have felt that, as a poet and emancipator, he was entitled to generous support. I once phrased this as follows: "we may postulate that he thought he was a kind of Augustan poet, in need of and deserving of a Maecenas in some form in recognition of his poetic eminence and his service to the commonweal."[28] A terser, truly inspired formulation appeared recently in a study uncommonly emancipated from the conventions of the Heine discourse: "mäzenatische Mischfinanzierung" (mixed financing under the patronage of a Maecenas).[29]

Heine's indifference to business matters extended consistently to the publishing business. With his skill in image management he managed to create, especially for posterity, the persona of a downtrodden, chronically impoverished poet, struggling to maintain himself against a rapacious publisher. In fact he appears to have been, work by work, one of the better paid serious German writers of his time and, on the whole, the best paid by Campe.[30] But, owing to his high standards and his meticulous way of working, he did not maintain the productivity of a professional writer. Despite the yards of shelf space taken up by Heine editions in our time, his total œuvre is quite compact, especially when compared with those of his contemporaries, some of whom, such as, for example, Karl Gutzkow, seem to have written unremittingly day and night. He did not professionalize himself in other ways very much either. He did not form alliances with other German writers, and the quality of his relations with French writers, which has been somewhat exaggerated for familiar reasons in our time, looks less rich if examined from the French side. He did not establish himself as a periodical editor, as his contemporaries often did, though he occasionally explored journalistic possibilities, such as his effort, if that is the word, in 1838, to found a German newspaper in Paris, "nachdem ich durch Uebermenschliche Beredsamkeit einen Esel gefunden der 150 000 Franks . . . riskiren wollte" (after having found, through superhuman eloquence, an ass . . . willing to risk 150,000 francs),[31] but this project seems as quixotic as Heine's alleged searches for employment in his late twenties, for it depended on Prussia's willingness to permit the newspaper's importation, which could not imaginably have been obtained. Heine's most potent ally in the business of publishing was obviously Campe. Heine knew this in some part of his mind, but he refused to conduct himself as though he did.

This brings us to the personal relationship of author and publisher. As in many marriages, it was asymmetrical. One might even think of the old adage that, in any love relationship, there is one who loves and one who condescends to be so treated. In this case the wooer was clearly Campe, at least in the early years. Repeatedly he tried to personalize the relationship with news of his private life and his business affairs. Heine almost never responded to initiatives of this kind, nor did he confide much in Campe in turn. He seems to have instinctively felt that the relationship had to be maintained on an adversarial footing, undiluted by sentiment. One notices in the marriage allusions that Campe employs them to urge harmony and cooperation, while Heine employs his for complaints of being ill-used. Heine constantly charged Campe with neglect, underpayment, inelegant book design, harboring enemies in the publishing house, and sacrificing the integrity of his texts to censorship. On this last point it became a kind of trope when he offered a new text to demand that it appear uncensored. He regularly implied that Campe could publish his works uncensored if he only would, and that he submitted them to the censorship only out of perversity and ill-will towards his author. He brought these charges into public print, in a detailed commentary in a newspaper in 1836 and an open letter titled *Schriftstellernöthen* (Writer's Tribulations) in 1839, accusing Campe of disloyalty and deceit, and questioning his competence and courage.[32] Campe at first tried to retain his patience: "Wir sind Freunde und verstehen uns, warum *dieser* Trödel!" (We are friends and understand one another, why *this* junk!)[33] but then obliquely threatened him with a duel.[34] He repeatedly tried to explain to Heine the economics of the publishing business, the facts of the censorship, and Heine's insecure standing with the public, but to no avail; Heine simply declined to engage in a dialogue on these matters, but continued to insist on the furor that his next work would arouse, promising writing that, as Campe put it, "mich in des Teufels Küche liefern soll" (is likely to deliver me into the devil's kitchen).[35]

The censorship was the most important issue between Heine and Campe, even more important than the differences over compensation, for as Heine lamented in one of his rare moments of clarity in the matter, "was hilft mir schreiben, wenn mir's nicht gedruckt [wird]?" (what good is it to write if it is not to be printed?)[36] The censorship was a device of the Metternichian regime to stop historical time.[37] The system had grown out of the Napoleonic Wars, which in turn had grown out of the French Revolution. Stability therefore required that there be no recurrence of revolution, and therefore no public discourse on political and governmental matters, no expressions of discontent, no criticism of any ruler or government, no discussions of constitutionalism or democracy. Forbidden also were the yearnings for the unification of Germany; patriotism was subversive because it implied the deposal of the rulers of the German states. The censorship had had a long history, but, in 1819, the assassination of the playwright August von Kotzebue, a conservative and a Russian agent, by a radical student provided the government with a pretext to tighten the censorship rules in the Carlsbad Decrees, which required that all publications under twenty signatures, or 320 pages in normal octavo, were to be subjected to precensorship before publication. The idea was that large books would not be read by the people, while the real danger lay in newspapers, pamphlets, and easily accessible short works. The effect can be seen in books of the time to this day: large type, wide margins, blank spaces, and twenty lines to the page.

At first the excisions of the censor were indicated by blank spaces or dashes. Heine satirized this practice in a famous chapter of *Das Buch Le Grand* consisting only of the words: "Die deutschen Censoren . . . Dummköpfe . . ." (The German censors . . . blockheads), separated by some ninety dashes;[38] elsewhere he suggestively inserted dashes where no excisions had been made, but in Prussia in 1826 and in all the German states in 1834 it became illegal to do even this, and type had to be expensively reset. This was an example of the continuous tightening of the censorship regulations throughout the years up to 1848. Also, in 1834 the rule that a book passed in any German state was admissible in any of the others was rescinded, so that Campe had to shop for a censor who would meet Prussian requirements and for printers willing to take chances. In December 1835 the German Confederation issued a ban on all writings, past, present, and future, against Heine and four other oppositional writers, collectively and loosely known as Young Germany, "deren Bemühungen unverholen dahin gehen, in belletristischen, für alle Classen von Lesern zugänglichen Schriften die christliche Religion auf die frechste Weise anzugreifen, die bestehenden socialen Verhältnisse herabzuwürdigen und alle Zucht und Sittlichkeit zu zerstören" (whose efforts tend openly to attack the Christian religion in this most impudent way, to denigrate existing social relations, and to destroy all discipline and morality, in belles-lettres accessible to all classes of readers); an explicit warning to the firm of Hoffmann und Campe was appended.[39] In December 1841 Campe did get into "the devil's kitchen": Prussia banned the whole firm of Hoffmann und Campe, giving the publication of Heine's works as a principal reason.[40] This time Campe was rescued literally by accident: in May 1842 a huge fire devastated the inner city of Hamburg and, as one of its charitable gestures toward the city, the Prussian government lifted the ban on Hoffmann und Campe.

Heine indicated little sympathy for Campe's troubles in these matters and sometimes not even a lucid understanding of his own. This is particularly evident in his initial inability to take the Young German ban of 1835 seriously. He persisted in regarding it as a misunderstanding, a confusion of his harmless, poetic self with Campe's other, offensive writers.

He wrote a letter to the Federal Assembly, complaining of having been condemned without a hearing, asserting the religious and moral qualities of his writing, and declaring his loyalty to the authorities.[41] For a time Campe was unable to persuade Heine of the futility of such initiatives and the seriousness of the situation. Not until he became persuaded of the need to cooperate with his publisher did they work together to seek a solution by evading and subverting the ban with works that at least appeared to be politically harmless.

A particularly impressive display of Heine's calculated deafness followed the public outrage generated by his book on Ludwig Börne. Heine originally demanded for the book, offered sight unseen, as usual, 2,000 marks banco;[42] Campe countered with an offer of 1,000 for the first printing and 1,000 for a second, probably speculating that there would not be a second. Campe prevailed, but as the storm over the book raged, Heine demanded a second printing so that he could have the remainder of the honorarium, despite Campe's insistence that the first printing was not selling well. Heine blamed the vociferous offense taken at his book on the machinations of Karl Gutzkow, whom he regarded as an enemy lodged in Campe's house; Campe wearily explained that Gutzkow had nothing like the power to generate such widespread outrage. No matter; in letter after letter Heine came back to his demand for a second printing and the dismissal of Gutzkow.[43]

Campe was himself a hard and devious man who was not above producing second printings for which he ought by rights to have paid, but on the whole he bore the burden of publishing Heine with fortitude. Although much has been written about Campe and his publishing house, the finances of Hoffmann und Campe are still not entirely transparent. While he may have more or less broken even with Heine, it seems clear that he did not get rich on him, since most of his books did not sell well or were balked by the censorship, and that the enterprise was secured with other kinds of publishing of such things as school textbooks and literary works of writers more prolific than Heine, such as some fifty volumes of Ernst Raupach's innumerable historical dramas. Campe was not an aesthete or an intellectual as one can see not only from his hasty, unkempt letters, but also from the one opusculum he wrote himself in which in 1832 he employed Schiller as a witness in the cause of freedom against the banning of Börne's Parisian letters.[44] But he seems to have had a perhaps partly subliminal sense that publishing Heine was a service to the welfare of the nation. One hint of this *e contrario* and almost *e silentio* is his unwillingness to publish Heine's commentary on a set of English fashion plates purportedly illustrating Shakespeare's female characters, though he did take some copies in commission.[45] The demurral was unusual, for he almost always, sometimes after stalling and haggling, agreed to publish Heine's books, often sight unseen. He seems to have sensed that *Shakspeares Maedchen und Frauen* (Shakespeare's Girls and Women) was a potboiler, which was exactly the way Heine thought of it, and that it therefore was not up to his standard even if it promised to sell pretty well, as it did. It is not significant for our purposes that Campe was mistaken about the book's value — it contains much that is interesting, notably the revaluation of Shylock, an early step in Heine's recovery of his Jewish identity; significant is only that Campe seems to have been protecting Heine's dignity as a major writer.

My third point concerns the most serious breach that occurred in the relationship. At a crucial historical moment, in April 1848, one month after the outbreak of the revolution in Berlin, Campe, the most loquacious of letter-writers, fell silent. Now the asymmetry of the marriage was reversed; Heine became the wooer. He wrote Campe a dozen pleading letters, but Campe, though he met his obligations punctually, sent not one line in reply for a full three years. The Heine scholars have confessed a remarkable bewilderment about this episode; for example, Höhn and Liedtke suggest that it "ist nicht einmal ganz klar, was Campe von 1848 bis 1851 bewogen hat, auf Heines dringliche Briefe nicht mehr zu antworten" (it is not even completely clear what induced Campe not to answer Heine's urgent letters from 1848 to 1851; Höhn/Liedtke, 29). As others have done, they speculate about a personal tiff. When Campe, late in life, had his only son, born in 1846, he asked Heine to stand godfather. Even if Heine could have evaded the standing order in Prussia for his arrest, his health would not have permitted him to travel, though Campe, inured by two decades of complaint, failed to grasp the seriousness of Heine's physical condition. Campe postponed the christening, finally holding it by proxy in February 1848. His announcement of the event in a letter of March 15 has a peevish undertone, especially as someone had started a rumor that Heine had refused the honor.[46] That this was the reason for the breach was later reported to Heine in a letter of Georg Weerth, not a source I would implicitly trust.[47] For this seems a rather petty motive for so drastic a move, and in fact there is another letter a month later in which Campe complains that none of his questions concerning Heine's collected edition and new editions of out-of-print works have been answered and that Austria has freed his works from censorship; then he adds, "Ich bitte mir diese Fragen *ungesäumt* zu beantworten" (I am asking you to answer these questions *without delay*).[48]

Campe's motivation here is not obscure. One of the most immediate consequences of the 1848 revolution was the collapse of the censorship regulations in one state of the German Confederation after another. This was the moment Campe had been waiting for; he was surprised by it, as he indicated in that earlier letter, dated March 15 but finished two days later: "Die Preße ist seit dem 8 d. hier frei und wird es auch soweit die deutsche Zunge reicht; freilich erwartete ich es langsamer und rein durch beßere

Einsicht der Regierungen — Kurz, wir haben es und das ist es, worauf ich für die unverstümmelte Herausgabe Ihrer Werke gewartet und gezögert habe" (The press is free here since the 8th of this month and will be as far as the German tongue extends; to be sure, I expected it more slowly and purely through the better judgment of the governments — anyway, we have it, and that is what I have waited for and why I delayed the unmutilated publication of your works).[49] With his professional acumen, he may have sensed, correctly, that the moment might not last indefinitely. What he meant with the "unverstümmelte Herausgabe Ihrer Werke" (unmutilated publication of your works) was not only new editions of individual works, but the collected edition, which had been a bone of contention for years. When he received no reply, he sent his ultimatum on April 18: he wanted answers to his questions *now*. When he did not get answers *now*, but more of Heine's complaints and dilatoriness, Campe fell silent. From his point of view, Heine had failed him as a partner at a moment essential to his *raison d'être*. The matter of the collected edition in particular is complicated and there are two sides to it, but, after all, Heine had sold him the rights to it eleven years earlier for 20,000 francs and never delivered it.[50] What drew Campe out of his sulk in 1851 was the prospect of a new book of poems, which was to become *Romanzero*; all he had ever wanted of Heine was that he should write books, preferably poetic and literary ones. Campe visited in Paris and finally was persuaded of the gravity of Heine's physical condition. The correspondence resumed; still, the marriage was not quite what it had been before. Heine almost immediately reverted to his customary pattern of self-righteous recriminations. To cite myself one more time: "Some of the adhesive, the fraternal substratum beneath all the combat, had crumbled out of their 'marriage,' and it could not all be put back in."[51]

The failure to perceive these matters accurately is owing, as it seems to me, to a zealous desire to appropriate Heine as new and modern, even as our contemporary, and as an ally of our own purposes and convictions. However that may be in general, the publishing relationship is not a suitable venue for it. Among the characteristics of modern publishing are author's royalties calibrated to sales figures, national and international copyright, and a reasonable degree of freedom of the press. In Heine's time authors sold books to publishers for a lump-sum honorarium per work or sometimes per edition. This system put the publisher at considerable risk, though it could be advantageous in the case of a good seller, as Heine's *Buch der Lieder* eventually came to be. The absence of effective copyright was a threat to the publisher's welfare and encouraged the greatest possible speed in the distribution process, for pirating was rife. A spectacular example in Heine's case was the publication of the unachievable collected edition by a Philadelphia pirate in 1855, which frustrated Campe, but he could do nothing about it except to try to prevent its reimportation into the German states. As for freedom of the press, the censorship was the single most significant consideration for the tactics of publishing Heine's works. It also accelerated the distribution process, as Campe endeavored to ship books so that they would appear in the shops on the same day all over Germany and, it was hoped, might have twenty-four hours of life before the confiscations began. The pirated edition of the collected works sold within a decade 18,000 sets in the United States,[52] more than any work of Heine in Germany during his lifetime except, possibly, the *Buch der Lieder*, thus an indication of what his success as an author might have been in the German-speaking countries if it had not been for the censorship. A further indication is the proliferation of Heine publications in every size and format from the 1860s through the Weimar Republic, too late, of course, to be of any use to the author.

Today's scholars want desperately to employ Heine in an indictment of capitalism and the commodification of literature, and, sometimes, to ascribe to him, on the one hand, an advanced mastery of the capitalist system to his advantage and, on the other, an advanced insight into it. I think this is a Marxist ghost in the machine, and of dubious relevance. Heine regarded capitalist investment and finance as a realm of magic. Despite his sometime friendship with the young Karl Marx, there is no indication that he absorbed anything of Marx's economic analysis. He was unable to grasp the concept of risk in investment. This became evident in the early 1850s in his long and persistent private and public campaign to humiliate and coerce the speculator Ferdinand Friedland into reimbursing him for a failed investment in a Prague gas-lighting scheme.[53] As for his publisher, Hoffmann und Campe was not really a capitalist enterprise. It had no investors, at least at that time, and operated as an artisanal shop, largely staffed with apprentices.

I have long thought that, in Heine studies, we might restrain ourselves somewhat from talking about our own preoccupations and, instead, look at him more closely on his own terms in his own context. His metaphorical marriage was more complex and more subtle than his literal one to "Mathilde," and tells us as much if not more about his sense of self and his sometimes overwrought devices for managing his affairs. Campe was by far the most important person in Heine's life, and if we try to perceive their marriage as accurately and fairly as we can, we will learn more about him than by fitting him into templates supplied by our own agendas.

Notes

[1] Julius Campe to Heinrich Heine, 23 March 1837, *Heinrich Heine Säkularausgabe*, ed. National Forschungs- und Gedenkstätten der klassischen deutschen Literatur in Weimar (after 1992, Stiftung Weimarer Klassik) and (to 1998) Centre National de la Recherche Scientifique in Paris (Berlin and Paris: Akademie-Verlag

and Editions du CNRS, 1970–), 25:37. Hereinafter cited as *HSA* with volume and page number.

[2] Campe to Heine, 18 November 1839, 21 August 1841, 28 January 1854, *HSA*, 25:227, 335; 27:155–56.

[3] See especially Campe to Heine, 23 October 1835, *HSA*, 24:353, where he expands the trope to all of Heine's works as a troublesome family, including "die ältesten Kinder, die Reisebilder, 2 Mädchen und 2 Knaben" (the oldest children, the *Travel Pictures*, two girls and two boys).

[4] Heine to Campe, 21 April 1854, *HSA*, 23:324, 326.

[5] On the history of the firm, see Gert Ueding with Bernd Steinbrink, *Hoffmann und Campe: Ein deutscher Verlag* (Hamburg: Hoffmann & Campe, 1981). Carl Brinitzer, *Das streitbare Leben des Verlegers Julius Campe* (Hamburg: Hoffmann & Campe, 1962) contains useful information about the family but is novelized and therefore to be used with caution.

[6] See especially Edda Ziegler, *Julius Campe — Der Verleger Heinrich Heines* (Hamburg: Hoffmann & Campe, Heinrich Heine Verlag, 1976). An informative and reasonable examination of Heine's finances, including his relationship with Campe, will be found in Michael Werner, *Genius und Geldsack: Zum Problem des Schriftstellerberufs bei Heinrich Heine* (Hamburg: Hoffmann & Campe, Heinrich Heine Verlag, 1978). Werner corrects some of Ziegler's figures.

[7] Richard S. Levy, *The Downfall of the Anti-Semitic Political Parties in Imperial Germany* (New Haven: Yale UP, 1975).

[8] Ute Kröger, "'Unsere Stadt ist kein Krähwinkel!' Die Düsseldorfer und 'ihr' Heine — vom Versuch, nach dem Denkmalsdebakel ein eigenes Heine-Verständnis zu pflegen," in *Das literarische Düsseldorf: Zur kulturellen Entwicklung von 1850–1933*, ed. Gertrude Cepl-Kaufmann and Winfried Hartkopf (Düsseldorf: Teubig, 1988), 59–66; Dietrich Schubert, *"Jetzt wohin?" Heinrich Heine in seinen verhinderten und errichteten Denkmälern* (Cologne: Böhlau, 1999).

[9] Inge Schlotzhauer, *Ideologie und Organisation des politischen Antisemitismus in Frankfurt am Main 1880–1914* (Frankfurt am Main: Kramer, 1989), 263–84.

[10] For a treatment of this topic that, for once, does not treat Kraus as a sacred cow, see Dietmar Goltschnigg, *Die Fackel ins wunde Herz: Kraus über Heine; Eine "Erledigung"?* (Vienna: Passagen, 2000).

[11] Robert Neumann, "Deutschland und Heinrich Heine," *C-V Zeitung*, 5 August 1927, 456.

[12] The fat conference volume, *Internationaler Heine-Kongreß Düsseldorf 1972. Referate und Diskussionen*, ed. Manfred Windfuhr (Hamburg: Hoffmann & Campe, Heinrich Heine Verlag, 1973), does not give an adequate picture of the turmoil. Not that those ill-disposed to Heine were paper tigers; the struggle to name the university for him took no less than twenty-one years.

[13] For an account of the events, see Jeffrey L. Sammons, "Review Essay: The Bicentennial of Heinrich Heine 1997: An Overview," *Goethe Yearbook* 9 (1999): 346–83, reprinted in Sammons, *Heinrich Heine: Alternative Perspectives 1985–2005* (Würzburg: Königshausen und Neumann, 2006), 245–76.

[14] Heinrich Heine, *Reise von München nach Genua*, chapter 31, *Historisch-kritische Gesamtausgabe der Werke*, ed. Manfred Windfuhr et al. (Hamburg: Hoffmann & Campe, 1973–97), 7/1:74. Hereinafter cited as *DHA*.

[15] Heinz Becker, *Der Fall Heine-Meyerbeer: Neue Dokumente revidieren ein Geschichtsurteil* (Berlin: de Gruyter, 1958). Jürgen Voigt attempts to obfuscate the matter by translating it into political and class terms, a good example of the protective devices of changing the subject; see Voigt, "Mäzen und Erpresser? Noch einmal zum 'Fall' Meyerbeer-Heine," *Zeitschrift für deutsche Philologie* 112, no. 4 (1993): 543–68. The most recent scholarly biography — Jan-Christoph Hauschild and Michael Werner, *"Der Zweck des Lebens ist das Leben selbst." Heinrich Heine: Eine Biographie* (Cologne: Kiepenheuer und Wisch, 1997), 398–400 — at least touches on the episode while eliding it. Becker's study is not in the bibliography.

[16] See the commentary to my translation of Heinrich Heine, *Ludwig Börne: A Memorial* (Rochester: Camden House, 2006).

[17] See Jeffrey L. Sammons, "Heine as *Weltbürger?* A Skeptical Inquiry," *Modern Language Notes* 101 (1986): 609–28, reprinted in Sammons, *Imagination and History: Selected Papers on Nineteenth-Century German Literature* (New York: Peter Lang, 1988), 97–122.

[18] A fresh beginning has been made by Klaus Deinet, "Heine und die Julimonarchie," *Internationales Archiv für Sozialgeschichte der deutschen Literatur* 32, no. 2 (2007): 55–92.

[19] Hans Hörling, *Heinrich Heine im Spiegel der politischen Presse Frankreichs von 1831–1841. Ansatz zu einem Modell der qualitativen und quantitativen Rezeptionsforschung* (Frankfurt am Main: Peter Lang, 1977).

[20] For one account of this still imperfectly understood episode, see Jeffrey L. Sammons, *Heinrich Heine: A Modern Biography* (Princeton, NJ: Princeton UP, 1979), 223–25.

[21] Dolf Oehler, "Heines Genauigkeit. Und zwei komplementäre Stereotypen über das Wesen der proletarischen Massen," *Diskussion Deutsch* 8 (1977): 258.

[22] Bodo Morawe, *Heines "Französische Zustände." Über die Fortschritte des Republikanismus und die anmarschierende Weltliteratur* (Beihefte zum *Euphorion*, 28. Heidelberg: Winter, 1997).

[23] Morawe, "'Sehet, alle Gottheiten sind entflohen. . . .' Heinrich Heine und die radikale Aufklärung," in *"Aber der Tod ist nicht poetischer als das Leben": Heinrich Heines 18. Jahrhundert*, ed. Sikander Singh (Bielefeld: Aisthesis, 2006), 73–120. For a long overdue critique of Morawe's fabrications from within Heine scholarship, see Klaus Deinet, "Heine und Frankreich — eine Neuordnung," *Internationales Archiv für Sozialgeschichte der deutschen Literatur* 32, no. 1 (2007): 114, 139n.68, and Deinet, "Heine und die Julimonarchie," 64–65.

[24] *"Der Weg von Ihrem Herzen bis zu Ihrer Tasche ist sehr weit": Aus dem Briefwechsel zwischen Heinrich Heine und seinem Verleger Julius Campe*, ed. with an introduction by Gerhard Höhn and Christian Liedtke (Hamburg: Hoffmann & Campe, 2007). This publication appeared in two versions. An earlier, shorter one, with the same title, dated 2005, was distributed as a "Freundesgabe" (gift for

friends) to mark the 150th anniversary of Heine's death on February 17, 2006. The more complete version is hereinafter cited as Höhn/Liedtke with page number.

[25] Gerhard Höhn, *Heine-Handbuch: Zeit, Person, Werk*, 3rd rev. ed. (Stuttgart: Metzler, 2004).

[26] Liedtke is the author of, among other things, a solid compact introduction, *Heinrich Heine* (Reinbek bei Hamburg: Rowohlt Taschenbuch Verlag, 1997), and the editor of a new volume in a once valuable, recently dormant series of collected studies, *Heinrich Heine: Neue Wege der Forschung* (Darmstadt: Wissenschaftliche Buchgesellschaft, 2000).

[27] Heinrich Heine, *Memoiren, DHA*, 15:63. The circumstances of the failure of young Heine's business, especially his father's efforts to extract credit from it, leading to his Uncle Salomon shutting it down, are not well known. See Sammons, *Heinrich Heine: A Modern Biography*, 45–46.

[28] Jeffrey L. Sammons, "Who Did Heine Think He Was?," *Heinrich Heine's Contested Identities: Politics, Religion, and Nationalism in Nineteenth-Century Germany*, ed. Jost Hermand and Robert C. Holub (New York: Peter Lang, 1999), 7; reprinted in Sammons, *Heinrich Heine: Alternative Perspectives*, 195–96.

[29] Ralph Häfner, *Die Weisheit des Silen: Heinrich Heine und die Kritik des Lebens* (Berlin: de Gruyter, 2006), 279.

[30] Höhn/Liedtke, 191–92.

[31] Heine to Giacomo Meyerbeer, 24 March 1838, *HSA*, 21:263.

[32] Heine to the *Allgemeine Zeitung* in Augsburg, 26 April 1836; to the *Zeitung für die elegante Welt*, 3 April 1839, *HSA*, 21:149–52, 308–18. The latter was printed in installments on 18, 19, and 20 April. It is characteristic that Höhn/Liedtke, though admitting that these charges were at least in part unjust, nevertheless justify them (90).

[33] Campe to Heine, 18 April 1839, *HSA*, 25:202. Not in Höhn/Liedtke.

[34] Campe to Heine, 22 May 1839, *HSA*, 25:212.

[35] Campe to Heine, 2 November 1832, *HSA*, 24:147.

[36] Heine to Campe, 1 September 1836, *HSA*, 21:160. Not in Höhn/Liedtke.

[37] A great deal has been written about the censorship, beginning with the last quarter of the nineteenth century, when scholars became distressed at the governmental repression of the drama and sought to expose the history of the struggle for freedom of expression. Among modern studies see Edda Ziegler, *Literarische Zensur in Deutschland 1819–1848. Materialien, Kommentare* (Munich: Hanser, 1983); Dieter Breuer, *Geschichte der literarischen Zensur in Deutschland* (Heidelberg: Quelle und Meyer, 1982); and Frederik Ohles, *Germany's Rude Awakening: Censorship in the Land of the Brothers Grimm* (Kent, OH: Kent State UP, 1992). For an excellent account of the struggles with the censorship of Hoffmann & Campe's greatest competitor, see Daniel Moran, *Toward the Century of Words: Johann Cotta and the Politics of the Public Realm in Germany, 1795–1832* (Berkeley: U of California P, 1990). For Heine in particular see Ute Radlik, "Heine in der Zensur der Restaurationsepoche," *Zur Literatur der Restaurationsepoche*

1815–1848. Forschungsreferate und Aufsätze, ed. Jost Hermand and Manfred Windfuhr (Stuttgart: Metzler, 1970), 460–89.

[38] *DHA*, 6:201.

[39] H. H. Houben, *Jungdeutscher Sturm und Drang: Ergebnisse und Studien* (Leipzig: Brockhaus, 1911), 63.

[40] Ueding, *Hoffmann und Campe*, 315–16.

[41] Heine to die Hohe Bundesversammlung in Frankfurt am Main, 28 January 1836, *HSA* 21:134–35.

[42] The mark banco was not a form of currency but a unit employed for banking and credit transactions in Hamburg; it was equal to approximately two French francs.

[43] See the commentary to Heine, *Ludwig Börne: A Memorial*.

[44] [Julius Campe], *Schiller's politisches Vermächtniß: Ein Seitenstück zu Börne's Briefen aus Paris* (Hamburg: Hoffmann & Campe, 1832).

[45] *Shakspeares Maedchen und Frauen mit Erlaeuterungen von H. Heine* (Paris: Delloye; Leipzig: Brockhaus und Avenarius, 1839).

[46] Campe to Heine, 15 March 1848, *HSA*, 26:221–22.

[47] Georg Weerth to Heine, 10 June 1851, *HSA*, 26:294.

[48] Campe to Heine, 18 April 1848, *HSA*, 26:223. Not in Höhn/Liedtke.

[49] Campe to Heine, 15 March 1848, *HSA*, 26:220–21.

[50] Contract *HSA*, 21:200–201. For an overview of the fifteen years of Heine and Campe balking one another over the collected edition, see Sammons, *Heinrich Heine: A Modern Biography*, 220–21. Höhn/Liedtke have a section subtitled "Das kurze Ringen um die Gesamtausgabe" (81–89; the brief wrestling over the collected edition), which was not brief; here and elsewhere some of the letters concerning the matter may be found, but by no means all of them. In a comment, Höhn/Liedtke blame Campe for the failure of the collected edition to appear, a quite typical example of editing the evidence in Heine's favor (81).

[51] Sammons, *Heinrich Heine: A Modern Biography*, 304.

[52] Robert E. Cazden, *A Social History of the German Book Trade in America to the Civil War* (Columbia, SC: Camden House, 1984), 312.

[53] Sammons, *Heinrich Heine: A Modern Biography*, 285–86.

8: At Wit's End: Frank Wedekind and the "Albert Langen Drama"

Mary Paddock

B Y MOST ACCOUNTS, the publisher Albert Langen (1869–1909) believed to the end in Frank Wedekind's ability as a playwright. Despite the unrelenting rancor that characterized their relationship — and repeated pleas from Langen's colleagues to let the "Sauhund" (bastard) Wedekind go — their professional relationship endured for nearly fifteen years.[1] Another of Langen's authors, Jakob Wassermann, characterized the relationship as one of "furioser Anziehung, von wildgewordener Freundschaft, von materieller Abhängigkeit auf der einen Seite, die sich in Beschimpfungen Luft machte, von Bewunderung und Wissen um die hohe Besonderheit auf der andern, die sich gern in Machtbeweisen und Dressurspäßen verleugnete" (tempestuous attraction, a crazed friendship on the one hand [based on] material dependence that gave vent to itself in verbal assaults, and on the other hand on recognition and awe of [the other's] distinctiveness, belied by power plays and games designed to keep him in line).[2]

What Wassermann at best only implies here, however, is that the mutually sadistic impulses to which he alludes were exacerbated to a great extent by the age-old conflict between art and commerce and "the fate of the artist in capitalist society" — the *Kunst-Mammon* (art vs. wealth for its own sake) dichotomy that had occupied Wedekind since before his first attempts at dramatic composition.[3] Langen's energetic focus on his other publishing enterprise, the weekly satirical journal *Simplicissimus*, and his reliance on what he viewed as Wedekind's Heine-esque satirical viewpoint to secure the journal's oppositional reputation (and thus increase its sales and advertising revenues) brought the dichotomy to the fore to a far greater extent than their author-publisher relationship alone would have done. From Wedekind's standpoint, it was intolerable that he should compose tendentious poetry for money to help Langen sell journals while his own serious work languished. While it would indeed be simplistic to reduce the complex author-publisher relationship exclusively to the *Kunst-Mammon* dynamic, the unquestionable personal and professional significance of this dichotomy for Wedekind makes it indispensable for understanding his troubled relationship with Langen and for mapping out the trajectory of his literary production.[4] The conflict was no doubt exacerbated by the emergence of mass media and the attendant encroachment of marketing tenets on public discourse that significantly influenced the publishing industry in the second half of the nineteenth century and had a decisive impact on the public campaign waged between Wedekind and Langen for more than ten years.

The long-standing acrimony between the author and his publisher intensified exponentially following the so-called *Simplicissimus* Affair of 1898, in which a poem by Wedekind attacking the Kaiser and a cover illustration by Thomas Theodor Heine caused the journal to be confiscated. This affair and its aftermath came, in a sense, to exemplify the *Kunst-Mammon* struggle for Wedekind. In an effort to engage with the artistic implications of this struggle, the author reworked the narrative of the affair in his dramas. Even Wedekind would later admit, however, that his fixation on Langen and the affair compromised his dramas' conceptual integrity.

There is no question that Wedekind's well-known artistic and personal complexities complicated virtually every personal relationship in which he was involved. The memoirs of his contemporaries refer almost invariably to Wedekind's "Zerwürfnisse" (quarrels) and his hot-and-cold relationships with various cohorts. Thus the characterization of Wedekind as a *Märtyrer* (martyr) to Langen's *Henker* (executioner) is indeed patently hyperbolic, but no less so than the view of Langen's "Märtyrertum" (martyrdom) at the hands of Wedekind or anyone else.[5] Indeed, as Wassermann indicates, Langen did his part to inflame the playwright's antagonistic inclinations. The protracted altercation between Wedekind and the *Simplicissimus* camp became a veritable morality play in which Wedekind and Langen represented *Kunst* and *Mammon*, respectively, and that played itself out in the press as well as in the playwright's literary work.[6] Both Wedekind and Langen consciously cultivated their own interpretations of their respective roles: Wedekind, the satanic yet principled artist, and Langen, the wealthy bon vivant, literary impresario, and gadfly of hypocrisy.

The younger of the two, Albert Langen, was the first to take steps consciously to fashion his public image. In the early 1890s, while Wedekind was entrenched in bohemian Paris having exhausted his modest inheritance from his father, Langen, a scion of a prominent Rhineland industrial family, led a lavish life as *Le petit Langéne*, cavorting with the Parisian *demimonde* as protégé of the charismatic con man and art forger Willy Grétor. The contacts Langen made during this time proved crucial when he recruited authors for his fledgling publishing house and, not long afterward, for *Simplicissimus*. But otherwise, as Langen would write later, he merely "played" the Bohemian for a few weeks at a time, "aus

Sport" (for sport).[7] Langen turned to publishing after his initial entrepreneurial enterprise — an art dealership — succeeded merely in transferring his inheritance to Grétor. Whether or not Grétor was, as legend would have it, behind the idea to found a publishing house to rehabilitate Langen into a "useful" person and thus free him from the "immoral" burden of inherited wealth, it was Grétor who introduced Langen to his first authors: Knut Hamsun, Bjørnstjerne Bjørnson, and of course Frank Wedekind, who became Langen's first German author with the publication of *Erdgeist* (Earth Spirit) in 1895.[8]

Langen's success in attracting these and other authors to his as yet unproven publishing house can be attributed in large measure to the aura of the wealthy, successful businessman that Langen, under Grétor's tutelage, learned to maintain his life long, regardless of the actual state of his finances at any given time.[9] This aura of wealth would become a perpetual source of conflict between Langen and Wedekind. In his memoirs, Langen colleague Korfiz Holm recounts an apparently recurring scenario in which Langen tries in vain to convince Wedekind that he does not have the funds at his disposal that Wedekind believes him to have. The author, in turn, cannot be dissuaded from his belief that "Für Ihren mühelos ererbten Mammon kaufen Sie sich die größten Künstler und die schönste Frau, aber unter Ihren Metzgerhänden wird alles zunichte: Künstler, Frau und Geld" (For your effortlessly inherited *Mammon* you buy the greatest artists and the most beautiful wife, only to have everything — artists, wife, and money — come to ruin in your butchering hands).[10]

Such sentiments would seem to render the claim that Wedekind was somehow "fascinated" by Langen an overstatement.[11] Unlike Willy Grétor, the "confidence man of culture," who served as the model for the character that Wedekind considered to be the best role he ever wrote, the eponymous figure of *Der Marquis von Keith* (The Marquis of Keith), the characters modeled on Langen, the "businessman of culture"[12] (Launhart in *Hidalla* and Sterner in *Oaha/Till Eulenspiegel*), are uniformly one-dimensional and emphatically uncharismatic.[13] In fairness, however, it must be noted that Langen did not become *dramatic* fodder for Wedekind until after the *Simplicissimus* scandal.

When Langen established *Simplicissimus* in Munich in 1896, Wedekind became one of his first authors; his story "Die Fürstin Russalka" (The Princess Russalka) led the first issue, and Wedekind remained a regular contributor until his work for the journal landed him in prison.[14] Wedekind's work for *Simplicissimus* was by and large mutually beneficial in that his satirical poems were very popular with readers and thereby helped to raise his own public profile and cultivate his notoriety as a *Bürgerschreck* (enfant terrible). But as Wedekind became increasingly frustrated at the lack of acceptance for his dramatic work, he complained about the "Lohnsklavenarbeit" (wage slave labor) coerced from him by Langen for

Simplicissimus while his more serious work went untended.[15] In a letter of July 1898 to his friend Beate Heine, the author portrays Langen as a greedy scandalmonger, gleefully wringing his hands at Wedekind's promise to employ his satirical talents to counter the recent ban on the sale of *Simplicissimus* in Prussian train stations.[16]

In late October 1898, as Wedekind prepared for the Munich première of *Erdgeist*, the so-called "Palästinanummer" (Palestine Issue) of *Simplicissimus* appeared with a cover illustration by Thomas Theodor Heine and a satirical poem titled "Im Heiligen Land" (In the Holy Land) signed by "Hieronymus," whom everyone knew to be Frank Wedekind. Wedekind's poem mocked the state pilgrimage to the Holy Land of the "Reise-Kaiser" (roving emperor), William II, with his enormous entourage and reportedly colossal wardrobe of outfits for every imaginable occasion (see fig. 8.1). When the "Palästinanummer" was confiscated, warrants were issued for the arrest of Heine, Wedekind, and Langen on the charge of *Majestätsbeleidigung* (lèse majesté). Heine, whose contract with Langen provided for this contingency, turned himself in, while Wedekind and Langen fled to Switzerland.

The Munich première of *Erdgeist* had been a disaster, but given that it was the first ever public theater performance of any of Wedekind's work in the nearly ten years since he had begun to write for the stage (with the first ever professional production of one of his plays — also *Erdgeist* — having taken place only in February of that year), the timing of the scandal for Wedekind's career as a playwright and actor could not have been more catastrophic. For him the affair represented a most immediate and spectacular collision of *Kunst* and *Mammon* in which his artistic aspirations were directly and fatally compromised by Langen's capitalist enterprise.

While this essay concerns itself largely with the consequences of Wedekind's inability to see beyond the personal dimension of the conflict, it is important to note that several social-cultural factors and trends also converged at this juncture in publishing history to raise the stakes further for all parties involved. The confiscation of the "Palästinanummer" points to the draconian censorship laws of Wilhelmine Germany that made the production of quality satire more challenging and its dissemination more risky. Wedekind's lack of theatrical success resulted to some degree from the public's initial rejection of his avant-garde themes and techniques, but the explicit sexuality of many of his earlier works caused the plays to be barred by the censors from the stage before the public could object. It is true that his plays did appear in print, but usually not without concessions to the censors, who deemed his works obscene.

The strict censorship laws presented not only obstacles to authors and publishers, but also opportunities to those — like Wedekind and Langen — who knew how to capitalize on them. Both men had participated in the aforementioned dawning of mass media and the advertising age

Im Heiligen Land

Berlin W.
(Zeichnung von E. Thöny)

Der König David steigt aus seinem Grabe,
Greift nach der Harfe, schlägt die Augen ein,
Und preist den Herrn, daß er die Ehre habe,
Dem Herrn der Völker einen Psalm zu weihn.
Wie einst zu Abisags von Sunem*) Tagen
Hört wieder man ihn wild die Saiten schlagen,
Indeß sein heßres Preis- und Siegeslied
Wie Sturmesbrausen nach dem Meere zieht.

Willkommen, Fürst, in meines Landes Grenzen,
Willkommen mit dem holden Ehgemahl,
Mit Geistlichkeit, Lakaien, Excellenzen,
Und Polizeibeamten ohne Zahl.
Es freuen rings sich die histor'schen Orte
Seit vielen Wochen schon auf deine Worte,
Und es vergrößert ihre Sehnsuchtspein
Der heiße Wunsch, photographiert zu sein.

Ist denn nicht deine Herrschaft auch so weise,
Daß du dein Land getrost verlassen kannst?
Nicht jeder Herrscher wagt sich auf die Reise
Ins alte Kanaan. Du aber fandst,
Du seist zu Hause momentan entbehrlich;
Der Augenblick ist völlig ungefährlich;
Und wer sein Land so klug wie du regiert,
Weiß immer schon im Voraus, was passiert.

Es wird die rote Internationale,
Die einst so wild und ungebärdig war,
Versöhnen sich beim sanften Liebesmahle
Mit der Agrarier sanftgemuten Schar.
Frankreich wird seinen Dreyfus froh empfangen,
Als wär auch er zum heilgen Land gegangen.
In Peking wird kein Kaiser mehr vermißt,
Und Ruße bält sogar der Anarchist.

So sei uns denn noch einmal hochwillkommen
Und laß dir unsre tiefste Ehrfurcht weihn,
Der du die Schmach vom heilgen Land genommen,
Von dir bisher noch nicht besucht zu sein.
Mit Stolz erfüllst du Millionen Christen;
Wie wird von nun an Golgatha sich brüsten,
Das einst vernahm das letzte Wort vom Kreuz
Und heute nun das erste deinerseits.

Der Menschheit Durst nach Thaten läßt sich
                                    stillen,
Doch nach Bewundrung ist ihr Durst enorm.
Der du ihr beide Durste zu erfüllen
Vermagst, seis in der Tropen-Uniform,
Sei es in Seemannstracht, im Purpurkleide,
Im Rokoko-Kostüm aus starrer Seide,
Sei es im Jagdrock oder Sportgewand,
Willkommen, teurer Fürst, im heilgen Land!

                                    Hieronymus

*) I. Könige I. 1—4.

„Wohin reisen de Leut' nach Palästina?"

Fig. 8.1. Hieronymus, "Im Heiligen Land,"
Simplicissimus 3.31 (1898): 245.

that began in earnest in the mid-nineteenth century and was in full swing by the beginning of the twentieth, Wedekind through his work as a copy editor for the spice giant Maggi and Langen as a publishing entrepreneur in a time when journals such as *Simplicissimus* proliferated throughout Europe. The heightened competition in a faster-paced, increasingly urbane environment compelled publishers to develop marketing strategies that enabled them to appeal to a mass readership.[17] At the same time, publishers relied increasingly upon revenue from commercial advertising to subsidize production costs; the popularity of satirical journals in particular ensured that advertisers would reach into more communities and expand their business.[18]

The publication of books did not offer quite the same commercial opportunities, and certainly while Wedekind's plays were not being produced, his books were not selling. As we shall see, both Langen and Wedekind showed time and again their inclination to make use of the various media at their disposal to market or defend their brand. For Wedekind, this meant primarily his artistic identity, but also the reputation he cultivated as enfant terrible that would keep his name and notorious personality before the public as he worked for the acceptance of his plays. For Langen, it meant maintaining his own reputation as a successful businessman, but also keeping *Simplicissimus* in the public eye as a journal that not only promoted avant-garde art and literature, but did so in clear opposition to the official aesthetic ideology of the Wilhelmine government.[19] The *Simplicissimus* affair proved to be a perfect storm, the inevitable convergence of all of these elements that would change the landscape permanently for all concerned. Predictably, the artist had the most to lose in this constellation.

In view of this, Wedekind's frustration at the effect of the scandal on his career is understandable, his allegation that Langen provoked the confiscation perhaps debatable; but his contention that Langen welcomed as well as profited by the scandal is not only plausible but supportable.[20] The circulation of the journal more than doubled within three weeks (from 26,000 to 58,000), and thanks at least in some measure to the exploitation of the affair by the journal's staff, eventually rose to nearly triple the pre-scandal number (67,000) two weeks after that. Thomas Theodor Heine stopped short of accusing Langen of provoking the confiscation, but he did express incredulity at the fact that Langen took no steps to protect anyone but himself: "Ich finde es sonderbar, dass Langen wohl Zeit gefunden hat vor seiner Abreise alle vorhandenen Photographien von sich zu vernichten aber nicht meine Briefe. — Ich bin jetzt blamiert bis auf die Knochen" (I find it peculiar that Langen apparently found the time before his departure to destroy all existing photographs of himself, but not my letters. — Now I am disgraced to the bone).[21] Equally frustrating was the fact that Langen promptly fled the country rather than take complete responsibility for the issue as he had promised.[22]

Langen's own words, which would later be used to support the Saxon Justice Ministry's case against him, reveal at a minimum his intent to capitalize on the scandal.[23] Only two days after leaving Munich, after the issue of *Simplicissimus* following the "Palästinanummer" had been confiscated preemptively (and was later found to contain a further incriminating illustration by Heine as well as another subversive poem by Wedekind), Langen was hardly able to contain his excitement. In a letter to his father-in-law, the eminent Norwegian author Bjørnstjerne Bjørnson (30 October 1898), Langen writes with the zeal of a post-war advertising magnate: "Die Tüchtigkeit ist nicht an den Ort gebunden. . . . Je toller, desto besser! Der Simplicissimus kommt seinem nächsten Ziel (die 100 000!) dadurch immer näher. Wenn die in München diese 2. Konfiskation nur richtig auszunützen verstehen. Jetzt sollte ich da sein!" (The ability [to exploit opportunity] is not bound to location! The more outrageous the better! Simplicissimus is getting ever closer to its next [circulation] goal (100,000!). Hopefully [the colleagues] in Munich will understand how to take advantage of this second confiscation! I should be there now!).[24]

And of course, with the help of Langen's direction from abroad, "the [colleagues] in Munich" did their best to capitalize on both Heine's arrest and pending incarceration as well as the flight of Langen and Wedekind. The first issue (3/33) to appear on the stands following the two confiscated issues bore the title: "Preßfreiheit" (Freedom of the Press). The following issue (3/34) showed a self-portrait of Heine on the cover with the text: "Wie ich meine nächste Zeichnung machen werde" (How I will draw my next illustration), depicting the artist in shackles at a drawing board, surrounded by police who watch his every move and even appear to guide his drawing hand. In issue 36, a poem appears that begins:

Wer reist so spät durch Nacht und Wind?
Herr Langen und Herr Wedekind.
So nachts zu reisen ist kein Genuß,
Und das kommt vom Hieronymus. (3/36)[25]

[Who rides so late through the night and wind? / Mr. Langen and Mr. Wedekind. / To travel thus at night is no pleasure / And that comes from Hieronymus.]

The "Simplicianische[r] Erlkönig" (Simplician Erlking) continues in this vein for twelve more stanzas; and in the same vein, issue after issue, the *Simplicissimus* staff continued to capitalize on the scandal.

Contrary to the depiction in the poem, Langen and Wedekind fled Germany separately, but they did spend much of their exile together, first in Zurich, then in Paris. Financially dependent upon Langen, Wedekind agreed to write a poem each week for *Simplicissimus* in exchange for what he admitted was a "kingly" sum.[26] Many of the poems Wedekind submitted were deemed unfit for publication, because they either were filled with the "etwas stinkige Atmosphäre Wedekindschen Nachtlebens" (the somewhat putrid atmosphere of Wedekind's nightlife) or were too politically abrasive.[27] Yet Wedekind soon complained that Langen put pressure on him to compose poems that would further incriminate him and thereby put a permanent end to his theatrical career.[28] In a letter to Bjørnson a week after Wedekind's incarceration in September 1899, Wedekind claimed that Langen "ging bewußt und systematisch darauf aus, das Geld für sein luxuriöses Leben dadurch zu gewinnen, daß er mein Glück, meine Freiheit und meine künstlerische Zukunft ausmünzte" (consciously and systematically sought to attain money for his luxurious life, by minting out my happiness, my freedom, and my artistic future).[29] If his impression was misguided, Langen did little to dispel it. In Paris Langen set up residence in a luxury ten-room apartment on the corner of the Avenue du Bois and the Rue de la Pompe, for which he employed a cook, two maids, a manservant, and a governess. Bjørnstjerne Bjørnson proclaimed the apartment the most beautiful he had ever seen.[30] Whatever financial difficulties may have faced Langen before and during his exile, his insistence on maintaining the appearance of the successful, carefree businessman obscured them, and this was of course by design.[31] However, the appearance of having sacrificed nothing while others sacrificed their freedom and jeopardized their livelihood was bound to engender resentment.

After eight months in exile, Wedekind returned to Germany to stand trial for *Majestätsbeleidigung*, and over the course of the trial, he reportedly threw himself on the mercy of the court. In his own defense Wedekind claimed that Langen exploited his desperate financial straits to coerce him to produce incriminating poems and sharpen their satire, and he attributed his limited ability to resist Langen's coercion to the stress associated with his preparations for the *Erdgeist* première. Most damning for Langen proved to be Wedekind's claim that Langen personally altered the poems prior to publication. Because Heine had made a similar claim with regard to the captions for his drawings, this allegation was upheld by the Saxon Ministry of Justice in Langen's case.[32]

From Wedekind's perspective, disavowing responsibility for a piece of satire that might have done much to further his reputation as enfant terrible was risky enough.[33] Still worse was the gossip circulating about him in Munich that seriously threatened to undermine the provocative image Wedekind strove to maintain.[34] Rumors such as the one spread by his own attorney of the author's "jämmerliches, kriecherisches Benehmen" (miserable, groveling behavior) before the court, or Heine's speculation that Wedekind was a "Lockspitzel" (agent provocateur) who sought to provoke legal attacks against the journal by publishing offensive poems, jeopardized the integrity of Wedekind's carefully cultivated notoriety.[35] As the former head copywriter for Maggi's advertising office and thus a

pioneer "ad man" of the emerging advertising age, Wedekind undoubtedly understood the implications of these rumors for the brand he had
worked to establish. In panic about his professional future, he occupied
himself in prison by writing defamatory and occasionally expletive-laden
letters to Langen, the *Simplicissimus* staff, and most notably to Bjørnson, such as the letter cited above. Unlike Heine, who after his release
essentially recanted his testimony from his own trial in two letters to be
included in Langen's case file, Wedekind made no such attempt to help
Langen return to Germany.[36]

Perhaps it was this refusal to cooperate as well as Wedekind's implication of Langen in his own crime and his adversarial behavior during his
confinement that caused Langen to refuse to send him any more money
and to cut off all unmediated contact with him for three years until Langen's return to Munich in 1903.[37] Not one to be ignored, Wedekind
for the most part refused to acknowledge the queries of Langen's inter-
mediaries, continuing instead to write antagonistic letters to Langen. In
one instance, when he received no reply from his publisher, Wedekind
tried to get his attention by writing to various theaters to annul whatever
contracts Langen had concluded with them. He also began to tease out
the idea for a play based on the *Simplicissimus* affair called *Der Witz* (The
Joke), a one-act piece he conceived for the nascent literary cabaret as a
counterpart to his commercially oriented 1897 play *Der Kammersänger*
(The Court Singer). But the play was not yet to see the light of day, and
Wedekind remained with Langen, despite his threats to change publishers.

Langen's return to Germany after nearly five years in exile was facilitated by his many well-placed connections, who wielded influence at the
highest levels of government. After an unsuccessful campaign to have
Simplicissimus nominated for a Nobel Peace Prize, Langen agreed to pay
a fine (a so-called *Bezeigungsquantum*) of 20,000 marks and promised
neither to reveal the conditions under which he was allowed to return
nor to resume his antimonarchist tone in *Simplicissimus.*[38] Langen was
certainly happy to pay the fine, preferring it to a full pardon, which, as
Ludwig Thoma suggested, might have compromised the provocative,
antiestablishment reputation of his journal.[39]

Shortly after returning to Munich, Langen resumed direct contact
with Wedekind, presumably unable to avoid him any longer. Within a
matter of days the publisher and his author were embroiled in a dispute
over — what else? — money. Langen's apparent reluctance to acquiesce
to Wedekind's request for a loan triggered the threat that the author
would resume work on his play-in-progress, "Hidallah," and publish it
elsewhere (25 May 1903): "Ich würde dann in diesem Falle das früher
von mir geplante Werk 'Hidallah' wieder Aufnehmen und würde dessen
Verwertung, wie mir kontraktlich freisteht, mit irgend einem anderen

Verlag oder auch Bühnenvertrieb abschließen. . . ." (I would [in the event
Langen did not loan him the money] take up the work "Hidallah" that I
had planned earlier and would seek, as my contract allows, to conclude an
agreement for its realization with some other publishing house or perhaps
theatrical agency. . . .).[40]
     Wedekind had threatened previously to take his work to another
publishing house and in this case finally did.[41] The more subtle implication, however, appears to be that Langen should have a stake in whether
Wedekind went public with the work or not. *Hidalla*, which Wedekind
originally gave the subtitle "Sein und Haben" (Being and Having), paints
an unflattering portrait of Langen in the figure of entrepreneur Launhart
(who represents "Haben" [having]). The transparent allusions to the *Simplicissimus* affair in the play, in which Launhart puts incriminating manuscripts of the protagonist Karl Hetmann (representing "Sein" [being])
into the hands of the police, hoping the scandal will increase his journal's
circulation, makes the association of Langen with the figure of Launhart
inevitable. In this play, which some consider to be the author's last major
work, Wedekind's version of the scandal plays a significant role but takes a
back seat to the larger theme of commercial exploitation of cultural ideals,
a slight variation on Wedekind's *Kunst-Mammon* preoccupation.[42]
     Prior to *Hidalla*, Wedekind had already invested a great deal of effort
into revising and indeed re-enacting his own performance in the *Majestätsbeleidigung* trial in order to rehabilitate his damaged public image or
brand. In his 1902 play, *So ist das Leben* (Such is Life), the deposed king,
Nicolo, stands trial on the same charge. However, rather than implicate
those who falsely accused him, the protagonist nobly argues against the
philosophical absurdity of *Majestätsbeleidigung* as a prosecutable crime, as
many intellectuals of Wedekind's day had done.[43] The eponymous narrator of Wedekind's popular cabaret song "Der Zoologe von Berlin" (The
Zoologist of Berlin) takes a similar tack. By positing a series of unflattering zoological analogies he suggests not only the illogic of the concept
of *Majestätsbeleidigung* as a crime, but also lampoons the Kaiser's well-
known personal peculiarities and impugns the efficacy of the judicial system that wastes its resources pursuing relatively harmless offenders.
     As one of the greatest celebrities of the literary cabaret, Wedekind was
able to earn desperately needed money after his release from his seven-
month incarceration, but he could also revise the narrative of the scandal
with "Der Zoologe," which *Simplicissimus* a few years earlier had deemed
too politically risky and declined to publish.[44] Through his cabaret performances, Wedekind could also reassert the audacity of the incriminating
poem "Im Heiligen Land" by performing a slightly revised musical version of it called "König David" (King David).[45]
     Wedekind's intense efforts to control his own public image had thus
been limited to revisiting and revising his own role in the scandal until the

play *Hidalla* brought his version of the affair — and Langen's involvement in it — to the stage. The *Simplicissimus* staff promptly retaliated with the weapon Wedekind feared most: ridicule. Before the theatrical premiere of *Hidalla* in February 1905, a caricature of Wedekind drawn by Heine appeared in *Simplicissimus* under the heading "Moderne Dichter" (Modern Poets), featuring the somewhat corpulent playwright standing nude before a full-length mirror and sighing in disgust: "Das verfluchte Fett verdirbt mir noch meinen ganzen Satanismus" (9/5 [1904]; This accursed fat is completely ruining my satanic persona) (see fig. 8.2). This caused Wedekind, whose already fragile sense of humor had been severely compromised by the scandal (as well as by his unpleasant girth), to cease contributing even occasional poems or texts to the journal. But he did not retire quietly.

Exactly what event caused Wedekind to return to the idea that had begun with *Der Witz*, now expanded and given the title *Oaha* (pronounced Óaha), is not clear. With the increasing acceptance of his work, Wedekind was no longer dependent upon freelance satire or cabaret performances, and he sought to be released once and for all from his contract with Langen. The timing of his work on the play also coincided with the appearance in 1907 of the essay "Der Bulldogg" (The Bulldog) in *Die Fackel* (The Torch), in which Karl Kraus, citing as his source Wedekind, whom he describes as an "in jeder Beziehung vortrefflicher Kenner der Langen'schen Verlegerseele" (in every respect an excellent connoisseur of Langen's publisher soul), takes Langen to task for using the artistic-minded *Simplicissimus* and the *Simplicissimus* brand as an advertising vehicle for Langen's new financial venture, Züst automobiles.[46] A further impetus was certainly the widely publicized "palace revolt" at *Simplicissimus* in 1906. In a preemptive public relations maneuver, Langen tried to spin the coup and his concession in the press as a magnanimous recognition of his staff's contribution to the journal's success, when in fact a dramatic mutiny by the journal's artists had led to its transformation into a limited liability corporation (GmbH) with the division of profits, as well as the expenses, between Langen and the artists.[47] The insistence of Thoma, Heine, and others on co-ownership of the journal certainly reflected its increased profitability, but also their growing dissatisfaction with the arrangement by which Langen made all decisions and reaped all rewards for their artistic commitment to the journal.[48]

Although Wedekind was largely successful at keeping to the high road with *Hidalla*, it is worth noting at this juncture that he was not above wielding a pen in the service of revenge, even when it meant using his literary work as a forum or vehicle for launching salvos. Indeed, one of his earliest plays, *Kinder und Narren* (Children and Fools), written in 1891 and later titled *Die junge Welt* (The World of the Young), was written in direct response to Gerhart Hauptmann's 1890 play *Friedensfest* (Peace Fest).

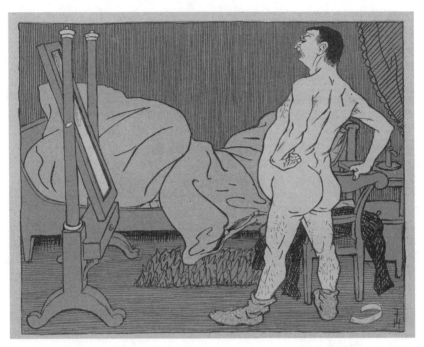

Fig. 8.2. Thomas Theodor Heine, "Das verfluchte Fett verdirbt mir noch meinen ganzen Satanismus," *Simplicissimus* 9.9 (1904): 85.

Wedekind held a life-long grudge against Hauptmann, who Wedekind believed had betrayed his confidence by using the dysfunctional Wedekind family as a model for the Scholz family in *Friedensfest*. Wedekind's play had been conceived as a discussion of the concept of women's liberation provoked by the work of Henrik Ibsen, but also as a gloss of sorts to the development of "realist," i.e., naturalist drama. This movement was represented predominantly by Hauptmann and would be a thorn in Wedekind's professional side for the first half of his career. In direct response to *Friedensfest*, Wedekind turned the figure of Ernst Ludwig Meier, originally a portrait of his friend Karl Henckell, into a caricature of Hauptmann. True to his modus operandi, the play was later revised to take a more rational approach and shed the emotional baggage of the first version.[49] Wedekind's *Die junge Welt* premiered (against his objections) in 1908, the same year he completed work on *Oaha*.

In contrast to the plays *Kinder und Narren* and *Die junge Welt*, and even to *Hidalla*, in which Wedekind's salvos against Hauptmann and Langen, respectively, were embedded within a larger substantive concept, the autobiographical content of *Oaha* was more overt. Still, Wedekind characterized his relationship to the material as merely a "Chronist" (chronicler), whom only the "power of the subject matter" compelled to immortalize the events in a play.[50] That the long-harbored bitterness toward Langen and *Simplicissimus* played a significant role is attested by the epigram to the play's first edition: "'Das verdammte Fett verdirbt mir meinen ganzen Satanismus — *Simplizissimus*'" [*sic*].[51] Unlike *Hidalla*, which in spite of its unflattering portrait of Langen puts at center stage the larger conflict inherent in the commercial exploitation of ideas rather than the sniping among the characters, *Oaha* obviously is designed to lampoon sensational events such as the *Simplicissimus* affair and the "palace revolt," to expose a few personal slights, and even to air Langen's marital difficulties. It also takes several of the *Simplicissimus* circle individually to task. Because it presented such a blatant defamation of prominent public figures, the drama was released only for a closed performance, after much debate, in 1911.[52]

Those parodied in *Oaha* did not wait for its debut to react to it. In 1908, when the comedy was first published — by Wedekind's new publisher, Bruno Cassirer, not Langen — *Simplicissimus* colleague Ludwig Thoma published his somewhat briefer dramatization of the infamous events in the journal (13/30 [October 1908]). The sketch titled "Der Satanist" (The Satanist) features Franz Wedelgrind, "ein satanischer Dichter" (a satanic poet), who tries to trade his reputation of "Satanist" for "Royalist" before judges in a Leipzig courtroom to defend himself against the charge of *Majestätsbeleidigung*, and blames his publisher for forcing him to choose between taking an antimonarchist stance or going hungry (see fig. 8.3). The satire is accompanied by a drawing by Olaf Gulbransson that depicts the still chunky Wedekind surrendering his false teeth to the judges.

Wedekind himself admitted that, from an artistic viewpoint, he did not have a "clear conscience" with regard to *Oaha*.[53] The deaths of Albert Langen, Bjørnstjerne Bjørnson, and the artists Rudolf Wilke and Ferdinand von Reznicek (in 1909 and 1910, respectively) so soon before the play's première made the satire all the more unseemly. Wedekind attempted to revise the work, as he did with many of his dramas, removing some of the more frivolous elements and incorporating more recent developments, most notably the fervent patriotism of the *Simplicissimus* staff at the outbreak of the First World War. He even allowed Georg Sterner, the Albert Langen figure, to prevail in the "palace revolt." However, the continued presence of scenes such as the slapstick *Klubsessel* (Club chair) scene, in which the character Bouterweck (Wedekind) literally falls victim to the playfully sadistic antics of Sterner (Langen) and staff, is evidence that the play continued to serve as a vehicle for airing the real-life indignities Wedekind had suffered at the hands of Langen, and perhaps for chipping away at Langen's "amiable" veneer.[54] Similarly, Wedekind declined to make any real concessions in his introspective assessment of the play later in life, citing instead conflicting interests to explain his evident

Fig. 8.3. Olaf Gulbransson, "Der Satanist," *Simplicissimus* 13.30 (1908): 490.

frustration as he chronicled events: he writes of "einen Verleger, dem damals sein Buchverlag weniger am Herzen lag als die von ihm begründete Zeitschrift. Mir hingegen lagen meine dramatischen Arbeiten mehr am Herzen als meine journalistische Tätigkeit" (a publisher whose publishing house was less important to him than his journal, whereas my dramatic works were closer to my heart than my journalistic endeavors).[55]

In the same essay, Wedekind complains that the Berlin critics proved incapable of looking beyond the biographical models for the play's characters to see the larger "artistic problem" of satire as the object of satire.[56] In leveling this critique, Wedekind implicitly demanded from the critics a level of detachment that the artist himself was unable to muster. His failure to distinguish the threat of monied interests from the person of Albert Langen and the detrimental effect of commercial concerns on artistic production from the indignities he suffered as an artist clearly exerted a deleterious influence on the integrity of the very art he strove to protect. Of course, Wedekind did go on to write several more plays before his own untimely death from complications due to surgery in 1918. None of the later works even alluded to the *Simplicissimus* affair, but neither did any of them attain the artistic stature of his pre-*Majestätsbeleidigung* work.

Wedekind never fully put this episode behind him. In the years that followed the première of *Oaha*, censorship eased significantly in pre-war Wilhelmine Germany, and Wedekind began at long last to reap the critical and financial fruits of his long years of work. Still, although he generated more revisions of this play than any other, culminating in the renamed *Till Eulenspiegel* of 1916, he never produced a satisfactory, definitive, end version of the play.[57] Because the playwright could not manage to wrest a work of critical or even comedic value from the low-brow exposé at its core, *Till Eulenspiegel* remains one of his weakest works.

Wedekind's obsession with the decade-long "Albert Langen-Drama" thus ended as it began: with satire, but worlds apart in terms of insight and trenchancy. What a difference a decade — and personal distance — can make! The final result of the drama was not the satire about satire as the object of satire, as the author would have it, but rather, as another Wedekind protagonist eventually came to realize, a *Beleidigung der eigenen Majestät* (insult to one's own majesty).

Notes

[1] All translations mine. Letter from Korfiz Holm to Albert Langen, 16 March 1900, in *Das Kopierbuch Korfiz Holms (1899–1903)*, ed. Helga Abret und Aldo Keel (Frankfurt am Main: Peter Lang, 1989), 188. In a letter written in 1899, Holm writes, "Wenn ich Ihnen meine aufrichtige Überzeugung sagen soll: lassen Sie ihn schwimmen, wenn er durchaus will" (55; If you want me to tell you my candid opinion: let him go if he wants to so badly).

[2] Although Wassermann had his own documented issues with Langen, the essential accuracy of his characterization has not been disputed by scholars on either side. Jakob Wassermann, *Lebensdienst: Gesammelte Studien, Erfahrungen und Reden aus drei Jahrzehnten* (Leipzig: Grethlein & Co.,1928), 325. See Abret and Keel, *Kopierbuch*.

[3] See Peter Jelavich, "Art and Mammon in Wilhelmine Germany: The Case of Frank Wedekind," *Central European History* 12 (1979): 203–36.

[4] Helga Abret, *Albert Langen: Ein europäischer Verleger* (Munich: Langen Müller, 1993), 402.

[5] Helga Abret has made it her goal to dispel the notion of an innocent Wedekind exploited by the ruthless Langen; see her "Frank Wedekind und sein Verleger Albert Langen," *Études germaniques* 60 (2005): 7. On Langen's "Märtyrertum," see J. A. Schmoll gen. Eisenwert, "Macht und Ohnmacht der politischen Karikatur," in *Simplicissimus: Eine satirische Zeitschrift. München 1896–1944. Mathildenhöhe Darmstadt. 24. Juni bis 13. August 1978*, ed. Carla Schulz-Hoffmann (Munich: Haus der Kunst, 1978), 20.

[6] Much of the feud on Langen's side was carried out by proxy, with the *Simplicissimus* staff doing much of the heavy lifting. This certainly contributed to the tension between the two.

[7] Letter to Dagny Bjørnson (15 May 1896), cited in *Im Zeichen des Simplicissimus: Briefwechsel Albert Langen-Dagny Björnson 1895–1908*, ed. Helga Abret and Aldo Keel (Munich: Langen Müller, 1987), 165.

[8] Thomas Theodor Heine, "Wie der Simplicissimus entstand," *Süddeutsche Zeitung*, 25/26 January 1958, Feuilleton.

[9] See Abret, *Albert Langen: Ein europäischer Verleger*, 45–47, and Ernestine Koch, *Albert Langen: Ein Verleger in München* (Munich: Langen-Müller, 1969), 32. See also Anton Sailer, "Glanz und Elend des 'Simplicissimus,'" in *Simplicissimus: Eine satirische Zeitschrift*, 36.

[10] Korfiz Holm, *Farbiger Abglanz* (Munich: Nymphenburger Verlagsbuchhandlung, 1947), 48 and 53, respectively.

[11] See Abret, *Albert Langen: Ein europäischer Verleger*, 404.

[12] Jelavich, "Art and Mammon," 226.

[13] Wedekind referred to the Marquis as the "Don Quixote of Pleasure." Frank Wedekind, "Was ich mir dabei dachte," in *Gesammelte Werke* (Munich: Müller, 1920–21), 9:429.

[14] Heine, who was involved with Langen in the initial conception of the journal, writes that Langen actively sought out rising literary stars to contribute to *Simplicissimus*; see Heine, "Wie der Simplicissimus entstand," 2.

[15] Frank Wedekind, *Der vermummte Herr: Briefe Frank Wedekinds aus den Jahren 1881–1917*, ed. Wolfdietrich Rasch (Munich: dtv, 1967), 77.

[16] Wedekind, *Der vermummte Herr*, 83.

[17] Ann Taylor Allen describes the visual impact of *Simplicissimus* in particular as a reflection of the more frenetic, fragmented existence of early twentieth-century city dwellers; see Allen, *Satire & Society in Wilhelmine Germany. Kladderadatsch and Simplicissimus, 1890–1914* (Lexington: UP of Kentucky, 1984), 37 and 44–45.

[18] Allen cites specifically the example of *Kladderadatsch*, an older and less controversial satirical journal, that began to print advertisements in 1860 which by 1866 had become "highly conspicuous" (*Satire & Society*, 29–30).

[19] Ibid., 43–44.

[20] Andreas Pöllinger, for one, asserts that it is "to be assumed" that Langen intentionally provoked the confiscation in order to increase circulation; see Pöllinger, ed., *Der Briefwechsel zwischen Ludwig Thoma und Albert Langen. 1899–1908. Ein Beitrag zur Lebens-, Werk- und Verlagsgeschichte um die Jahrhundertwende* (Frankfurt am Main: Peter Lang, 1993) 1:65.

[21] Letter to Korfiz Holm (14 November 1898) StB München, HsAbt., Nachlaß Korfiz Holm (cited in Pöllinger, *Der Briefwechsel zwischen Ludwig Thoma und Albert Langen*, 1:56–57).

[22] Pöllinger, *Der Briefwechsel zwischen Ludwig Thoma und Albert Langen*, 1:64.

[23] Helga Abret and Aldo Keel, eds., *Die Majestätsbeleidigungsaffäre des "Simplicissimus"-Verlegers Albert Langen* (Frankfurt am Main: Peter Lang, 1985), 101.

[24] Helga Abret, "Unveröffentlichte Briefe von Albert Langen an Bjørnstjerne Bjørnson," *Skandinavistik* 2 (1983): 139 (cited in Abret, *Im Zeichen*, 69). Within

a week of his arrival in Zurich, Langen wrote to his wife (5 November 1898), "Daß Heine im Gefängnis sitzt, ist für den Simplicissimus eine Riesenreklame" (That Heine is sitting in prison is an enormous advertisement for *Simplicissimus*); see Abret, *Im Zeichen*, 189.

[25] The poem is signed "Iste," a pen name of Ludwig Thoma, who would later become the interim editor of *Simplicissimus*.

[26] Letter to Beate Heine (wife of Ibsen Theater director Carl Heine), 7 January 1899, in Frank Wedekind, *Gesammelte Briefe*, ed. Fritz Strich (Munich: Müller, 1924), 1:328.

[27] Letter from Korfiz Holm to Albert Langen, 7 March 1899; see Abret and Keel, *Kopierbuch*, 45, and Holm, *Farbiger Abglanz*, 75. One such "abrasive" poem was "Der Zoologe von Berlin," which is discussed below.

[28] Letter to Beate Heine, 12 March 1899 (*Gesammelte Briefe*, 1:338–39). This letter shows that Abret's claim ("Frank Wedekind und sein Verleger Albert Langen," 26) that Wedekind's letters gave contradictory portrayals of his situation is only partially accurate, since Beate Heine received both positive and negative letters. Thus he did not always conspicuously tailor the message to the reader.

[29] 28 September 1899, *Gesammelte Briefe*, 2:16–17.

[30] B. A. Björnson-Langen, *Aulestad tur-retur*, 10 (cited in Abret, *Im Zeichen*, 80); see also Abret, *Albert Langen*, 78.

[31] Abret, *Albert Langen*, 81–83.

[32] Abret and Keel, *Majestätsbeleidigungsaffäre*, 100.

[33] Several scholars have debated whether Wedekind, as he himself testified in his *Majestätsbeleidigung* trial, had no intellectual affinity for his political satire. See Willy Schumann, "Frank Wedekind — Regimekritiker? Einige Überlegungen zur 'Majestätsbeleidigung' in den 'Simplicicissimusgedichten,'" *Seminar* 15, no. 4 (1979): 235–43; and Paul Günter Krohn, "Frank Wedekinds politische Gedichte," *Neue deutsche Literatur* 6 (1958): 85–95. Hans Wagener argues that Wedekind was painfully naïve when it came to politics ("Frank Wedekind: Politische Entgleisungen eines Unpolitischen," *Seminar* 15 [1979]: 244–50), while Wedekind biographer Artur Kutscher concedes that Wedekind was more politically astute and engaged than the author himself admitted but maintains that Wedekind was, at most, a "Stimmungspolitiker" (politician of the current mood; *Frank Wedekind: Sein Leben und seine Werke* [Munich: Langen-Müller, 1922/31; Repr. AMS Press, NY, 1970], 2:17 and 20, respectively).

[34] *Gesammelte Briefe*, 2:23, 25, and 37. Evidently gossip about Wedekind began immediately after he fled to Zurich. See his letter to Richard Weinhöppel, 14 November 1898, in *Gesammelte Briefe*, 1:319, and to Beate Heine, 2 November 1899, in *Gesammelte Briefe*, 2:23.

[35] Reported third-hand by Korfiz Holm to Albert Langen (20 June 1900); see Abret and Keel, *Kopierbuch*, 198. In spite of Wedekind's obviously volatile personality, and his claims that his long-time friend and attorney Kurt Hezel had been bribed by Langen to represent him so poorly, he seldom held a permanent grudge against anyone he at one time considered a friend. His 1912 play *Herakles* is dedicated warmly to Kurt Hezel. For Heine's speculation, see Pöllinger, *Der Briefwechsel zwischen Ludwig Thoma und Albert Langen*, 2:444.

[36] Abret and Keel, *Majestätsbeleidigungsaffäre*, 53, 65, and 66, respectively.

[37] Wedekind acknowledges receipt of the notice that Langen saw no reason to send him any more money in a letter to his friend Beate Heine dated 16 September 1899. See also K. Holm to A. Langen, 15 September 1899, in Abret and Keel, *Kopierbuch*, 135. Wedekind complains to Langen about the latter's three-year silence in a letter dated 25 September 1903 (*Gesammelte Briefe*, 2:109–10), and again on 27 April 1904 (*Gesammelte Briefe*, 2:117).

[38] This endeavor appears to have begun as a cynical tactic to force the hand of the German government by making a cultural hero of the journal, in line with Thoma's suggestion that Langen fake his own death so that he could return to Germany without fear of prosecution (Pöllinger, *Der Briefwechsel zwischen Ludwig Thoma und Albert Langen*, 1:310). However, Langen evidently did not give up on the idea of the Peace Prize, even long after he had returned to Germany, as he indicates in a 1908 letter to Ludwig Thoma (Pöllinger, *Der Briefwechsel zwischen Ludwig Thoma und Albert Langen*, 1: 402). The sum of the *Bezeigungsquantum*, which equaled approximately five times the annual salary paid Ludwig Thoma in 1901 (Pöllinger, *Der Briefwechsel zwischen Ludwig Thoma und Albert Langen*, 2:821), was set so high because of the wide-spread perception of Langen as a wealthy entrepreneur, and to offset some of the profit Langen reaped as a result of the scandal (Pöllinger, *Der Briefwechsel zwischen Ludwig Thoma und Albert Langen*, 2:452).

[39] Ludwig Thoma writes on 6 November 1902 to Langen: "Und ich meine, wenn der König von Sachsen so wohlwollend gesinnt ist, können Sie schlimmsten Falles durch den Justizminister erfahren, ob Sie nicht auf die selbe Strafe wie Heine und Wedek. rechnen dürfen, 6 Monate Festung. Das wäre mir persönlich lieber, als Begnadigung, die Sie doch sans phrase in eine etwas schiefe Stellung bringt. Natürlich wünsche ich Sie [*sic*] Ihnen ja aufrichtig — aber ich meine man 'nur'" (And I am of the opinion that, if the King of Saxony is so favorably disposed, you could in the worst case scenario ascertain from the Minister of Justice whether you might be able to count on receiving the same penalty as Heine and Wedekind, [i.e.] six months fortress incarceration. That would be for me personally preferable to a pardon, which simply put will place you in a somewhat inconsistent position. Naturally, I fervently hope you get it [i.e., the pardon], but I'm just saying). Cited in Pöllinger, *Der Briefwechsel zwischen Ludwig Thoma und Albert Langen*, 1:384.

[40] Cited by Koch, *Albert Langen*, 138; Abret, *Albert Langen*, 161 (citing Hanns Floerke, *Der Albert Langen Verlag*. Typescript, Durchschlag im Deutschen Literaturarchiv in Marbach/N. Nachlaß Gustav Pezold). In "Frank Wedekind und sein Verleger Albert Langen," Abret indicates that the original letter is in the Handschriftenabteilung der Stadtbibliothek München.

[41] Letter dated 3 April 1902 and cited in Abret, "Frank Wedekind und sein Verleger Albert Langen," 30.

[42] One critic noted after seeing the play that the author's personal antipathy toward the charlatan Launhart lent that figure contour at least, while the others, regrettably, receded blandly into the mist. See Siegfried Jacobsohn, *Schaubühne 1*, 1905–1906, 117–19. Cited in Günter Seehaus, *Frank Wedekind und das Theater* (Munich: Laokoon, 1964), 554.

[43] See Abret and Keel, *Majestätsbeleidigungsaffäre*, 7–13.

[44] Holm, *Farbiger Abglanz*, 75.

[45] Mary M. Paddock, "Redemption Songs or How Frank Wedekind Set the Simplicissimus Affair to a Different Tune," *German Studies Review* 28 (2005): 245–64.

[46] *Die Fackel* 9 (1907): 230–31. The connection is suggested in Frank Wedekind, *Werke: Kritische Studienausgabe*, ed. Hans-Jochen Irmer et al. (Darmstadt: Häusser, 2003), 8:396.

[47] Abret praises Langen's advertisement as a "Meisterstück verlegerischer Diplomatie" (masterpiece of publisher diplomacy); see Abret, *Im Zeichen*, 125, and *Albert Langen*, 113 . Langen printed the notice in *Simplicissimus* 10/48 (1906), and it appeared around the same time in newspapers throughout Germany. A week later, follow-up articles reported that the decision had been the result of a coup rather than of Langen's magnanimity (Polizei-Behörde/Politische Polizei, Staatsarchiv Hamburg, 331/S5458).

[48] Allen, *Satire & Society*, 39.

[49] It is not clear whether Wedekind was aware that while he was in exile in Paris, *Friedensfest* was being staged in Munich at the Münchner Schauspielhaus, the site of the hard-fought *Erdgeist* première that might have led to wider acceptance of his dramatic work had it not been brought to an abrupt halt by the *Simplicissimus* confiscation. It seems unlikely that Wedekind, as the theater's former dramaturge, would not have known what was happening there. See the *Münchener Neueste Nachrichten* 51/539 (22 November 1898). The play was scheduled for December 2, 1898.

[50] Wedekind, "Was ich mir dabei dachte," 435. See also his letter to Alfred Kerr in January 1909, *Gesammelte Briefe* 2:213–14.

[51] "The damn fat is completely ruining my satanic persona ~ Simplicissimus." Cf. Frank Wedekind, *Werke: Kritische Studienausgabe*, 8:11. Wedekind frequently inserted this sort of contextual marginalia in his published literary work, more as a commentary on his frame of mind than on the specific work to which they were appended. The proof is that he tended to omit the epigrams in later editions of the works.

[52] In fact, because the play's only potential appeal lies in what Seehaus has called its "problematic interest" to those familiar with the events depicted and with Wedekind's own performance in the role of Sterner, the comedy has yet to be staged before an audience unfamiliar with the events and figures. See Seehaus, *Frank Wedekind und das Theater*, 627.

[53] Letter to Alfred Kerr, *Gesammelte Briefe*, 2:213–14 (cited in Seehaus, *Frank Wedekind und das Theater*, 625).

[54] Frank Wedekind, *Oaha. Gesammelte Werke*, 5:205–6. The incident from which this scene stems is recounted in Holm, *Farbiger Abglanz*, 80, where, not surprisingly, Wedekind is depicted as taking great umbrage at an innocent mistake.

[55] Wedekind, "Was ich mir dabei dachte," 436.

[56] Wedekind, "Was ich mir dabei dachte," 448.

[57] Seehaus, *Frank Wedekind und das Theater*, 625.

IV. Elite Culture, Mass Culture, and the Medium of the Book

9: *Bildung* for Sale: Karl Robert Langewiesche's Blaue Bücher and the Business of "Reading-Up"

Katrin Völkner

IN THE TURBULENT FIRST DECADES of the twentieth century, forces across Germany's political and religious spectrum surprisingly found common ground in one area: educators, theologians, and politicians all emphasized the importance of encouraging Germany's masses to embrace the country's venerable tradition of *Bildung* for the sake of the nation.[1] Faced with the rise of modern consumer culture and its new forms of entertainment, conservative, communist, and liberal leaders alike called on every German to frequent local libraries and bookstores in order to seek out Goethe, Schiller, and other highlights of German *Bildung*. The broadly accepted belief was that "reading up" and engaging in Germany's cultural traditions would not only improve every individual but bolster the young nation's strength by steeling the masses against the influences of mass culture and by displaying Germany's cultural power. The results of these efforts were mixed at best. Publishers such as Reclam who offered cheap versions of the classics flourished, but so did distributors of dime novels, movies, and other forms of entertainment considered inferior by the educated elite. People flocked to cheap lending libraries to satisfy their reading desires and often ignored the recommendations of clerics, union leaders, and educators. Yet despite their limited success, the attempts to control the cultural behavior of the masses turned out to be long-lived and continued to dominate cultural discourses during the Weimar Republic.[2] These efforts illuminate the powerful polarity that was constructed between mass culture and high culture, the former often described as seductive or even dangerous, the latter seen as something akin to salvation.

This seemingly polarized cultural landscape provides the backdrop for my analysis of Karl Robert Langewiesche's successful *Blaue Bücher* (Blue Books). Langewiesche (1874–1931) thoroughly confused his contemporaries when in 1902 he announced his new publishing house with the following words: "Mein liebstes Ziel wird es sein, moderne, vornehme Massenartikel zu schaffen. . . ." (My foremost goal will be to create modern, sophisticated mass products).[3] German cultural critics and the publishing world greeted Langewiesche's announcement with skepticism, calling the idea of *vornehme Massenartikel* (sophisticated mass products) an oxymoron. But within a short time Langewiesche had achieved the nearly impossible in cultural production: his products convinced cultural critics and consumers alike, making his young publishing company an instant success. Within little more than a decade he had sold millions of books, although he only published a few titles each year.[4] The brand Blaue Bücher became a household name for several generations in Germany and a common sight on many bookshelves.[5] Critics and fellow publishers celebrated his books as an important contribution to the German cultural landscape and expressed their amazement at the quality of the books given their affordable prices. Precisely this straddling of the ostensibly insurmountable culture/consumerism divide renders this publisher and his cultural products a fascinating case study.

In the following I will argue that Langewiesche's books and publishing practices offer insight into cultural processes and products that could only have developed at a time when new modes of production and consumption interacted with nineteenth-century cultural discourses and practices. The rare combination of commercial success and critical acclaim that Langewiesche's books achieved resulted from the creation of hybrid products whose mechanisms and effects on consumers and critics can only be understood if we consider the book's material as well as textual traits. In that regard my analysis is indebted to the growing field of book history, for which an examination of the complex interplay of the book's materiality, textuality, and embeddedness in broader cultural and social values is central.[6] I will not only look at Langewiesche as a publisher who modernized the book trade, I will also briefly analyze some of the titles he published. This multi-layered examination renders visible an uneasy alliance of mass culture and high culture in Langewiesche's products and allows us to trace some of the tensions and contradictions that arose when consumer culture co-mingled with *Bildung*. At the center of my argument will be the claim that Langewiesche's books helped people navigate consumer modernity while at the same time providing them with important cultural capital in the form of access to book culture and discourses relevant to the German *Bildungsbürgertum* (educated bourgeoisie).

As we will see, Langewiesche implemented the newest marketing and publishing strategies while carefully conserving other traditions that preceded the rise of consumer capitalism. Langewiesche's books paid tribute to nineteenth-century ideals such as *Bildung* and Germany as a cultured nation, and propagated these ideas as correctives against modern society. By establishing lines of continuity, I will demonstrate that Langewiesche's Blaue Bücher can be seen as providing elements of stability while their very character as hybrid products renders them examples of the complex cultural and economic transitions occurring at the beginning of the twentieth century.

The hybrid character of the books stems from their presenting bourgeois values (such as originality, the autonomy of art, the inward cultivation of personality) as constant ideals while at the same time challenging them through the use of techniques of standardization and rationalization to produce and distribute the books.[7] For example, the concepts of "originality" and "authenticity" necessarily had to take on a different meaning when presented in a mass-produced and standardized format. In general, many of Langewiesche's books embody the tensions that had to be negotiated when *Bildung* became commercialized. They faced the dilemma of propagating inward reflection and immaterial values while in their very nature as commodities they had to encourage such "outward" activities as spending and consuming. An analysis of Langewiesche's strategy of interweaving tradition and innovation illuminates the complex interplay of *Bildung* and consumer culture in Germany in which discourses of *Bildung* were used both to facilitate and to control consumer culture.[8]

Despite his relative obscurity in the early twenty-first century, Karl Robert Langewiesche became a well-known and admired cultural force during his lifetime (1874–1931). Into the 1960s authors praised him as a brilliant visionary whose innovations had influenced the German publishing world for decades. He is credited as the creator of an entirely new type of book and as the inventor of the modern book cover.[9] In his *Geschichte des Buches und des Buchhandels* (1962; History of the Book and the Book Trade), Friedrich Uhlig lists Langewiesche along with Eugen Diederichs and Anton Kippenberg as the main innovator of the book industry at the beginning of the twentieth century.[10] Uhlig and other post-1945 book experts underline Langewiesche's unique and modernizing approach and point to his determination to standardize and streamline book production at a time when the book industry showed resistance to incorporating principles of the new consumer-driven economy.[11]

In order to understand what effects Langewiesche had on the culture of selling books, one needs to recall certain key features of the German book trade at the beginning of the twentieth century. The rise of mass-produced print material presented new challenges for Germany's "traditional" book trade, which resisted embracing components of consumer capitalism. This is evident in statements of the Börsenverein Deutscher Buchhändler, the powerful trade organization that represented the interests of book dealers and publishers (and still does). In such publications as the *Börsenblatt für den deutschen Buchhandel* (German Book Trade Gazette), the book trade fashioned itself as the true arbiter of German culture and presented producers and publishers of magazines and dime novels as a dangerous threat to German culture. Consistently, members of the book trade downplayed any economic interest they might have in the production, distribution, and selling of books. They drew a clear distinction between the book and other commodities as the following quotation from a manual for booksellers illustrates: "Wem das Buch eine eben solche Ware ist, wie der Kaffee und Zucker, der bemühe sich um den Vertrieb dieser Waren, an welchem Geschäft durchgehends mehr zu verdienen ist, als am Handel mit dem, was den geistigen Bedürfnissen des Publikums frommen soll" (People who consider the book a commodity just like coffee or sugar should deal in these considerably more profitable goods rather than trade in articles that are to enrich the intellectual needs of the public).[12] People in the book trade commonly differentiated the book from other commodities, and this differentiation often led to the conclusion that books ought not to be marketed like other commodities, a fact that has to be kept in mind when we analyze Langewiesche's juggling of culture and commerce.

At first glance Langewiesche's endeavor strikes one as just another attempt in Wilhelmine Germany to enlighten the masses by offering up real "Kultur." In an autobiographical sketch Langewiesche declares that his life's mission was to serve the masses by educating them through culture. The tone of his text resembles the often paternalistic approach that the *Volksbildungsbewegung* (movement to educate the masses) took when trying to persuade the "masses" to read up to the level of the *Bildungsbürgertum*. But there is one big distinction between the efforts of *Volksbildungsvereine* (organizations to educate the masses) and Langewiesche's endeavor: as an entrepreneur of a newly founded publishing house, Langewiesche *had* to reach his audience if he wanted to have a viable business. Studies on readership at the beginning of the twentieth century show, for example, that unions' efforts to persuade their members to read political and classical literature had limited success.[13] While Langewiesche wanted to create affordable culture for the masses, he also had to be sure to make a profit.

In order to gain access to a mass market, Langewiesche decided to employ marketing strategies that were increasingly used within the burgeoning consumer society but, as mentioned above, had been sparsely used in the book trade. One has to distinguish here of course between books that carried cultural capital because they were considered culturally valuable and various other reading materials. The former were only sold in bookstores, whereas books such as crime novels and romance fiction could be purchased through peddlers, at train stations, and even from vending machines.[14] Only "proper books" qualified as cultured reading, and as an 1899 guide to book culture underlines, the *possession* of such books was an important component of being a sophisticated German:

Es schickt sich nicht, seiner Tochter eine Aussteuer für 10 000 bis 100 000 Mark anzuschaffen und dabei den Bücherschrank zu vergessen. Es schickt sich nicht, Kommerzienrat zu sein und einen vollen Weinkeller, aber einen leeren Bücherschrank zu haben. Es schickt sich nicht, nach Patchouli . . . zu duften und schmierige Leihbibliotheksbände zu lesen.[15]

The importance placed on book possession and the kind of content presented within the covers is crucial for understanding Langewiesche's commercial and critical success. He devised a type of book that was affordable for a relatively wide audience and presented content that gave the readers of his books access to discourses and concepts integral to a German bourgeois sensibility at the beginning of the twentieth century.

The title of the very first book Langewiesche published leaves no doubt about his intention to distinguish his books from reading material that might be considered superficial entertainment. In 1902, after announcing in the *Börsenblatt* his intention to publish "sophisticated books for the masses," he chose as his first title a collection of writings by the nineteenth-century British philosopher and historian Thomas Carlyle (1795–1881) entitled *Arbeiten und nicht verzweifeln* (1902; Work and Do Not Despair).[16] This phrase was not only the title of Langewiesche's first published book, it became his corporate identity. He chose it as a motto to be printed under a drawing of a sculptor at work, and this logo could be found in all his books, letterhead, and advertising materials.[17] The phrase even adorned the entrance to the building that housed his private and business quarters in Königstein/Taunus (and still does).[18]

It was Carlyle's concept of work as an ennobling force that provided Langewiesche with a thematic focus for this very first publication. Carlyle had been published before in German but only in multi-volume editions. For *Arbeiten und nicht verzweifeln* Langewiesche edited selections of Carlyle's writings to produce an anthology that combined short aphorisms and longer passages, thus giving readers the possibility of reading selectively. The book's main message advocates work and self-discipline as salvation and exalts a puritan work ethic.

The celebration of labor, which valorizes work and saving over idleness and consumption, had been identified by Max Weber as the paradoxical core of modern capitalism in his seminal work *Die protestantische Ethik und der Geist des Kapitalismus* (1905; The Protestant Ethic and the Spirit of Capitalism). In choosing "Arbeiten und nicht verzweifeln" as the theme for his self-presentation and initial publication, Langewiesche displayed his dedication to the Protestant work ethic identified by Weber and shifted the focus away from such common associations with mass culture as conspicuous consumption and pleasure. The book's format of short passages that encourage re-reading, combined with a moralistic-religious tone, recalls that of *Erbauungsliteratur* (edifying and morally uplifting reading material), an important genre in the eighteenth and nineteenth centuries. Historians of reading have observed that *Erbauungsliteratur* represented the main source of reading for large parts of the population, in particular in rural areas and smaller cities.[19] Texts like *Arbeiten und nicht verzweifeln* continued a tradition of reading that scholars refer to as *Wiederholungslektüre* (repetitive reading) and that they contrast to a more "modern" way of reading that developed with the rise of the novel at the end of the eighteenth century. Such scholars as Erich Schön have argued that people who only owned a few books revered them as a source of authority and used the often religious content of the books for practical advice and moral sustenance.[20] With *Arbeiten und nicht verzweifeln* Langewiesche could appeal to readers who favored a more repetitive reading style and were more familiar with reading shorter, more popular texts (such as those in almanacs, religious literature, and magazines and newspapers).

In the foreword to the book, Langewiesche gives another reason why he opted for aphorisms and excerpts: he hints at "modern readers" who have the ability and experience to read longer works but do not have the time. These kinds of readers need a type of book that can be used more easily. At the same time, the sober content and the aphoristic style distinguish *Arbeiten und nicht verzweifeln* from books considered "too easy" to consume such as romance and detective fiction. Langewiesche's book could not be devoured like other mass-produced literature; rather, it lent itself to controlled reading with the intention of providing an uplifting message.

With the publication of *Arbeiten und nicht verzweifeln* as his first book, Langewiesche signaled that he was dedicated to offering "serious" literature that could deliver moral advice to readers and that was more than entertainment. The numerous reviews of the book show that he gained the respect of critics who praised not only the book's content but also its material quality and design.[21] *Arbeiten und nicht verzweifeln* turned out to be a bestseller that sold more than 300,000 copies.[22]

How then was it possible that Langewiesche's books were almost instantly recognized as valuable cultural objects while also successfully penetrating new markets of readers? The answer has to be sought in the complex interplay of the content of the books, their status as aesthetic objects, and the way they were marketed to potential readers. An analysis of Langewiesche's marketing apparatus reveals the status of his books as commodities of modern consumer culture and shows how his marketing strategies introduced consumers and booksellers alike to some crucial characteristics of consumer modernity. But Langewiesche was also mindful of the book trade's continued resistance to applying modern marketing methods to books because of a fear that they would endanger the status of the books as cultural assets. How did he negotiate tensions between consumption and availability and a desired air of exclusivity and degree of distinction?

It turned out to be useful that Langewiesche was a small publisher who could only publish a few titles each year and thus could not be seen as flooding the market with his books. As the publishing house remarked in its marketing materials, "Der Verlag bringt wenige mit Sorgfalt aus-gewählte Werke aus den Litteraturgebieten [*sic*]: Lebensführung, Welt-anschauung, Bildende und Redende Kunst" (The publisher offers a few carefully chosen books in the areas of leading one's life, Weltanschauung, fine and oratory arts.)[23] Langewiesche thus focused on non-fiction titles and somewhat vague subject areas that nevertheless underline an empha-sis on self-improvement and *Bildung*. The books were offered in two different formats: art books, which consisted mainly of high-quality illus-trations and very little text, came in a larger format, while the other titles were regular-sized books.

Langewiesche quickly proceeded to standardize his book produc-tion and marketing in several ways. The standard price of 1.80 marks played an important role in positioning the books in the cultural land-scape: they were cheaper than most hard-bound books but more expen-sive than dime novels or Reclam books, which made them affordable but not cheap. In fact, Langewiesche was disappointed in the merely moderate success of the books with the working class and therefore later started a separate series called *Der Eiserne Hammer* (The Iron Hammer) and targeted at workers.

One reason for the books' relative affordability was that Langewie-sche printed 10,000, 20,0000, or 40,000 thousand copies at a time. By 1916 he had sold more than two million books, sales which, given that he published only a few titles a year, were unmatched in German publish-ing.[24] Commentators pointed out time and again that the quality of these books was extraordinary and unprecedented for the price, especially for illustrated volumes.

The bulk of the marketing efforts was guided by the realization that the market segment Langewiesche wanted to tap into consisted partially of readers who had not necessarily had contact with the traditional book trade; among other things, these readers did not frequent bookstores. Since Langewiesche was committed to working with the traditional book trade (as opposed to selling the books directly to consumers), he devised measures that rendered the bookstores more consumer-friendly. He also recognized the importance of the bookseller as a mediator in the pro-cess of turning interested readers into buyers of books. Therefore, most of his efforts at communication attempted either to lower the threshold required to get window-shoppers to enter the bookstore or to help book-sellers with the presentation of Langewiesche's products.

Shopping generally underwent a transformation at this time, from a process of entering a store to buy a specific product to the possibility of walking into a store without the intent to purchase something. Warren Breckman convincingly links this change to the rise of the department store in the 1890s and 1900s and the emergence of new public spaces and shopping as a "peculiarly modern pastime."[25] Just as a Baedeker travel guide to Berlin had to explain to visitors to the new department store Wertheim that they need not make purchases, Langewiesche wanted to ensure potential buyers that it was acceptable simply to look at his books first.[26] In that regard Langewiesche contributed to a change in the behavior of consumers and in the character of bookstores. He helped to transform the latter into more public spaces that gradually became part of a modern shopping experience.[27]

An important step in this process was the introduction of the "Scheibenplakat" (window display poster) that Langewiesche sent to booksellers along with detailed descriptions on how and where to hang the posters. To our modern eye the poster seems small (about letter-size) and text-heavy, but in its day it provided crucial pieces of information right in the window of the bookstore: it displays the book's price, provides a few highlights of its content, and spells out that customers should feel free to have a look at the book inside the store (see fig. 9.1). Some posters specifically mentioned that there was no obligation to buy.

But the most important sign that Langewiesche's books were products of rising consumer modernity was Langewiesche's decision to brand his books. Starting in 1908, most of his books appeared under the heading of "Die Blauen Bücher," with standardized blue covers and a standardized price of 1.80 mark (see fig. 9.2). The branding process made his books easily recognizable and secured consumer loyalty by helping readers, who were faced with 30,000 new German titles each year, select a book.[28] Branding streamlined the marketing and appearance of a set of diverse titles under the umbrella of Blaue Bücher. Topics covered in the Blaue Bücher in the first few years alone ranged from Baroque architecture to modern child-rearing, and from Swedish art to the role of German culture in the world. Many of the titles went through numerous editions and were popular well into the Nazi years and beyond (see the appendix to this article for an overview of selected Blaue Bücher titles.)[29]

Even though Langewiesche was one of the first publishers to implement branding in such a systematic manner, others had deployed similar mechanisms before him. In 1885 the publisher Carl Engelhorn had started "Engelhorns Allgemeine Romanbibliothek" (Engelhorn's Universal Library of Novels), a series that published a new novel every week. The books had a standardized price and appearance (red bindings), and they soon came to be known as the "Rotröcke" (red coats).[30] Langewiesche may have been inspired by the success of the Engelhorn series and their unofficial brand name. It is also very likely that Langewiesche was familiar with the French "Bibliothèque Bleue" (Blue Library) — one of the first examples of a mass-produced book series. The Bibliothèque Bleue consisted of small-formatted, cheap booklets that reached a mass audience in nineteenth-century France. Titles published represented the whole

Wir jungen Männer! 1.⁸⁰Mk.

)

Wie ein roter Faden zieht fich das fexuelle Problem durch das Leben des jungen Mannes vor der Ehe. Da ift niemand, der an der Wahl vorbeikommt, ob er das Roß fein will, das ein wilder Reiter jagt und hetzt, oder ob ER der Reiter fein und mit ruhiger Hand die Zügel führen will. Und für jeden werden Stunden kommen, in denen das Schickfal feines Lebens von der Selbftbeherrfchung eines einzigen Augenblicks abhängt: das in kurzer Zeit durch ganz Deutfchland verbreitete Buch: „Wir jungen Männer" bringt dazu, dem fexuellen Problem frei und gerade ins Auge zu fehen. Es wird da nicht „gefcholten"! Es wird auch nicht „gepredigt" und „ermahnt". Aber es wird von Natürlichem natürlich gefprochen und die Dinge bei ihrem geraden Namen genannt. In nüchternen Zitaten findet fich dazwifchen, was medizinifche Autoritäten von diefen Dingen fagen. So ift es ein Buch voll fchonungslofer Wahrheit u. ein Wort an den felbftändigen, feiner Kraft u. feines Gefchlechtes fich bewußten jungen Mann. Das bereits im 75. Taufend erfchienene Buch wird gern zur Anficht vorgelegt.

Fig. 9.1. Scheibenplakat (poster), *Wir jungen Männer*. Langewiesche Archive, Frankfurt am Main, HA/BV 51: Drucksachen 1907.

spectrum of nineteenth-century reading: religious and didactic texts, advice literature, songbooks, fables and fairy-tales, and novels, constituting in the words of one book historian a true *Volksbibliothek* (people's library).[31] What differentiates Langewiesche's project from predecessors like the Bibliothèque Bleue is its insistence on sophistication and aesthetic appeal, a characteristic that to date had been absent from cheap series and the many efforts of the various educational groups.[32]

In 1908 Langewiesche used the busy Christmas season to launch the Blaue Bücher as a brand. In addition to printing the brand name Blaue Bücher on the books' covers, he used posters and statements that communicated the character and direction of the brand and introduced the Blaue Bücher as a concept that had its own coherence and intentions. In one of these texts, Langewiesche specified that with the Blaue Bücher he wanted to reach an audience that crossed political and religious boundaries and hoped to appeal to readers who often did not find the time to read "wahrhaft lesenswerte Bücher" (books truly worth reading). The statement also provided reassurance to potential readers that the books would be comprehensible because they dealt with real-life issues and not with abstractions. Throughout this advertisement Langewiesche tried to strike a balance between presenting his books as accessible to an audience beyond the *Bildungsbürger*, yet distinguished enough to qualify as worthwhile reading matter.

The existence of contradictory impulses becomes particularly visible in the volumes of "Die Welt des Schönen" (The World of Beauty), an illustrated, larger-format series that was also published under the brand

Fig. 9.2. Book Cover, *Die Schöne Heimat: Bilder aus Deutschland*
(1916 ed.). Author copy.

Blaue Bücher. The books in this series featured high-quality reproductions of paintings, sculptures, architecture, and photographs of landscapes and national monuments. Text mainly appeared in the form of prefaces or appendixes and was subordinated to the images and thereby made optional to read. This ploy was intended to attract a whole new set of readers, and advertisements show that Langewiesche also had the international market in mind when conceptualizing the series. The increasing importance of images mirrored developments in other media, for example, the transformation that occurred in the magazine landscape with the rise of such magazines as the *Berliner Illustrirte Zeitung*, which lent photographs a privileged status and created stories around them. Indeed, the photographic image gained a new authority as a carrier of reality.

The use of innovations in printing technologies and a high volume of publication (around 30,000 per printing) enabled Langewiesche to offer these large-formatted books for the same low price as his non-illustrated Blaue Bücher. The highly acclaimed inaugural volume, *Griechische Bildwerke* (Greek Sculptures), published in 1907, reinforced his position as a reputable publisher of high-quality, low-cost books. Critics unanimously celebrated this new effort as an unprecedented achievement in publishing and lauded the technical perfection and simple beauty of the volume.

Griechische Bildwerke assembled 140 photographs of classical Greek sculptures (see fig. 9.3). The photographs were preceded by an introduction that praised Greek antiquity as the golden age of an aesthetic of naturalness and of ethical thinking, and the book reflected the importance that Greek ideals had played since the end of the eighteenth century for discourses on *Bildung*. *Griechische Bildwerke* held up Greek antiquity as an embodiment of artistic, intellectual, and physical perfection.[33] In enthusiastic reviews of *Griechische Bildwerke*, commentators emphasized the naturalness and organic beauty found in Greek art, sometimes implying that contemporary culture lacked true beauty and aesthetic taste.

The unevenness of celebrating the "timelessness," "authentic culture," and "naturalness" of Greek culture in a mass-produced book was a level of reflection that was absent from the reviews. While Walter Benjamin later famously observed the loss of a work of art's "aura" in the age of mechanical reproduction, these reviewers paradoxically welcomed Langewiesche's mass-produced photography book of Greek sculptures as a new chance to return to tradition and timeless beauty. How was it possible that Langewiesche's books, unlike other products of mass culture, were not seen as a threat to bourgeois culture and their potential to challenge the meaning of core concepts such as "authenticity" went unnoticed? One possible answer lies in the cohesive image Langewiesche created for his books with messages that emphasized continuity and tradition rather than change and innovation. Through his marketing materials, choice of subject matter, and the small number of titles published each

WAGENLENKER AUS DELPHI. ERSTE HALFTE DES 5. JAHRH.
(Nach einem Gipsabguß des Bronzeoriginals.) Delphi.

Fig. 9.3. "Wagenlenker aus Delphi" (Driver from Delphi), *Griechische Bildwerke* (Düsseldorf: Karl Robert Langewiesche, 1907), 13.

year, Langewiesche presented his books as tools of edification for hard-working people, and they were not perceived as "mere" commodities or simply a source of entertainment. The following excerpt from a review exemplifies the kind of language used in conjunction with his books:

> Wie alles, was Langewiesche herausgibt, in bezug auf Inhalt und Stoff vornehm ist und den Zweck hat, dem Bedürfnis nach Freude und Schönheit nachzukommen, so auch dieser Band. Dem Verleger ist vor allem daran gelegen, recht vielen den Besitz guter und schö-ner Bücher zu ermöglichen und durch sie veredelnd und verfeinernd auf das deutsche Volk zu wirken.[34]

The theme of improvement and enjoyment through exposure to a book's aesthetic and moral values was also accentuated in two other bestsell-ing illustrated volumes. *Der Stille Garten: Deutsche Maler des ersten und zweiten Drittels des 19. Jahrhunderts* (1908; The Quiet Garden: Ger-man Painters of the First Two Thirds of the Nineteenth Century) and *Das Haus in der Sonne* (1909; The House in the Sun) show no traces of modernity. Instead, they focus on a celebration of the bourgeois home and spaces untouched by industrial culture. *Der Stille Garten* is a compila-tion of one hundred nineteenth-century portrait and landscape paintings, including such artists as Caspar David Friedrich, Ludwig Richter, Phillip Otto Runge, and Moritz von Schwind. The book encourages a contem-plative mood and inner reflection by including paintings of interior spaces with idyllic nature scenes, and portraits, many of them of children. The paintings conjure up romantic notions of the individual in harmony with nature and present interior spaces as a sanctuary of tranquility and reflec-tion, suggesting them as a respite from the perceived discord of indus-trial times (see fig. 9.4). Harmonious visions of bourgeois life also form the focal point in *Das Haus in der Sonne*, which gathers sixty-six illustra-tions and paintings (fifty in black and white and sixteen in color) by the Swedish artist Carl Larsson. Like *Der Stille Garten* the book became a commercial success, with 100,000 copies already sold a year after publica-tion.[35] Apart from celebrating family life in the Swedish countryside, the book integrates other topics that were of interest to Germans around the turn of the century, such as *Heimatkunst* (regional art), child-rearing, and a general fascination with Nordic countries and culture.[36]

Most importantly, *Das Haus in der Sonne* and *Der Stille Garten* both offered a model of reassurance in rapidly changing times by assert-ing the stability of the bourgeois home and presenting spaces seemingly untouched by any transformation connected with industrialism and modernity. Langewiesche used their message of simple, immaterial plea-sures for material purposes, launching a Christmas advertising campaign that marketed them together as "Ein Haus mit Garten" (A House with a Garden). Sold in a gift box, the two books not only gave consumers the

Fig. 9.4. "Die Stickerin" (The Embroiderer) by Georg Friedrich Kersting, *Der Stille Garten*, 6th ed. (Königstein: Karl Robert Langewiesche, 1913), 25.

chance to purchase a respectable yet affordable present, but carried the promise of access to a better, more joyful life full of sunshine.

Whereas the illustrated series "Die Welt des Schönen" was intended to lead readers to refinement and a harmonious way of living through exposure to art, another set of Blaue Bücher addressed more directly how to strive for moral growth and character improvement. The two instant bestsellers, Hans Wegener's *Wir jungen Männer: Das sexuelle Problem des gebildeten Mannes vor der Ehe; Reinheit, Kraft und Frauenliebe* (1906; We Young Men: The Sexual Problem of the Educated Man before Marriage; Purity, Strength, and the Love of Women) and Heinrich Lhotzky's *Das Buch der Ehe* (1911; The Book of Marriage) are examples of Blaue Bücher that combine a religious tone with the concrete advice of modern self-help books. Both books were written by theologians, and they weave issues of sexuality and shifts in gender roles into an ultimately tradition-affirming narrative.

Given the title of Wegener's book, it is not surprising that the text is culturally conservative and that it prescribes marriage as the only space for sexuality. At the same time the book fashions sexuality as a natural force that needs to be discussed openly and freely and that has the potential to function as a transformative power not only for the individual but for society. The text negotiates embracing sexuality as an essential part of a person while setting up mechanisms to control and police it. While the focus of the early editions is first on the male individual and then on his relationship to society, later editions shift more and more to the individual's roles and duties within the "Volksgemeinschaft" (national and racial community). In the 1941 edition Wegener tells the reader that he was loyal to the Führer long before he came to power and he still proudly wears his SA uniform. In this edition, *völkische* and anti-Semitic rhetoric abound.

Another author with a background as a theologian and pastor in essence provided the sequel to Wegener's book. Heinrich Lhotzky's *Das Buch der Ehe* appeared in 1911 and was also published in numerous editions into the 1940s. It sold more than 300,000 copies. Like Wegener's book, *Das Buch der Ehe* has a strong undercurrent of biology as a force that propels society forward. Biology can also justify the existence of a natural order such as two distinct and complementary genders for which marriage is the perfect state. While these books offer some concrete advice for the individual reading them, they also have to be seen as part of a narrative that strives to stabilize the German nation by strengthening individuals' values and by inserting these individuals into a larger whole.

A year after Lhotzky's *Buch der Ehe* was published, Langewiesche's endeavor took a decidedly nationalist turn. The topics of the books shifted from an emphasis on how art and culture could aid the individual in his or her quest for moral growth and self-improvement to what role culture played in strengthening Germany as a nation. This change became particularly apparent in the publication of Paul Rohrbach's *Der deutsche Gedanke in der Welt* (1912; German Thought in the World), but also in Langewiesche's decision to limit the illustrated Blaue Bücher to subjects covering German art and art history. Other bestselling books that represented the preoccupation with the question of German national culture and its historical and current status included *Deutsche Burgen und Feste*

Schlösser (1913; German Castles and Forts) and the immensely popular *Die Schöne Heimat. Bilder aus Deutschland* (1915; Beautiful Homeland. Images from Germany [see fig. 9.2]). Langewiesche attributed this new focus to changes in his personal interests, but it is of course also an expression of an intensifying nationalism among the German population.[37]

Despite the range of topics the Blaue Bücher covered, some dominant themes can be identified. Many of them emphasize "the true," "the real," and "the natural" and thus portray notions of authenticity and naturalness as the core of the harmonious individual. Even though the books were the products of modern consumer culture, modernity was largely absent from their pages, revealing the tensions that arose when *Bildung* was offered for sale in mass-produced books. *Bildung*, by definition, could not simply be purchased. It was conceptualized as an organic process that happened over time and required the individual to improve morally, emotionally, and intellectually and to strive for a balanced personality. Books certainly had played an important role in this process, and the Blaue Bücher conveyed the idea of the harmonious individual that was consistent with nineteenth-century ideas of *Bildung*. The Blaue Bücher could not guarantee access to a better, more educated life, but they did provide access to symbolic capital, and they kept alive hopes that "reading up" might actually work.[38]

Appendix

Selected Blaue Bücher titles, their year of publication, and circulation figures:

1902 Thomas Carlyle, *Arbeiten und nicht verzweifeln* (Work and Do Not Despair), 33rd edition in 1942; 301,000 copies published by 1942.

1904 *Von Rosen ein Krentzelein: Alte deutsche Volkslieder* (A Little Wreath Made of Roses: Old German Songs), 12th edition in 1942, with 83,000 copies published by 1942; new edition in 1959.

1906 Hans Wegener, *Wir jungen Männer: Das sexuelle Problem des jungen Mannes vor der Ehe; Reinheit, Kraft und Frauenliebe* (We Young Men: The Sexual Problem of the Young Man Before Marriage: Purity, Strength, and Love of Women), 26th edition in 1942, with 283,000 copies published.

1907 *Griechische Bildwerke* (Greek Sculptures), 12th edition in 1942, with 196,000 copies published.

1908 Heinrich Lhotzky, *Die Seele deines Kindes* (Your Child's Soul), 23rd edition in 1942, with 304,000 copies published.

1908 *Der Stille Garten: Deutsche Maler des ersten und zweiten Drittels des 19. Jahrhunderts* (German Painters of the First Two Thirds of the

Nineteenth Century), 15th edition in 1940, with 286,000 published copies.

1909 Carl Larsson, *Das Haus in der Sonne* (The House in the Sun), 19th edition in 1940, with 336,000 copies published by 1940; 20th–40th editions 1955–2006.

1910 Wilhelm Pinder, *Deutsche Dome* (German Cathedrals), 17th edition in 1942, with 300,000 copies published by 1942; 26th edition in 1969, with 455,000 copies published by 1969.

1911 Heinrich Lhotzky, *Das Buch der Ehe* (The Book of Marriage), 17th edition in 1941, with 300,000 copies published.

1912 Paul Rohrbach, *Der deutsche Gedanke in der Welt* (German Thought in the World), 16th through 18th editions in 1942, with 222,000 copies published.

1913 *Deutsche Burgen und Feste Schlösser aus allen Ländern deutscher Zunge* (German Castles and Forts from all German-Speaking Countries), 13th edition in 1942, with 278,000 published; 16th edition in 1968, with 328,000 by 1968.

1915 *Die Schöne Heimat: Bilder aus Deutschland* (Beautiful Fatherland: Images from Germany), 13th edition in 1941, with 345,000 copies published; 31st edition in 1970, with 619,000 copies published by 1970.

Notes

I would like to thank Hans-Curt Köster and Gabriele Klempert, both of the Karl Robert Langewiesche Nachfolger Hans Köster Verlagsbuchhandlung, who generously opened their workplace and home to me so that I could gain access to archival material on Langewiesche. The Karl Robert Langewiesche archive is one of the few publishing archives in Germany that survived the Second World War in a nearly intact state. At the time I did my research, a large part of the archival material was still housed in the original Langewiesche home; other parts were held by the Archiv des Börsenvereins des Deutschen Buchhandels e.V. My thanks go also to Hermann Staub of the Börsenverein, who helped me gain access to the archival material at the Börsenverein and whose article on Karl Robert Langewiesche (see the bibliography in this volume) introduced me to this publisher and his archive. In the meantime, all material of the Karl Robert Langewiesche archive up to 1956 is held by the Börsenverein Archive, which is now housed at the Deutsche Nationalbibliothek in Frankfurt am Main.

[1] See Georg Bollenbeck for an illuminating discussion on how diverse political forces saw themselves as the "true" heir of *Bildung*; Bollenbeck, *Bildung und Kultur: Glanz und Elend eines deutschen Deutungsmusters* (Frankfurt am Main: Insel, 1994), 13–15. See also Jennifer Jenkins, *Provincial Modernity: Local Culture and Liberal Politics in Fin-de-Siècle Hamburg* (Ithaca, NY: Cornell UP, 2003), on the role of *Bildung* and aesthetic education in creating a moral citizenry.

[2] See Gideon Reuveni, *Reading Germany: Literature and Consumer Culture in Germany before 1933* (New York: Berghahn, 2006), especially chapter 5, "The Struggle over Reading: Studies of Reading and the Fight against Schund- und Schmutzschriften" (221–73).

[3] *Börsenblatt für den Deutschen Buchhandel*, 2 May 1903, 3755.

[4] Stefan Paul calculates that Langewiesche had sold more than two million books by 1916; see Paul, "Der Verlag Karl Robert Langewiesche im Ersten Weltkrieg" (Master's thesis, University of Tübingen, 1992), 17.

[5] The books can still be easily found in almost any German used bookstore, and many people born in the 1940s and '50s remember not only seeing them on their parents' bookshelves but looking at them regularly.

[6] Book history, in the words of Joan Shelley Rubin, "requires discerning relationships between material conditions, social structures, and cultural values — relationships that establish the meanings print forms carry as they pass from author to reader"; see Rubin, "What Is the History of the History of Books?" *The Journal of American History* September 2003, http://www.historycooperative.org. turing.library.northwestern.edu/journals/jah/90.2/rubin.html (1 Nov. 2008). For other introductions to the growing field of book history, see, e.g., the 2006 special issue of *PMLA*, *The History of the Book and the Idea of Literature*, ed. Seth Lerer and Leah Price, *PMLA* 121, no.1 (January 2006), and David Finkelstein and Alistair McCleery, introduction to *The Book History Reader*, 2nd ed. (London: Routledge, 2006), 1–4.

[7] My thinking in this regard has been influenced by Janice Radway and her conceptualization of middlebrow culture; see Radway, *A Feeling for Books: The Book-of-the-Month Club, Literary Taste, and Middle-Class Desire* (Chapel Hill: U of North Carolina P, 1997). For a longer discussion of how the concept of middlebrow culture can prove useful for discussing German culture, see my dissertation, "Books for a Better Life: Publishers and the Creation of Middlebrow Culture in Wilhelmine Germany" (PhD diss., Duke University, Durham, NC, 2001).

[8] On the conflicted relationship the German *Bürgertum* had with consumption, see Warren Breckman, "Disciplining Consumption: The Debate about Luxury in Wilhelmine Germany, 1890–1914," *Journal of Social History* 24 (1991): 485–505.

[9] In a laudatio published in the *Börsenblatt* in honor of Langewiesche's twenty-fifth publishing anniversary, the author praises Langewiesche as a brilliant inventor and leader and cites the book cover and other marketing materials as examples. See "Ein Vierteljahrhundert 'Die Blauen Bücher,'" *Börsenblatt für den deutschen Buchhandel*, May 5, 1927. Reprinted in Karl Robert Langewiesche, *50 Jahre Verlagsarbeit* (Königstein/Taunus: Langewiesche, 1952), 47.

[10] Friedrich Uhlig, *Geschichte des Buches und des Buchhandels* (Stuttgart: Poeschel, 1962), 81.

[11] See also Hans Ferdinand Schulz, *Das Schicksal der Bücher und der Buchhandel* (Berlin: de Gruyter, 1960), 161–64, and G. K. Schauer, *Geschichte des deutschen Buchumschlages im 20. Jahrhundert* (Königstein/Taunus: Langewiesche, 1962), 13.

[12] Georg Hölscher, *Der Buchhändler* (Leipzig: Paul Beyer, n.d.), 4. All translations are my own unless otherwise indicated.

[13] For an overview of workers' reading tastes see, e.g., A. Pfannkuche, *Was liest der deutsche Arbeiter? Auf Grund einer Enquete beantwortet* (Tübingen: Mohr, 1900).

[14] For an overview of the German publishing field around 1900, see Reinhard Wittmann, *Geschichte des deutschen Buchhandels: Ein Überblick* (Munich: C. H. Beck, 1991), 271–300.

[15] "It is not proper to provide your daughter with a dowry of 10,000 to 100,000 marks and forget the bookshelf. It is not proper to be a distinguished businessman with a full wine cellar but to have an empty bookshelf. It is not proper to smell of patchouli but to read sleazy literature from the lending library"; Ludwig Hamann, *Der Umgang mit Büchern und die Selbstkultur* (Leipzig: Ludwig Hamann Verlag, 1899), 66.

[16] Langewiesche chose this title himself, and it is a translation back into German of a line from a Goethe poem that Carlyle had translated as "work and dispair [*sic*] not." Cf. Cecilia Lengefeld, *"Der Maler des glücklichen Heims." Zur Rezeption Carl Larssons im wilhelminischen Deutschland* (Heidelberg: Winter, 1993), 18.

[17] For an excellent resource on the publishing history of Karl Robert Langwiesche, see Gabriele Klempert, *"Die Welt des Schönen." Karl Robert Langewiesche 1902–2002. Eine hundertjährige Verlagsgeschichte in Deutschland* (Königstein/Taunus: Karl Robert Langewiesche Nachfolger Hans Köster Verlagsbuchhandlung, 2002).

[18] Langewiesche founded his company in Düsseldorf but moved to Königstein, a small town near Frankfurt am Main, in 1912.

[19] Cf. Rolf Engelsing, *Analphabetentum und Lektüre: Zur Sozialgeschichte des Lesens zwischen feudaler und industrieller Gesellschaft* (Stuttgart: Metzler, 1973), 89.

[20] Erich Schön, *Der Verlust der Sinnlichkeit oder die Verwandlung des Lesers: Mentalitätswandel um 1800* (Stuttgart: Klett-Cotta, 1987) 40, 41.

[21] The folder with reviews in the Langewiesche archive contains about 130 reviews of *Arbeiten und nicht verzweifeln.*

[22] Klempert, *Welt des Schönen*, 218.

[23] Text on Langewiesche letterhead. Langewiesche Archiv, Frankfurt am Main, HA/BV 51: Drucksachen 1905/1906.

[24] Paul, *Verlag Karl Robert Langewiesche*, 17.

[25] Breckman, "Disciplining Consumption," 496.

[26] For the Baedeker reference, see Breckman, "Disciplining Consumption," 503.

[27] Even though Langewiesche was very loyal to the traditional book trade and never sold directly to consumers, he nevertheless realized the importance of using new channels of distribution. Despite the fact that representatives of the booktrade often deemed department stores inappropriate retail outlets for books, Langewiesche sold his books at department stores such as Wertheim and Tietz, possibly attracting a set of customers who did not frequent bookstores.

[28] With 31,281 books published in 1910 and 34,871 in 1913, Germany published the highest number of books in the world; see Wittmann, *Geschichte des deutschen Buchhandels*, 271.

[29] An overview of all titles published between 1902 and 2002 can be found in Gabriele Klempert's history of the Langewiesche publishing house; see Klempert, *"Die Welt des Schönen,"* 218–49.

[30] Peter de Mendelssohn, *S. Fischer und sein Verlag* (Frankfurt am Main: Fischer, 1970), 515.

[31] Rudolf Schenda, "Bibliothèque Bleue im 19. Jahrhundert,"in *Studien zur Trivialliteratur*, ed. Heinz Otto Burger (Frankfurt am Main: Vittorio Klostermann, 1968), 143.

[32] In his dissertation Langewiesche's contemporary Helmut von den Steinen notes of "Die Blauen Bücher" that the combination of high aesthetic standards and a dedication to *Volksbildung* was highly unusual in the publishing industry. Helmut von den Steinen, "Das moderne Buch" (PhD diss., University of Heidelberg, 1912), 35.

[33] Hermann Glaser describes the German preoccupation with Greek culture as a fetishism that reached its height as a result of the work of such archeologists as Heinrich Schliemann. The display of Greek reproductions, for example, became a common sight in many bourgeois homes. See Hermann Glaser, *Bildungsbürgertum und Nationalismus: Politik und Kultur im Wilhelminischen Deutschland* (Munich: dtv, 1993), 51.

[34] "Everything Langewiesche publishes is sophisticated in regard to content and material and serves the purpose of fulfilling the need for joy and beauty. This is true of this book as well. It is of particular importance to the publisher to have the effect of ennobling the German people and making them more sophisticated"; from a 1907 review in "Die Leserin," folder HA/BV 51: "Rezensionen: Griechische Bildwerke, Archiv des Langewiesche Verlags im Historischen Archiv des Börsenvereins des Deutschen Buchhandels," Deutsche Nationalbibliothek, Frankfurt am Main.

[35] The book has been in print since 1909 and still is (last edition, 2006).

[36] Lengefeld, *"Der Maler des glücklichen Heims,"* 6.

[37] The publisher Eugen Diederichs, for example, also moved away from questions of inner edification to an emphasis on the German *Volk* and ideas of a national, ethnic, and cultural community around the same time.

[38] In a fascinating article on modern advice and non-fiction literature, Timo Heiderdinger argues that consumers of advice literature choose precisely titles that represent a social and cultural class to which they do not necessarily belong but to which they strive to belong; see Heiderdinger, "Der gelebte Konjunktiv. Zur Pragmatik von Ratgeberliteratur in alltagskultureller Pespektive," in *Sachbuch und populäres Wissen im 20. Jahrhundert*, ed. Andy Hahnemann and David Oels (Frankfurt am Main: Peter Lang, 2008) 97–108. Lengefeld, *"Der Maler des glücklichen Heims,"* 7–108.

10: The Weimar Literature Industry and the Negotiations of *Schloss Gripsholm*

Theodore F. Rippey

REVIEWING ALFRED WEBER'S *Die Not der Geistigen Arbeiter* (The Crisis of Intellectual Workers) in the venerable literary and cultural journal *Die neue Rundschau* in 1923, Samuel Saenger observed with dismay that authors of his day were erratically chasing down every "Verdienstmöglichkeit" (opportunity to earn money). Leisure, the "Nährboden für jede Geistbetätigung" (nourishing basis for any intellectual activity) had been obliterated from writers' lives, leaving a "Gelände . . . mit armen, gehetzten, in der Angst vor dem Gespenst der Notdurft herumirrenden Geschöpfen bedeckt, die dem reinen Dienst am Geist verloren sind" (landscape covered with poor, agitated beings, wandering astray, in fear of the specter of bare necessity, lost to the pure service of the spirit).[1] Eight years later, however, one of the Weimar Republic's best-known authors began a letter to his publisher as follows:

> Lieber Meister Rowohlt,
> auf dem neuen Verlagskatalog hat Sie Gulbransson ganz richtig gezeichnet: still sinnend an des Baches Rand sitzen Sie da und angeln die fetten Fische. Der Köder mit 14% honorarfreien Exemplare ist nicht fett genug — 12 sind auch ganz schön. Denken Sie mal ein bißchen darüber nach und geben Sie Ihrem harten Verlegerherzen einen Stoß. Bei 14% fällt mir bestimmt nichts ein — ich dichte erst ab 12%.[2]

What happened in the time that elapsed between these two quotations? What unfolded in the life of the mind, the cultural landscape, and the transactions between authors, industry, and readers that could allow Kurt Tucholsky (1890–1935) to be so glib in 1931 about the exact same convergence of ideas, aesthetics, and commerce that elicited such desperation from Samuel Saenger (1864–1944) in 1923? Should not the intensifying unemployment and the looming depression of 1931 have represented a threat equally dire to that of the inflation that beset Germany just as the dust from the uprisings of 1918–19 was starting to settle?

The Saenger remarks spring from a *crisis of the book* which — at least in the eyes of the literary establishment — gripped Germany in the wake of the First World War. An expression of the persistent fantasy of a literary world detached from capitalism, the crisis, to those who conceptualized and publicly discussed it, was a threat to the very foundations of Germans' shared identity as a people of poets and thinkers. A close reading of Saenger's words reveals his principal preoccupation with transhistorical matters, even as he laments the historically contingent problem. That this or that poet starves is unfortunate, naturally, but the real catastrophe inherent in writers stalked by the specter of need is the ideal, not material, loss of the service that socially, politically, and economically untethered writing — and Saenger clearly believes that there once was such a thing — renders to the transcendent *Geist*.

One assumes that Tucholsky, on the other hand, has no interest in that *Geist*, unless it can guarantee him that the royalty-free copies of his next book will be limited to twelve percent of the run. Driving a hard bargain with his publisher, Ernst Rowohlt, he precedes the passage quoted above by dangling some bait of his own: a tentative statement of openness to writing a "summer story" that German readers might welcome as a change from politics and current affairs. Rowohlt, champion of "the bibliophile's book for the common reader," sees high demand for an attractively bound, witty, light-hearted volume; Tucholsky wants a payoff on as many copies as possible. To Saenger's eye, literature would surely be lost in the exchange, and Tucholsky's use of *dichten*, the hallowed verb for literary writing, would be solely regarded as provocation.

Dichten, in the more colloquial sense of "to fabricate," has already begun: the correspondence with Rowohlt, which opens Tucholsky's *Schloss Gripsholm*, is as fictional as the narrative that follows, all part of a game that Tucholsky initiates as the story opens. This game is predicated on a perceptive reader, who will become wise to it and participate. How one plays that game determines how one judges the book. Is this German lovers' getaway to the Swedish countryside sheer frivolity, significant only in its sexism, political indifference, and cynical profit motive? Or is it a masterly rendering of heavy content in light form, an oblique yet devastating account of the late-Weimar social reality it flees, an unusual hybrid of commercial viability and artistic legitimacy?

In what follows, I will dodge my own questions by responding "yes" to all of the above. I analyze the text as a realm in which an interrelated set of cultural-, sexual-, and corporal-political tensions manifest but do not resolve themselves, positioning both author and reader as observer-participants in the conflicts the text portrays. My reading understands *Schloss Gripsholm* as a paradigmatic response to the crisis of the book. Tucholsky's summer story reflects an approach to writing and publishing that accepts the book's commodity status and exploits that status as financial and literary opportunity. A literary experiment in a popular register, *Schloss Gripsholm* heightens awareness of the contingency of feelings, draws attention to the relationship between individual sensibilities and collective corporality, and opens the door to new ways of experiencing the relationship between language as self-composing material and the social composition of power.

Schloss Gripsholm also offers evidence of Tucholsky's strengthening conviction that the book as a medium offered the greatest chance for creative and communicative freedom in the Weimar public sphere, even as his confidence in writing as a lever of social influence waned. This conviction did not blind Tucholsky to the compromises that writing a popular novel entailed, and *Schloss Gripsholm*, I argue, involves two kinds of negotiation. The first is intransitive: communicating in pursuit of compromise. This negotiation is associated with the financial motives of publishers and authors, market dynamics, and readers as consumers — all the factors at work in the correspondence between "Tucholsky" and "Rowohlt" at the book's outset. The second form of negotiation is transitive: navigating difficult obstacles or treacherous paths. This form interlinks with how the text deals with corporality, sensibility, language, gender, and poesis in the context of late-Weimar modernity. These two processes of negotiation are inextricable, as wrong moves in one invariably threaten to undermine both.

Literature, Industry, Crisis

If everything else was in crisis in the early 1920s, then why not the book as well? As Gideon Reuveni's illuminating study *Reading Germany* shows, there was widespread perception during the postwar inflation of a threat to the ennobling reading and writing culture fostered by the educated bourgeoisie over the course of the long nineteenth century.[3] Far from bringing salvation, the economic stabilization of the mid-1920s apparently only made matters worse. In his 1926 essay "Bemerkungen zur Bücherkrise" (Observations on the Book Crisis), for example, publisher Samuel Fischer lamented, "Man treibt Sport, man tanzt, man verbringt die Abendstunden am Radioapparat, im Kino, man ist neben der Berufsarbeit vollkommen in Anspruch genommen und findet keine Zeit ein Buch zu lesen" (One engages in sport, dances, spends the evening at the cinema or listening to the radio; outside working hours, everyone is so occupied that no one has time to read a book).[4]

As a classically educated publisher, Fischer believed in an intrinsic value of books. As a German, he anguished over what the apparent collapse of reading culture meant for the nation in general. The soaring popularity of cinema and increasing stature of radio (both media designed for collective reception) meant an erosion of the literary clubs, book-reading evenings, and public library programming that had formed the nucleus of the German bourgeoisie's efforts to organize itself as a literary public, neighborhood by neighborhood, throughout the Wilhelmine period. The end of such activity was ominous for Fischer and for many others who shared his cultural attitudes. Fischer saw the non-commercialized bourgeois literary associations as the means of fostering a communal sense (*Gemeinschaftsgefühl*) of German culture. As Reuveni argues, "The associations had made reading into a social event and the book into an instrument for bringing people together."[5] At stake was thus not merely an appreciation of this or that canonized author, but the very concept and lived reality of a German cultural community.

Fellow publisher Reinhard Piper elaborated Fischer's point, seeing the turn toward new entertainment culture as a symptom of the collapse of the bourgeois individual.[6] Piper's concerns are a specific manifestation of the general discourse about Germany's transformation into a mass society during the Weimar period and the anxieties it frequently perpetuated regarding the erasure of individual distinctions that the mass represented.[7] For Piper, the amorphous mass lacked the intellectual autonomy and sovereign decision-making that were hallmarks of the individual that was forged as the bourgeoisie came to dominate public life over the course of the nineteenth century.[8] As in Fischer's comments, we see in Piper's a much more deeply seated fear: the crisis of the book was not really about books; it was about the end of the world as they knew it.

Amid all the hand-wringing about a book culture in collapse, Weimar Germany's reading culture — defined in economic terms — was on the rise. As Reuveni shows, the number of bookstores, publishing houses, and titles in print all increased during the Weimar years, continuing a general trend of book-market expansion that, even taking occasional dips into account, had accelerated from the late eighteenth century onward. For example, the number of titles published per year, after hitting a low of 14,910 in 1917, rose to 32,345 in 1920 and reached 37,866 by 1927. Household expenditure records show increased reading budgets for families across class lines in the Weimar years. As Reuveni concludes, "In the post-war years, reading became an integral part of daily life of all strata of society, and books became available as never before."[9]

This boom was the latest consequence of sweeping shifts in literature as a social-cultural system brought on, as Ute Maack argues, by the industrialization of publishing and the general modernization of German society since the early 1900s.[10] In such systemic shifts, Russell Berman has located the foundation of a set of economic and aesthetic transformations in literary writing through which authors came to see themselves no longer as autonomous artists but as craftsmen under increasing economic pressure, forced to write, in Berman's phrase, "for the book market," even as they yearned to serve purposes that transcend systems of commodity production and exchange.[11] As Berman argues, the emergence of a literary market liberated literature from the "exigencies of religion and politics which had prevailed in the pre-secularized . . . literature of the courtly-absolutist period."[12] At the same time, the book trade became a potential threat to literary independence as the writer became subject to the complicated tangle of publisher, wholesaler, and retailer bottom lines — not to mention reader pocketbooks and the popular tastes that underlay the purchase.

Reuveni's and Berman's investigations both shed light on a paradoxical situation in which more books published plus more people reading equals bad news for literature. The dilemma leaves those interested in literature to choose between defeatist retreat, radical conservatism, or a re-imagination of literary activity more in tune with the times. Kurt Tucholsky and Ernst Rowohlt are two examples of option three. Making that choice was simple enough; orienting oneself in a new literary world was something else again.

Tucholsky knew the territory, in any case. Even before the war, he had made a splash on the literary scene with *Rheinsberg, ein Bilderbuch für Verliebte* (1912; Rheinsberg, a Picture-Book for Lovers), and his work during the 1920s for such publications as the *Vossische Zeitung, Berliner Tageblatt,* and (most importantly) the cultural-political weekly *Die Weltbühne* (The World Stage) had made him one of the best-known satirists and commentators in the Weimar press. He was also a tireless book critic, and as Maack shows, his approach to book criticism reveals his sense of the new conditions of reception that the literature industry creates.[13]

In one 1929 installment of "Auf dem Nachttisch" (On the Nightstand), an ongoing set of brief takes on recently published works, Tucholsky's comments about leaning towers of books growing on his nightstand, bed, and shaving table humorously allude to the profusion of new titles in print. The overwhelming quantity leads Tucholsky to ask who publishes, buys, and reads all these volumes, and why some are selected for publication over others.[14] The questions are both rhetorical and unanswerable, given the magnitude and complexity that Weimar book production has reached — it is a landscape that can no longer be surveyed. On the reception side, as Maack argues, the educated bourgeois groupings of the nineteenth century were superseded by a heterogeneous, subculturally divided reading public in the 1920s.[15] Tucholsky's criticism shows awareness of the emergence of such subcultural readerships that establish themselves not via the grass-roots book evening or literary club, but through selective book buying, reading, and discussion. The "Auf dem Nachttisch" series models such a practice by making informed comment on selected titles without asserting infallible critical command of all literary production or claiming final authority in matters of taste. The critic, ultimately just another reader in a fragmented public, must avoid playing "das Literaturpäpstlein" (the little literary pope), as Tucholsky puts it.[16]

The commercialization and industrialization of publishing meant the transformation of reading culture into consumer culture. That sea-change, in the eyes of some publishers, simply meant the death of German literature. Others, seeing their hands forced, chose to bifurcate their operations, developing commercially viable lists and courting mass readerships in order to finance publication of those vessels of the German intellectual and spiritual heritage that, in their view, had to be held above the fray of the mass production and consumption. Still others chose to re-think the book as an object in which intellectual or aesthetic value would not be mutually exclusive with commercial value. Even as the lament of the book crisis reached a crescendo, some Weimar-era authors and publishers were already set on producing a type of book that would meet aesthetic, critical, and economic demands simultaneously. Rowohlt, Piper, Fischer, and other houses that cultivated the image of the cultural publisher (*Kulturverlag*) were, before the emergence of professional marketing discourse about brand identity, essentially in the process of becoming commercial brands.[17] *Rheinsberg* proved that in Tucholsky, Rowohlt's brand had a high-caliber performer. That set the stage for *Schloss Gripsholm*, but repeating the pre-war success required making the commodity appealing and the story meaningful to an interwar world.

Gripsholm I: Language and Location

The world of *Schloss Gripsholm* reveals itself first in Berlin via the fictional Rowohlt-Tucholsky exchange discussed briefly above. Some further excerpts:

> Rowohlt, 8 Juni: Wie Sie wissen, habe ich in letzter Zeit allerhand politische Bücher verlegt, mit denen Sie sich ja hinlänglich beschäftigt haben. Nun möchte ich doch aber wieder einmal die 'schöne Literatur' pflegen. Haben Sie gar nichts? Wie wäre es denn mit einer kleinen Liebesgeschichte? . . . Die befreundeten Sortimenter sagen mir jedesmal auf meinen Reisen, wie gern die Leute so etwas lesen.

> Tucholsky, 10 Juni: Ja, eine Liebesgeschichte. . . . In der heutigen Zeit Liebe? Lieben Sie? Wer liebt denn heute noch? Dann schon lieber eine kleine Sommergeschichte.

> Rowohlt, 12 Juni: Die Leute wollen neben der Politik und dem Aktuellen etwas, was sie ihrer Freundin schenken können. . . . Ich denke an eine kleine Geschichte, nicht zu umfangreich, . . . zart im Gefühl, kartoniert, leicht ironisch und mit einem bunten Umschlag. (*SG* 148–50)[18]

This exchange both links the summer story (with a wink) to the epistolary novel and satirizes the interpenetration of commercial and aesthetic concerns in Weimar publishing. Moreover, it reveals elective affinities between product planning, marketing strategies, and traditional notions of gender. We have politics and related weighty, intellectual content for men; light, attractively packaged, feelings-oriented material for women (who, in this instance, enter the literary market only via men's generosity). It also suggests some central themes that Tucholsky explores in this book, specifically the moment when authentic emotional intimacy becomes a problem for ironic contemplation, the relationship of personal erotic life to encompassing political life, and the textual and discursive construction of identity.[19] These explorations test the generic and medial potential of *Schloss Gripsholm*, just as they test the assumptions that underlie the fictional Rowohlt's remarks.

For Lydia and Kurt, the lovers in *Schloss Gripsholm*, discursive production or reproduction (citation, hybrid vernaculars, role play) turns language into a medium of experiment with gender, power, and a flexible set of selves. In the double remove of the fictional vacation, such experimental poesis is liberating. This double remove constitutes a significant qualifier, and the fact that such liberation remains strictly virtual provides ammunition for those who would deride the book as escapism. But in what follows, I will show how the text repeatedly conveys awareness of that qualification through the temporal and spatial dislocation, hybrid discourse, and construction of scenarios that, even within the eminently recognizable fictional world, are openly unreal.

We can begin to get at all of these issues by analyzing the relationship of language, eroticism, and subjectivity in *Schloss Gripsholm*. The erotic life that offers itself in this text is not reducible to sexuality, and poesis assumes forms in these pages that fall beyond the bounds of more strictly defined, literary poesis. Reading pleasure stems frequently from the lovers' banter and romantic interludes, and in the story's interplay of words and bodies, *Schloss Gripsholm* both affirms and negates traditional constructions of femininity and masculinity that circumscribed the icon of the New Woman embodied by Lydia. Particularly striking here are "Missingsch," a mixture of Low and High German that Kurt understands but only Lydia masters, and the frequency with which Lydia ironizes Kurt's attempts to speak in the traditionally coded masculine voice of reason and authority.

Moments after the narrator posts his last letter to Rowohlt, he heads by taxi to pick up "the princess" (his most common term of endearment for Lydia). His punctuality surprises her. "Du bischa all do?" (*SG* 152; Du bist ja schon da? / You're here already?), she blurts out as he arrives, introducing us to her idiolect in her very first utterance and setting the tone that characterizes their playful debates, in which they engage as equals throughout the narrative. Kurt describes Lydia's "Missingsch" thus:

> Das Plattdeutsche kann alles sein: zart und grob, humorvoll und
> herzlich, klar und nüchtern und vor allem, wenn man will, herrlich
> besoffen. Die Prinzessin bog diese Sprache ins Hochdeutsche um,
> wie es ihr passte — denn vom Missingschen gibt es hundert und
> aberhundert Abarten, von Friesland über Hamburg bis nach Pom-
> mern. (*SG* 155)[20]

Any human being who achieves speech is subject to language, and
decades of inquiry into language in social use have charted the double
subjection that results when language becomes a means of reinforcing
imbalances of power along gendered lines. Kurt is an ironic patriarch,
frequently capable of laying a finger on his sexist tendencies and reflect-
ing critically on their construction. But even were he of the most severely
conservative stripe, "Missingsch" would be a field in which he would
constantly find himself on the defensive. The description of the regional
idiom is itself rich in meaning: "Missingsch" is both localizable and unlo-
calizable, coextensive with a region bounded by a fluid frontier, existing
in myriad variations. It is a vernacular that Lydia, like a literary author,
uses as material, harnessing its potential and directing its flow according
to her design, finding freedom in being subject to a language in which
she is exceptionally proficient. As Kurt and Lydia travel toward Sweden,
they thus literally move through the heart of her linguistic territory. The
transition between Germany and abroad, between professional life and
vacation, unfolds on her turf.

In their intertwined strands of discourse, Kurt and Lydia frequently
demonstrate how gendered speakers can use the very language to which
they are subject as a means of slipping beyond the bounds of linguistically
rooted gender convention. The games get underway even before the pair
arrive at the station, when Lydia asks, "Ist es wirklich so kalt da oben?"
Kurt responds, "Es ist doch merkwürdig . . . Wenn die Leute in Deutschland an Schweden denken, dann denken sie: Schwedenpunsch, furchtbar
kalt, Ivar Kreuger, Zündhölzer, furchtbar kalt, blonde Frauen und furchtbar kalt. So kalt ist es gar nicht." Lydia: "Also wie kalt ist es denn?" Kurt:
"Alle Frauen sind pedantisch." Lydia: "Außer dir!" Kurt: "Ich bin keine
Frau." Lydia: "Aber pedantisch!" (*SG* 153)[21]

The exchange has a nonsensical air but presents an intriguing logic
problem, the resolution of which guarantees that Lydia will outflank
Kurt. Kurt opens with a classic essentialist maneuver: all women are *x*.
Lydia's retort both rejects the categorical assertion and, raising the ante,
counterfactually asserts the male interlocutor as an exception to the
alleged rule of female pedantry. Placed in such an extraordinary position, Kurt must make a comparatively pedantic move — restatement
of the obvious — to return the conversation to reality. This proves the
conclusion that Lydia immediately offers, a conclusion that connects

him (woman or not) to the group from which he meant to distinguish himself with his original assertion.

If language often serves as a means of endowing socially constructed (thus alterable) hierarchies with an air of natural immutability, this kind of verbal sparring exposes the dynamic, comparatively open struggle that each discursive interchange potentially constitutes. Lydia's inventive linguistic subjectivity, evolving in interlocution with Kurt, becomes discursive poesis: a self-production through speech. As she dialogically draws and re-draws her identity, she resists the tendency by narrator or reader to reduce her to a mere object.

Throughout the opening chapters, the speakers are both mobile and relatively isolated (on the deck of a ship, in a train compartment, in a taxi). They are passengers, not anchored in social space but moving through it. This freedom, coupled with Lydia's active co-construction of her and Kurt's discursive relationship, stands in contrast to the gender distinctions inherent in the fictional Rowohlt's comment about light, non-political material that "people" (to his way of thinking, men) can buy for their girlfriends. That comment is shaped by conventions of gender that identify women as passive consumers of language, call for male guidance into the sphere of German letters, and restrict women's access to serious intellectual forums. Tucholsky's depiction of the Lydia-Kurt relationship suggests tactics for destabilizing such conventions from within, even as its displacement of the couple to the realms of fiction and vacation displays sensitivity to the practical difficulty of such destabilization in his Weimar readers' historical reality.

Places that become non-places recur throughout the story. Consider this account of a walk home after swimming:

> Dann krochen wir langsam zurück durch den Wald. . . . An jeder Schneise blieben wir stehn und hielten große Reden; jeder tat so, als ob er dem anderen zuhörte, und er hörte ja auch zu, und jeder tat so als bewunderte er den Wald, und er bewunderte ihn ja auch — aber im allertiefsten Grunde, wenn man uns gefragt hätte: wir waren nicht mehr in der großen Stadt und noch nicht in Schweden. Aber wir waren beieinander. (*SG* 181)[22]

This is one of many passages that can be read as an empty vignette yet is also layered with significance. First, consider the presence of colloquial lexical items ("krochen" for moving at a slow pace, "stehn" instead of *stehen* [to stand]) amid the assiduous grammatical correctness of the syntax and structures (the subjunctive especially). The conventions of more casual oral communication commingle with the precise conventions of formal writing, yielding a hybrid print language that can register as a conversation but nonetheless displays its formal artifice. Indeed, that display pulls the colloquial devices into the orbit of stylistic deliberation: words that, in isolation, strike the ear as unconscious choices emerge as part of a careful process of textual planning and execution.

The relationship between the characters in the woods reflects a similar paradox of mediated immediacy. They walk side by side, talk to one another, listen to one another, *are* together — and yet there is a conscious degree of staging to it all. Here the book exposes that strange juncture at which the historical and social contingency of emotion becomes suddenly apparent: even genuine feelings no longer feel genuine; actual communication and acting as if one were communicating are simultaneous and interlinked. But the loss of a naïvely felt authenticity turns out to be a gain. The characters lose their sense of fixed location in the liminal space of the forest, which holds both the familiar metropolis and the foreign vacation land at a distance. The distinction between the intuitive and the deliberative fades, opening new possibilities for talking together and being together, that is, for self-production, intimacy, and pleasure achieved via shared discourse. And the vignette, by virtue of its interactivity with other episodes in the story, comes into focus as a form well suited to exploring these new dynamics.

Gripsholm II: Text, Body, Sense

The episodes I have discussed so far, though saturated with playfulness and pleasure, are neither physical nor emotional in a way that evokes traditionally defined romance. Kurt-as-narrator clearly yearns for *physical* intimacy, but just as he questions the possibility of unscripted, authentic love in modern times, he is also apparently incapable of achieving intimacy without some degree of conscious staging. Let us consider a paradigmatic evening walk vignette during which Lydia laments that she has never seen the northern lights, something she always wanted to do as a child. Enter the narrator:

> Blaßblau wölbte sich der Himmel über uns; an einer Stelle des Horizonts ging er in tiefes Dunkelblau über, und da, wo die Sonne vorhin untergegangen war, leuchtete es gelbrosig, . . . "Lydia," sagte ich, "Wollen wir uns ein Nordlicht machen?" — "Na . . ." "Sieh mal," sagte ich, und deutete mit dem Finger nach oben, "siehst du, siehst du — da — da ist es!" // Wir sahen beide fest nach oben — wir hielten uns an den Händen, Pulsschlag und Blutstrom gingen von einem zum andern. In diesem Augenblick hatte ich sie so lieb wie noch nie. Und da sahen wir unser Nordlicht. (*SG* 187)[23]

The fictional Ernst Rowohlt would have surely detected girlfriend-gift material here, and if that description — in all its implications — is fitting, then this would be a particularly ripe moment for critical assault. Literary purists in Tucholsky's day, nostalgic for a time when writers ostensibly worked unfettered by economic concerns, would here detect an author doing a businessman's bidding, producing text under the guise of literature that has only commercial viability, no literary merit. Champions of the avant-garde would find an utter lack of radical aesthetic experiment, thus no basis for critical interest. A critic principally attuned to problems of gender would find sexism in the guise of romance, isolating in the scene a structure under which a woman's long-desired fulfillment becomes possible only with a man's guiding hand. And proponents of progressive, politically engaged art would read the scene as ignorant of the problems of the day, thus affirmative of the status quo.

The first and second critiques rely on tenuous claims: that art was once independent of commercial or other social conditions, that only avant-garde art warrants critical attention, and that the high/low distinction is insoluble. The third and fourth critiques are more cogent: the structural sexism is indisputable, as is the lack of explicit reference to the political tensions of the times. But while these charges stick, they leave a significant dimension of the scene untreated.

The northern lights vignette is not shy about being written for the market, but this should not distract us from the way it lightly, somberly renders the pain one experiences upon achieving the knowledge that childhood innocence is a fiction, only to realize that this knowledge does not make the desire to restore innocence disappear. Without raising his voice, the narrator conveys the thrill born of that fleeting moment in which a person-to-person coupling obliterates everything that took that innocence away — even words. Yet in its depiction of the achievement of happiness via fantasy-fueled perception, the scene becomes a document of the practical impossibility of that happiness. Once again, the paradoxical element asserts itself; but this time, instead of inhabiting an in-between territory or a place that does not exist, the characters see something that is not actually there. They commune via touching flesh, a mutual feeling of pulse, and a synchronous, creative act of *observation*, generating a synchronized sensory perception and bi-corporal flow that they stand just beyond, even as it overcomes them.

This is a defining scene for *Schloss Gripsholm* because it works in the register of emotion and sensation yet invites a reader response that is analytical as well as visceral. One is tempted to dismiss it as a recycling of a stock situation that stirs base sensations but remains devoid of the combined aesthetic and intellectual complexity characteristic of literary art. But the layering of the scene thwarts that impulse, coaxing the reader toward the narrator's observer-participant relationship with the depicted sentiments. The creation of the northern lights is thus both a genre-romance cliché and a confrontation with emotion as an epistemological problem, set up in such a way that the one cannot be extricated from the other. As it both bows to genre convention and uses convention as a means of raising the kind of complex questions genre fiction is generally accused of ignoring, the text demonstrates that it does not fall into the trivial, stock-romance category. Obliquely, but perhaps more important, it also questions whether critiques that employ labels like "trivial" and discredit genre fiction out of hand pay due attention to the subtleties of texts and intelligence of readers condemned as unsophisticated.

A later scene raises the erotic ante with a much-anticipated sexual encounter between Lydia, Kurt, and their friend Sibylle (Billie), who has been visiting for a few days. The narrative account covers barely a half-page, but it is rich in meaning, as this passage suggests:

> Wir flüchteten aus der Einsamkeit der Welt zueinander. Ein Gran Böses war dabei, ein Löffelchen Ironie, nichts Schmachtendes, sehr viel Wille, sehr viel Erfahrung und sehr viel Unschuld. Wir flüsterten, wir sprachen erst übereinander, dann über das, was wir taten, dann nichts mehr. Und keinen Augenblick ließ die Kraft nach, die uns zueinander trieb; . . . nun waren wir bewußt geworden, ganz und gar bewußt. (*SG* 243)[24]

How would the Kurt Tucholsky of *Deutschland, Deutschland über alles* (1929; Germany, Germany above Everything), who proclaimed that there was nothing outside politics, have assessed the politics of this passage? Does the recalled progression from speech to silence, through which the trio achieves total *consciousness*, signal a giving-up on language, thus an anticipation of the prolonged public silence that marked the last years of Tucholsky's life? (Just as the summer story's itinerary charts the author's path into exile?) In their attempt to find in each other's arms a remedy for the atomization of modern life, are Lydia, Kurt, and Billie, like Kracauer's revue fans, immersing themselves in the corporal and thus perpetuating the very conditions from which they seek refuge?[25]

There is escapism and defeatism here, and these do add up, de facto, to conservatism. But such passages also demonstrate a keen interest in tackling via fiction the problematic relationship between the corporal and the intellectual and its intertwining with politics, sexual and otherwise, at this juncture of modern history. As in the northern lights scene, we find the distance of the observer-narrator, as well as the engulfing corporal immediacy of the erotic. Kurt is explicit about the ironic mode of communion, and the reflective discourse on self (talking about each other) and erotic pleasure (talking about what we were doing) seems to persist, driving the threesome not toward a purely instinctual mode of being but toward consciousness. And again, observation is never decoupled from participation. As Kurt recalls, "Vieles habe ich von dieser Stunde vergessen — aber eins weiß ich noch heute: wir liebten uns am meisten mit den Augen" (*SG* 243; I have forgotten much of that hour — but there is one thing I am sure of still today: we loved each most with our eyes).

One might take such a remark as proof of scopophilia fueled by a patriarchal desire for control, but such a reading would not do justice to the subtleties of the scene or to its function in the paradoxical synthesis of closeness and separation — what Walter Delabar describes as "the dual condition of intimacy and distance" — that marks the text from the opening moment.[26] The characters, the setting, the action, and the experiences of all these via reading are all subject to the writer's choices — but Billie and Lydia are no more on scopophilic display for the reader than they are under Kurt's control in the scene. As captivated as Tucholsky the critic was by Freud, *Schloss Gripsholm* amounts to more than psychoanalytic paint-by-numbers.[27] The desire to objectify and possess is unquestionably felt by the male narrator, but in the way he ironically frames that impulse, he invites the reader into a dialogue about how such desire relates to more broadly and deeply felt needs for wholeness and control that modernity simply will not satisfy. Hence the northern lights. Hence the climactic sex scene, which has little to do with sex per se and more to do with the utopian quality of synchronized sensuality.

As the lovers' tale explores the positive potential of hearts beating as one, the story of the child and Frau Adriani demonstrates the perils. Adriani's principal pleasure comes from ruling: she imposes her will violently, by her words or by her hand, and is pleased when this aggression shapes her charges (thus her world) to her liking. Inevitably, the child's story collides with the lovers'. While out for a stroll with Kurt's friend Karlchen, Kurt and Lydia stumble upon a girls' home. In a predictable contrivance, a girl shoots out of a side door as they approach. Noticing the wanderers, she darts into their arms. They learn that the girl's name is Ada Collin and that she is suffering terribly at the hands of Adriani, who herself then promptly demands that they return Ada to her rightful custodian. The child returns tearfully into Adriani's clutches, and Kurt observes retrospectively, "Die Frau riss abermals an dem Kind; sie riss wie an einer Sache; ich fühlte: sie meinte nicht das Mädchen, sie meinte ihre Herrschaft über das Mädchen" (*SG* 213; The woman jerked the child toward her again, as if seizing a thing; I felt: she didn't mean [to punish] the child personally, she meant to express her rule over the girl).

The use of the verb *fühlen* (to feel) is striking here: it is at the level of the senses that Kurt recognizes the matron's brutal reduction of child to object. We can describe his initial response to the witnessed injustice as aesthetic, provided we understand that term as designating the whole field of sensory impression and response. The encounter violently disrupts the *Gripsholm* sensibilities, the patterns of aesthetic recognition and response that the novel has modeled up to this point. In fact, the confrontation reveals a very specific (and perhaps untenable) sensibility which, anchored in the realms of corporal sensation and emotion, nonetheless involves an irreducibly analytical, cognitive element as well. What follows the colon in the citation just made is, after all, too cerebral to be considered a feeling.

The Adriani encounter sends Kurt into a daydream that extends the exploration of how some human beings can reduce others to suffering-material, such that the suffering can be witnessed with great aesthetic pleasure and yield a sense of personal fulfillment. Compare this description of the coliseum with the erotic passages discussed above: "Das Tier Masse wälzte sich in einem Orgasmus von Lust. Es gebar Grausamkeit. Was hier vor sich ging, war ein einziger großer schamloser Zeugungsakt der Vernichtung — das süße Abgleiten in den Tod, der anderen" (*SG* 216; The mass animal writhed in an orgasm of lust. It gave birth to atrocity. It was one great shameless procreation of destruction — the sweet slide into death, that of others). The sweet slide, fueled by the Roman masses' daily regimens of frustration and humiliation, culminates in a sensation so intense as to become hyper-fulfillment: "Es war wie Liebeserfüllung, nur noch ungestümer, noch heißer, noch zischender. Wie eine spitze Stichflamme stieg die Lust aus den viertausend Menschen — sie waren *ein* Leib, . . . sie waren die Raubtiere, die die Menschen dort unten zerfleischten, und sie waren die Zerfleischten (*SG* 216; It was like a consummation of love, but it was hotter, more hissing, stormier. Like an explosive flame, the lust rose from the four thousand people. They were *one* body; . . . they were the predators that tore the flesh from the human beings below, and they were the mangled). It is not much of a stretch to identify this passage as the book's most explicitly sexual, and in painting this picture the narrator depicts the brutal result of the elective affinity formed between socially embedded, misshapen libidinal impulses and the mass spectacle in Roman (obliquely, Weimar German) society.

The strongly negative charge of this scenario contrasts with the positive valence of the lovers' interludes, raising the question of whether any of the positive erotic dynamics that play out in the remove of the fictional vacation are transferable to the conveniently (but, as the story demonstrates, only temporarily) elided mass society. This question casts a further assumption inherent in the fictional Rowohlt's girlfriend-gift remark in the opening correspondence into critical relief: the love story may exist alongside politics and current events, but the two are inseparable, even if what links them runs underground. For relations of power matter in the bedroom, and erotics and aesthetics matter in the public sphere. The book does anything but flee its author's historical reality, even if that reality is hidden in plain view.

In retrospect, we see that reality as marked by a dizzying array of mass configurations and myriad violent confluences of aesthetics and politics, variations of the nexus that cinematically concretizes in the above-mentioned daydream of the coliseum. The main problem with such violence, at least as Kurt sees it, is its capacity to spread epidemically from one population to the next, regardless of people's conscious politics. Snapping out of the dream, Kurt draws a deep breath while suddenly springing to his feet, surprising Karlchen and Lydia.

> Plötzlich spürte ich dieselbe Lust an der Zerstörung, am Leiden der anderen; diese Frau leiden machen zu können. . . . Mit einem kalten Wasserstrahl löschte ich das aus, während ich ausatmete. Ich kannte den Mechanismus dieser Lust: sie war doppelt gefährlich, weil sie ethisch unterbaut war; quälen, um ein gutes Werk zu tun. (*SG* 217)[28]

Given Kurt's sudden lust for the suffering of another, one can view the daydream as a hinge between the child's story and the lovers' interludes. It reveals the overlap of the matrices of sensation that characterize the intimate, pleasurable interplay of bodies on the one hand and the staging of suffering as mass spectacle on the other.

There is a particular, misogynistic dimension to Kurt's general, anti-authoritarian thoughts on Adriani. This becomes most crassly apparent when, as Ada packs her things to leave with her rescuers, Kurt and Lydia, he and Adriani catch each other's eye. He comments retrospectively, "In diesem Blick war so viel körperliche Intimität, dass mir graute" (*SG* 253; I was horrified by how much physical intimacy there was in that glance). After their eyes meet, he veers into speculation that this bitter harpy could be put on the road to recovery by a steady regimen of heterosexual sex: "Und in diesem Augenblick öffnete sich mir eine tiefe Schlucht: diese Frau war niemals befriedigt worden, niemals. Durch mein Gehirn flitzte jenes zynische Rezept: Rp. Penis normalis, dosim: Repetatur!" (*SG* 253; And in this moment an abyss opened before me: this woman had never been satisfied, never. A cynical prescription shot through my brain: Rx: penis normalis, in repeated doses!)[29] Here again, as with Kurt's paternal antics in his relationship with Lydia or the quip by the fictional Rowohlt about people buying books for girlfriends, we see the persistence of a diffuse sexism that finds expression in concentrated bursts throughout the book, a tendency that persists in opposition to the emancipatory dynamics of Lydia and Kurt's discursive relationship.

Among other things, this sexism is itself an expression of the anxiety over a total dissolution of order, of the fear that keeps the teasing of gender hierarchy (and hierarchies generally) from becoming a thoroughgoing dismantling. The Kurt-Adriani exchange of glances — a combination of observation and intimacy that structurally doubles yet emotionally inverts the visual relations of Kurt, Lydia, and Billie — suddenly erodes the difference between the narrator and the tyrant. This erosion elicits a brutal response, and that response takes explicit recourse to an unmistakable sign of the imperiled difference. This need to conserve or restore distinction is a characteristically modern symptom of a situation in which the impulse to push beyond established boundaries (or the recognition that such boundaries are losing force) exists in an uneasy balance with the need to guard against chaos via schemes of classification and organization. As Helmut Lethen argues, the social enforcement of such schemes is particularly strong when "stable external bounds of convention fall away; when the dissolution of familiar limits, axes, and roles is feared."[30] *Schloss Gripsholm* demonstrates the persistence of such fear regarding femininity and masculinity, even as it ironizes patriarchal ways of seeing, thinking, and acting.

Tucholsky's text thus exposes but cannot fully overcome the schematizing trend that Lethen describes. As Kurt's immediate corrective to his prescription idea makes clear, the underlying problem is the desire for power felt by human beings (*SG* 253), a desire intensified by a world driven by mechanisms that operate beyond individual control. In his encounters with and thoughts on Adriani, Kurt draws two lines: one that separates him from her and one that connects him to her. They must both contemplate a world in which the security of the order they know is compromised.

"Read books!" The Late-Weimar Public Sphere and the Modernity of *Schloss Gripsholm*

There is no world-changing optimism in Kurt and Lydia. They picture their non-vacation reality as something they are subject to, not an object over which they, as subjects, could exert shaping force. If the intricately structured artifice I have discussed over the balance of this essay suggests anything, it is that Tucholsky *the novelist* issues no marching orders for the solution of problems of gender, subjectivity, or collective corporality. Rather, the text draws attention to how those problems take shape in attitudes and ideas, find expression in language, and feel in discursive and physical interaction. Instead of a declaration issued, there is an invitation extended to aesthetic participation that positions the reader to sense, in a conscious way, erotic configurations of feeling and thought. These are at once potentially productive and destructive, depending on how human subjects manage to channel them into experience in each distinct juncture of social space and historical time. These configurations become a sensible realm of playful breaking-down, a comparatively open expanse that tests pervasive schematization, with an airy but not vacuous atmosphere and an absence of interest in direct political influence that does not mean an absence of political ramifications. The value of *Schloss Gripsholm* lies not in gravity, but in questions raised regarding the substance of lightness.[31]

To call Tucholsky the *Gripsholm* author a novelist is, however, somewhat problematic. The book consciously avoids traditional generic distinction, just one of the ways in which it is "crammed together," as Tucholsky put it in a response to a critic who complained that Gripsholm was a batch of loosely related formal and thematic components. The book's components are refined, but their assemblage reveals seams: the two narrative strands, at first glance, do not connect well; and the intergeneric text is too long to be a short story, too short to be a novel, and too frequently digressive to be a *Novelle*. An entertaining read, it is also an uncomfortable fit, a book clothed like a short novel that reveals itself to be a series of subtly recorded experiential scenes interspersed with essayistic reflection. In this combination of report and comment, it shows commonalities of orientation and method with Tucholsky's journalism. There is little point in framing the fiction as a mechanistic re-activation of the journalistic project in a different register, but his various forums and texts did not exist in isolation. In fact, over the course of the 1920s increasingly apparent problems in periodical publishing intensified Tucholsky's interest in being a writer *of books*.[32]

Tucholsky was well attuned to the precarious position of left-critical journalism in the Weimar period, having witnessed the state's aggressive pursuit of his colleague Carl von Ossietzky, who had faced charges multiple times for his critique of the German military. While Tucholsky worked on *Gripsholm*, Ossietzky was waylaid by legal proceedings that began with charges of betraying military secrets in August 1929. In October 1930 — that is, a good two years before the Nazi accession to power — Tucholsky and Ossietzky met in Hindås, Sweden (where Tucholsky had been living since January), to discuss the relocation of *Die Weltbühne*. Ossietzky was found guilty in 1931, and his eighteen-month prison sentence further underlined the increasingly draconian posture assumed by broad sectors of the republican government (the judiciary in particular) vis-à-vis the press. Tucholsky observed these developments at close range, and he recognized them as a threat both to his means of material sustenance and to his more overtly political writing.

In addition, even as he remained an active *Publizist*, Tucholsky, like many Weimar authors, was becoming increasingly skeptical of a concept of writing (literary or journalistic) as a consequential lever of direct political influence.[33] Ossietzky's tribulations only fueled such skepticism, and in its preoccupation with the personal and the elision of the overtly political, *Schloss Gripsholm* presents evidence of this shift in thinking. The book avoids any possibility of making a social statement, which insulates it from censorial or prosecutorial aggression and conveys a growing conviction that the book, as a medium, is ill-suited to such activist intervention.

The book, in summer story form, is well-suited for superimposing semantic layers and for catalyzing sensory interactivity between literary and non-literary reality via the textuality and discursivity that connect the two. And light as it may be, *Schloss Gripsholm* as a book calls for a more sustained, concentrated reading practice than Tucholsky's short-form prose requires. These are the formal factors that interlink with those political factors, of which Tucholsky was acutely aware. In a 1931 commentary on state restriction of media content, he issued an admonition to readers that could apply to his own writing as well: "Lest Bücher! Sie sind kleine Insel der Freiheit im Meer der Zensur" (Read books! They are small islands of freedom in an ocean of censorship).[34] Tucholsky's recognition of the industrialization of literature was sober and complete.[35] He nonetheless maintained that the book was a medium of creative expression and aesthetic communication *comparatively* free of the political and institutional strictures placed on periodical publishing, radio broadcasting, and the cinema.

Schloss Gripsholm was in its fourth printing inside a year, overshooting every preceding Tucholsky book (including *Rheinsberg* and the controversial, widely sold *Deutschland, Deutschland über alles*).[36] It also fared well with critics: between May and August 1931 the book was reviewed in nearly two dozen prominent venues, and the tone of the reviews was overwhelmingly positive.[37] If Tucholsky the political commentator found himself increasingly hemmed in, he found in the summer story a means to converse with a broad, enthusiastic audience.

Peter Jelavich's book *Berlin Alexanderplatz* presents a case study of the degrees-of-freedom model that Tucholsky describes. Jelavich argues that the broad range of experimental, cosmopolitan, left-leaning undertakings associated with the term "Weimar culture" was "largely defunct by the end of 1931," having fallen victim to the fear and brutality cultivated by an extreme right that the republican government was too ill-equipped, incompetent or simply disinclined to halt.[38] Much of Tucholsky's late-Weimar work suggests that he was an unusually aware witness of the premature cultural death that Jelavich depicts. Tucholsky grasped that it was not simply censorship; it was the effective collapse of the late-Weimar public sphere that necessitated a retreat to books as the last island of freedom.

Schloss Gripsholm is a paradoxical island. The book's fictive contrivance is omnipresent yet occasionally pushed to a vanishing point: literary reality remains manifestly, openly constructed, even as it becomes — in moments — indistinguishable from real life. This flowing together, which is also a collision, is not avant-gardistic confrontation: *Schloss Gripsholm* is inventive, but only within the framework of convention. Its lack of radical formal moves makes it anything but high-modern; and in its bows to the market, self-conscious acceptance of commodity status, and implicit rejection of the autonomous negative capability claimed by the literary avant-garde, it seems to anticipate the most politically inert strains of postmodernism.

But a fair reading cannot overlook that the text both emerges from and grapples with aesthetic and political dimensions of the cultural death that Jelavich analyzes, and this attention to the historical moment marks the text as thoroughly modern. Its modernity, to draw on a theoretical insight by Miriam Hansen, is vernacular. Hansen argues that "different forms of mimetic experience and expression, of affectivity, temporality, and reflexivity, a changing fabric of everyday life, sociability, and leisure" emerge in an age of industrialization and mass consumption. Vernacular modernism engages these emergent forms in a way that "combines the dimension of the quotidian, of everyday usage, with connotations of discourse, idiom, and dialect, with circulation, promiscuity, and translatability."[39] In analyzing how the sensibilities of Tucholsky's characters inform their response to self, other, and surroundings; how the games they play in the remove of the vacation critically illuminate the working world that lies in the distance; and how they experience intimacy and generate identities through discourse, I have sought to emphasize the vernacular-modernist qualities of *Schloss Gripsholm*.

Considering this text at the late-Weimar nexus of the history of feelings, the history of literature, and the history of the book brings into focus what such a vernacular-modernist move makes possible: a highly *accessible* textual field, on which sensibilities less compatible with violent authority and oppressive social structures become recognizable and appropriable. The conditions for that field's coalescence were not favorable at the left-critical periphery of German letters; the summer story made such a field possible through negotiation from within the literary-industrial mainstream. The text, exactly because of the aesthetic choices that made it commercially viable, found broad resonance in a fractured literary public. That such literature could directly influence the reality beyond the page is a notion that Tucholsky had relinquished by 1931, but *Schloss Gripsholm* reads in retrospect as evidence that the gains to be had from writing for the book market in the final phase of the Weimar Republic were significant, even if not world-changing. Negotiation is a mode of struggle, but it is not about total victory.

Notes

[1] Samuel Saenger, "Die Not der geistigen Arbeiter," *Die neue Rundschau* 34 (1923): 276, qtd. in Anton Kaes, "Schreiben und Lesen in der Weimarer Republik," in *Literatur der Weimarer Republik 1918–1933*, ed. Bernhard Weyergraf (Munich: Hanser, 1995), 39. Saenger edited the *Neue Rundschau*. All translations are mine unless otherwise noted.

[2] "Dear Master Rowohlt, Gulbransson has captured you perfectly on the new catalog cover: there you sit on the bank of the brook, contemplative, catching

the fat fish. The bait with the fourteen percent royalty-free copies that you're dangling isn't fat enough — twelve percent is also a nice figure. Think it over a bit and give your cold publisher's heart a nudge. At fourteen percent, I surely won't be able to think up anything — I start versifying at twelve percent." Kurt Tucholsky, *Schloss Gripsholm*, in *Texte 1931*, vol. 14 of Kurt Tucholsky, *Gesamtausgabe: Texte und Briefe*, ed. Sabina Becker (Hamburg: Rowohlt 1998), 151. Subsequent citations will use the abbreviation *SG* and the page number and will appear parenthetically in the body of the text. *Castle Gripsholm*, Michael Hofmann's translation of *Schloss Gripsholm*, was originally published as *Schloss Gripsholm: A Summer Story* in 1985 (London: Chatto & Windus) and is currently available in a 2004 edition (Woodstock, NY: Overlook Press) distributed by Penguin Group. In keeping with the analytical purposes of this essay, I am using my own, more literal translations.

³ Gideon Reuveni, *Reading Germany: Literature and Consumer Culture before 1933* (New York: Berghahn, 2006).

⁴ Samuel Fischer, "Bemerkungen zur Bücherkrise," in *S. Fischer Verlag: von der Gründung bis zur Rückkehr aus dem Exil*, ed. Friedrich Pfäfflin (Marbach: Deutsche Schillergesellshaft, 1985), 357, qtd. in Gideon Reuveni, "The 'Crisis of the Book' and German Society after the First World War," *German History* 20, no. 4 (2002): 444. Fischer's essay was originally published in *Die Literarische Welt*, the Rowohlt-backed literary and cultural weekly edited by Willy Haas.

⁵ Reuveni, "The 'Crisis of the Book' and German Society," 445.

⁶ See Reinhard Piper, "Das Buch und der Mensch von heute," *Börsenblatt für den deutschen Buchhandel* 93 (1926): 1537, qtd. in Reuveni, "The 'Crisis of the Book' and German Society after the First World War," 449.

⁷ See Helmut Lethen and Bernhard Weyergraf, "Der Einzelne in der Massengesellschaft," in Weyergraf, *Literatur der Weimarer Republik 1918–1933*, 636–72. Gustave Le Bon's *Psychologie des Foules* (1895; The Crowd: A Study of the Popular Mind) gave the masses great currency as a topic in intellectual discourse across Europe. It was available in German by 1906, and Freud's debt to Le Bon is evident (and acknowledged) in the 1921 text *Massenpsychologie und Ich-Analyse*, *Gesammelte Werke*, vol. 13 (Frankfurt am Main: Fischer, 1998), 71–161; English translation: *Group Psychology and the Analysis of the Ego* (New York: Norton, 1990).

⁸ Reuveni, "The 'Crisis of the Book' and German Society," 449.

⁹ Ibid., 443.

¹⁰ Ute Maack, "Warum schreibt das keiner? Kurt Tucholskys Literaturkritik," in *Kurt Tucholsky: Das literarische und publizistische Werk*, ed. Sabina Becker and Ute Maack (Darmstadt: Wissenschaftliche Buchgesellschaft, 2002), 245.

¹¹ Russell Berman, "Writing for the Book Industry: The Writer under Organized Capitalism," *New German Critique* 29 (1983): 39–56.

¹² Ibid., 40.

¹³ For analysis of *Rheinsberg*, see Sascha Kiefer, "'Meine ganze Jugend': Kurt Tucholskys *Rheinsberg* (1912)," in Becker and Maack, *Kurt Tucholsky*, 17–46;

and Dirk Grathoff, "Kurt Tucholskys *Rheinsberg*: Die Inszenierung der Idylle im Rekurs auf Theodor Fontane und Heinrich Mann," *Monatshefte* 88, no. 2 (1996): 197–216. On the development of *Die Weltbühne*, see Gunther Nickel, *Die Schaubühne/Die Weltbühne: Siegfried Jacobsohns Wochenschrift und ihr ästhetisches Programm* (Opladen: Westdeutscher Verlag, 1996).

[14] Tucholsky, "Auf dem Nachttisch," *Die Weltbühne* 25, no. 9 (1929): 337, qtd. in Maack, "Warum schreibt das keiner? Kurt Tucholskys Literaturkritik," 245.

[15] Maack, "Warum schreibt das keiner? Kurt Tucholskys Literaturkritik," 245.

[16] Tucholsky, "Die Aussortierten," in *Texte 1931*, 22–26. Maack makes a compelling case that Tucholsky's criticism ultimately seeks to determine the possibilities of a modern literature of society ("moderne Gesellschaftsliteratur") suitable to the Weimar Republic's fragmented public sphere ("fragmentierte Öffentlichkeit"). See Maack, "Warum schreibt das keiner? Kurt Tucholskys Literaturkritik," 255.

[17] Reuveni, *Reading Germany*, 47–48.

[18] "Rowohlt, 8 June: As you know, I've published all sorts of political books lately, which you have given due treatment. Now I'd like to get back to cultivating *belles lettres*. Don't you have anything? How about a little love story? . . . Whenever I'm in the field, all my bookseller friends tell me how much people enjoy reading that kind of thing.

Tucholsky, 10 June: Right, a love story . . . Love, in this day and age? Are you capable of love these days? Is anyone? I think I'd really prefer a little summer story.

Rowohlt, 12 June: Alongside their politics and current events, people want something that they can give their girlfriend as a gift . . . I'm thinking of a little story, not too lengthy, . . . with a tender feel to it, a touch ironic, with a colorful cover."

[19] In this essay, I use "discourse" and "discursive" in the basic sense of language in spoken use.

[20] "Low German can be everything: tender and coarse, humorous and hearty, clear and sober and, above all, beautifully drunk, when one wants it to be. The princess twisted this language into High German as she pleased — the strains of 'Missingsch' number in the hundreds, from Frisia via Hamburg to Pomerania."

[21] Lydia asks, "Is it really so cold up there?" Kurt responds, "It's a funny thing. . . . When people in Germany think about Sweden, they think: Swedish glogg, horribly cold, Ivar Kreuger, matches, horribly cold, blond women and horribly cold. Really, it's not all that cold." Lydia: "How cold is it, then?" Kurt: "All women are pedantic." Lydia: "Except you!" Kurt: 'I'm not a woman." Lydia: "But you're pedantic!"

[22] "Then we crawled slowly back through the woods. . . . We stopped at each forest aisle and gave big speeches. Each of us acted as if he were listening to the other, and each actually was listening; each acted as if he were marveling at the forest, and we did actually marvel. But on the most fundamental level, if someone

had asked us — we were no longer in the big city, and we were not yet in Sweden. But we were together."

[23] "The pale blue sky arched above us; at one point on the horizon it shifted into a deep dark blue, and there, where the sun had gone down, it glowed yellow-rose . . . 'Lydia,' I said, 'Should we make our own Northern Lights?' — 'What are you . . .' 'Look,' I said, pointing my finger to the sky above, 'See? Do you see? There it is!' // We both looked up intently — we held each other's hands, pulse and blood flow coursing back and forth between us. At this moment, I loved her more than ever. And then we saw our Northern Lights."

[24] "We fled from the loneliness of the world to one another. There was a hint of mischief in it, a spoonful of irony, no trace of yearning, a lot of will, a lot of experience, a lot of innocence. We whispered, we talked at first about each other, then about what we were doing, then nothing more. And at no moment did the force driving us toward one another fade; . . . now we had become conscious, totally and completely conscious."

[25] See Siegfried Kracauer, "Das Ornament der Masse," 1927, *Aufsätze 1927–1931*, Schriften 5:2, ed. Inka Mülder-Bach (Frankfurt am Main: Suhrkamp, 1990), 57–67.

[26] Walter Delabar, "Eine kleine Liebesgeschichte: Kurt Tucholskys *Schloss Gripsholm: eine Sommergeschichte*," in Becker and Maack, *Kurt Tucholsky*, 137.

[27] Tucholsky comments at length and with enthusiasm on the new Freud edition, calling it "elf Bände, die die Welt erschütterten" (eleven volumes that shook the world), in an installment of "Auf dem Nachttisch," in *Texte 1931*, 258–61.

[28] "Suddenly I felt the same appetite for destruction, a desire for the suffering of others, to be able to make this woman suffer. . . . I extinguished the feeling with a stream of cold water as I exhaled. I knew the mechanism of this desire. It was doubly dangerous because of its ethical undergirding: torture in the name of doing good."

[29] The "cynical prescription" is attributed to Viennese gynecologist Rudolf Chrobak in Freud's essay "Zur Geschichte der psychoanalytischen Bewegung" (On the History of the Psycho-Analytic Movement). See Sigmund Freud, *Gesammelte Werke*, vol. 10 (Frankfurt am Main: Fischer, 1999), 43–113, or *Standard Edition*, vol. 14 (New York: Norton, 1990), 3–80.

[30] Helmut Lethen, *Verhaltenslehren der Kälte: Lebensversuche zwischen den Kriegen* (Frankfurt am Main: Suhrkamp, 1994), 10–11.

[31] For insight into Tucholsky's concept of literary lightness, see Sabina Becker, "Gegen deutsche 'Tiefe' und für poetische 'Leichtigkeit': Kurt Tucholskys und Walter Hasenclevers Komödie *Christoph Kolumbus oder die Entdeckung Amerikas* (1931/32)," in Becker and Maack, *Kurt Tucholsky: Das literarische und publizistische Werk*, 143–72.

[32] Kiefer, Maack, and Becker all discuss Tucholsky's aspiration for success as a book author in their respective articles cited above.

[33] For an examination of this shift, see Dieter Mayer, "Aktiver Pessimismus: Kurt Tucholskys *Deutschland Deutschland über alles* (1929)," in Becker and Maack, *Kurt Tucholsky*, 67–114.

[34] Tucholsky, "Die Rotstift-Schere," in *Texte 1931*, 285.

35 Tucholsky, "Kritik als Berufsstörung," in *Texte 1931*, 440.

36 Kurt Tucholsky, *Deutschland, Deutschland über alles* (Berlin: Neuer Deutscher Verlag, 1929).

37 See "Kommentar," in *Texte 1931*, 583.

38 Peter Jelavich, *Berlin Alexanderplatz: Radio, Film, and the Death of Weimar Culture* (Berkeley: U of California P, 2006), xi.

39 Hansen, "The Mass Production of the Senses: Classical Cinema as Vernacular Modernism," *Modernism/Modernity* 6, no. 2 (1999): 60.

Fig. 11.1. The collector Eduard Fuchs. Ullstein Bild, reprinted with the kind permission of the Granger Collection, New York.

11: "It would be delicious to write books for a new society, but not for the newly rich": Eduard Fuchs between Elite and Mass Culture

Ulrich Bach

> *The lustful escapades of Don Juan were not just an unusual young man's unusual adventures. . . . Notwithstanding his numerous affairs, he is sensitive to his own feelings. He is not truly loving but in need of reassurance that he is wanted and loveable. In essence he is lonely and forever trying to gain reassurance from what our young Don Juan described as objects.*
>
> — Werner Münsterberger, *Collecting*[1]

WHILE WERNER MÜNSTERBERG'S fictitious Don Juan collects women for ephemeral emotional comfort, Eduard Fuchs collected transient yet contingent material history in the most literal manner. It is precisely this collecting passion that Walter Benjamin reflects on in his seminal essay "Eduard Fuchs, der Sammler und Historiker," first published in *Zeitschrift für Sozialforschung* (Journal for Social Research) in 1937.[2] For Benjamin, Fuchs is a historian of objects and a pioneer in the field of material art history. That is to say, Fuchs the collector represents both the fetishistic antiquarian *and* the stellar historical materialist.[3]

It is widely known that Benjamin called for a revolutionary aesthetics in the age of mass reproducibility, but he also elevated the solitary, individual book collector to the lofty position of a passionate gatekeeper of memory. Every passion, he writes, "grenzt ja ans Chaos, die sammlerische aber an das der Erinnerungen" (borders on the chaotic, but the collector's passion borders on that of memories).[4] The tension between Benjamin's conflicting positions — *the masses as opposed to the individual as the force of history* — is reflected in the difference between public and private collections. In both cases the collectibles are wrested from history because they are taken out of a continuum and placed in an artificial teleology. But public collections are socially more acceptable — because of their accessibility to students and scholars — than private collections with restricted access to the public. In both cases, however, the institutional *and* private collectors' reverence for their objects helps to facilitate a unique engagement with history.

Benjamin's opposing positions on the masses versus the individual as the force of history are also reflected in Fuchs's theory of artistic production. The collector sees artistic production as the dialectical relation between Marxism and psychoanalysis. On the one hand Fuchs upholds his Marxist belief that social conditions produce artistic expression; on the other hand he argues, in keeping with Freud, that individual sexual urges are the driving force of genuine creativity. In what follows I will examine how Fuchs sought to mediate between elite and mass culture by utilizing his private collections in his book publications to foster his political agenda.

Collecting as Cultural Praxis

Before I turn to Fuchs the collector, some remarks about the cultural praxis of collecting are in order. Collecting, it could be argued, is partly motivated by the desire to overcome mortality and to create a legacy beyond death. In the Middle Ages the Christian worldview considered death merely a passage to another sphere, a view that obviated a preoccupation with collecting. Furthermore, the lack of expendable income and mass-produced goods among the majority of Europe's peoples kept the passion for collecting from gripping Europe before the Renaissance.[5] While Renaissance collectors represented their prestige, taste, and riches through the sheer wealth of objects acquired, by the eighteenth century collectors attempted to give the praxis of collecting wider meaning within an ideal system: collectibles were arranged and categorized in order to generate new meaning. As Michel Foucault has demonstrated, this moment of ordering represents an epistemological shift: "The documents of this new history are not other words, texts, or records, but unencumbered spaces in which things are juxtaposed: herbariums, collections, gardens."[6] In others words, collectors and the fledging historical associations of the eighteenth century no longer relied on handed-down natural scientific texts, but turned their attention instead to objects in their natural surroundings. Their scientific approach to collecting went hand in hand with a desire to create a historical consciousness, or as Susan A. Crane puts it, "[T]he associations began to amass collections of architectural fragments, coins, weapons, costumes, heraldry, documents, manuscripts, and more: anything that, when viewed, inspired that shared, exalted feeling of historical consciousness."[7]

In the wake of the French Revolution, public collections and museums were established in Germany, and collectors started to perceive their collectibles as means to order history and knowledge.[8] According to Eckhardt Köhn, by the end of the nineteenth-century private German collectors sought to achieve a "personal relationship" with their collectibles, an affective attachment to their trophies.[9] They arranged their collections according to criteria of aesthetic judgment and became passionate about their objects.

Up to the present day the collector is affectively bound to his trophies, and although the collector strives for order, the objects and their polyphonic narratives threaten to throw the collector into an abyss of unruly memories. This unruliness is only balanced by a strict order that manifests itself in every individual collectible. Hence, each individual collectible speaks to a collector who is not primarily interested in the use value of the object. While objects of everyday life can be used, only collectibles can be possessed. With the former objects one seeks to assert practical control over reality; with the latter one aims for something divested of its objective function. As Jean Baudrillard puts it,

> The objects of our lives, as distinct from the way we make use of them at a given moment, represent something much more, something profoundly related to subjectivity: for while the object is a resistant material body, it is also, simultaneously, a mental realm over which I hold sway, a thing whose meaning is governed by myself.[10]

The collection not only opens an imaginary space governed by the collector, this space prefigures the collector's own mind. History and the provenience of the collectible unfold in the hands of the collector and make the entire passage visible, that is, its passage through historical time and space before its arrival in this collection. Benjamin describes this phenomenon as follows: "Kaum hält der Sammler die Gegenstände in seinen Händen, so scheint er inspiriert durch sie hindurch, in die Ferne zu schauen" (As the collector holds the objects in his hands, he seems to be seeing through them into their distant past, as though inspired).[11] Accordingly, the collector comprehends not only the historical fate of the object, but also knows about its hidden structure and the relationship of the objects to each other.

This intimate knowledge enables the collector to arrange the collectibles into a new meaningful order. For Benjamin, collecting against the grain is a truly anarchic and destructive achievement that creates new functional relationships for the objects. The collector's intimate knowledge of his objects, combined with a subversive protest against the typical and classifiable, renders collecting a dialectical praxis that has the ability to achieve an alternative historical order.[12] In this vein, Fuchs ordered his exquisite possessions anew with every consecutive book publication, thus satisfying his apparently exhibitionistic urge to show his collectibles to the public. Inasmuch as he was interested in the dissemination of visual arts, Fuchs focused his collecting on such "Massenkunst" (art for the masses) as caricature and on the material conditions of its reception and reproduction. In doing so he subverted the appreciation of beauty, harmony, and smooth surface appearance that had characterized bourgeois art.

Fuchs's collections encompassed nineteenth-century French caricature and paintings by Honoré Daumier and Henri de Toulouse-Lautrec, as well as twentieth-century German art by Max Slevogt, John Heartfield, and George Grosz. His passion for Daumier led him to Slevogt, whose Don Quixote drawings Fuchs considered as exquisite as Daumier's Cervantes illustrations.[13] His extensive studies in art history gave him authority over a wide variety of fields such as ancient ceramics, Japanese masks, and Chinese sculptures. He also possessed a sizeable library of art-historical reference books, comprising 6,000 to 8,000 titles, among them many first and special editions.[14] Throughout his life Fuchs maintained a friendly relationship with many of the contemporary artists he collected. Most notably, he traveled together with Slevogt, whose work he collected, to Egypt and Sudan in the spring of 1914.

In 1933, upon the National Socialist seizure of power, Fuchs was forced to leave Germany and move to Paris; he had to leave almost all of his collection and reference library behind in Berlin, where it was shortly broken up. In catalogue 197, the auction company C. G. Boerner of Leipzig auctioned off — on behalf of the new German authorities — 481 artifacts of Fuchs's various collections: furniture, porcelain, and thirty-two paintings by Slevogt. The remainder — 799 items of East Asian art, sculptures, and other miscellany — went on the block a year later.[15] Fortunately, Fuchs could save his unique Daumier paintings. It was this small part of his erstwhile stellar art collection that secured him and his wife a decent existence in exile.

By the time Benjamin wrote his essay on Fuchs — in the late 1930s — the historical situation in Europe had become increasingly hopeless for leftist intellectuals. Exiled in Paris, Fuchs was unable to continue to publish his counter-history of art. He never fully recovered from the loss of his possessions, and his publishing activities ceased with his death in Paris in 1940. Yet the dire historical circumstances seem to have inspired Benjamin to portray Fuchs as a collector with a unique approach to the material history of art despite his being bereft of his possessions and position. Suffice it to say that in Benjamin's essay on Fuchs, the concept of collecting no longer revolves around individual memory, fate, and magic, but emphasizes the social relevance of art for the masses. Tellingly, the essay concludes with Fuchs's ideal of anonymous popular art expressed in his book on Chinese Ceramics.[16] In this study, Fuchs dissociates himself from the cult of the individual artist and instead praises art that would not reveal the name of its creator.[17]

Fig. 11.2. Daumier room in the Villa Fuchs. Ullstein Bild, reprinted with the kind permission of the Granger Collection, New York.

Eduard Fuchs: A Collector's Life

Born near Stuttgart in 1870, Eduard Fuchs started an apprenticeship in a print shop as a teenager.[18] He joined the Socialist Workers' Party (precursor of the SPD) and became a politically engaged journalist, during which time he repeatedly came into conflict with the law and was incarcerated numerous times for *lèse majesté* or for distributing socialist propaganda.[19] With the abolition of the *Sozialistengesetz* (socialist law) in 1890, he could become an accountant for the *Münchner Post* and then in 1892 editor-in-chief for the left-leaning satiric Munich weekly *Süddeutscher Postillon*, in which function he revised the paper's antiquated didactic style and popularized the journal through humor and a tinge of eroticism. During the 1890s he lived in Schwabingen, Munich's bohemian quarter, where he befriended such literary luminaries as Frank Wedekind, Christian Morgenstern, and Franziska Gräfin von Reventlow.

It was in Munich that Fuchs began to follow his obsession with book- and art-collecting, and on journeys throughout Europe he paid visits to innumerable antiquarian bookshops and art galleries. His various collections, which he utilized for a string of publications on art, caricature, and sexual mores, soon became widely known. The year 1898 saw his first *Mappenwerk* (illustrated publication) entitled *1848 in der Karikatur*

SAMMLUNG E. F., BERLIN

DAUMIER – GRAPHIK

KULTURGESCHICHTE

NR. 619

VERSTEIGERUNG DURCH

C. G. BOERNER IN LEIPZIG

AM MONTAG, DEN 23. MAI 1938

NACHMITTAGS 3 UHR

UND AM DIENSTAG, DEN 24. MAI 1938

VORMITTAGS 10 UHR

Fig. 11.3. Cover of catalog for the Fuchs collection auction of
May 23–24, 1938. Author copy.

Fig. 11.4. Vestibule of the Villa Fuchs with porcelain collection. Ullstein Bild, reprinted with the kind permission of the Granger Collection, New York.

Fig. 11.5. Study (Slevogt room), Villa Fuchs. Ullstein Bild, reprinted with the kind permission of the Granger Collection, New York.

(1848 in Caricature). Soon expanding the scope and theme of caricatures, he dedicated a volume exclusively to the representation of women: *Die Frau in der Karikatur* (1906; Woman in Caricature).

Upon moving to Berlin in 1901, Fuchs worked as a freelance writer, dedicating his full attention to cultural history and at the same time vying for the attention of the scientific community. Shortly before the outbreak of the First World War, he distanced himself from the revisionist tendencies of the Social Democratic Party, and in return the party's press steadfastly ignored his increasingly popular *Illustrierte Sittengeschichte* (1908–12; Illustrated History of Mores and Customs). Over the course of the war, Fuchs joined the proletarian anti-war movement and became affiliated with the Spartacists, associating with such radical political figures as Karl Liebknecht, Rosa Luxemburg, and Clara Zetkin. Perhaps as a result of his political engagement, he published only one book during the war, *Der Weltkrieg in der Karikatur* (1916; The World War in Caricature), an exclusively socio-economic study that uncharacteristically neglected his customary emphasis on eroticism.

The cultural liberalism of the Weimar Republic fostered some of his best publications, namely the three-part set *Geschichte der erotischen Kunst* (1908, 1923, 1926; History of Erotic Art) and *Die grossen Meister der Erotik* (1930; The Great Masters of the Erotic), and enabled him to live a comfortable life surrounded by his exquisite collections in a Berlin-Zehlendorf villa designed by Mies van der Rohe. His modernist residence reflects his increasing interest in progressive art and aesthetics. Although Fuchs's publications show little trace of avant-garde art,[20] Fuchs's collecting patterns moved from erotic caricatures to German impressionist paintings and finally to Soviet avant-garde art. His preference for Mies van der Rohe's abstract *Revolutionary Monument* (1926) over Rodin's figurative *Génie de la Guerre* (1879; Genius of War) as a memorial to the victims of the November revolution of 1918 in Berlin-Friedrichsfelde was a salient expression of his new way of seeing art.[21]

Eduard Fuchs and Erotic Art

As a cultural historian and egalitarian, Fuchs strove for the enlightenment of the masses by shifting his critical attention to such popular art forms as political and erotic caricature. The steady flow of royalties from his publications enabled him, as an elitist collector, constantly to extend his private collection. He primarily perceived his books, as one of his biographers Thomas Huonker puts it, "as comments to show off his beloved collectibles."[22] Benjamin, however, sees Fuchs's true accomplishment in his consistent emphasis on techniques of reproduction for the transfer of visual art within a society, which, Benjamin remarks, are "made possible through the reading of the iconographic, in the observation of mass produced art, [and] in the study of reproduction techniques."[23] In this respect, Fuchs was not merely a collector and historian of his objects, but through his persistent research focus on the technical reproducibility of visual art for the masses he opened up the new field of material art history. That is to say, Fuchs did not merely produce art books en masse; more importantly, he reproduced ephemeral art such as caricature via the more enduring medium of the book. In this manner he found a new medium to educate his readers in material art appreciation. Fuchs, like Benjamin, hoped that mechanical reproduction could emancipate art from its confining bourgeois structure and that it would become politically engaged.

Perhaps the best example of Fuchs's social engagement is his early book publication *Karikatur der Europäischen Völker* (1901; Caricature of the European Peoples). For this social history he used caricatures from all over Europe and elevated prints of caricature and even ephemeral newspaper clippings to veritable documents of political art. For the first volume alone he selected 500 from over 68,000 pages of illustrations from his own collection, and he did not reproduce these illustrations again in other publications.[24] This arduous selection process shows how judiciously Fuchs used his collection and ultimately rendered his publications equally unique. Only through his selection and configuration did caricature find its readers and become known as politically engaged art. With the skillful combination of two interrelated modes of knowledge, namely collecting and publishing, Fuchs created a new epistemological order; by collecting and publishing political caricature, he questioned the underlying conditions that constituted the moral code of Imperial Germany. By doing so, he changed art historical discourse just as he created a new political awareness in his time.

Fuchs's hugely successful multi-volume *Sittengeschichte* is concerned with the historical development of cultural customs. Apart from mundane everyday life and the morality of society, he paid special attention here to the history of eroticism and sexuality. The first installment on the "Renaissance" was put on the market featuring no fewer than 450 illustrations. Although publishing ventures like this needed huge investments, the sales of the *Sittengeschichte* turned out to be immensely profitable for Albert Langen, Fuchs's publishing house, in the years to come. The book historian Helga Abret describes the allure of the *Sittengeschichte* as follows: "the erotic, the sexual, cunningly presented with true expertise, was in accordance with the taste of the wealthy bourgeoisie."[25] With the *Sittengeschichte* Fuchs earned over a million reichsmarks in royalties and at the same time pioneered material art appreciation.[26]

In spite of his unquenchable appetite for art and books, Fuchs was painfully aware that his luxurious coffee-table books were more likely to decorate living rooms in bourgeois villas than to be read voraciously to shreds in working-class kitchens. In the preface to one of his publications, he lamented that writing books that can only be purchased by wealthy people comes close to literary prostitution.[27] Moreover, this dichotomy between proletarian impetus and bourgeois reception is traceable in Fuchs's intellectual development as a cultural historian. In 1908, in the first volume of *Geschichte der erotischen Kunst* he underscores the social conditions of art and culture:

> Es steht heute fest . . ., dass es in letzter Linie immer die allgemeinen wirtschaftlichen Interessen sind, die den gesellschaftlichen Lebens-prozess der einzelnen Völker und Klassen bedingen. . . . Rechtsan-schauungen, Sittlichkeitsbegriffe und Künste einer Zeit sind nur das ideologische Widerspiel der ökonomischen Basis der betreffenden Zeit und wechseln darum — *das ist die entscheidende Logik!* — folge-richtig auch mit dieser.[28]

Fuchs apparently applied Marxist theory to the artistic and cultural realms, and he saw in historical materialism nothing less than a natural law; but in his thinking about culture he balanced the natural law of art and culture with a law of vitality that proposes sensuality as the driving force of art.

Unlike Kant's disinterested pleasure, for Fuchs and many artists of his generation, sensuality points directly to the sexual roots of art and aesthetics. Unsurprisingly, Frank Wedekind, one of the most provocative dramatists before the First World War, was Fuchs's friend and colleague at the Munich publishing house Albert Langen.[29] In fact, during the fin-de-siècle the thematic interest of art and literature seems to have shifted rapidly from social to psychological, especially erotic topics. Suffice it to say that if we were to apply Fuchs's unmediated sensuality to — let's say — erotic literature, we would invariably end up with pornography.

Given his fondness for social formations, it is hardly a surprise that Fuchs saw in the orgy the most worthy cultural achievement. According to him the orgy is the pinnacle of human exuberance, which runs coun-ter to the philistine's desire for moderation. After all, he claimed, it is the orgy that distinguishes us from the animal world: "Der schöpferische Mensch kennt den Begriff des Genug überhaupt nicht. Aber gerade diese Sehnsucht nach Übermass ist das Göttliche in ihm. Denn nur das Über-mass an Expansionsdrang im Wünschen findet neue Wege" (The creative human being doesn't know the concept of "enough.") But it is precisely the longing for excess that makes him divine. Only excess of expansively impulsive wishes opens new venues).[30] And the genuine artist does not respect the concept of enough. Only the opposite, namely the longing for excess, opens new venues for artistic progress. By the time Fuchs pub-lished the second volume of *Erotische Kunst* in 1923, he had come to see individual sexuality — and not social conditions — as the driving force behind creative art: "Jeder Künstler will mit dem Werk, das er aus einem eigenen inneren Antrieb schafft, sich 'befriedigen' oder 'sich ausleben', wie der allgemein übliche Ausdruck lautet. Das Schaffen und Gestalten eines Kunstwerkes ist also für seinen Schöpfer ein sublimierter, erotischer Akt" (Every artist wants to "satisfy" himself or "live life to the full" — as people generally formulate it — with the work that he creates out of his own inner impulse. The creation and formation of a work of art is for its creator an act of sublimated eroticism).[31]

For Fuchs art became an act of sublimated eroticism. The emphasis here on drive and fantasy reflects his study shortly before, during, and after the First World War of psychoanalytical literature by Freud, Alfred Adler, and Wilhelm Stekel. Like Adler, Fuchs saw in the inferiority complex the prime motivation for artistic creation, but unlike the then popular Zionist Max Nordau, he did not posit a causal relation between art and degeneration; instead Fuchs assessed the inability to sublimate as a sign of pathological neuroticism. However, by applying Adler's individual psychology to the process of artistic creation, he did not intend to renounce his Marxist convictions. For Fuchs, Freud's insistence on libido as the encompassing human drive signified a negation of all social factors, and negating the masses as a historical agent, Fuchs cautioned, would drive the psychoanalytical movement into a cul-de-sac. Instead, he preferred a psychosexual model of the human being in which individuals propel the social progress of the masses forward.

Hence, Fuchs sought to establish a dialectical relation between psychoanalysis and Marxism to explain the condition of art and culture: "Die Liebe und der Hunger sind, von der Natur zusammengekoppelt, die allgewaltigen Diktatoren und Former der Weltgeschichte. . . . Erst wenn beide zusammen sind, ergibt sich ein Ganzes. Der eine Teil kann und darf den anderen niemals ignorieren, geschweige denn negieren" (Love and hunger, put together by nature, are the all-powerful dictators and shapers of world history. . . . Only when both are brought together will a whole be achieved. One part should never ignore, let alone negate, the other part).[32] Fuchs's aspiration to form a dialectical relationship between individual psychology and Marxist theory attracted Max Horkheimer's attention, and in January 1935 Horkheimer asked Benjamin to write an article about Fuchs for the *Zeitschrift für Sozialforschung*. Although Horkheimer saw in Fuchs a lesser psychologist than Freud, he praised him for his long-standing, committed, "historical orientation" and open-minded social psychology, which was allegedly free of Freud's discontent.[33]

Cultural Books versus Mass-Produced Books

Fuchs's attempt to mediate between individual psychology and social theory, or in other words between elite and mass cultures, was paralleled by the development of the modern German book market at the end of the long nineteenth century. The rapid demographic and economic growth before the First World War led to mass-produced books for everyone published alongside exclusive art books for wealthy individual collectors. In his 1912 study of the modern book, Helmut von den Steinen juxtaposes the *cultural* book to the *mass-produced* book. Although this classification covers only a partial reality, both market segments appeared at the time in extreme forms: luxurious private press printings were offered next to Nick Carter penny magazines.

A new type of cultural publisher sought, moreover, to live among his authors, support them, and organize a movement whereby he could influence public opinion through their books. This new type of publisher wanted to be a productive element, an integral factor in the literary production of his authors. Perhaps the most successful such cultural publisher was Samuel Fischer. He understood his enterprise as something far beyond economic ends. In 1911 he declared, "To impress onto the public new values, even unwanted ones, is the most important and beautiful mission of the publisher."[34]

Unsurprisingly, Fuchs's publisher, Albert Langen, also belonged to this group of innovative publishers. Working from bohemian Munich at the turn of the century, Langen was primarily interested in such Scandinavian and French modernists as Knut Hamsun and Guy de Maupassant. Launching the richly illustrated satirical journal *Simplicissimus* in 1896, he showed an extraordinary sensibility to the needs of the educated middle class. The journal acting as a political and moral opponent of the reactionary Wilhelminian empire, its print-run rose from 15,000 to 85,000 copies within eight years.

Considering their mutual interest in aesthetics and politics, one can easily see an elective affinity between Langen and Fuchs. They started to collaborate as early as 1905, and the first fruit of their business relationship was the volume on *Die Frau in der Karikatur* (1906), which first appeared in twenty installments, followed by an illustrated book publication. Despite the high price of twenty-five reichsmarks, the sales of the book were so successful that the publisher requested another illustrated book, the aforementioned *Sittengeschichte*. Fuchs, his collections, and his books were at the forefront of the "discovery" of eroticism in Germany at the beginning of the twentieth century. Armed with new insights pertaining to sexuality, desire, and repression, Fuchs sought to popularize Freud's ideas and render them accessible to the book-buying public. In fact, those publications were not only important from an aesthetic point of view, they had political significance for the society at the time. Individual eroticism was not indicative of an apolitical inward turn, but was seen by authors like Fuchs and publishers like Langen as a continuation of the political struggle against the Wilhelminian bourgeoisie and their attempt to restrict freedom of expression.[35]

This may explain why Fuchs, although clearly against any sort of elitism, agreed in 1909 to publish supplements of the *Sittengeschichte* separately and for subscribers only in order to avoid the looming threat of censorship. Throughout his life as a publicist in Germany, Fuchs had had to deal with conservative watchdogs. At the beginning of his career he was threatened by the introduction of the "Lex Heinze" in 1899, a law ostensibly against matchmaking and pimping. In reality the law sought to prohibit all printed matter that was unruly and would violate the "natural sense of shame." According to this perfidious law, almost all plays at the turn of the century by Fuchs's friend Wedekind were denounced as "unzüchtig" (licentious) and could not be staged publicly in Germany.[36]

Three decades later, during the Weimar Republic in 1926, conservative lawmakers introduced the "Schmutz- und Schundgesetz" (law against filth and smut), which was intended to prohibit penny publications. Allegedly, the cheaply produced booklets appealed to base human instincts such as the wish for drugs, sex, and pornography and would destroy respect for state authority. This law sought to abolish the Weimar constitutional right of freedom of expression.[37] Some of Germany's leading intellectuals denounced the law as mere pretext to suppress intellectual freedom.[38] On 6 December 1926, Fuchs organized a formal protest with other leftist writers of the *Schutzverband Deutscher Schriftsteller* (The Federation for the Protection of German Writers) against the law.[39] But in the end, on 18 December 1926, the Reichstag passed it.[40] For the remaining years of the Weimar Republic, Fuchs and his colleagues fought an increasingly uphill battle against the moral and political repression that culminated in the National Socialist seizure of power in March 1933.

Bourgeois Bibliophiles

Beyond the riveting political, economic, and technological developments at the beginning of the twentieth century, Siegfried Kracauer explained mass consumption of books in sociological terms: "Das Proletariat greift in der Hauptsache zu Büchern abgestempelten Inhalts oder liest nach, was ihm die Bürgerlichen schon vorgelesen haben. Immer noch ist es das Bürgertum, das einigen Schriftstellern zweifelhaften Ruhm bringt und unbezweifeltes Vermögen" ("The proletariat primarily reaches for books whose contents have been given a stamp of approval, or else it reads up on what the bourgeoisie has already read. It is still the bourgeoisie that accords certain authors dubious fame and indubitable wealth).[41] Kracauer refers here to such successful Weimar authors as Erich Maria Remarque, Frank Thiess, and Stefan Zweig. For Kracauer, all these authors emphasize individualism and idealism, which results in an exciting melodrama for the masses. As a politically engaged author whose proletarian convictions happened to appeal to his bourgeois customers, Fuchs was not a target for Kracauer's criticism. But despite their desire to emulate the bourgeoisie in style and taste, the proletarian masses could not afford Fuchs's richly illustrated *Sittengeschichte*.

Fuchs owed his commercial success to a different group of book buyers: the bibliophiles. His popularity among Germany's booklovers was underscored by his own publications in the *Zeitschrift für Bücherfreunde* (Journal for Bibliophiles) between 1897 and 1902.[42]

In the first three decades of the twentieth century, no fewer than thirty clubs for book collectors were founded in all parts of Germany. In 1913 the "Society of Bibliophiles" alone already counted over 900 members, and in 1932 the "Soncino Society: Friends of the Jewish Book" had no fewer than 650 members.[43] A diverse network of communication, bibliophilic lectures, and journals such as *Imprimatur* and *Philiobiblon* buttressed this plethora of bibliophilic organizations and "created a blossoming landscape of book lovers."[44] In response to the currency devaluation after the First World War, investments in "Sachwerte" (tangible assets) increased, and middle- and upper-middle-class book buyers became ardent collectors and bibliophiles. The modish prevalence of book collecting intensified to a point that led the eminent book designer Paul Renner to speak of a "new snobbism for renowned and speculative book objects."[45] In this elitist environment, the commercial success of Fuchs's publications was guaranteed.[46] But these blossoming bibliophilic landscapes lasted only a few years, and by 1930 book sales were plummeting in response to the worldwide economic crisis.

Conclusion

As we have seen, Fuchs consistently had to negotiate between his socially engaged publishing agenda and his individual obsession to collect. Undoubtedly his massive success with bourgeois readers helped to found his own collections, but at the same time this success broadened the gap between him and his intended readership, the working class. As long as Fuchs resided in Berlin, his collections of caricatures and erotic art preserved a literal, material presence of the past. Fuchs managed to combine two interrelated modes of knowledge, namely collecting and publishing books. By collecting and publishing political caricature, Fuchs shifted the art historical discourse even as he created a new political awareness in his time. At the same time, he was a guardian of his objects, and since his research focused on the technical reproducibility of visual art for the masses, he opened up the new field of material art history. With the dissolution of his collections in Berlin, however, the foundation for his work was permanently destroyed.

For Benjamin, memory, possession and happiness are central to the collector's motivation. The collector does not live solely in time and space — Benjamin argues — he exists in and through his collection.

Hence, collecting offers a unique possibility for the collector's memory, that is, to be at peace with his fate. Fuchs surely lost this peace of mind in his forced Parisian exile. Moreover, he lost the opportunity to display his collectibles in his book publications. In this respect, Fuchs was not merely an obsessive seducer in need of reassurance like Münsterberger's Don Juan, even if his desire to collect and publish satisfied an exhibitionistic longing to safeguard his treasures for the public.

Notes

[1] Werner Münsterberger, *Collecting: An Unruly Passion; Psychological Perspectives* (Princeton, NJ: Princeton UP, 1994), 12.

[2] See Walter Benjamin, "Eduard Fuchs, der Sammler und der Historiker," in *Gesammelte Schriften,* ed. Rolf Tiedemann and Herrmann Schweppenhäuser (Frankfurt am Main: Suhrkamp, 1972), 2/2:465–505. For the English translation, see Walter Benjamin, "Eduard Fuchs, Collector and Historian," in *Selected Writings,* vol. 3 1935–1938, ed. Michael W. Jennings et al. (Cambridge, MA: Belknap Press of Harvard UP, 2002), 260–302. These editions will henceforth be cited as *GS* and *SW* with volume and page numbers.

[3] See Michael Steinberg, "The Collector as Allegorist: Goods, Gods, and the Objects of History," in *Walter Benjamin and the Demands of History,* ed. Michael Steinberg (Ithaca, NY: Cornell UP, 1996), 88.

[4] Walter Benjamin, "Ich packe meine Bibliothek aus," *GS* IV/1, 388. "Unpacking my Library," trans. Harry Zohn, *SW* II, 486.

[5] See Philipp Blom, *To Have and to Hold: An Intimate History of Collectors and Collecting* (New York: The Overlook Press, 2002), 238. Blom argues, furthermore, that "[I]n *Saturn und die Melancholie* Raymond Klibansky and Fritz Saxl have given an elegant exposition of the Church's opposition to curiosity and its polemic against it. Intelligence, it was felt, should be concentrated on contemplation of divine mysteries, not on fruitless chases for temporal frivolity."

[6] Michel Foucault, *The Order of Things: An Archaeology in the Human Sciences* (London: Routledge, 2002), 142–43.

[7] Susan A. Crane, *Collecting and the Historical Consciousness in Early Nineteenth-Century Germany* (Ithaca, NY: Cornell UP, 2000), 17.

[8] On the topic of institutional collecting in Germany, see James J. Sheehan, *Museums in the German Art World: From the End of the Old Regime to the Rise of Modernism* (Oxford: Oxford UP, 2000).

[9] "Gegen Ende des 19. Jahrhunderts tritt in Deutschland ein veränderter Typus des Sammlers hervor, dem es einzig und allein um die von Burkhardt beschriebene 'innerliche' Beziehung zu den Gegenständen seines Begehrens geht." (Toward the end of the nineteenth century a different type of collector emerged who is concerned only with his affective relationship to the objects of his desire.) Eckhard Köhn, "Sammler," in *Benjamins Begriffe,* ed. Michael Opitz and Erdmut Wizisla (Frankfurt am Main: Suhrkamp, 2002), 2:697.

[10] Jean Baudrillard, "System of Collecting," in *Cultures of Collecting*, ed. John Elsner and Roger Cardinal (London: Reaction Books, 1994), 7.

[11] Benjamin, "Bibliothek," *GS* 4/1:389; "Library," *SW* 2:487.

[12] Walter Benjamin, "Rezension von Max von Boehns *Puppen und Puppenspiele* (1929)," in *GS* 3:216; "Die wahre, sehr verkannte Leistung des Sammlers ist immer anarchistisch, destruktiv. Denn dies ist ihre Dialektik: Mit der Treue zum Ding, zum Einzelnen, bei ihm Geborgenen, den eigensinnigen, subversiven Protest gegen das Typische, Klassifizierbare zu verbinden" (The true, but often overlooked, accomplishment of the collector is always anarchic and destructive. Because this is its dialectic: the collector's faithfulness to the unique, well-preserved object is combined with an obstinate, subversive protest against the typical and classifiable [my translation]).

[13] See Benjamin, "Eduard Fuchs," *GS* 2/2:478–49. "Eduard Fuchs," trans. Howard Eiland and Michael Jennings, *SW* 3:289.

[14] Ulrich Weitz, *Eduard Fuchs: Sammler, Sittengeschichtler, Sozialist* (Stuttgart: Stöffler & Schütz, 1991), 341.

[15] For a detailed description of the auction proceedings, see Weitz, *Eduard Fuchs*, 421–23.

[16] Eduard Fuchs, *Dachreiter und verwandte chinesische Keramik des XV. bis XIII. Jahrhunderts* (Munich: Albert Langen, 1924), 45. "Nicht der letzte Ruhm der chinesischen Dachreiter ist es, dass es sich in ihnen um eine . . . namenslose Volkskunst handelt. Es gibt kein Heldenbuch, das von ihren Schöpfer zeugt" (It is not the least of the glories of Chinese turrets that they are products of an anonymous popular art. There is no heroic folk book that mentions their creator [my translation]).

[17] See Benjamin, "Eduard Fuchs," *GS* 2/2:505. "Eduard Fuchs," *SW* 3:284.

[18] For further biographical information, see Peter Gorsen, "Wer war Eduard Fuchs?" *Zeitschrift für Sexualwissenschaft* 19, no. 3 (2006): 215–33.

[19] Ibid., 217; "Während der 1886 bis 1887 absolvierten Lehrjahre begegnete [Fuchs] revolutionär gesinnten Schriftsetzern und schloss sich dem anarchistischen Flügel der illegalen Sozialdemokratie an. Fuchs verfasste zwei anarchistische Flugschriften und verbüsste 1888 wegen 'Majestätsbeleidigung', 1889 wegen 'Verbreitung sozialistischer Druckschriften' eine Gefängnisstrafe von jeweils fünf Monaten" (During his apprenticeship in 1886 and 1887, Fuchs met revolutionary-minded typesetters and joined the anarchic wing of the illegal Social Democratic Party. Fuchs wrote two anarchic leaflets and was detained twice, for *lèse majesté* [1888] and "distribution of socialist print material" [1889], for five months each time [my translation]).

[20] See ibid., 221.

[21] Weitz, *Eduard Fuchs*, 416–19.

[22] Eduard Fuchs, *Illustrierte Sittengeschichte in sechs Bänden*, ed. Thomas Hounker (Frankfurt am Main: Fischer, 1985), 1:13.

[23] Benjamin, "Eduard Fuchs," *SW* 3:269; "Eduard Fuchs," *GS* 2/2:479; "Das geschieht in der Deutung des Ikonographischen, in der Betrachtung der Massenkunst, in dem Studium der Reproduktionstechnik."

[24] See Benjamin, "Eduard Fuchs," *GS* 2/2:491; "Eduard Fuchs," *SW* 3:276.

[25] Helga Abret, *Albert Langen: Ein Europäischer Verleger* (Munich: Langen Müller, 1993), 268; "Das Erotische, das Sexuelle, raffiniert und mit wirklicher Kunstkennerschaft dargestellt, entsprachen dem Geschmack einer bestimmten kaufkräftigen Schicht des Bürgertums."

[26] Weitz, *Eduard Fuchs*, 300.

[27] "Bücher schreiben, die in der Hauptsache nur noch von Leuten mit ungeheuer gesteigerten Einkommen gekauft werden können, das ist literarischer Huren-dienst. Wenigstens empfinde ich es so. Für eine neue Menschheit schreiben, müsste köstlich sein, nicht aber für die neuen Reichen" (To write books which can only be purchased by wealthy people is nothing but literary prostitution. At least that is how I feel. It would be delicious to write books for a new society, but not for the newly rich [my translation]); preface to Eduard Fuchs, *Die Juden in der Karikatur* (Munich: Albert Langen, 1921), qtd. by Weitz, *Eduard Fuchs*, 468.

[28] "It has become clear today that the societal processes of all peoples and classes foremost depend on general economic interests. Interpretation of law, the moral codex, and the arts are merely ideological repercussions of the economic basis of a given time, and — that is decisive logic — they change accordingly"; Eduard Fuchs, *Geschichte der erotischen Kunst* (Munich: Albert Langen, 1912), 2.

[29] Wedekind's play *Frühlings Erwachen* (1891; Spring's Awakening) attacks the moral hypocrisy and social conservatism of fin-de-siècle Germany. The play deals with the awakening sexual urges among a group of German students and caused a scandal at the time, as it contains scenes of homoeroticism and masturbation, as well as references to abortion.

[30] Eduard Fuchs, *Geschichte der erotischen Kunst: Das individuelle Problem. Erster Teil* (Munich: Albert Langen, 1923), 283.

[31] Ibid., 126.

[32] Ibid., 35.

[33] See Benjamin, "Anmerkungen," *GS* II/3, 1319. Horkheimer's letter to Benja-min 1/28/1935: "Es wäre eine schöne Gelegenheit, darzutun, wie der psycholo-gisch viel primitivere Apparat, dessen sich Fuchs bedient, infolge des Umstandes, dass er von Anfang an die richtige historische Orientierung besaß, ihn in der Sozi-alpsychologie viel weitsichtiger machte als Freud, in dessen Schriften die Verzwei-flung in der bestehenden Wirklichkeit als das Unbehagen eines Professors zum Ausdruck kommt." (It would be a nice opportunity, to present how Fuchs's psy-chologically more primitive apparatus, due to the fact that he possessed from the start the right historical orientation, is more clear-sighted in terms of social psy-chology than Freud's. His writings express the despair over the present reality as a professorial discontent [my translation].)

[34] Peter de Mendelssohn, *S. Fischer und sein Verlag* (Frankfurt: Fischer, 1970), 47; "Dem Publikum neue Werte aufzudrängen, die es nicht will, ist die schönste und wichtigste Mission des Verlegers."

[35] See Karl Riha, "Zur Entdeckung des Erotischen um die Jahrhundertwende — Am Beispiel von Eduard Fuchs und Franz Blei," in *Annäherungsversuche: Zur Geschichte*

und Ästhetik des Erotischen in der Literatur, ed. Horst Albert Glaser (Bern: Paul Haupt, 1993), 302–4.

[36] See Reinhard Wittmann, *Geschichte des deutschen Buchhandels* (Munich: C. H. Beck, 1991), 276.

[37] "Article 118 of the Constitution of the Weimar Republic contains the important statement: 'Within the limits laid down by general legislation, every German has the right to freedom of expression by spoken, written, and printed word, by the visual image or other means.' Also: Censorship is not practiced"; Wolfgang Beutin et al., *A History of German Literature*, 4th ed. (London: Routledge, 1993), 443.

[38] Thomas Mann wrote: "Every literate and knowledgeable person recognizes that the need to protect our youth from filth and trash . . . is nothing more than a pretext. The law drafters want to use the law's penetrating power against freedom, against intellect itself"; qtd. by Eric D. Weitz, *Weimar Germany: Promise and Tragedy* (Princeton, NJ: Princeton UP, 2007), 107.

[39] Weitz, *Eduard Fuchs*, 411.

[40] "It took three readings and a fractured majority before the government could muster the requisite votes in the Reichstag. But the bill did pass"; Weitz, *Weimar Germany*, 107.

[41] Siegfried Kracauer, "Über Erfolgsbücher und ihr Publikum," in *Das Ornament der Masse* (Frankfurt am Main: Suhrkamp, 1977), 67; Siegfried Kracauer, "On Bestsellers and their Audience," in *The Mass Ornament: Weimar Essays*, trans. Thomas Y. Levin (Boston: Harvard UP, 2005), 92.

[42] Weitz, *Eduard Fuchs*, lists four essays on caricatures in this bibliophilic journal, 489–90.

[43] See Ulrich Heider, "Die Soncino-Gesellschaft der Freunde des jüdischen Buches e.V. (1924–1937)," *Aus dem Antiquariat* 6 (2007): 405.

[44] "'Eine glückliche Vermischung . . .': Zum Verhältnis von Bibliophilie und Antiquariat im ersten Drittel des 20. Jahrhunderts"; Ernst Fischer, *Aus dem Antiquariat* 1 (2002): 18.

[45] Qtd by Wulf D. von Lucius, "Buchgestaltung und Buchkunst," in *Geschichte des deutschen Buchhandels im 19. und 20. Jahrhundert: Die Weimarer Republik 1918–1933 Teil 1*, ed. Ernst Fischer and Stephan Füssel (Munich: K. G. Saur, 2007), 335.

[46] Having weathered the morally repressive Wilhelminian Empire and the upheavals of the First World War, the *Illustrierte Sittengeschichte* was as late as 1930 the book most often requested by members of parliament in the exclusive Berlin Reichstag library; see Weitz, *Eduard Fuchs*, 301.

Bibliography

THIS BIBLIOGRAPHY IS CONFINED TO secondary sources cited in the essays. Primary sources are cited in full in the notes in the individual essays.

Abret, Helga. *Albert Langen: Ein europäischer Verleger.* Munich: Langen Müller, 1993.

———. "Frank Wedekind und sein Verleger Albert Langen." *Études germaniques* 60 (2005): 7–51.

Abret, Helga, and Aldo Keel, eds. *Die Majestätsbeleidigungsaffäre des "Simplicissimus"-Verlegers Albert Langen.* Frankfurt am Main: Peter Lang, 1985.

———. *Im Zeichen des Simplicissimus: Briefwechsel Albert Langen-Dagny Björnson 1895–1908.* Munich: Langen Müller, 1987.

Albisetti, James C. *Schooling German Girls and Women: Secondary and Higher Education in the Nineteenth Century.* Princeton, NJ: Princeton UP, 1998.

Allen, Ann Taylor. *Satire & Society in Wilhelmine Germany.* Kladderadatsch *and* Simplicissimus, *1890–1914.* Lexington: UP of Kentucky, 1984.

Anderson, Benedict. *Imagined Communities: Reflections on the Origins and Spread of Nationalism.* London: Verso, 1991.

Applegate, Celia. "The Mediated Nation: Regions, Readers, and the German Past." In *Saxony in German History: Culture, Society, and Politics, 1830–1933,* edited by James Retallack, 33–50. Ann Arbor: U of Michigan P, 2000.

Askey, Jennifer, "Reading as Women, Reading as Patriots: Nationalism, Popular Literature, and Girls' Education in Wilhelminian Germany." PhD diss., Washington University in St. Louis, 2003.

Barth, Dieter. "Das Familienblatt—ein Phänomen der Unterhaltungspresse des 19. Jahrhunderts. Beispiele zur Gründungs- und Verlagsgeschichte." *Archiv für Geschichte des Buchwesens* 15 (1975): 121–316.

Baudrillard, Jean. "System of Collecting." In *Cultures of Collecting,* edited by John Elsner and Roger Cardinal, 7–24. London: Reaction Books, 1994.

Bauer, Werner M. "Der Verleger und Drucker Joseph Vinzenz Degen und Johann Baptist Wallishausser und ihre Stellung in der österreichischen Literatur ihrer Zeit." In *Die Österreichische Literatur: Ihr Profil an der Wende vom 18. zum 19. Jahrhundert (1750–1830),* edited by Herbert Zeman, 179–203. Graz: Akademische Druck und Verlagsanstalt, 1979.

Becker, Heinz. *Der Fall Heine-Meyerbeer: Neue Dokumente revidieren ein Geschichtsurteil.* Berlin: de Gruyter, 1958.

Becker, Sabina. "Gegen deutsche 'Tiefe' und für poetische 'Leichtigkeit': Kurt Tucholskys und Walter Hasenclevers Komödie *Christoph Kolumbus oder die Entdeckung Amerikas* (1931/32)." In Becker and Maack, *Kurt Tucholsky*, 143–72.

———. "Kommentar 51." In *Texte 1931: Kurt Tucholsky Gesamtausgabe Texte und Briefe 14*, edited by Sabina Becker, 552–601. Hamburg: Rowohlt, 1998.

Becker, Sabina, and Ute Maack, ed. *Kurt Tucholsky: Das literarische und publizistische Werk*. Darmstadt: Wissenschaftliche Buchgesellschaft, 2002.

Belgum, Kirsten. "Critique of the Parvenu Interior: Friedrich Spielhagen and Eugenie Marlitt." Chapter 4 in *Interior Meaning: Design of the Bourgeois Home in the Realist Novel*, German Life and Civilization 9, 103–27. New York: Peter Lang, 1992.

———. "E. Marlitt: Narratives of Virtuous Desire." In *A Companion to German Realism 1848–1900*, edited by Todd Kontje, 259–82. Rochester, NY: Camden House, 2002.

———. *Popularizing the Nation: Audience, Representation, and the Production of Identity in* Die Gartenlaube, *1853–1900*. Lincoln: U of Nebraska P, 1998.

Bending, Stephen. "Re-Reading the Eighteenth-Century English Landscape Garden." In *An English Arcadia: Landscape and Architecture in Britain and America*, edited by Guilland Sutherland and Harriet Ritvo, 379–99. San Marino, CA: Huntington Library, 1992.

Benjamin, Walter. "Anmerkungen." In *Gesammelte Schriften* 2/3, 1319.

———. "Eduard Fuchs, Collector and Historian." In *Selected Writings* 3, 260–302. Translated by Howard Eiland and Michael W. Jennings.

———. "Eduard Fuchs, der Sammler und der Historiker." In *Gesammelte Schriften* 2/2, 465–505.

———. "Ich packe meine Bibliothek aus." In *Gesammelte Schriften* 4/1, 388–96.

———. "Rezension von Max von Boehns *Puppen und Puppenspiele* (1929)." In *Gesammelte Schriften* 3, 213–18.

———. "Unpacking my Library." In *Selected Writings* 2, translated by Harry Zohn, 486–93.

———. *Gesammelte Schriften*. Edited by Rolf Tiedemann and Herrmann Schweppenhäuser. Frankfurt am Main: Suhrkamp, 1972.

———. *Selected Writings*. Edited by Michael W. Jennings et al. Cambridge, MA: Belknap Press of Harvard UP, 2002.

Berman, Russell. "Writing for the Book Industry: The Writer under Organized Capitalism." *New German Critique* 29 (1983): 39–56.

Berry, Christopher. *The Idea of Luxury: A Conceptual and Historical Investigation*. Cambridge: Cambridge UP, 1994.

Bessell, Georg. *100 Jahre Kippenberg-Schule 1859–1959*. Bremen: Illing Lüken, 1959.

Beutin, Wolfgang, et al. *A History of German Literature*. 4th ed. London: Routledge, 1993.

Biesalski, Ernst-Peter. "Die Entwicklung der industriellen Buchbinderei im 19. Jahrhundert." In *Gebunden in der Dampfbuchbinderei: Buchbinden im Wandel des 19. Jahrhunderts*, 61–98. Wolfenbüttler Schriften zur Geschichte des Buchwesens 20. Wiesbaden: Harrassowitz, 1994.

Blom, Philipp. *To Have and to Hold: An Intimate History of Collectors and Collecting*. New York: The Overlook Press, 2002.

Bollenbeck, Georg. *Bildung und Kultur: Glanz und Elend eines deutschen Deutungsmusters*. Frankfurt am Main: Insel, 1994.

Bonter, Urszula. *Der Populärroman in der Nachfolge von E. Marlitt: Wilhelmine Heimburg, Valeska Gräfin Bethusy-Huc, Eufemia von Adlersfeld-Ballestrem*. Würzburg: Königshausen & Neumann, 2005.

Borchert, Angela, and Ralf Dressel, eds. *Das* Journal des Luxus und der Moden*: Kultur um 1800*. Heidelberg: Winter, 2004.

Bosse, Heinrich. *Autorschaft ist Werkherrschaft: Über die Entstehung des Urheberrechts aus dem Geist der Goethezeit*. Paderborn: Schöningh, 1981.

Bourdieu, Pierre. *La distinction: critique sociale du jugement*. Paris: Éditions de Minuit, 1979.

Breckman, Warren. "Disciplining Consumption: The Debate about Luxury in Wilhelmine Germany, 1890–1914." *Journal of Social History* 24 (1991): 485–505.

Breuer, Dieter. *Geschichte der literarischen Zensur in Deutschland*. Heidelberg: Quelle und Meyer, 1982.

Brinitzer, Carl. *Das streitbare Leben des Verlegers Julius Campe*. Hamburg: Hoffmann & Campe, 1962.

Brunken, Otto. "Überblick." In *Handbuch zur Kinder- und Jugendliteratur: Von 1800 bis 1850*, edited by Otto Brunken, Bettina Hurrelmann, and Klaus-Ulrich Pech, cols. 285–318. Stuttgart: J. B. Metzler, 1998.

Brunken, Otto, Bettina Hurrelmann, Maria Michels-Kohlhage, and Gisela Wilkending. *Handbuch zur Kinder- und Jugendliteratur: Von 1850 bis 1900*. Stuttgart: J. B. Metzler, 2008.

Cazden, Robert E. *A Social History of the German Book Trade in America to the Civil War*. Columbia, SC: Camden House, 1984.

Collison, Robert. *Encyclopaedias: Their History Throughout the Ages*. New York: Hafner Publishing Co., 1966.

The Complete Encyclopedia of Illustration. New York: Park Lane, 1979. Reprint of *Iconographic Encyclopaedia of Science, Literature, and Art*. New York: R. Garrigue, 1851.

Crane, Susan A. *Collecting and the Historical Consciousness in Early Nineteenth-Century Germany*. Ithaca, NY: Cornell UP, 2000.

Crowley, John. "The Sensibility of Comfort." *The American Historical Review* 104, no. 3 (1999): 749–82.

Cunnington, C. Willett. *English Women's Clothing in the Nineteenth Century*. New York: Dover Publications, Inc., 1990.

Darnton, Robert. "Histoire du livre — Geschichte des Buchwesens: An Agenda for Comparative History." *Publishing History* 22 (1987): 35–41.

———. "What Is the History of Books?" *Daedalus*, Summer 1982: 65–83.

————. "'What is the History of Books?' Revisited." *Modern Intellectual History* 4, no. 3 (2007): 495–508.

de Bolla, Peter. "The charm'd eye." In *Body and Text in the Eighteenth Century*, edited by Veronika Kelley and Dorothea von Mücke, 89–111. Stanford, CA: Stanford UP, 1994.

Deinet, Klaus. "Heine und Frankreich — eine Neuordnung." *Internationales Archiv für Sozialgeschichte der Literatur* 32, no. 1 (2007): 111–52.

Deinet, Klaus. "Heine und die Julimonarchie." *Internationales Archiv für Sozialgeschichte der Literatur* 32, no. 2 (2007): 55–92.

Delabar, Walter. "Eine kleine Liebesgeschichte: Kurt Tucholskys *Schloss Gripsholm: eine Sommergeschichte*." In Becker and Maack, *Kurt Tucholsky*, 115–42.

Douglas, Mary, and Baron Isherwood. *The World of Goods: Towards an Anthropology of Consumption*. 2nd ed. London: Routledge, 1996.

Ehlers, Swantje. *Der Umgang mit dem Lesebuch: Analyse — Kategorien — Arbeitsstrategien*. Baltmannsweiler: Schneider Verlag Hohengehren, 2003.

Encylopédie I, ed. Alain Pons. Paris: Flammarion, 1986.

Engelsing, Rolf. *Analphabetentum und Lektüre: Zur Sozialgeschichte des Lesens zwischen feudaler und industrieller Gesellschaft*. Stuttgart: J. B. Metzler, 1973.

Estermann, Alfred, and Peter Uwe Hohendahl, eds. *Literaturkritik. Band 4. 1848–1870*. Vaduz: Topos-Verlag, 1984.

Estermann, Alfred. *Die Gartenlaube (1853–1880 [-1944]) A-*. Vol. 3, bk. 1 of *Inhaltsanalytische Bibliographien deutscher Kulturzeitschriften des 19. Jahhunderts*. Munich: K. G. Saur, 1995.

Finkelstein, David, and Alistair McCleery. Introduction. *The Book History Reader*. 2nd edition. Edited by David Finkelstein and Alistair McCleery, 1–4. London: Routledge, 2006.

Fischer, Ernst. "'Eine glückliche Vermischung . . .': Zum Verhältnis von Bibliophilie und Antiquariat im ersten Drittel des 20. Jahrhunderts." *Aus dem Antiquariat* 1 (2002): 18–26.

Fischer, Samuel. "Bemerkungen zur Bücherkrise." In *S. Fischer Verlag: von der Gründung bis zur Rückkehr aus dem Exil*, edited by Friedrich Pfäfflin, 357–60. Marbach: Deutsche Schillergesellschaft, 1985.

Flik, Reiner. "Kultur-Merkantilismus? Friedrich Justin Bertuchs 'Journal des Luxus und der Moden' (1786–1827)." In Borchert and Dressel, *Das Journal des Luxus und der Moden: Kultur um 1800*, 21–55.

Foucault, Michel. *The Order of Things: An Archaeology in the Human Sciences*. London: Routledge, 2002.

Freud, Sigmund. "Zur Geschichte der psychoanalytischen Bewegung." In *Gesammelte Werke*, vol. 10, 43–113. Frankfurt am Main: Fischer, 1999; English translation: "On the History of the Psychoanalytic Movement." In *Standard Edition*, vol. 14, 3–80. London: Vintage, 2001.

————. *Massenpsychologie und Ich-Analyse*. In *Gesammelte Werke*, vol. 13, 71–161. Frankfurt am Main: Fischer, 1998; English translation: *Group Psychology and the Analysis of the Ego*. New York: Norton, 1990.

Fritzsche, Gustav. *Seinen Gönnern, Freunden und Mitarbeitern aus Anlaß seines 25jährigen Geschäftsjubiläums am 4. März 1889 gewidmet.* n.p.: n.p., 1889.

Gamper, Michael. *"Die Natur ist republikanisch": Zu den ästhetischen, anthropologischen und politischen Konzepten der deutschen Gartenliteratur im 18. Jahrhundert.* Würzburg: Königshausen & Neumann, 1998.

Gay, Peter. "Experiment in Denial: A Reading of the *Gartenlaube* in the Year 1890." In *Traditions of Experiment from the Enlightenment to the Present*, edited by Nancy Kaiser and David E. Wellbery, 147–64. Ann Arbor: U of Michigan P, 1992.

Gerhardt, Claus W. "Die Wirkungen drucktechnischer Neuerungen auf die Buchgestaltung im 19. Jahrhundert." In *Buchgestaltung in Deutschland 1740 bis 1890: Vorträge des dritten Jahrestreffens des Wolfenbüttler Arbeitskreises für Geschichte des Buchwesens in der Herzog August Bibliothek Wolfenbüttel, 9. bis 11. Mai 1978*, edited by Paul Raabe, 146–80. Hamburg: E. Hauswedell, 1980.

Gettmann, Royal A. "The Author and the Publisher's Reader." *Modern Language Quarterly* 8, no.4 (1947): 459–71.

Gilpin, William. *An Essay upon Prints. Containing remarks upon the principles of Picturesque Beauty.* London, 1786.

Glaser, Hermann. *Bildungsbürgertum und Nationalismus: Politik und Kultur im Wilhelminischen Deutschland.* Munich: dtv, 1993.

Goldfriedrich, Johann. *Geschichte des Deutschen Buchhandels vom Beginn der Fremdherrschaft bis zur Reform des Börsenvereins im neuen Deutschen Reiche, 1805–1889.* Leipzig: Verlag des Börsenvereins der Deutschen Buchhändler, 1913.

Goltschnigg, Dietmar. *Die Fackel ins wunde Herz: Kraus über Heine; Eine "Erledigung"?* Vienna: Passagen, 2000.

Gorsen, Peter. "Wer war Eduard Fuchs?" *Zeitschrift für Sexualwissenschaft* 19, no. 3 (September 2006): 215–33.

Grathoff, Dirk. "Kurt Tucholskys *Rheinsberg*: Die Inszenierung der Idylle im Rekurs auf Theodor Fontane und Heinrich Mann." *Monatshefte* 88, no. 2 (1996): 197–216.

Grosse, Eduard. "Deutsche Bucheinbände der Neuzeit," *Papier-Zeitung.* 1898. Reprint, Leipzig: Leipziger Buchbinderei-Actiengesellschaft, 1898.

Gruber, J. G. *C. M. Wielands Leben.* 1827. Reprint, Hamburg: Hamburger Stiftung zur Förderung von Wissenschaft und Kultur, 1984.

Gruppe, Heidemarie. *"Volk" zwischen Politik und Idylle in der "Gartenlaube" 1853–1914.* Europäische Hochschulschriften 19, no. 2. Bern: Herbert Lang, 1976.

Häfner, Ralph. *Die Weisheit des Silen: Heinrich Heine und die Kritik des Lebens.* Berlin: de Gruyter, 2006.

Hansen, Miriam Bratu. "The Mass Production of the Senses: Classical Cinema as Vernacular Modernism." *Modernism/Modernity* 6, no. 2 (1999): 59–77.

Häntzschel, Günter. "'Für fromme, reine und stille Seelen': Literarischer Markt und 'weibliche' Kultur im 19. Jahrhundert." In *Deutsche Literatur von Frauen*, edited by Gisela Brinker-Gabler, 2:119–28. Munich: Beck, 1988.

Hauschild, Jan-Christoph, and Michael Werner. *"Der Zweck des Lebens ist das Leben selbst." Heinrich Heine: Eine Biographie.* Cologne: Kiepenheuer und Witsch, 1997.

Heider, Ulrich. "Die Soncino-Gesellschaft der Freunde des jüdischen Buches e.V. (1924–1937)." *Aus dem Antiquariat* 6 (2007): 401–11.

Heiderdinger, Timo. "Der gelebte Konjunktiv. Zur Pragmatik von Ratgeberliteratur in alltagskultureller Perspektive." In *Sachbuch und populäres Wissen im 20. Jahrhundert,* edited by Andy Hahnemann and David Oels, 97–108. Frankfurt am Main: Peter Lang, 2008.

Heller, Otto. "Women Writers of the Nineteenth Century." In *Studies in Modern German Literature*, 229–95. Boston: Ginn & Company, 1905.

Hoffmann-Scholl, Rosemary. "Die Buchillustration im 18. Jahrhundert." In *Buchgestaltung in Deutschland 1740 bis 1890*, edited by Paul Raabe, 39–53. Hamburg: Dr. Ernst Hauswedell & Co., 1980.

Hofmann, Else. *E. Marlitt: Ein Lebensbild.* Edited by Fayçal Hamouda. Arnstadt: Edition Marlitt, 2005.

Hohendahl, Peter Uwe. *Literarische Kultur im Zeitalter des Liberalismus, 1830–1870.* Munich: C. H. Beck, 1985.

Höhn, Gerhard. *Heine-Handbuch: Zeit, Person, Werk.* 3rd rev. ed. Stuttgart: J. B. Metzler, 2004.

Hölscher, Georg. *Der Buchhändler.* Leipzig: Paul Beyer, n.d.

Hörling, Hans. *Heinrich Heine im Spiegel der politischen Presse Frankreichs von 1831–1841: Ansatz zu einem Modell der qualitativen und quantitativen Rezeptionsforschung.* Frankfurt am Main: Peter Lang, 1977.

Houben, H. H. *Jungdeutscher Sturm und Drang: Ergebnisse und Studien.* Leipzig: Brockhaus, 1911.

Hübscher, Arthur. *Hundertfünfzig Jahre F. A. Brockhaus, 1805–1955.* Wiesbaden: F. A. Brockhaus, 1955.

Hugo, Victor. *The Hunchback of Notre Dame.* 1831. Introduction by Elizabeth McCracken. Revised translation and notes by Catherine Liu. The Modern Library. New York: Random House, 2002.

Hurrelmann, Bettina. "Lesesozialisation." In *Sozialisation — Lebenslauf — Biografie,* edited by Imbke Behnken and Jana Mikota. Weinheim: Juventa (2009).

Hurrelmann, Bettina, Susanne Becker, and Irmgard Nickel-Bacon. *Lesekindheiten: Familie und Lesesozialisation im historischen Wandel.* Weinheim: Juventa, 2006.

Jäger, Georg, ed. *Das Kaiserreich 1871–1918.* Vol. 1, pts. 1 and 2 of *Geschichte des deutschen Buchhandels im 19. und 20. Jahrhundert.* Frankfurt am Main: Buchhändler-Vereinigung GmbH, 2001, and MVB, 2003, respectively.

———. "Reclams Universal-Bibliothek bis zum Ersten Weltkrieg: Erfolgsfaktoren der Programmpolitik." In *Reclam 125 Jahre Universalbibliothek: Ein Almanach*, 19–45. Stuttgart: Philipp Reclam Jun., 1967.

———. "Der Schulbuchverlag." In *Das Kaiserreich 1871–1918*, 1/2:62–102.

———. "Der Verlagsbuchhandel." In *Das Kaiserreich 1871–1918*, 1/1:197–215.

———. "Der Verleger und sein Unternehmen." In *Das Kaiserreich 1871–1918*, 1/1:216–80.

———. "Das Zeitschriftswesen." In *Das Kaiserreich 1871–1918*,1/2:368–89.

Jäger, Georg, and Monika Estermann. "Geschichtliche Grundlagen und Entwicklung des Buchhandels im Deutschen Reich bis 1871." In Jäger, *Das Kaiserreich 1871–1918*, 1/1:17–41.

Janzin, Marion, and Joachim Güntner. *Das Buch vom Buch: 5000 Jahre Buchgeschichte*, 3rd ed. Hannover: Schüter, 2007.

Jarrett, David, Tadeus Rachwał, and Tadeaus Sławek. *Geometry, Winding Paths, and the Mansions of Spirit*. Katowice: Wydawnictwo Uniwersytetu Ślaskiego, 1997.

Jelavich, Peter. "Art and Mammon in Wilhelmine Germany: The Case of Frank Wedekind." *Central European History* 12 (1979): 203–36.

———. Berlin Alexanderplatz: *Radio, Film, and the Death of Weimar Culture*. Berkeley: U of California P, 2006.

———. *Munich and Theatrical Modernism: Politics, Playwriting, and Performance 1890–1914*. Cambridge, MA: Harvard UP, 1985.

Jenkins, Jennifer. *Provincial Modernity: Local Culture and Liberal Politics in Fin-de-Siècle Hamburg*. Ithaca, NY: Cornell UP, 2003.

Joeres, Ruth-Ellen Boetcher. "*Die zweite Frau*, Popular Culture and the Analytical Categories of Gender and Class." Chapter 6 in *Respectability and Deviance: Nineteenth-Century German Women Writers and the Ambiguity of Representation*, 219–55. Chicago: U of Chicago P, 1998.

Jordan, John O., and Robert L. Patten, eds. *Literature in the Marketplace: Nineteenth-Century British Publishing and Reading Practices*. Cambridge: Cambridge UP, 1995.

Junghanß, Christina. "'Es ist ein Unglück vor die teutschen Handwerksleute, daß sie gar keinen Unternehmungsgeist besitzen [. . .]' Bertuch als Wirtschaftsförderer." In *Friedrich Justin Bertuch (1747–1922): Verleger, Schriftsteller und Unternehmer im Klassischen Weimar*, edited by Gerhard R. Kaiser and Siegfried Seifert, 301–7. Tübingen: Niemeyer, 2000.

Kaes, Anton. "Schreiben und Lesen in der Weimarer Republik." In *Literatur der Weimarer Republik 1918–1933*, edited by Bernhard Weyergraf, 38–64. Munich: Hanser, 1995.

Kastner, Barbara. "Statistik und Topographie des Verlagswesens." In Jäger, *Das Kaiserreich 1871–1918*, 1/2:300–67.

Keiderling, Thomas. *F. A. Brockhaus 1905–2005. Band 2 der Festschrift F. A. Brockhaus 1805–2005*. Leipzig: F. A. Brockhaus, 2005.

Kiefer, Sascha. "'Meine ganze Jugend': Kurt Tucholskys *Rheinsberg* (1912)." In Becker and Maack, *Kurt Tucholsky*, 17–46.

Klempert, Gabriele. *"Die Welt des Schönen." Karl Robert Langewiesche 1902–2002. Eine hundertjährige Verlagsgeschichte in Deutschland.* Königstein/Taunus: Karl Robert Langewiesche Nachfolger Hans Köster Verlagsbuchhandlung, 2002.

Koch, Ernestine. *Albert Langen: Ein Verleger in München.* Munich: Langen-Müller, 1969.

Köhn, Eckhard. "Sammler." In *Benjamins Begriffe,* edited by Michael Opitz and Erdmut Wizisla, 695–724. Frankfurt am Main: Suhrkamp, 2002.

Könnecke, Gustav. *Bilderatlas zur Geschichte der deutschen Literatur.* Marburg: Ewert, 1887.

Kontje, Todd. "Eugenie Marlitt: The Art of Liberal Compromise." Chapter 6 in *Women, the Novel, and the German Nation 1771–1871,* 183–201. Cambridge: Cambridge UP, 1998.

———. "Marlitt's World: Domestic Fiction in an Age of Empire." *German Quarterly* 77, no. 4 (2004): 408–26.

———. *Women, the Novel, and the German Nation 1771–1871: Domestic Fiction in the Fatherland.* Cambridge: Cambridge UP, 1998.

Korte, Hermann. "Lyrik im Unterricht." In *Grundzüge der Literaturdidaktik,* edited by Klaus-Michael Bogdal and Hermann Korte, 203–16. 4th ed. Munich: dtv, 2006.

Kracauer, Siegfried. "On Bestsellers and Their Audience." In *The Mass Ornament: Weimar Essays,* translated by Thomas Y. Levin, 89–98. Boston, MA: Harvard UP, 2005.

———. "Das Ornament der Masse." 1927. In *Aufsätze 1927–1931. Schriften* 5:2, edited by Inka Mülder-Bach, 57–67. Frankfurt am Main: Suhrkamp, 1990.

———. "Über Erfolgsbücher und ihr Publikum." In *Das Ornament der Masse,* 64–74. Frankfurt am Main: Suhrkamp, 1977.

Kräupel, Irmgard. "Buchausstattung." In *Lesewuth, Raubdruck und Bücherluxus: Das Buch in der Goethezeit,* edited by Jörn Görres, 148–203. Düsseldorf: Goethe-Museum Düsseldorf, 1977.

Kreuzer, Helmut, ed. *Deutschsprachige Literaturkritik 1870–1914. Eine Dokumentation.* 3 vols. Frankfurt am Main: Peter Lang, 2006.

Kröger, Ute. "'Unsere Stadt ist kein Krähwinkel!' Die Düsseldorfer und 'ihr' Heine — vom Versuch, nach dem Denkmalsdebakel ein eigenes Heine-Verständnis zu pflegen." In *Das literarische Düsseldorf: Zur kulturellen Entwicklung von 1850–1933,* edited by Gertrude Cepl-Kaufmann and Winfried Hartkopf, 59–66. Düsseldorf: Teubig, 1988.

Krohn, Paul Günter. "Frank Wedekinds politische Gedichte." *Neue deutsche Literatur* 6 (1958): 85–95.

Kutscher, Artur. *Frank Wedekind: Sein Leben und seine Werke* 2. Munich: Langen-Müller, 1922/31. Reprint, New York: AMS Press, 1970.

Kwass, Michael. "Ordering the World of Goods: Consumer Revolution and the Classification of Objects in Eighteenth-Century France." *Representations* 82 (Spring 2003): 87–114.

Langewiesche, Karl Robert. *50 Jahre Verlagsarbeit*. Königstein/Taunus: Langewiesche, 1952.

Lengefeld, Cecilia. *"Der Maler des glücklichen Heims": Zur Rezeption Carl Larssons im wilhelminischen Deutschland*. Heidelberg: Winter, 1993.

Lerer, Seth, and Leah Price, eds. The History of the Book and the Idea of Literature. Special issue, *PMLA* 121, no. 1 (January 2006).

"Lesebücher für Volks-, Mittel- und höhere Mädchen-Schulen." *Centralblatt für die gesamte Unterrichtsverwaltung in Preußen* 17, no. 2 (1875): 105–7.

Lethen, Helmut, and Bernhard Weyergraf. "Der Einzelne in der Massengesellschaft." In Weyergraf, *Literatur der Weimarer Republik 1918–1933*, 636–72.

Lethen, Helmut. *Verhaltenslehren der Kälte: Lebensversuche zwischen den Kriegen*. Frankfurt am Main: Suhrkamp, 1994.

Levy, Richard S. *The Downfall of the Anti-Semitic Political Parties in Imperial Germany*. New Haven: Yale UP, 1975.

Liedtke, Christian. *Heinrich Heine*. Reinbek bei Hamburg: Rowohlt Taschenbuch Verlag, 1997.

———, ed. *Heinrich Heine: Neue Wege der Forschung*. Darmstadt: Wissenschaftliche Buchgesellschaft, 2000.

Lucius, Wulf D. v. "Anmut und Würde: Zur Typographie des Klassizismus in Deutschland." In *Von Göschen bis Rowohlt: Beiträge zur Geschichte des deutschen Verlagswesens*, edited by Monika Estermann and Michael Knoche, 33–61. Wiesbaden: Otto Harrassowitz, 1990.

———. "Buchgestaltung und Buchkunst." In *Geschichte des deutschen Buchhandels im 19. und 20. Jahrhundert: Die Weimarer Republik 1918–1933*, vol. 1, edited by Ernst Fischer and Stephan Füssel, 315–40. Munich: K. G. Saur, 2007.

Luhmann, Fritjof. "Wandlungen der Buchgestaltung am Ende des 18. Jahrhunderts." In *Buchgestaltung in Deutschland 1740–1890*, edited by Paul Raabe, 89–104. Hamburg: Dr. Ernst Hauswedell & Co., 1980.

Maack, Ute. "Warum schreibt das keiner? Kurt Tucholskys Literaturkritik." In *Kurt Tucholsky: Das literarische und publizistische Werk*, edited by Sabina Becker and Ute Maack, 245–76. Darmstadt: Wissenschaftliche Buchgesellschaft, 2002.

Marshall, David. "The Problem of the Picturesque." *Eighteenth Century Studies* 35, no. 3 (2002): 413–37.

Mayer, Dieter. "Aktiver Pessimismus: Kurt Tucholskys *Deutschland Deutschland über alles* (1929)." In Becker and Maack, *Kurt Tucholsky*, 67–114.

McGovern, Charles F. *Sold American: Consumption and Citizenship, 1890–1945*. Chapel Hill: U of North Carolina P, 2006.

Mendelssohn, Peter de. *S. Fischer und sein Verlag*. Frankfurt am Main: Fischer, 1970.

Menz, Gerhard. *Die Zeitschrift: Ihre Entwicklung und ihre Lebensbedingungen; Eine Wirtschaftsgeschichtliche Studie*. Stuttgart: Poeschel, 1928.

Meyer, Thorsten. "Zwischen sozialer Restriktion und ökonomischer Notwendigkeit: Konsum in ökonomischen Texten der Frühen Neuzeit." In *"Luxus und Konsum" — Eine historische Annäherung*, edited by Reinhold Reith and Torsten Meyer, 62–81. Münster: Waxmann, 2003.

Miller, Daniel. *Material Culture and Mass Consumption*. Oxford: Blackwell, 1987.

Moran, Daniel. *Toward the Century of Words: Johann Cotta and the Politics of the Public Realm in Germany, 1795–1832*. Berkeley: U of California P, 1990.

Morawe, Bodo. *Heines "Französische Zustände." Über die Fortschritte des Republikanismus und die anmarschierende Weltliteratur*. Beihefte zum *Euphorion* 28. Heidelberg: Winter, 1997.

———. "'Sehet, alle Gottheiten sind entflohen. . . .' Heinrich Heine und die radikale Aufklärung." In *"Aber der Tod ist nicht poetischer als das Leben." Heinrich Heines 18. Jahrhundert*, edited by Sikander Singh, 73–120. Bielefeld: Aisthesis, 2006.

Moretti, Franco. *Graphs, Maps, Trees: Abstract Models for a Literary History*. New York: Verso, 2005.

Müller-Michaels, Harro. "Konzepte und Kanon in Lesebüchern nach 1945." In *Das Lesebuch: Zur Theorie und Praxis des Lesebuchs im Deutschunterricht*, edited by Swantje Ehlers, 6–21. Baltmannsweiler: Schneider Verlag Hohengehren, 2003.

Müller-Wolff, Susanne. "Über Englische Gärten, französische Landsitze und den 'Park bey Weimar.' Gartenkunst." In Borchert and Dressel, *Das Journal des Luxus und der Moden: Kultur um 1800*, 227–42.

Muensterberger, Werner. *Collecting: An Unruly Passion; Psychological Perspectives*. Princeton, NJ: Princeton UP, 1994.

Neumann, Peter. "Herstellung und Buchgestaltung." In Jäger, *Das Kaiserreich 1870–1918*, 1/1:170–96.

Neumann, Robert. "Deutschland und Heinrich Heine." *C-V Zeitung*, 5 August 1927, 456–57.

Nickel, Gunther. *Die Schaubühne/Die Weltbühne: Siegfried Jacobsohns Wochenschrift und ihr ästhetisches Programm*. Opladen: Westdeutscher Verlag, 1996.

Nipperdey, Thomas. *Deutsche Geschichte 1800–1866: Bürgerwelt und starker Staat*. Munich: C. H. Beck, 1983.

Oehler, Dolf. "Heines Genauigkeit. Und zwei komplementäre Stereotypen über das Wesen der proletarischen Massen." *Diskussion Deutsch* 8 (1977): 250–71.

Oesterle, Günter, and Harald Tausch, eds. *Der imaginierte Garten*. Göttingen: Vandenhoeck & Ruprecht, 2001.

Ohles, Frederik. *Germany's Rude Awakening: Censorship in the Land of the Brothers Grimm*. Kent, OH: Kent State UP, 1992.

Paddock, Mary M. "Redemption Songs or How Frank Wedekind Set the Simplicissimus Affair to a Different Tune." *German Studies Review* 28 (2005): 245–64.

Paul, Stefan. "Der Verlag Karl Robert Langewiesche im Ersten Weltkrieg." Master's Thesis, University of Tübingen, 1992.

Peterson, Brent O. *History, Fiction, and Germany: Writing the Nineteenth-Century Nation*. Detroit, MI: Wayne State UP, 2005.

Pierce, Jason A. "The Belle Lettrist and the People's Publisher: or, the Context of *Treasure Island*'s First-Form Publication." *Victorian Periodicals Review* 31, no. 4 (Winter 1998): 356–68.

Piltz, Anton Ernst Oskar. "Zur Geschichte und Bibliographie der encyklopaedischen Literatur insbesondere des *Conversations-Lexikon*." In *F. A. Brockhaus in Leipzig, Vollständiges Verzeichnis der von der Firma F. A. Brockhaus in Leipzig seit ihrer Gründung durch Friedrich Arnold Brockhaus im Jahre 1805 bis zu dessen hundertjährigem Geburtstage im Jahre 1872 verlegten Werke. In chronologischer Folge mit biographischen und literarhistorischen Notizen*. Leipzig: F. A. Brockhaus, 1872–75, xxxviii–xl.

Piper, Ernst. "Das Buch und der Mensch von heute." *Börsenblatt für den deutschen Buchhandel* 93 (1926): 1537.

Pöllinger, Andreas, ed. *Der Briefwechsel zwischen Ludwig Thoma und Albert Langen, 1899–1908: Ein Beitrag zur Lebens-, Werk- und Verlagsgeschichte um die Jahrhundertwende. Teil 1*. Frankfurt am Main: Peter Lang, 1993.

Price, Leah. "Introduction: Reading Matter." In The History of the Book and the Idea of Literature, edited by Seth Lerer and Leah Price. Special issue, *PMLA* 121, no. 1 (2006): 9–16.

Radlik, Ute. "Heine in der Zensur der Restaurationsepoche." In *Zur Literatur der Restaurationsepoche 1815–1848. Forschungsreferate und Aufsätze*, edited by Jost Hermand and Manfred Windfuhr 460–89. Stuttgart: J. B. Metzler, 1970.

Radway, Janice A. *A Feeling for Books: The Book-of-the-Month Club, Literary Taste, and Middle-Class Desire*. Chapel Hill: U of North Carolina P, 1997.

Rarisch, Ilsedore. *Industrialisierung und Literatur: Buchproduktion, Verlagswesen und Buchhandel in Deutschland im 19. Jahrhundert in ihrem statistischen Zusammenhang*. Berlin: Colloquium Verlag, 1976.

Reagin, Nancy R. *Sweeping the German Nation: Domesticity and National Identity in Germany, 1870–1945*. Cambridge: Cambridge UP, 2007.

Reuveni, Gideon. "The 'Crisis of the Book' and German Society after the First World War." *German History* 20, no. 4 (2002): 438–61.

———. *Reading Germany: Literature and Consumer Culture in Germany before 1933*. New York: Berghahn, 2006.

Riha, Karl. "Zur Entdeckung des Erotischen um die Jahrhundertwende — Am Beispiel von Eduard Fuchs und Franz Blei." In *Annäherungsversuche: Zur Geschichte und Ästhetik des Erotischen in der Literatur*, edited by Horst Albert Glaser, 301–19. Bern: Paul Haupt, 1993.

Rubin, Joan Shelley. "What Is the History of the History of Books?" *The Journal of American History*, September 2003. http://www.historycooperative.org.turing.library.northwestern.edu/journals/jah/90.2/rubin.html (1 Nov. 2008).

Sailer, Anton. "Glanz und Elend des 'Simplicissimus.'" In *Simplicissimus: Eine satirische Zeitschrift. München 1896–1944. Mathildenhöhe Darmstadt. 24. Juni bis 13. August 1978*, edited by Carla Schulz-Hoffmann, 35–52. Munich: Haus der Kunst, 1978.

Sammons, Jeffrey L. "Heine as *Weltbürger*? A Skeptical Inquiry." *Modern Language Notes* 101 (1986): 609–28. Reprinted in Sammons, *Imagination and History: Selected Papers on Nineteenth-Century German Literature*, 97–122. New York: Peter Lang, 1988.

———. *Heinrich Heine: Alternative Perspectives 1985–2005*. Würzburg: Königshausen und Neumann, 2006.

———. *Heinrich Heine: A Modern Biography*. Princeton, NJ: Princeton UP, 1979.

———. "Review Essay: The Bicentennial of Heinrich Heine 1997: An Overview." *Goethe Yearbook* 9 (1999). Reprinted in Sammons, *Heinrich Heine: Alternative Perspectives*, 245–76.

———. "Who Did Heine Think He Was?" In *Heinrich Heine's Contested Identities: Politics, Religion, and Nationalism in Nineteenth-Century Germany*, edited by Jost Hermand and Robert C. Holub, 1–24. New York: Peter Lang, 1999. Reprinted in Sammons, *Heinrich Heine: Alternative Perspectives*, 189–206.

———. *Wilhelm Raabe: The Fiction of the Alternative Community*. Princeton, NJ: Princeton UP, 1987.

Sarkowski, Heinz. *Das Bibliographische Institut: Verlagsgeschichte und Bibliographie, 1826–1976*. Mannheim: Bibliographisches Institut, 1976.

Schaefer, Helma. "Leipziger Verlagseinbände des 19. Jahrhunderts als Gegenstand einbandkundlicher Forschung." In *Das Gewand des Buches: Historische Bucheinbände aus den Beständen der Universitätsbibliothek Leipzig und des Deutschen Buch- und Schriftmuseums der Deutschen Bücherei Leipzig*, 147–58. Leipzig: Universitätsbibliothek, 2003.

Schäfer, Roland. "Die Frühgeschichte des Großen Brockhaus." *Leipziger Jahrbuch zur Buchgeschichte* 3 (1993): 69–84.

Schauer, G. K. *Geschichte des deutschen Buchumschlages im 20. Jahrhundert*. Königstein/Taunus: Langewiesche, 1962.

Schenda, Rudolf. "Alphabetisierung und Literarisierungsprozesse in Westeuropa im 18. und 19. Jahrhundert." In *Sozialer und kultureller Wandel in der ländlichen Welt des 18. Jahrhunderts*, edited by Ernst Hinrichs and Günter Wiegelmann, 1–20. Wolfenbütteler Forschungen 19. Wolfenbüttel: Herzog August Bibliothek, 1982.

———. "Bibliothèque Bleue im 19. Jahrhundert." In *Studien zur Trivialliteratur*, edited by Heinz Otto Burger, 137–53. Frankfurt am Main: Vittorio Klostermann, 1968.

———. *Volk ohne Buch: Studien zur Sozialgeschichte der populären Lesestoffe 1770–1910*. Studien zur Philosophie und Literatur des neunzehnten Jahrhunderts 5. Frankfurt am Main: Vittorio Klostermann, 1970.

Schlotzhauer, Inge. *Ideologie und Organisation des politischen Antisemitismus in Frankfurt am Main 1880–1914*. Frankfurt am Main: Kramer, 1989.

Schmidt-Glintzer, Helwig. Introduction. In *Gebunden in der Dampfbuchbinderei: Buchbinden im Wandel des 19. Jahrhunderts*. Wolfenbüttler Schriften zur Geschichte des Buchwesens 20. Wiesbaden: Harrassowitz, 1994.

Schmoll gen. Eisenwert, J. A. "Macht und Ohnmacht der politischen Karikatur." In *Simplicissimus: Eine Satirische Zeitschrift. München 1896–1944. Mathildenhöhe Darmstadt. 24. Juni bis 13. August 1978*, edited by Carla Schulz-Hoffmann, 13–22. Munich: Haus der Kunst, 1978.

Schön, Erich. *Der Verlust der Sinnlichkeit oder die Verwandlung des Lesers: Mentalitätswandel um 1800*. Stuttgart: Klett-Cotta, 1987.

Schubert, Dietrich. *"Jetzt wohin?" Heinrich Heine in seinen verhinderten und errichteten Denkmälern*. Cologne: Böhlau, 1999.

Schulz, Gerd. "Das Klassikerjahr 1867 und die Gründung von Reclams Universal-Bibliothek." In *Reclam 100 Jahre Universal-Bibliothek: Ein Almanach*, 11–28. Stuttgart: Philipp Reclam Jun., 1967.

Schulz, Hans Ferdinand. *Das Schicksal der Bücher und der Buchhandel*. Berlin: de Gruyter, 1960.

Schumann, Willy. "Frank Wedekind — Regimekritiker? Einige Überlegungen zur 'Majestätsbeleidigung' in den 'Simplicissimusgedichten.'" *Seminar* 15 (1979): 235–43.

Seehaus, Günter. *Frank Wedekind und das Theater*. Munich: Laokoon, 1964.

Sengle, Friedrich. *Die Formenwelt*. Vol. 2 of *Biedermeierzeit*. Stuttgart: J. B. Metzler, 1972.

Sheehan, James J. *Museums in the German Art World: From the End of the Old Regime to the Rise of Modernism*. Oxford: Oxford UP, 2000.

Siems, Renke. "Gesprochene Schrift: Zu Kurt Tucholskys Erzählprosa." In *Kurt Tucholsky: Das literarische und publizistische Werk*, edited by Sabina Becker and Ute Maack, 213–44. Darmstadt: Wissenschaftliche Buchgesellschaft, 2002.

Slater, Don. *Consumer Culture and Modernity*. Cambridge: Polity, 1997.

Smith, Woodruff. *Consumption and the Making of Respectability 1600–1800*. London: Routledge, 2003.

Sprenger, Bernd. *Das Geld der Deutschen: Geldgeschichte Deutschlands von den Anfängen bis zur Gegenwart*. Paderborn: Ferdinand Schöningh, 1991.

St Clair, William. *The Reading Nation in the Romantic Period*. Cambridge: Cambridge UP, 2004.

Staub, Hermann. "'Arbeiten und nicht verzweifeln.' Das Archiv des Verlags Karl Robert Langewiesche (Königstein) im Historischen Archiv des Börsenvereins (Frankfurt)." In *Von Göschen bis Rowohlt: Beiträge zur Geschichte des deutschen Verlagswesens*, edited by Monika Estermann and Michael Knoche, 336–68. Wiesbaden: Otto Harrassowitz, 1990.

Steinberg, Michael. "The Collector as Allegorist: Goods, Gods, and the Objects of History." In *Walter Benjamin and the Demands of History*, edited by Michael Steinberg, 88–118. Ithaca, NY: Cornell UP, 1996.

Steinen, Helmut von den. "Das moderne Buch." PhD Dissertation, University of Heidelberg, 1912.

Storey, John. *Cultural Consumption and Everyday Life*. Oxford: Oxford UP, 1999.

Tatlock, Lynne. "Eine amerikanische Baumwollprinzessin in Thüringen: Transnationale Liebe, Familie und die deutsche Nation in E. Marlitts *Im Schillingshof* (1879)." In *Amerika und die deutschsprachige Literatur nach 1849. Migration — kultureller Austausch — frühe Globalisierung*, edited by Christof Hamann, Ute Gerhard, and Walter Grünzweig, 105–25. Bielefeld: transcript, 2008.

———. "Domesticated Romance and Capitalist Enterprise: Annis Lee Wister's Americanization of German Fiction." In *German Culture in Nineteenth-Century America: Reception, Adaptation, Transformation*, edited by Lynne Tatlock and Matt Erlin, 153–82. Rochester, NY: Camden House, 2005.

———. "Gendering Fashion and Politics in the Fatherland: Willibald Alexis' 'Doppelroman' *Die Hosen des Herrn von Bredow*." In *Autoren damals und heute: Literaturgeschichtliche Beispiele veränderter Wirkungshorizonte*, edited by Gerhard P. Knapp, 232–55. Amsterdam: Rodopi, 1991.

———. "'In the Heart of the Heart of the Country': Regional Histories as National History in Gustav Freytag's *Die Ahnen* (1872–80)." In *A Companion to German Realism (1848–1900)*, edited by Todd Kontje, 85–108. Rochester, NY: Camden House, 2002.

———. Introduction to *From a Good Family*, by Gabriele Reuter, translated by Lynne Tatlock. Rochester, NY: Camden House, 1999.

———. "Realist Historiography and the Historiography of Realism: Gustav Freytag's *Bilder aus der deutschen Vergangenheit*." *The German Quarterly* 63, no. 1 (1990): 59–74.

———. "Regional Histories as National History: Gustav Freytag's *Bilder aus der Deutschen Vergangenheit (1859–67)*." In *Searching for Common Ground: Diskurse zur deutschen Identität 1750–1871*, edited by Nicholas Vazsonyi, 161–78. Cologne: Böhlau, 2000.

Teistler, Gisela, ed. *Bestandskatalog der deutschen Schulbücher im Georg-Eckert-Institut erschienen bis 1945. Teil 1: Lese- und Realienbücher, einschließlich Fibeln*. Hannover: Hannsche Buchhandlung, 1997.

Ueding, Gert, with Bernd Steinbrink. *Hoffmann und Campe: Ein deutscher Verlag*. Hamburg: Hoffmann und Campe, 1981.

Uhlig, Friedrich. *Geschichte des Buches und des Buchhandels*. Stuttgart: Poeschel, 1962.

Ungern-Sternberg, Wolfgang von. "Schriftstelleremanzipation und Buchkultur im 18. Jahrhundert." *Jahrbuch für Internationale Germanistik* 8, no.1 (1976): 72–98.

van Dülmen, Andrea. *Das irdische Paradies: Bürgerliche Gartenkultur der Goethezeit*. Cologne: Böhlau, 1999.

Völkner, Katrin. "Books for a Better Life: Publishers and the Creation of Middlebrow Culture in Wilhelmine Germany." PhD dissertation, Duke University, Durham, NC, 2001.

Vogel, Martin. "Recht im Buchwesen." In Jäger, *Das Kaiserreich 1871–1918*, 1/1:122–38.

Voigt, Jürgen. "Mäzen und Erpresser? Noch einmal zum 'Fall' Meyerbeer-Heine." *Zeitschrift für deutsche Philologie* 112, no.4 (1993): 543–68.

Wagener, Hans. "Frank Wedekind: Politische Entgleisungen eines Unpolitischen." *Seminar* 15, no.4 (1979): 244–50.

Weyergraf, Bernhard, ed. *Literatur der Weimarer Republik 1918–1933*. Munich: Hanser, 1955.

Weitz, Eric D. *Weimar Germany: Promise and Tragedy*. Princeton, NJ: Princeton UP, 2007.

Weitz, Ulrich. *Eduard Fuchs: Sammler, Sittengeschichtler, Sozialist*. Stuttgart: Stöffler & Schütz, 1991.

Werner, Michael. *Genius und Geldsack: Zum Problem des Schriftstellerberufs bei Heinrich Heine*. Hamburg: Hoffmann & Campe, Heinrich Heine Verlag, 1978.

Wilkending, Gisela. "Erzählende Literatur." In *Handbuch zur Kinder- und Jugendliteratur: Von 1850 bis 1900*, edited by Otto Brunken, Bettina Hurrelmann, Maria Michels-Kohlhage, Gisela Wilkending, col. 279–760. Stuttgart: J. B. Metzler, 2008.

———. "Die Kommerzialisierung der Jugendliteratur und die Jugendschriftenbewegung um 1900." In *Schund und Schönheit: Populäre Kultur um 1900*, edited by Kaspar Maase and Wolfgang Kaschuba, 218–51. Cologne: Böhlau, 2001.

Windfuhr, Manfred, ed. *Internationaler Heine-Kongreß Düsseldorf 1972: Referate und Diskussionen*. Hamburg: Hoffmann und Campe, Heinrich Heine Verlag, 1973.

Wischermann, Ulla. *Frauenarbeit und Presse: Frauenarbeit und Frauenbewegung in der deutschen illustrierten Presse des 19. Jahrhunderts*. Munich: Sauer, 1983.

Wittmann, Reinhard. "Die bibliographische Situation für die Erforschung des literarischen Lebens im 19. Jahrhundert (1830–1880)." In *Buchmarkt und Lektüre im 18. und 19. Jahrhundert: Beiträge zum literarischen Leben 1750–1880*, 232–52. Studien und Texte zur Sozialgeschichte der Literatur 6. Tübingen: Max Niemeyer, 1982.

———. *Geschichte des deutschen Buchhandels: Ein Überblick*. Munich: C. H. Beck, 1991.

Wurst, Karin. *Fabricating Pleasure: Fashion, Entertainment, and Consumption in Germany 1780–1830*. Detroit, MI: Wayne State UP, 2005.

———. "Fashioning a Nation: Fashion and National Costume in Bertuch's Journal des Luxus und der Moden." *German Studies Review* 28, no. 2 (May 2005): 367–86.

Wurzbach, Dr. Constant von, ed. *Biographisches Lexikon des Kaiserthums Oesterreich*. Vol. 10. Vienna: Die kaiserlich-königliche Hof- und Staatsdruckerei, 1863.

Ziche, Paul. "'Auf eine wohlfeile und bequeme Art einen anschaulichen Begriff von einer Wissenschaft zu geben.' Beschreibung im 'Journal des

Luxus und der Moden' in der Mechanik und Wissenschaft um 1800." In Borchert and Dressel, *Das* Journal des Luxus und der Moden: *Kultur um 1800*, 243–60.

Ziegler, Edda. *Julius Campe — Der Verleger Heinrich Heines.* Hamburg: Hoffmann & Campe, Heinrich Heine Verlag, 1976.

———. *Literarische Zensur in Deutschland 1819–1848. Materialien, Kommentare.* Munich: Hanser, 1983.

zum Hingst, Anja. *Die Geschichte des Großen Brockhaus: Vom Conversationslexikon zur Enzyklopädie,* mit einem Geleitwort von A. G. Swierk. Wiesbaden: Harrassowitz Verlag, 1995. 23–25.

Contributors

JENNIFER DRAKE ASKEY is Assistant Professor of German at Kansas State University. Her research and publications have been in the area of nineteenth-century schools and children's literature. She is currently working on a book-length project dealing with nationalist historical fiction and biography for young readers during the Wilhelmine Empire.

ULRICH E. BACH is Assistant Professor of German at Texas State University. His research focuses on late nineteenth- and early twentieth-century literary culture and exile studies. An antiquarian bookseller by training, he has written about the emigration of Jewish-German booksellers to England and the USA. More recently, he has published an article on Leopold von Sacher-Masoch in the *German Quarterly*. Essays on Franz Blei's exile and on the émigré publishing house Philosophical Press will appear in a forthcoming volume of John Spalek's series, Deutschsprachige Exilliteratur.

KIRSTEN BELGUM is Associate Professor of German at the University of Texas at Austin. She has published on German Realism, the popular press in the nineteenth century, and issues of German-American cultural transfer. These publications include *Popularizing the Nation: Audience, Representation, and the Production of Identity in* Die Gartenlaube, *1853–1900* (1998). She is currently working on a book-length study of the origins and legacy of the *Encyclopaedia Americana* in the nineteenth century.

MATT ERLIN is Associate Professor of Germanic Languages and Literatures at Washington University in St. Louis. He is the author of *Berlin's Forgotten Future: City, History, and Enlightenment in Eighteenth-Century Germany* (2004) and the co-editor, together with Lynne Tatlock, of *German Culture in Nineteenth-Century America: Reception, Adaptation, Transformation* (2005). He has also published articles on a variety of topics related to late eighteenth- and early nineteenth-century German culture. He is currently completing a book on luxury and the novel in the German Enlightenment.

JANA MIKOTA is Lecturer for German Literature at the University of Siegen. Her research focuses on children's and youth literature of the nineteenth and twentieth centuries, nineteenth-century women writers, and historical and current canons of reading. Her publications include *Alice Rühle-Gerstel: Ihre kinderliterarischen Arbeiten im Kontext der Kinder- und Jugendbücher der Weimarer Republik, des Nationalsozialismus und des Exils* (2004). She is currently completing her habilitation project "Canons of Reading at Higher Girls' Schools 1870–1933."

MARY PADDOCK is Associate Professor of German and Assistant Dean of Arts and Sciences at Quinnipiac University. Her primary fields of research and publication are lyric performance and persona construction. She has presented papers and published articles on turn-of-the-century literary cabaret in Germany, Frank Wedekind, medieval German courtly lyric, and Walther von der Vogelweide. She is currently working on a monograph with the working title "Frank Wedekind: Satire, Scandal, and Satanism."

THEODORE F. RIPPEY is Associate Professor of German at Bowling Green State University. His research areas include Weimar and exile literature and film, reading, sound, the concept of the mass, and the relationship between aesthetics and politics. His book-length study on aural experience and German modernity (in progress) focuses in part on Kurt Tucholsky's textualization of speech.

JEFFREY L. SAMMONS is Leavenworth Professor Emeritus of Germanic Languages and Literatures at Yale University. His most recent book publications are *Heinrich Heine: Alternative Perspectives 1985–2005* (2006); a translation with commentary, *Heinrich Heine, Ludwig Börne: A Memorial* (2006); and *Kuno Francke's Edition of* The German Classics *(1913–15): A Critical and Historical Overview* (2009).

LYNNE TATLOCK, Hortense and Tobias Lewin Distinguished Professor in the Humanities at Washington University in St. Louis, has published widely on German literature and culture from 1650 to the 1990s. Recent book publications include *German Culture in Nineteenth-Century America* (2005), co-edited with Matt Erlin, and *Catharina Regina von Greiffenberg: Meditations on the Incarnation, Passion, and Death of Jesus Christ* (2009). She is preparing a study of the translation, marketing, and reading of popular novels by German women in postbellum America.

KATRIN VÖLKNER is Lecturer of German and European Studies Advisor at Northwestern University. Her research and publications have focused on the use of technology in foreign language teaching and on book history and popular culture in the nineteenth and twentieth centuries as reflected, for example, in her dissertation "Books for a Better Life: Publishers and the Rise of Middlebrow Culture in Wilhelmine Germany." She is also a co-founder of The Public Square (www.thepublicsquare.org), an organization that promotes participatory democracy and creates spaces for public conversations.

KARIN A. WURST is Professor of German and Dean of the College of Arts and Letters at Michigan State University. Her research interests include eighteenth-century literature and culture, visual culture, and literary and cultural theory. She has published on Lessing, Lenz, women authors of the eighteenth century, fashion and changing love paradigms in literary texts, and on material culture. Her books include *Unpopular Virtues: J. M. R. Lenz and the Critics; A Reception History* (1999) with Alan Leidner, *Frau und Drama im achtzehnten Jahrhundert* (1991), and *Fabricating Pleasure: Fashion, Entertainment, and Consumption in Germany (1780–1830)* (2005).

Index